RESTLESS GIANT

MUSIC IN AMERICAN LIFE

*A list of books in the series appears
at the end of this book.*

Restless Giant

THE LIFE AND TIMES OF
JEAN ABERBACH AND
HILL AND RANGE SONGS

BAR BISZICK-LOCKWOOD

UNIVERSITY OF ILLINOIS PRESS
Urbana, Chicago, and Springfield

FRONTISPIECE: Joachim "Jean" Aberbach.
Courtesy of Susan Aberbach.

Library of Congress Cataloging-in-Publication Data
Biszick-Lockwood, Bar.
Restless giant : the life and times of Jean Aberbach
and Hill and Range Songs / Bar Biszick-Lockwood.
p.   cm. — (Music in American life)
Includes bibliographical references and index.
ISBN 978-0-252-03507-4 (cloth : alk. paper) —
ISBN 978-0-252-07694-7 (pbk. : alk. paper)
1. Aberbach, Joachim Jean.
2. Music publishers—United States—Biography.
3. Hill and Range Songs (Firm)
I. Title.
ML427.A24B57   2010
070.5'794092—dc22   2009020121
[B]

Contents

PREFACE

Hill and Range Songs is arguably one the most important and influential popular music publishing houses in history. Born of keen business acumen and a genuine love for indigenous American music, it was established in late 1944 by Viennese immigrant Joachim "Jean" Aberbach and his brother Julian. Together, they recognized country and western, blues, and gospel music as lucrative business opportunities, and as popular music genres deserving of wider exposure. Over the next twenty years the company produced more than three hundred chart hits. In so doing, they were responsible for having a direct impact on popularizing new song forms, promoting the careers of some of America's best loved popular performers, changing industry laws and practices, and assuring fair payment to songwriters.

This book is a biography of one of those brothers. Shortly after Jean Aberbach's death in May 1992, I was recommended by veteran music publisher, Lou Levy, to Jean's widow Susan as a potential biographer. I was acting as Lou's administrative assistant at that time, helping him on various deals related to copyright renewals and music publishing company sales. From the start, I was apprehensive. While I am a trained musicologist, I had only a few minor scholarly publishing credits to my name. But even in his later years, Lou was an unparalleled dealmaker, and for better or worse, convinced both Susan and me that my music research background and work with him made me right for this job. Neither Susan nor I had any idea what we were getting ourselves into.

Over the past sixteen years I have grown to know and love this man I never met. Life took me in many different directions over that time, as I struggled to complete this work. Things proceeded slowly but never stopped. Waking or sleeping, I was always thinking about Jean and his adventures. Now, looking back several careers and almost two decades later, I am stunned by the mere thought of finishing this. I will be forever grateful to Susan Aberbach, whose infinite patience I surely did not deserve. The only comfort I can offer in retrospect is that Jean believed a man continues to live when he is fondly remembered by others. Since I pondered Jean every single day for almost two decades, I'm not so sure he would have thought this long delay such a bad thing after all.

I was fortunate to have access to his sketch memoir notes, along with an archive of well-kept corporate records, and Jean's daybooks for some pivotal years. Few people actually thought Jean would complete his autobiography—he moved much too fast for all the mundane details such a task requires. But we can be grateful that before he abandoned the effort, he left us with a list of stories he would have included, as well as a preface detailing exactly what kind of book he wanted to write: "There are really two types of memoirs—those that are the dry, factual business of history, of figures, etc. Then there are the ethical memoirs—the ones that preach how one's children should lead their lives. But kids today don't want to hear about such things. Therefore, I would rather tell these stories in a pleasurable, lighthearted way, in hopes that, when confronted with a similar situation, these stories might come to mind. They are serious, philosophical stories which are funny only upon first sight. They are really models for life that can be referred to time and again, as the need arises."

And so I have written a book the way I imagine Jean wanted to write it. This presented challenges, because what the above passage clearly tells us is that Jean did not want to write a dry, historical book about music publishing, about Hill and Range Songs, Inc., or about his role in the lives of key popular figures like Elvis Presley. Instead, Jean wanted to use these rich topics as a backdrop to illuminate things he thought much more interesting and important.

This endeavor took on a much larger perspective when the appalling lack of literature about the music publishing profession became clear. When I began my research in the early 1990s, music publishers—if mentioned at all—showed up in popular literature as ancillary figures in works about or by popular performers. Their contributions to an artist's career were rarely mentioned, but they were always spotlighted when their actions ended up benefiting themselves at the expense of a performer, even when that was the legal arrangement between them. The impression that gave was that music publishers were nothing more than loan sharks and artistic parasites. But I knew otherwise. My time with Lou brought me into contact with all the people still around in the profession from that time, and I discovered that there was a story behind every one of them. These were artistic people, as highly creative and passionate in their profession as were the performers and songwriters they serviced. So long was his tenure in it, I thought Jean's life offered a rare opportunity to narrow this gap in music history literature by raising the visibility of this greatly under-studied, under-documented profession and the people in it.

So strong was the negative perception about music publishers that over the years several people actually questioned why I would want to waste my time writing about such people—particularly the Aberbach brothers. Their aloofness and persistent success understandably raised suspicions among their colleagues and competitors. They kept such a low profile that gossip and myths abounded. How could Jean and Julian have built this enormous private international music empire without employing unscrupulous business practices, swindling their songwriters, and twisting the arms of America's most beloved performing artists?

What little I did find written about the Aberbach brothers painted them as copyright predators who exercised dictatorial control over performing artists and songwriters. The former turned out to be true—but the same can be said of virtually every good music publisher, that being the measure of success in this profession. But the latter characterization—that they exercised unreasonable control over their artists—did not ring true. I simply could not reconcile how so many of our best-loved and most honorable, genteel, and respected songwriters and performing artists could have retained the Aberbach brothers as business partners for their entire lifetimes, if they had been such scoundrels!

I set out to solve this mystery by trying to understand who one of these brothers really was. Of course, I wanted to know what attracted Jean to this profession, and why he excelled at it. But to really understand what a music publisher was required going deeper. I needed to understand Jean's motivations, and how—when presented with challenges—this man reacted to the world around him. In other words, my goal was to see the world through his eyes, to equip us with just enough industry knowledge that we could ask ourselves—"what would I, as a music publisher, have done?" So if the reader is looking for a populist biography, one filled with light anecdotes and personality characterizations, this is not it. Some subjects don't lend themselves to that sort of discussion, and Jean is one of them. Jean's personality only truly comes alive when seen against the backdrop of the business of music. In that context, we can participate in his life rather than just read about it.

This work also challenges some long-held beliefs. For instance, it has long been thought that the Aberbach brothers had to buy off the people around them to do well in business. Some also believe that they had a stranglehold on material available to Eddy Arnold and Elvis Presley. In the end, what I believe I show—and what Jean clearly wanted to convey—is that truth is a matter of perception. When these events are put into proper context, it becomes hard to ignore the fact that self-interest motivated *all* the participants in this complex play—even our most beloved artists.

Julian (left) and Jean
Aberbach (right)
with music teacher,
ca.1918. Courtesy of
Susan Aberbach.

Nevertheless, there is also plenty of "dark matter" throughout the book, if one chooses to see it. Jean Aberbach and his brother were no saints. They were simply astute businesspeople who used every available means—up to and including the "gray" areas of the law—to obtain the best business advantage for themselves and their artistic partners.

My entire aim in this endeavor was to discover and document the truth as best I could discern it through tangible evidence and firsthand accounts. I had the privilege of interviewing almost everyone alive who knew Jean, and I believe the material amassed is sufficient in quantity and consistency as to justify the conclusions. When there was not sufficient evidence to warrant a conclusion, then I did not draw one. At times that can lead to uncertainty, but I would rather that than make up history to fill out a story that may not be true.

Another challenge this book presented is how best to characterize Jean's brother and lifelong partner. While Julian's contributions cannot be understated, the nature and approach the book took—as an exploration of one man's life to illuminate his profession—did not lend itself to producing a work that always allowed me to focus equal attention on Julian's unique accomplishments.

I was fortunate to have three very long and frank discussions with Julian before he died. I leveraged every bit of his insights and included all his verifiable accomplishments in this work. Jean would not have had it any other way. He loved his brother dearly and never would he have tolerated a work that detracted in any way from Julian's accomplishments, or that diminished the tremendous contributions he made to their mutual success.

I believe I have presented a fair picture of the relationship between Jean and Julian and, from an examination of the facts, given credit where credit was due to each brother. I also think I make clear throughout that these two brothers were inseparable, and to a large extent interchangeable, in their work. In that sense, one could say that this is a book about the Aberbach brothers, but that to preserve the approach of the book it takes the point of view of only one of them.

Jean knew how difficult it is to tell a "true" story. Fact and opinion become mixed as we look backward in time. While we can be diligent in seeking out and confirming dull historical facts, what mattered to Jean was the point, not the date or spelling of a name. Being a trained historian, I can't help but be bothered when not every date or event can be confirmed absolutely by multiple sources, or that multiple recollections don't match perfectly in detail. But each time I was confronted with such problems, Jean always brought me back to the point.

In his memoir sketches Jean advises the reader to look for what he calls the "red thread" in each of these stories—the essence of it all, the most important thing. He reminds us that the truth will always be the same, but that human beings are interpretive creatures. The meaning of these stories will likely be

Julian (left) and Jean Aberbach (right), 1990. Courtesy of Rampage Studios.

different for each of us. And he admits that, as an interpretive creature himself, we are not likely to find the definitive version of a story from him either. A twice-told tale is always a different story, as the second storyteller adds his own personal embellishments.

In the end, I think what matters is that we are given a rare chance to explore a complex man living in his complex times. We come to understand the kind of man Jean was, and what mattered to him. We get a chance to live his world through his eyes and see what it took to excel in a highly competitive, greatly misunderstood profession that shaped popular culture for more than half a century. I don't think Jean would disapprove. Above all, he wanted his book to come alive, to engage readers and to have some personal impact. Wherever he is, I am sure he hopes readers will enjoy his life just as much as he did, and perhaps learn something of value from his experiences that could be useful to their own.

In other words, Jean believed history is good, but meaning is better. The "point" is not the factual truth, but the ultimate truth, and what value it might have to the reader in the context of his own life. Wherever he is, I believe Jean doesn't care so much that this is a book about him. Jean cares more that this is a book about you.

ACKNOWLEDGMENTS

I am indebted to the following persons for providing their recollections of Jean and his times: Al Berman, Alan Harrill, Anne-Rachel Aberbach, Ben Weisman, Bob Summer, Cecelia Zembrano, Charlie Grean, Chet Atkins, Cindy Walker, David Aberbach, Don Robertson, Doodle Owens, Ed Cramer, Eddy Arnold, Fernando Botero, Frankie Laine, Freddy Bienstock, Friedrich Hundertwasser, Grelun Landon, Hank Snow, Fred Fox, Jason Aberbach, John Schmetterling, Johnny Bienstock, Joram Harel, Julian Aberbach, Justin Tubb, Lamar Fike, Leonard Feist Jr., Lou Levy, Mike Stoller, Milton Rudin, Mitch Miller, Nick Firth, Norman Tyre, Susan Aberbach, Thea Zavin, Tom Levy, Vincent Scuderi, and Winfield Scott.

Thanks to Mick Booth for background on Campbell, Connelly; to Lawrence Zwisohn for background on early western music; and to Walter Zeisl for Aberbach genealogy. I want to also tip my hat to the many unsung heroes of the internet—people like Archie Gramble, whose enthusiasm for music compels them to share the unique and hard-earned fruits of their passion freely with others.

Thanks also to the Aberbach families for access to the Corporate Records of Hill and Range Songs, Inc., to the Country Music Hall of Fame and Museum, and the Graceland Foundation.

Special thanks to Peter Guralnick for his inspiration and years of encouragement, to Ronnie Pugh for his valuable feedback, and to Alanna Nash and Paul Kingsbury for supporting the greater exposure of the Aberbach brothers' legacy in country music literature.

Thanks to Mike Gunderloy for supporting me during the early years of research, and to soul mates like Detrik Hohenegger, who never lost faith in me. Special thanks to my wonderful husband Bryan Lockwood who, it turns out, is an amazing editor! He is my eleventh-hour hero, and had a strong hand in making this text as good as it could be.

Special thanks to Dr. Mary Jane Corry, State University of New York at New Paltz, who inspired me to follow a path in musicology. Her genuine, humble professionalism, her devotion to her students, her grace and enthusiasm have been a lifelong inspiration (MJ, this one's for you!). And thanks to Dr. Kay Shelemay and Dr. Edward Rosen, for encouragement during my NYU graduate career.

I could not have completed this work without the continued support, encouragement, infinite patience, and faith of Susan Aberbach. She is undoubtedly a "patron of the arts" to have suffered my creative development for so many years on this project. While I can't bring back those years, I hope there was some measure of joy in watching this work, however slowly, come together. Thank you for letting me discover all the wonderfulness that was your beloved Jean, on my own, one piece at a time. I hope we've made him proud.

RESTLESS GIANT

CHAPTER I

No Wrong Turns

Vienna had always been a crown jewel of the Holy Roman Empire. It was strategically situated on the powerful Danube River—a major trade route to the Black Sea, itself the gateway to the Mediterranean and the rest of the civilized Christian world. Encouraged by this influx of strangers and goods, the city grew into a powerful trading hub between East and West, and within its markets precarious neutrality prevailed.

Vienna flourished as a center for the arts and culture, becoming one of the most opulent and progressive cities in the world. To support the aristocracy, an extensive service class emergèd, and the Aberbach family was part of it. They had come from a region of Poland then encompassed by the Austro-Hungarian Empire, Jean Aberbach's father and mother having been born and partly raised in Bolechow and Choroskow, respectively, before moving to Vienna. His grandfather died of tuberculosis at the age of forty-two, leaving his grandmother a widow with seven children dependent to some extent on her brother.

Among these original seven children was Aron Adolf—affectionately known as Dolfi. He courted Anna Schmetterling, then fourteen, and—never forgetting the crowded living conditions and destitute circumstances of his youth—vowed not to marry until he was financially secure. There was good opportunity in Vienna, and some of the aristocratic prosperity began to trickle down to this new business class. Dolfi worked in the credit field, selling jewelry on monthly terms. He was successful enough that, in 1902, Dolfi and Anna were wed.

But the world around them was swiftly changing. By the first decade of the twentieth century, the Austro-Hungarian kingdom had extended its reach over Slovakia, the Czech Republic, and parts of Poland, Romania, Slovenia, Croatia, Bosnia, and Herzegovina. The empire's awesome power—especially when viewed in partnership with its Teutonic ally Germany—was much feared by the rest of Europe, especially by France, whose awareness of the growing military force just beyond its borders made it particularly uneasy. Territorial squabbles over trade routes and the rights to raw materials in Africa further heightened the unease. Internally, the Austro-Hungarian Empire was experiencing its own problems as well. Inspired by the popular governments in France and elsewhere, a growing nationalism was chipping away at the Habsburg dynasty—especially in Serbia, where the dissenters were becoming overtly militant.

It was into this tumultuous world that Joachim "Jean" Aberbach was thrust on August 12, 1910. Born in Vöslau, he was the second of two children gratefully conceived after seven long years of disappointment that nearly destroyed the marriage. He followed his brother Julian, eighteen months his senior, who had been born on February 8, 1909.

Dolfi continued to build modest wealth until the outbreak of World War I, precipitated by the 1914 assassination in Sarajevo of Habsburg heir Archduke Franz Ferdinand by a Serbian nationalist. A man of no privilege but much ambition, Dolfi pursued lucrative opportunities during the war years. He founded a factory that manufactured leather goods for the Austro-Hungarian army—belts, saddles, and strap parcels used to carry provisions. The demand was so great that he added two other factories. By this time the Aberbachs were enjoying a fairly high standard of living despite a wartime economy, and their successful credit and manufacturing enterprises had even led to a partnership in one of the local banks. As the empire buckled under the weight of war, astute Viennese businessmen like Dolfi began to look for ways to protect their profits. They invested their savings in tangibles like real estate, fearful that the growing political instability might rob them of their hard-earned wealth.

Jean, only four at the time, spent much of World War I in Vienna. But as the conflict progressed, the family retreated to the resort town of Marienbad to escape the dispiriting atmosphere. The conflict had gone badly, and when it ended the empire was dissolved and its territories carved up for the victors. Austria was reduced to a fraction of its size and the economic effects were disastrous. Inflation reduced many fortunes to dust. Luckily Dolfi managed to

Jean Aberbach with his nurse, ca. 1911. Courtesy of Susan Aberbach.

Anna, Dolfi, Julian, and Jean Aberbach, ca. 1924. Courtesy of Susan Aberbach.

weather the storm of devalued currency, working-class uprisings, and social distress by leveraging his real-estate holdings to raise the capital he needed to reopen his factories. One site was retooled to make inexpensive shoes and another turned out only those of the highest quality. Two others were refitted to manufacture luggage.

Dolfi personifies the venerable tradition of the Viennese tradesman. Conducting business during dangerous times required knowledge, creativity, and confidence. Dolfi was a master diplomat who knew that best advantage is obtained by knowing your opponents and putting them at ease. Therefore, a practical education for his sons was essential, and it included mastering multiple languages, gaining appreciation of various cultures, and maintaining high standing in local society. These activities would occupy Jean and Julian throughout their youth.

Although the boys enjoyed a very comfortable lifestyle, they never felt rich. Haunted by his impoverished youth, Dolfi allocated money only to necessities—never to luxuries. No mention was ever made of household servants or luxurious extravagances, but the boys had several private tutors. Jean would eventually master five languages.

Jean and Julian were eighteen months apart in age, but they might as well have been biological twins. The two seemed to know instinctively what the other was thinking. Where their opinions and attitudes differed, it was in a way that was most often complementary. They would explore ideas exhaustively from different perspectives and when there were disagreements they solved them quickly without a hint of tension. While both had plenty of ego to show the world, they felt no need for fruitless competition between themselves. Throughout their youth, they had mutual respect for each other. They were, in fact, the best of friends.

School presented little challenge for Jean. He could absorb material far faster than the classroom pace, and so he was accelerated one grade and joined Julian's class. To bring a little adventure to his studies, he progressively made it more difficult for himself by reducing the amount of time he allowed himself for learning the material. Only then could he be sure he was progressing—learning to work better, smarter, and faster than his peers.

Julian was the very same way. He could absorb the material quickly and would then become bored. This was very bad for their teachers. The boys looked like twins and often wore the same clothes. They took great pleasure in impersonating one another and confusing their teachers. For subjects in which they excelled, one could take the other's tests and not be noticed.

Eventually their classroom behavior became completely unmanageable. The more inept the teacher was, the bolder the boys became. Known as "the professor murderers," by their junior high school years, their pranks were legendary. To preserve what integrity was left of the Vienna public school system, the boys were finally separated and sent to different institutions. When they reached high school grade, however, there was no choice except to reunite them in the classroom at the Hundert Akademie—the commercial trade school that taught business skills.

By this time the boys were thoroughly disenchanted with schooling. They kept their grades up despite the fact that they were spending less and less time in the classroom. To fund their leisure time, Julian began charging their less fortunate cousins for the use of their home's indoor shower! At first they tried to hide their truancy from their father, but after a while it became obvious that they were not returning to school. One morning Dolfi stormed in, rousted them from bed, and declared, "That's it! You either go to school—or you work."

They landed jobs with a linen company that sent salesmen to remote alpine regions. Jean and Julian teamed up. They went away to the Tyrol Mountains for several months, selling sheets and pillowcases door to door in the resort villages and to the farmers' wives in the mountains surrounding Innsbruck.

On doorsteps of modest homes in the Tyrol, Jean and Julian Aberbach discovered their talent—the ability to sell anything. Alone, each of the boys had enough talent and confidence to rope in a sale. But together it became almost impossible to resist them. They worked the sale, volleying between them and assuming supporting roles as needed. If they warmed up to Jean, then Julian stepped into the shadows; other times Julian would take the lead role. Everything depended on making the customer comfortable enough to part with money. The two boys did quite well, but after a while the novelty wore off. Surely they were meant for greater things than this common, mundane, relatively low-paying work. They returned to Vienna to think things over.

Back in Vienna, Jean felt the walls closing in. He wanted to travel. Both he and Julian read voraciously, and an especially exciting subject for them was America. Books, newspaper accounts, and magazines told fascinating stories of America's Wild West—the dusty deserts and sweeping plains, wagon trains and gun-slinging buckaroos. Jean dreamed about going there someday.

His chance came unexpectedly. After living for a time with Dolfi's family, his orphaned cousin Ida had gone to America. There she met and married a hardworking Hungarian named Louie Terner. Louie worked in a bottle-washing factory and became wealthy after selling a huge quantity of bottles to the company that later became Kraft Foods. Ida and Louie had five children while under the care of her personal gynecologist Dr. Hamilton (first name unknown), who would travel with them. Dr. Hamilton took a liking to Jean while on a trip to Vienna in 1928 and invited him to come back to America with them.

Jean was thrilled! America was everything he had hoped and more. Frédéric Auguste Bartholdi's majestic bronze Statue of Liberty, the magnificent skyscrapers, the massive bridges over the East and Harlem rivers, and the underground subways were all monuments of modern technology that had no equal in Vienna. Jean had come during the school year and enrolled in courses, but he never completed them. Instead he secured a job in a furrier's shop, where he learned the skill of selecting quality pelts for coats and stoles. Six months later, the Terners closed up their Brooklyn house and left for their summer home in the country. Apparently Jean stayed for a while, but he eventually returned to Vienna, probably compelled by the devastating events after the great stock market crash in October 1929. Jean was fortunate to have experienced America at the height of its prosperity. After he tasted its freedom and adventure, things would never be the same for him again.

Back in Vienna, Jean tried to reintegrate into society but found it difficult. While Julian moved gracefully among Viennese society, Jean was straining at the bit. Except for a failed scholarly career, some fur pelts, and few Tyrolian bed linens, he was acutely aware that his life was unremarkable. Every day he bent farther and farther under the weight of waiting for his career to begin.

In the end, Jean couldn't contain his impatience. Armed with a letter of reference from his kind friend Dr. Hamilton, Jean boarded a sooty train for Berlin one morning, ready to meet the rest of his life. He had no idea what to expect. He had never before visited Berlin, but for months had dreamed of escaping there, urged on by a fabulous letter from a relative, on whose hospitality he would depend until he could find a job and a suitable living situation.

Unfortunately, when he arrived, he did not find his friend swimming in money. In fact, by this time the poor boy had hocked most everything he owned at the neighborhood pawnbroker. He could not support himself, let alone put up Jean for any length of time. After a fitful night's sleep, Jean had more or less recovered from his shock.

Berlin was a place of affluence, purpose, and opportunity. Bereft of cash, Jean was nevertheless flush with youthful ambition. Confident that great and prosperous things were shortly in store for him, he headed directly to the Kurfürstendamm (familiarly known as the Ku'Damm)—the main street. Rather than seeking a reasonably priced room in a moderate district, he cast caution to the wind and arranged credit for a high-priced apartment. The cost was absurd—but then, so was his situation. The irony was delicious and he savored every moment.

Wandering the seedy streets in the nightclub district, he found himself drawn to a building with large windows. There was a good deal of activity in and out of the front door, mostly by groups of attractive, well-dressed women. Jean stepped into the Kakadu dance hall and scanned the interior with interest. There were far too many women for the number of men. In fact, the odds were remarkably favorable! There never seemed a moment that a young man wasn't dancing. It was not long before he was approached by the proprietor: "A young, elegant gentleman like you would do well in a place like this. How would you like a job?"

The very first money Jean Aberbach made was as an escort dancer at the Kakadu dance hall. It seemed altogether outrageous to him that he should be paid money to do what he enjoyed most and what came naturally to him—dancing day and night with an endless parade of wealthy and attractive women—but Jean attacked this challenge with no less vigor than he would any other in his life. It took only a day or two to learn the tricks of the trade. He observed—with some amusement—how the other dancers competed to attract the best-looking women and capture the best tips. Their chief weapon was a skillful lesson in practical economy—a large sausage down their trousers by day became their dinner at night!

Although the ladies were thrilled with him, the proprietor was not. Jean was too quick to charm, whisking the wealthy ladies off to the dance floor before they had a chance to order food and drinks which translated into the better part of the Kakadu's profit margin. Jean was a fantastic charmer and a good enough dancer, but he was altogether bad for business. Perhaps a less enthusiastic temperament for customer service was required for this profession.

So sometime in 1931, Jean retrieved Dr. Hamilton's letter of reference and made his way to the address he found in it. At the top of the stairs, he mistakenly turned left instead of right and entered the offices of Will Meisel, a well-known composer of popular operettas and film music. Most people would have politely apologized and left, but Jean recognized his mistake had opened the door to an opportunity. His intelligence, wit, and self-confidence made a good impression, and he was hired on the spot as a production assistant.

It always amused Jean that his career was launched by accidentally stepping inside the wrong office. Embracing a mistake turned out to be exactly what was needed to jump-start his career in music. His boundless ambition blinded him to the fact that he was inexperienced and destitute. Instead, he saw the world around him as full of possibilities. He dreamed big, trusted his abilities, gave himself up to the moment, and was presented with the opportunity he needed. By the time he was working for Will Meisel, there was one thing of which he was certain: If you trust your instincts, in life there will be no wrong turns.

CHAPTER 2

Happenstance

J ean gained his earliest apprenticeship in music publishing at the offices of Will Meisel. The company had been established as a music publishing and production house for Meisel's theater and film-score work. Sometimes confused with Edmund Meisel, the composer for the German adaptation of Serge Eisenstein's groundbreaking Russian film *Battleship Potemkin* (1926), Will Meisel was a craftsman rather than an artist and is best remembered as an impresario and influential businessman. He created countless serviceable popular songs, film scores, and serious operettas, but none are historically significant. Instead, he became one of the most powerful music businessmen in the country and was closely connected to the German performing rights society, Gesellschaft für musikalische Aufführungs- und mechanische Vervielfältigungsrechte (GEMA).

In his role as music production assistant, Jean got a fast education in the business of music, some appreciation for the laws governing it, and broad exposure to artist management and music production techniques for orchestra and film. The profession offered plenty of opportunity. By 1931, the Universum-

Dedicated portrait,
Will Meisel, 1962.
Courtesy of Susan
Aberbach.

Film-Aktiengesellschaft (UFA)—Germany's centralized film agency—had built a powerful entertainment cartel with its European allies to protect against losing profits to Hollywood filmmakers. These alliances were built on contractual agreements that included music as a new and lucrative area of film. As a result, royalty rights administration for the use of music in film was growing quickly.[1] Apparently Jean excelled in this work and before long was being listed in movie credits, to the surprise and delight of his parents, who attended showings back in Vienna.

During the year Jean worked for Meisel, the world around him was changing. Social unrest in Berlin was growing at an alarming pace, but he hardly seemed to notice. Like most of the general populace intent on their daily lives,

Jean ignored the warning signs of a nation moving rapidly toward a disturbing future. Since the European depression, set off by America's stock market crash of 1929, Adolf Hitler's National Socialist German Workers (Nazi) party had been gaining public support, campaigning on a platform that attributed Germany's economic problems to a combined Jewish-Communist plot. Between 1928 and 1930, Nazi party representation in the Reichstag had gone from 28 to 107 seats. Fueled by growing unemployment, fear of Communism, and racial hatred, the political group gained momentum. Jean could not have avoided hearing the speeches, witnessing the acts of intimidation performed by the party youth corps, or seeing the frighteningly massive rallies. But he barely showed a hint of his Jewish heritage in his features, nor did he consort with Jews exclusively or engage in a profession that might have suggested he was a Jew. What could happen? Even in his own profession, the power of the Nazi party had become starkly apparent. When the American film *All Quiet on the Western Front*— a sensational war novel that had been overwhelmingly popular as a book in Germany—was shown in December 1930, Nazi party members took offense at the unfavorable portrayal of the German army and the film's pacifist theme. Intent on stopping the performance, Dr. Joseph Goebbels mobilized a massive demonstration to disrupt the theater district. Several of his operatives interrupted the showing with catcalls and released white mice, snakes, and stink bombs in the theater. Five days later, the film was officially banned to guard the safety of theatergoing patrons.

One morning Jean wandered into a local barber shop and noticed an entertaining patron there. Jacques Rosenberg was the director of the French office of English music publisher Campbell, Connelly & Co. Ltd. He was a likable fellow who had a knack for attracting good fortune. When a local owner of a Parisian department store fell in love with the Dolly Sisters, a popular singing group, the charming Mr. Rosenberg collected a handsome second income delivering two huge flower bouquets to the girls every morning on his behalf. His outgoing business style mirrored a flamboyant personal life, and his loyal staff learned quickly to cover his indiscretions. Very often, visitors asking after him would be told he had stepped out of the office but was just across the street and would be back shortly. Though it was the truth, his secretary neglected to tell the client that the only thing across the street was a whorehouse!

Rosenberg had come to Berlin to investigate the possibility of representing Meisel's work in France. He must have been impressed with Jean, because over the snips of the barber shears, Rosenberg offered Jean a job opportunity: "Come to Paris! What, are you crazy? How long do you think it will be before Hitler takes over?" Jean was surprised, but he was doing well enough at Meisel and was enjoying his work. He graciously declined.

Though flattered by the event, before long Jean was caught up in the business of the day. Later that same day Jean had business in the motion picture district and once again ran into Rosenberg. Impressed by the serendipity of the encounter, they continued their conversation from the morning. Jean was now completely convinced that the hand of fate was distinctly pointing in the direction of Paris and he would be a fool not to follow it. The arrangements were made on the spot—a commission of 3.5 percent of the gross if Jean would place Campbell, Connelly & Co. songs in French film and theater.[2]

Jean's Berlin apprenticeship had taught him many things. But the lessons he gathered about life dwarfed even the vast business knowledge he had acquired there. In fact, he may owe his life to that casual barbershop encounter. Only a month or two after Jean arrived in Paris, Hitler assumed control of the Reichstag and began to exert authoritarian control over every facet of German life and industry. He effectively nationalized the film industry and began reorganizing it to meet his growing propagandistic aims, placing creative resources such as composers and filmmakers at his exclusive disposal. By February 1933, Hitler had suspended all constitutional guarantees of personal liberties, including secrecy of mail, property rights, freedom of the press, and the right to assemble. Decrees limiting access to education and the right to hold public office were but precursors to the coming horrors.

It was sobering to think that in a single moment a casual barbershop encounter might abruptly transform into an escape hatch. The world had unraveled before him, and he nearly failed to see it. He would not forget this lesson. Years later he would write, "Until your very last moments, you should lead a conscious, self-examined life. You should take the time to turn around and look behind you . . . to reflect on it, and to try to figure out what has happened behind your backside!!"[3]

CHAPTER 3

The Revolving Door

The music publishing industry did not operate very differently in Paris from the way it did in Berlin. By law, when a lyricist and composer registered a copyright for their song, they were then entitled to collect a fee each time the song was played in public. Music publishers acted as their agents, promoting their songs and overseeing the collection and distribution of these "performance right" revenues. Although new distribution media like phonograph recordings and film were beginning to offer exciting new revenue streams, the most lucrative means of generating performance revenue was placing works with orchestra leaders at high-quality hotels and theaters, who would perform these pieces for live audiences and for broadcast radio. Publishers employed promotional salesmen—in America, known as song pluggers—who would induce bandleaders to perform their songs. This type of endorsement was known as a plug. If they were successful at obtaining plugs, the publishers received a percentage of the performance royalty and paid a commission to the song plugger.

The English music publishing firm of Campbell, Connelly & Co. Ltd. had been created by James Campbell and Reg Connelly, who had gained some recognition in the United States with "Good Night, Sweetheart," cowritten by Campbell, Connelly, and Ray Noble. They also wrote one of the world's greatest standards, "Try a Little Tenderness," with Harry Woods. The firm was founded in 1925 on the success of another song they had cowritten with dance band leader Hal Swain called "Show Me the Way to Go Home." They followed this enormous success with others, slowly building up their catalog until they had earned the respect and the means to join the ranks of established music publishers on Denmark Street, London's equivalent of the neighborhood in New York City around 28th Street commonly referred to as Tin Pan Alley where most songwriters and composers worked. Having attended school in the United States, they naturally developed relationships with American music publishers of the day who began representing their works—among them De Sylva, Brown & Henderson (from whom they acquired the rights to represent "Sonny Boy" in foreign territories), Famous Music, Harms Inc., Robbins Music Corp., and Shapiro Bernstein & Co. Ltd.

By the late 1930s, James Campbell and Reg Connelly were a formidable force in the world of music publishing. They readily embraced the film industry by teaming up with Gaumont British and Gainsborough Pictures to bring over songwriting teams from America to write music for their productions. Campbell, Connelly's foreign branch offices monitored the promotion and representation of their song catalog and collected royalties on them in their foreign territories.

Jean was hired as a song plugger for Campbell, Connelly. In his promotional role, he developed strong relationships with the leading figures in Parisian theater at that time. Although he may have been hired specifically because of his experience with music in film, the fact that his pay was on a straight commission basis (and that he came to know all these individuals), suggests he was probably doing general catalog exploitation work as well. He made a living at this, but there was no security.

Julian arrived from Vienna at midyear 1932, Jean having arranged a position for him at the firm. Julian quickly absorbed the catalog highlights and the general acquisition and selling techniques. Jean took him around and introduced him to all the important industry people. Julian quickly fell into the rhythm of Paris nightlife and before long there seemed to be an Aberbach behind every bandstand.

Together again, the Aberbach brothers could do what they did best—an utterly charming, two pronged, sales assault. Working as a team, their warm, personal approach, quick wit, and similar looks had a memorable impact. Theater owners, film producers, and orchestra leaders quickly learned that it didn't matter which one you were talking to because they traded follow-up between them as convenience dictated. They used each other as a foil—showing up on alternating days, for instance, to engage in casual conversation that would subliminally remind the person of the details of the other brother's deal. In these ways, it was not much different from selling linens in the Tyrol.

The prestige of their positions offered access to the most powerful people in music, theater, and film. They would need these contacts when they moved off on their own. At the time, however, they were just a couple of typical young professionals hustling for a living, overspending their budgets, and living hand to mouth. As in any big city, the cost of living in Paris was high and became higher every month as Europe moved inevitably toward war. They were required to frequent high-class establishments—theaters and hotels—to seek their opportunities, and most of their available cash was used to appear successful and creditworthy so that owners, composers, film directors, and orchestra leaders might take the young men seriously. Little was left over for actual living expenses.

This did not bode well when the rent came due, but the boys were resourceful. They had not paid their rent at the Hotel Belmont for some time and knew they were about to be evicted. They also knew that the restaurant and the hotel owners were partners. The partners had had a falling out and were not speaking to one another. So every time one of the partners asked if the brothers had paid the rent, they replied they had paid it to the other. They knew this could not go on for very long, and so they sent all their laundry out for cleaning and packed everything else they could fit in a single suitcase. By the time they reached the lobby, the bellman had already been notified and was instructed to stop them. Lucky for them, there was a revolving door that separated the lobby from the restaurant. Jean trapped the man inside as Julian made his escape, and then Jean himself sprinted away!

After working for only three months, Julian left Campbell, Connelly to get the brothers' own business underway, while Jean stayed on to generate the operating income they would continue to need until their business became profitable. This was the best possible arrangement, and it would be repeated time and again as their joint careers moved forward. Jean would attain a prestigious position at a major music publishing house and generate operating capital to sustain them while Julian forged ahead to establish their own business. This approach afforded some level of financial security during the business start-up phase while preserving access to resources, information, and individuals that would have been otherwise out of their reach.

During the day, Jean would go off to Campbell, Connelly to pursue the acquisition of background music for film, while Julian would do the same on behalf of the Aberbach brothers' new firm. At night, they scoured the streets, theaters, and industry haunts in search of song properties that would generate fast money. Opportunities were scarce, and before long it looked as though they might soon have need of another revolving door.

Then one day Julian shared lunch with a Dutch woman who happened to own a townhouse but was leaving to join her new boyfriend in South America for at least a year. She was looking for someone who would take care of the townhouse while she was away. When Jean arrived home that night, he was delighted to hear that they would be taking up residence in new, spacious quarters located in a wonderful neighborhood. There were three floors, and so their living quarters and office could be located on entirely separate floors, and except for yearly taxes and typical maintenance costs, they could occupy it rent-free. Encouraged by this turn of events, they took on a secretary to assist Julian with the day-to-day affairs.

It was 1934 when they moved into the townhouse and almost immediately things began to look up. In casual socializing with the head of the French performing rights society known as SACEM (Société des Auteurs, Compositeurs, et Éditeurs de Musique), the loose-tongued gentleman let slip a little known copyright rule that benefited film dialogue writers but had never been exercised. Jean and Julian quickly moved to incorporate a new company they called the Société Entertainment Musicale Internationale (SEMI), and Julian began contacting the most important dialogue writers in France, offering to approach SACEM on their behalf to collect the royalty money to which they were lawfully entitled. For their efforts, the brothers would keep one-third of any money collected.

The stakes were enormous. Thousands of films had been produced and shown in France since 1927, when sound began to be added to film—and none of the money had ever been distributed to these writers. Jean and Julian had to work quickly to secure the most prolific writers before competition arose. As soon as the venture took off, Jean quit his job at Campbell, Connelly and he and Julian worked exclusively on researching film credits, locating and signing film dialogue writers, and preparing and sending enormous royalty claims to the stunned performing rights society.

Although the SEMI venture was completely lawful, SACEM and its regular members were not happy about it. SACEM was a nonprofit agency that distributed all the royalty money it collected to its entire pool of members according to set percentages, except those retained for operating expenses. The unexpected addition of dialogue writers increased the number of claimants, thereby significantly reducing the amount each member received. The more members, the less money each one got. Also, although dialog writers had never made a claim for royalties before, when the guidelines were first enacted they had been given a very fair percentage position. Not only had Jean and Julian substantially reduced royalties for all other SACEM members, but they were making substantial claims connected to years already past for money that had probably never been set aside. Overnight, SACEM found itself under siege. The irony was that Jean and Julian had armed themselves with the society's own policies! SACEM endured several months of chaos before it did the only thing it could do: *change the law*. Its board of directors altered their policies, severely reducing the percentage amount that could be claimed by a dialogue writer.

The gold rush was over by 1935, but the Aberbach brothers had made a killing. Spiraling inflation suggested that the best way to protect their profits was to invest in Vienna real estate. With their cousin's help they bought two apartment buildings there with funds that today would equal several million dollars.

By the time administration of film dialogue rights became only marginally profitable, Jean and Julian were already engaged in other areas of business. They had captured the rights to some background music—even the right to add lyrics to the background music of *Betty Boop* films in Italy. Jean had also arranged to represent some important American music publishing companies in France and Italy—including Peer International, as well as the venerable firm of E. B. Marks.

During this time, they became acquainted with a well-known Parisian playwright named Jacques Deval. He regarded his newest work, *Tovarich* (a lighthearted farce about two members of the Russian royal family masquerading as servants in Paris) as little more than a throwaway piece. When the October 1933 debut met with great popular acclaim, the brothers approached him about the rights to produce the work outside France. The deal, partnered with Parisian music publisher Éditions Salabert, gave them the right to mount *Tovarich* in Austria, Germany, and Switzerland.

The piece was enormously successful in Germany and eventually played in more than 100 theaters throughout the country. According to Robert E. Sherwood in his *Tovarich Notes,* Adolf Hitler was urged by friends to see the work. Before consenting to buy a ticket, he commissioned the German Embassy in Paris to investigate Deval's background for traces of Semitism. When assured there were none, the Führer saw the delightful play—and then saw it twice more, apparently quite tickled by it. One wonders what he might have done had he known that Jean Aberbach and his brother Julian had bankrolled the performances and would profit handsomely by it!

As a consequence of the SEMI venture, it became clear that if Jean and Julian intended to continue their work in France, the going would not be easy. Even though the Grand Master of the powerful French Lodge of Masons had intervened on their behalf, they had permanently alienated the majority of French music publishers. After all, they were Austrian foreigners who had cleverly robbed domestic publishers of a profitable domestic opportunity. They had even made enemies of most of the industry's composers and songwriters— everyone except a small pool of film dialogue writers. Without the goodwill of key figures in the French film, music, and theater industries, expanding their firm in France would be an uphill battle not worth fighting. In 1935 they sold SEMI to their American client Ralph Peer.

While *Tovarich* was successful, royalty collection and distribution was slow. Whether for dramatic or musical properties, it would take a year, possibly two, before the money generated by *Tovarich* would trickle back to them. In the meantime, they still needed to eat, keep a roof over their heads, and generate new business. With all their funds tied up in real estate, there was only a small cushion to live on while they planned their next move.

Jean knew exactly what he wanted to do. By 1936, Hitler had invaded the Ruhrgebiet, which provided even greater reason to return to America. At least one member of the family should set up residence there and apply for citizenship, in the event that a safe haven might be needed for the family. He contacted their venture partner Salabert, who provided passage and purpose. Jean was assigned to promote the works of Pyotr Ilich Tchaikovsky in American film and theater.

As Jean steamed across the Atlantic, he had a chance to reflect on all that had happened. It had been an interesting apprenticeship. He had managed to fall into a business that he found both challenging and satisfying. He had gone from being a starving escort dancer to a successful businessman in the space of only a few years. During that time, he had learned many things. Some of

Jean Aberbach,
ca. 1939. Courtesy
of Susan Aberbach.

his best fortune had been obtained through lucky accident. It would be best to remain alert to other such opportunities. But it was the success of SEMI that proved most illuminating. It taught him that you can defeat an opponent merely by knowing him and finding his weaknesses. By scrutinizing SACEM's own policies Jean and Julian found a lucrative opportunity that was being ignored by everyone else. It was not unlike their hotel experience. As they had with the unfortunate bellhop, the Aberbach brothers had trapped SACEM in a revolving door of its own design.

CHAPTER 4

Destiny

Jean arrived in the New York during 1936, anxious to begin his new job and expecting that before long he would be established and secure. Unfortunately, the Salabert assignment to represent Tchaikovsky in the United States turned out to be completely unprofitable. Through prior agreement, Chappell Music—America's largest music publishing firm—exclusively represented Salabert in the United States, and so he could collect royalties only when Tchaikovsky was performed in Canada. Chappell did not, however, represent the works for film. When these rare occasions arose, Jean could collect a fee and retain a percentage to supplement the meager $50 per week stipend that Salabert provided for his services.

Jean was twenty-six years old. He and Julian had made a fortune in the last two years, all of which was tied up in Vienna real estate. He took a modest room in a boardinghouse and was living frugally, spending most of his time competing with swindlers and sweethearts for the use of the busy pay phone in the lobby. It was like starting all over again.

The New York Jean had come to was still reeling from the aftermath of the Great Depression. The political difficulties in Europe had disrupted normal channels of trade, and business was suffering as America tried to remain passive and neutral in light of the escalating world events. The declining economy was painfully apparent everywhere except two places—Broadway and Hollywood. The theaters were lit six nights a week, plus matinees. It was the golden age of Tin Pan Alley, and writers like George and Ira Gershwin, Cole Porter, and Irving Berlin were turning out their finest work. They were generating a fortune from clever songs that were popularized in long-running Broadway plays and reproduced in sheet music, on disc, and over the radio. This was not the work Jean was very familiar with or contracted to do. The work he had secured through Salabert—indeed the work he was best qualified to do—was not happening in New York. It was happening in Hollywood.

As soon as sound was wedded to film in 1927, the Hollywood motion picture industry bought up the major publishing catalogs—among them Robbins Music, Miller Music, and Leo Feist, Inc. They then lured hordes of the best production songwriters to Hollywood. By the summer of 1929, there were 320 songwriters and composers working on Hollywood movie lots.

Jean was highly qualified to succeed in Hollywood, but there is no indication he went west during this period. Instead, he stayed in New York and spent his time gathering information about American copyright practice and getting to know who was who in the American music publishing world. Things were different here—the whole style of business practice as well as the laws. There was a striking informality in the way things were done. Most deals were consummated with a handshake. If he was going to make an impact here, he had better do his homework.

The year in America went by very slowly. Elsewhere in the world, however, things were moving very fast. In defiance of the Versailles treaty, Hitler began rebuilding the German army a year before Jean had left. Just as he set foot on American soil, German troops were sent to occupy forbidden demilitarized territory in the Rhineland. China was engaged in a desperate war to rid the mainland of the Japanese, Italy had invaded Abyssinia, and Franco, aided by Italy and Germany, had laid siege to Madrid. Now Hitler was openly threatening Czechoslovakia and parading his cock feathers just outside the Austrian border, while independent bands of Nazi thugs practiced terrorism within it. Jean's world back home was in chaos and his family was in danger.

By late 1937, Vienna was a sad imitation of the grandeur Jean had known as a young boy. Shortly after their humiliating World War I defeat, the Austrian power base had been seized by the socialist left, who instituted a series of social reforms admired throughout the world, subsidized with money bled from the wealthy aristocrats and business barons. As the standard of living and educa-tion of workers increased, so did their agitation against the privileged classes. In 1932 Engelbert Dollfuss (aligned with a group supported by Italy's Fascist dictator Benito Mussolini) had taken power and adopted a series of repressive measures, including outlawing the Nazi, Communist, and Social Democratic parties. He abolished freedom of speech and dissolved the Parliament. However extreme these measures seemed, the Jewish businessmen—Dolfi Aberbach among them—had no choice but to stand by their chancellor, knowing that Mussolini's support was the only thing that stood between them and the forced annexation of Austria by Hitler's Germany. After two years, the social unrest had culminated in an unsuccessful armed uprising of Austrian workers in February 1934, and for four days the streets and suburbs of Vienna ran red with blood. Dollfuss was finally assassinated the following July by a renegade Nazi group in an attempted takeover. The regime recovered under a new chancellor, but the country remained deeply divided and relations between the classes were extremely fragile. At this point, Austria's supposed ally Mussolini was partnering with Hitler to support Franco in his Spanish Civil War. In the shabby salons, barons and businessmen whispered of the return to prosperity and privilege, but how could they really believe it, now that the wolf was at the door?

After a year in America, Jean's representation of Salabert properties was up for renewal, and in the spring of 1937 he returned to France to renegotiate his contract. It had been a long and difficult stay, and while he was determined to return to the United States, it had to be under better circumstances. Through his affiliation with Salabert he had became familiar with its American representative Chappell Music and met its renowned director, Max Dreyfus. He was certain he could obtain a job with the firm if his arrangements with Salabert did not improve. Jean redoubled his resolve when Julian took him home to his new, extravagant Paris apartment. While Jean had been living in squalor in America, Julian was enjoying an extravagant lifestyle in Paris, thanks to a recent turn of events.

Initially, things had not gone well for Julian. During the SEMI period, the Aberbach brothers had enjoyed the very highest standard of living. When the Dutch woman returned to reoccupy her townhouse, Jean and Julian relocated to an upscale neighborhood on Montmartre, where they took rooms at the Hotel Alcina, whose other residents included performing stars like Édith Piaf and Lucien Boyer. SEMI supplied the necessary ready cash, and they were also generating money elsewhere—in Germany with *Tovarich,* and in Italy with the *Betty Boop* lyrics. In the latter territory, Jean also had arranged to have his name included as author/composer on these new arrangements, although it's unclear exactly whether he contributed creatively to the works. Nevertheless, this meant the Aberbach brothers were also collecting songwriter royalties from the CIA—

Julian Aberbach.
Courtesy of Susan
Aberbach.

Italy's performing rights agency for music and lyric writers. Therefore, at the time Jean left for America the year before, it seemed there would be plenty of money for Julian to draw on while he looked around for other opportunities.

Spiraling economic problems caused countries around the world to adopt policies limiting foreign money exchange. One by one, in swift succession, the United States, Great Britain, France, Germany, and Italy unexpectedly stopped money flow across their borders. All the profits the Aberbachs had made through SEMI were invested in Vienna real estate, and they could not obtain the generous amounts they had collected in Germany and Italy. Overnight Julian had no job and no money. He was finally evicted from the posh Montmartre residence, reduced for a short time to borrowing a friend's apartment for sleep during the day while he wandered the streets at night like a common tramp.

Finally he engaged a shady Italian broker, who delivered most of the money generated in Italy in cash after extracting an outrageous commission. While the remainder was still an enormous amount of money for that time, who knew how long it would last? He immediately took work with Salabert, representing the use of its catalog music for film and also checking that the royalty amounts provided from the performing rights society were correct. Between the money collected from Italy and the money he was generating at Salabert, Julian could once again afford a luxurious lifestyle. On the other hand, because of the bans on the international flow of money, Jean could not take any of the money they had collected out of France, nor was Salabert prepared to offer him a better deal.

Jean did not like what he saw and felt on that trip. Austria had become a divided and deeply demoralized nation after the assassination of Chancellor Dollfuss. Mussolini, now cooperating with Hitler, could not be trusted. While Hitler declared Austria would not be annexed without consent, no one believed him. It was widely believed that the Führer would take Austria without a shot being fired.

Things were not much better in France. The crippling depression caused the price of agricultural goods to drop and a government rent subsidy program to fail. Thousands of unemployed workers began living on their savings. At the same time, the country was gripped by scandal and disaster: a major train wreck, a public bond fraud, and politically charged investment swindles. Finally, the Popular Front won control, and the rival political parties—Communist, Radical-Socialist, and Socialist—joined them to preserve the Republic from Fascism. They began implementing promising progressive social reforms that thrilled the general public. Now, only two years later, these efforts were floundering, the result of internal party quarreling. Its factions were unable to agree on a united response to the growing threat of war. There was no time left to wait and watch. War was clearly imminent, and the lives of his family were at risk. Jean returned to New York, probably in the summer of 1937, and immediately began preparing affidavits for Julian, his parents, and some close relatives so they could join him in America.

Jean was not alone in his concerns. By this time, thousands of Austrian Jews had emigrated to find peace and prosperity elsewhere. By far, the preferred destination was the United States. Obtaining a visa was complicated and the journey, dangerous. Nevertheless, by the spring of 1938, the mass exodus was clearly apparent. New York night clubs and coffee shops like the Café Vienna became more crowded week after week with Jewish musicians, singers, and artists who had fled Nazi repression in Europe to seek better fortunes in America. Jean's good friend and composer, Fritz Spielman, who would later go on to write the popular American standard "Paper Roses" (1955, with Janice Torre), was among them.

Spielman was a well-known composer of popular songs, light-hearted farces, and musical plays in Vienna. He was making a name for himself and a good living when the winds of politics blew his way. The composer was engaged to be married when it became clear that the racist Nazi juggernaut would make it impossible for him to provide for a family if he stayed in Vienna.

There was no direct route to the United States in March 1938. Spielman and his wife-to-be bought Cuban transit visas and paid the expensive steamship passage, selling all they each owned. They were promptly married in Cuba, and after some anxious time they landed at Ellis Island.

It was not long before they felt at home. Many of the Spielmans' close friends were already here, and because of Fritz's formidable piano skills and good humor, they helped him find work almost immediately. He quickly advanced to the top spot at the Café Vienna. All the young refugees from Austria and Hungary would come to share pastry and coffee—maybe a little light dinner. Afterward, they would dance. During the week he would play his Victor Borge–style comedy songs because he thought it would raise people's spirits. But on Sundays, the Café Vienna would swing with the popular jazz tunes of the day.

He had not known Jean in Vienna, and as he recalls it, their first encounter in America was a bit unnerving. During one Sunday session, Fritz noticed a young man in a shabby coat. Jean had been there all day, arriving just after they began to play and settling down at a small table in the far corner. He had not moved for several hours but just kept staring at the bandstand. Sometimes, Jean would glance over at the composer's wife then back at the band-stand again.

At first Fritz thought he was simply waiting for someone, but it soon became obvious that Jean was there by himself. But he had not danced—not one single tune! And there were many single girls who would have welcomed it. He just sat, nursing his coffee, looking serious, observant. Now he was writing—writing . . . on his shirt cuff! *Who but a madman would do such a thing?*

As he put his full attention on this crazy man, Fritz's mind raced. *Perhaps he is from immigration —had they done something wrong? Maybe he was here to send them back!* Suddenly, Jean was up and moving swiftly across the room, taking long strides—moving toward Mary. *Toward Mary!* As he bent over her, Fritz was frantic. Jean was huge! Six feet, maybe more! He completely obscured little Mary, and he was talking, talking, talking. Fritz expected shy Mary was scared half to death. "Excuse me!" he demanded as he came upon them. They looked up, Jean at first serious—then he broke into a playful grin. "Fritz! Fritz Spielman!" he said in a high-pitched, excited voice. "I know you! I know everything about you!"

"And you are . . . ?" Fritz asked. "Do you know Aberbach?" the man replied. "Yah, yah, Vienna Aberbachs," Fritz said. "Well! I am Jean!" He grabbed Fritz's hand and pumped it warmly. "Jean Aberbach!" breathed Fritz—"a crazy man . . . who writes on his shirt!" Jean glanced at his soiled cuff. "Yes, yes," he replied, dismayed. "I lose many shirts this way. But I never forget!" he laughed.

To Spielman's amazement, Jean then proceeded to enumerate, one by one, all the places he had played in Vienna, and all the songs he had written that had become somewhat popular there. "Now, Fritz," Jean said seriously. "I can help you here. I have attained a good position with the best music publisher in the world. If you have a song coming up, Fritz," he said confidentially, "I am at Chappell these days, although I'm more on the show tunes. In fact, I am in charge of a whole division" Jean continued. "I tell the song pluggers, 'Take this song to Guy Lombardo, take this song to Bob Crosby. . . . Fritz, if you have a song, remember, you must come to me," Jean said, taking his hand. "Of course," Fritz replied. "But Aberbach. I have one question for you. If you are doing so well at this music publisher's business, then why is your coat so shabby?" Fritz was still just a little suspicious. Jean roared with laughter. "Well," he quipped, "Sometimes people give me a dime!"[1]

Jean was indeed doing well, and, frankly, could not care less what people thought of his attire. After leaving Julian in Paris in the middle of 1937, he had returned to New York disappointed that he had been unable to take any money they had collected in France back to America. He immediately approached Max Dreyfus for work to supplement his arrangement with Salabert. Dreyfus hired him as a song plugger and Jean could not have been happier. He was safe in New York, working for the biggest music publishing company in the world, and reporting to Max Dreyfus, someone who is, even now, generally regarded as the best music publisher the world has ever seen.

Born near Baden, Germany, Max Dreyfus immigrated to the United States at the age of fourteen, determined to make his fortune as a pianist and composer. When his biggest-selling song met with only moderate public success, he decided instead to become a rich publisher of America's art music, the songs

Max Dreyfus. Courtesy of the Max and Victoria Dreyfus Foundation.

for musical theater. His early work was as a demonstration pianist and song plugger with the firm of Howley, Haviland & Dresser. Dreyfus later worked for the Witmarks, and for T. B. Harms Company, whose theater music holdings dated back to the Civil War and included the works of American folk composer Stephen Foster. By the time Tom Harms died, Max and his brother Louis owned a large interest in the company. Around 1904, the firm devoted itself to promoting the music of Jerome Kern, who later also became a major shareholder in the company, foreshadowing a future practice of co-ownership with some of his songwriters.

Later, Max would acquire the companies of De Sylva, Brown & Henderson, Green & Stept, Remick Music, and George Gershwin's New World Music. Around this time, Max and his brother Louis opened Harms, Inc.—solely owned by them—and through it purchased the American subsidiary of a respected British publishing company, the merger resulting in Chappell-Harms, Inc. They would use this company as the song repository for all their songs except those connected to stage production works.

Max Dreyfus was a hands-on publisher. Early in his career he had become skilled at turning associate Paul Dresser's sketchy melodies and ideas into viable songs. Schooled in nearly every aspect of the creative profession—writer, composer, song plugger—Max became a formidable music publisher, drawing the very best music talent around him and personally overseeing their work. He guided and advised almost every major important writer in American musical theater—Jerome Kern, Rudolf Friml, George Gershwin, and Richard Rodgers and Lorenz Hart—and was involved in almost all the successful Broadway shows produced during the 1920s. At the same time, he launched the careers of some of the industry's best music men, schooling them in the art of song plugging and copyright management. His power and influence virtually dominated the show tune business. He maneuvered himself into the enviable position of controlling both the means of production and that of promotion, so great was his power over the Broadway producers.

Max was also the most powerful member on the American Society of Composers, Authors and Publishers (ASCAP) board, established in 1914. From a business perspective, ASCAP was a publisher's dream—a nonprofit organization that would police music copyright distribution channels, collect and distribute performance royalties to its author, composer, and publisher members, and pay for itself! Like the French SACEM organization, ASCAP acted as a watchdog of public copyright use, collecting royalties from theaters and radio stations and distributing those funds to the lyricists and composers who had registered their songs with it. As a nonprofit organization, it distributed all the funds it received by set percentages based on classes of membership that depended on criteria such as performance frequency, venue prestige, and membership seniority, keeping a percentage of the gross revenue to cover operating expenses. As far as Max was concerned, ASCAP freed the publisher from time-consuming tasks, cost him nothing, and increased his revenues. What could be better?

Max had been installed as a founder-director, and he remained loyal to the organization throughout its difficult formative years. By virtue of their seniority, his firms maintained the highest ASCAP rating and therefore received the most revenues. He kept a watchful eye on the society's progress, often introducing motions and measures that would protect his interests.

By 1915 the growing new radio and film industries began to challenge Broadway's monopoly on music promotion. Suddenly, songs that could be heard only on the Broadway stage were being performed on radio and as accompaniment to film. Since ASCAP was not equipped to police these new media, performances yielded no revenue for its creators or the publishers that represented them. Feeling this cheapened his properties and discouraged people from attending theater (an industry he was heavily invested in), Max responded by lobbying the ASCAP board to authorize restrictions on radio play for his copyrights, which he exercised liberally.

In contrast, Max's response to the film industry threat was like a good, strategic game of chess. Warner Brothers wanted to circumvent copyright royalty payments to publishers entirely. They could do so by acquiring or creating large libraries of music copyrights they alone would control. In this way, they could avoid paying anyone for the use of music in their films. Max owned the most valuable popular song tune catalog in the business. He recognized the futility of avoiding the motion picture trend. So when Warner Brothers, the biggest, most successful film company, offered to buy the Harms catalog for a staggering price, and sweetened the deal with a directorship on the board of its combined holding company, which also included a retainer for consulting, there was no question whether he would accept the offer. During the summer of 1929 he received $8.5 million from Warner Brothers for the Harms catalog—retaining $4 million personally for himself and his brother.[2]

With the funds he had secured from the Harms deal, his brother Louis went out and bought his publishing firm's parent corporation, Chappell & Co., in Britain, and together he and Max reopened its subsidiary branch in America.[3] Not only did it solidify their position in the American market but it forced entry into the European market as well. By acquiring a controlling share of Chappell & Co. in Britain, Max became a pivotal force in the development of Euro-American music publishing royalty relations. Owning this prestigious British firm allowed him to enter the European music publishing society with considerable power and to pressure European rights societies into cooperative royalty arrangements. Through his efforts, America's ASCAP realized its first royalty revenues collected on American songs performed overseas.[4]

Max's response to Warner Brothers was a classic case of business strategy. Max was motivated as much by power as by money. He understood that as film companies bought up all the big publishers, they were at the same time also acquiring the majority of votes on the ASCAP board. Soon Hollywood would dominate ASCAP. Either they would vote the organization out of existence or, if made to suffer its existence due to antitrust actions, they would exert strong influence over its policies to favor their own goals. To make sure Hollywood's goals would be aligned with his own, it made sense to cash in with Warner and assume an influential position on the board of its new holding company, which included seven other major catalogs as well as his own. Doing this not only put money in his pocket but also ensured he would have a hand in the fate of ASCAP. That mattered to him, because with the money he got from the deal, the Dreyfus brothers went out and bought an interest in an international catalog. Max then arranged for royalties generated overseas to be collected and distributed to him through ASCAP. This strengthened ASCAP against the film interests by demonstrating its potential to bring taxable revenue into the country. This was the kind of deal Max liked, a win by strategy. No matter which way the wind blew, he remained standing—and at the very top of the mountain.

Some history books remember Max as a prodigious gambler, advancing as much as $15,000 (nearly $200,000 in today's money) toward productions his writers were involved in.[5] Even those gestures were driven by strategy, not by chance. During the 1920s Broadway theater was the most important vehicle for song exploitation and, without a show, there was little, if any, chance his copyrights would become enormous popular hits. Collaborating with proven production writers on works he personally oversaw, with confidence in his own abilities to judge the quality of a work and anticipate public reaction and with the superb job of exploitation by his seasoned professional staff, the odds tended to be in his favor on such investments. It was almost assured that the show would be a success, and that at least one or two of the songs would be big-selling hits.

Max understood that the best way to attract great talent—and to keep it— was to offer slightly more than his competitors. He was criticized by other publishers for offering royalty rates greater than the customary two cents per copy of sheet music and one-third of phonograph royalties to his writers.[6] With no significant competition and with enormous money rolling in throughout the 1920s, he could afford to put cash toward shows and be fair and generous with his writers.

Underneath, he was driven by a ruthless agenda that was often obscured by the totality of his brilliant creative success. Selective actions sometimes pitted him directly against his peers. For instance, he rejected membership in the Music Publishers Protective Association (MPPA), an organization of his peers meant to encouraging fairness and ethical practices in the profession and to act as a lobbying force with government. While almost every other publisher opted in, Max rejected membership because he made far better money negotiating the use of his music in film than he otherwise would have received under the compulsory MPPA rate.[7]

Max was a strategist, not a gambler, and these traits are what most attracted Jean to him. Where copyright ownership was concerned, Max was masterful in selling his *cut-in* strategy—a kickback scheme whereby songwriters agreed to allocate part of their author royalties in exchange for preferred treatment by key professionals who could make or break a hit song. Max convinced songwriters that the best means of getting their songs in front of the public was to provide tangible incentive to people who could make their works successful. This might include deejays, singers, or the publishers themselves. Individuals were listed as cowriters of the song even though they may have had nothing whatsoever to do with the creation of the work, so they could share in the royalties if the song became a hit. In this way, everyone was invested in the property and motivated by personal gain to help make it successful. This practice virtually guaranteed Max's dominant hold on the Broadway production machine.

By the time Jean joined Chappell, however, Broadway was not the monopolistic power it had once been. Both radio and film now shared, if not exceeded, Broadway's importance as song promotion vehicles.[8] As Broadway's absolute power declined in the 1930s, so had Max's hold on the industry to some extent. He was still the most influential Broadway publisher, but there was less industry money to be made there than there had been a decade before. Max knew this and was looking for experienced staff to help maintain his hold on Broadway and to expand his influence in film and radio.

Max recognized Jean's unique experience in this area and took an immediate liking to him.[9] Jean had a proven track record, having worked with Campbell, Connelly & Co. in Paris, and Max had observed his efforts in the United States as an independent agent for Salabert.[10] Jean was singularly driven, a tireless worker, and a fast learner who had quickly attained a high level of understanding of American copyright law and its attractive loopholes. After only a short time at song plugging, Max installed Jean in a managerial position where he oversaw an entire division devoted to show music exploitation and property acquisitions. This gave him a free hand to pursue copyrights and catalogs wherever he saw opportunities. Some of these opportunities came from the most unexpected places.

Publisher Leo Feist had sold the bulk of Leo Feist, Inc., to filmmaker Metro-Goldwyn-Mayer (MGM) in 1935 but retained the educational catalog and some other minor areas as well. The educational division was put in the hands of his son, Leo, Jr., but the energetic young man found it hopelessly boring. So Leo,

Jr., began to publish some contemporary music as well. Somehow he got to know the acclaimed Russian classical composer Igor Stravinsky, whose *Rite of Spring* and *Firebird Suite* are considered symphonic masterpieces of the twentieth century. Now, twenty-five years later, Stravinsky was bent on becoming a Tin Pan Alley songwriter.

Young Leo thought this was just the funniest thing! In the year during which Stravinsky had premiered his magnificent *Symphony in C*, he was also frequenting smoky jazz clubs and other popular music haunts, desperately hoping something would sink in. He did write a pop tune and kept hounding Leo, Jr., to get a lyric written for it. Jean apparently caught wind of this and invited himself by one day. Jean and Leo agreed to a one-year deal for exclusive representation with Chappell, no advance on royalties, with continuation pending on the publisher's ability to successfully obtain a performance.

Some opportunities paid off, but this was not one of them. Try as he might, Igor Stravinsky was hopeless as a Tin Pan Alley writer. That he tried at all given his towering reputation in serious music is surprising. But that he failed is testament to the unique creative talent that was required to write a successful pop tune. Not everyone had that talent—not even one of the most highly trained and respected composers of the twentieth century. And without that talent Jean had nothing to promote. The term of their Chappell agreement lapsed quietly.

Jean loved working for Max. He was in the center of the most exciting pool of talent in the music industry. Max had every important Broadway writer under contract—Sigmund Romberg, writer of *The Student Prince,* Jerome Kern of *Show Boat* fame, and Richard Rodgers and Oscar Hammerstein II, whose *Oklahoma!* later won a Pulitzer Prize. They used to assemble right outside his office, trade jokes and stories, and discuss their projects. On weekends they would often gather at Max's house in Brewster, New York, to relax, fiddle with new tunes, and just enjoy each other's company.

Jean could not have been happier. Whether spending Sundays at the Café Vienna or with Max at his comfortable home in Brewster, whether rubbing elbows with orchestra leaders at nightclubs, or taking part in light-hearted banter with Broadway luminaries outside his office door, Jean was finally sure he was exactly where he was meant to be. He was certain of it. While Max's decisions sometimes perplexed his colleagues, Jean understood them immediately, reducing them to logical chess moves, a game he knew and played well. Jean was already analyzing these masterful moves in preparation for the day he might make his own name for himself in the business: *Look for seasoned talent with proven track records. . . . Money follows power. . . . When necessary, pay a little more than the fellow down the road.* Jean wore his shabby, unassuming coat and quietly gathered up Max's dimes of wisdom as they dropped from his pocket. Not one bit of Max's brilliance was lost on him.

CHAPTER 5

Eye of the Needle

While Jean's career flourished at Chappell, trouble was brewing across the sea. With the growing concern over the influx of immigrants to Paris and the hateful propaganda about Jews propagated by the Nazi party, there was already serious talk in the French government about conducting a census and restricting movement of nonresidents in order to assert more control over them. During the early months of 1939, Julian's immigration number came up. He thought it best to leave quietly. He declared that he deserved a vacation and would like to see the World's Fair in New York, scheduled to open April 30, 1939. Although Salabert's wife believed he would never return, her husband granted the retreat, and Julian departed for the United States, probably arriving sometime in April 1939.

Things in Vienna were even more serious. On threat of becoming another besieged Madrid, Austrian chancellor Kurt von Schuschnigg had signed a document on February 12, 1938, lifting bans on Nazism. The embittered Schuschnigg would later admit he had signed Austria's death warrant. Four weeks later, the chancellor was in prison and German Nazis were patrolling the streets of

Vienna. Since everything that Dolfi and Anna had worked for their whole lives was in Vienna, there was great incentive to stay and try to work with the new government, but the situation quickly got worse.

A repressive regime was quickly installed and a systematic purge of Jews and other "undesirables" was under way. How Dolfi and Anna managed to endure there for more than a year is a mystery, but Dolfi's standing in the community may have had something to do with it. Those in power knew that financial and worker management skills like Dolfi's were temporarily needed to help preserve order and productivity during the transfer of power. They also knew that men like Dolfi had the resources and connections to buy their way into exile once they had exhausted their usefulness. When the time came, Nazi officers would be happy to take their money and property and assist them in the emigration process.

The situation was very different for Jean's cousin, John Schmetterling. While Jean and Julian had pursued business, John had studied law. Young, educated Jewish teachers, lawyers, and political activists were most feared by the Reich, for they were articulate, trusted, and able to refute the Nazi propaganda and mobilize the masses.

As long as other countries were willing to accept them and their passage could be arranged, the Nazi regime cordially assisted in the deportation of Jews. They oversaw the process of transfer papers, visa purchase, and transport fees, keeping prices standardized and the process orderly. This ensured the steady and peaceful transport of "undesirables" from German-occupied areas, and made sure that the maximum possible assets would be left behind for seizure.

Shortly after Julian arrived in New York, the brothers had pooled their money and purchased visas and passage for their parents. Leaving everything they owned behind, Anna and Dolfi made their way through Bremen to Hamburg with transit papers, landing documents, and vessel tickets in hand, confident that they would soon reach the safety of Cuba, where they could stay until their U.S. immigration quota numbers came up.

Unfortunately, by this time receiving countries like the United States and Palestine had exceeded their immigration quotas and had closed their doors to foreign exiles. The Gestaatspolizei, or Gestapo—anxious to promote the exodus of Jews by any possible means—connived with German steamship operators and South American officials and began authorizing the sale of illegal visas that allowed the refugees to leave the occupied territories but did not guarantee a entry at a destination country.

Such was the case for the passengers of the ill-fated steamship *St. Louis*. On May 13, 1939, 936 passengers set sail from Hamburg for Cuba.[1] Cuba—a preferred port because of its convenient proximity to the United States—had already accepted a disproportionately high number of refugees compared to other, richer nations. The island was overrun with almost 10,000 displaced foreigners and its economy was feeling the strain.[2] On May 5, the Cuban president invalidated all but twenty-two landing certificates that had been previously approved by the Cuban State, Labor, and Treasury departments. Anna and Dolfi Aberbach's certificates were among those rejected.

Some days before the boat docked in Havana, Jean and Julian were there to meet them and to make arrangements for their temporary stay. Having used most of their available cash to secure passage for their parents, they had to transport themselves to Miami by bus. When they finally arrived, they took a hydrofoil to Cuba, where they waited for the ship to arrive.

A few days out from port, there were signs of trouble. Telegrams had been sent to the ship's captain by Cuban authorities, who expressed serious doubt about the validity of the passenger's landing papers. Panic swept the ship. Some fell ill with worry, one died. Fearful that the Cuban government would use the dead passenger's body as an excuse to bar the ship from port, the unfortunate man was given a burial at sea. Although the liner arrived safely at Havana port on May 27, 1939, only those passengers with preauthorized visas were allowed to disembark, while the remaining (more than 900, including 400 women and children) looked on in despair.

After a few days, it became clear that there was little to do except wait and pray. Jean and Julian managed to rent a small boat, which transported them to the side of the vessel. A newspaper photographer recorded the scene as they stood in the boat waving to Anna and Dolfi, who are high above them on the ocean liner rail, the distance too great to communicate in any other way.

This heartbreaking scene was played out again and again over the course of the next few agonizing days. Scores of friends and relatives on these small boats wept helplessly as they shouted words of encouragement to their frantic loved ones high above. On May 31, a lawyer traveling with his wife and children slit his wrists and jumped overboard. The ship's captain wired Cuban authorities that he feared a wave of suicides if he was forced to leave port. Nevertheless the ship was forced to remove itself from Havana port on June 2, to linger just off the coast of Miami.

By June 8 the *St. Louis* was being referred to as the "saddest ship afloat," with its "cargo of human despair." Cuba remained unmoved and the United States, upholding its staunch neutrality, could not be swayed despite the fact that 734 of its passengers—including Anna and Dolfi—already had confirmed identification numbers on the American immigration quota list.

The ship was forced to begin the tortuous journey back to Europe. As the ship steamed eastward across the Atlantic toward Hamburg, a volunteer committee was formed to patrol the decks to prevent further suicide attempts. Meanwhile, the captain weighed the enormous risk of deliberately running aground off the English coast rather than returning to Germany.

NEVER SAY DIE, Havana Jews shout to their banished friends.

Jean Aberbach ("myself") and Julian Aberbach ("my brother Julius") on a small boat docked next to the ocean liner *St. Louis* off the coast of Havana, Cuba, June 2, 1939. This photo appeared in the *Miami Herald*.

As the vessel neared the British Isles, an arrangement was made for Belgium, the Netherlands, Britain, and France to each take approximately 250 passengers. While much of the world breathed a sigh of relief, little did anyone know that most of these people could only delay, not escape, their fate. While most Americans were only just becoming aware of Nazi racial oppression, members of the immigrant Jewish community knew only too well that the passengers were doomed if they were forced to return to German soil.

Jean and Julian were not willing to accept that in all probability they had seen their parents for the last time. As soon as they returned to New York, Julian booked passage on the steamship *Normandy* back to Europe. He met his parents at Bologne-sur-Mer, where they had been transported after landing in Antwerp, and he brought them to Paris, where they would wait as they would have in Cuba, until their American immigration numbers came up.

By this time there were 200,000 Jews living in Paris, a large portion of which were refugees from Germany and Austria.[3] Anti-Semitism had been growing in Paris throughout the 1930s, as had suspicion of any immigrants and visitors. As a result, the Jews from the *St. Louis* were not welcome in Paris. Instead Julian was forced to make arrangements for them to stay at a bed and breakfast outside Paris. Meanwhile, Julian took up residence at a Paris hotel.

Away from the petit-bourgeois community on Montmartre he was used to, Julian began to feel the full force of anti-Semitism in the capital. The new radical premier Édouard Daladier was determined to make life as uncomfortable for Jews in Paris as possible. He ordered that residence papers held by alien Jews be replaced with expulsion orders suspended only in exchange for temporary residency permits that required weekly renewal. In order to avoid routine police checks, Julian led a clandestine life while friends and associates brought in food and ran errands for him.[4]

Eight weeks later, upon Germany's invasion of Poland on September 3, 1939, France declared war on the aggressor. By virtue of the forced annexation of Austria to Germany, Julian graduated from being a tolerated foreign guest to an enemy alien. The country immediately undertook to identify and detain all visitors of Germanic descent as possible enemy sympathizers and potential spies. No longer working and without permanent residence papers, Julian could claim no valid reason for his continued presence there. Once gas masks were issued to French citizens, who were instructed to carry them with them at all times, it became impossible to hide. After barely escaping internment by deliberately contracting influenza, he collected the necessary exit papers, hid as much money as possible in a money belt, and fled Paris, making his way through France to Spain and finally Portugal. He secured passage from Lisbon and arrived back in the United States on November 1, 1939.

They managed to relocate their parents to Bordeaux, a major port city in southwestern France, which had access to the Atlantic for oceangoing vessels via the Bay of Biscay and to the Mediterranean through a series of canal locks. It was far safer than Paris and was the most likely place from which to depart. A U.S. consulate was there and the brothers encouraged Anna and Dolfi to plead their case to the authorities while they did what they could from the States.

Dolfi and Anna Aberbach's immigration quota numbers came up shortly thereafter. They escaped the jaws of war only three months before Hitler began his assault on Western Europe. After a year of anxiety and frustration, deception and fear, they arrived safely in New York, probably in February 1940.

The next few years would show that Anna and Dolfi's chances had been little better than trying to pass an elephant through the eye of a needle. Of more than 900 men, women and children returned to Europe aboard the *St. Louis*, 288 took refuge in Great Britain. The rest were distributed across Belgium, the

Netherlands, and France. Only those that landed in Britain—and the few like Anna and Dolfi who managed some other escape, were to survive. Most of the rest perished in German concentration camps over the next few years. Of approximately 300 Aberbach relations, only twenty were left. As if disappointed, fate taunted Anna and Dolfi one last time when the ocean liner that had carried them safety struck a mine and sank on its return voyage.[5]

CHAPTER 6

Ambition

After their parents arrived, the family moved north of the city to a suburb called Inwood. All four were dependent on Jean's salary at first, but before long Julian found a job selling toiletry cases to army post exchanges and chains of variety stores. In the meantime, Dolfi attended night school for English, returning home to teach each lesson to Anna. Soon after, he landed a job as an agent for the sale of low-cost paintings for domestic decoration to the chain stores.

Their domestic bliss was shattered when, on December 7, 1941, prompted by the devastating bombing of Pearl Harbor, President Franklin Delano Roosevelt declared war on Japan. America entered a conflict that had been going on for years, and the country was keenly aware from the start that it had joined the losing side. But by this time the newspapers and newsreels had familiarized the public with the conflict, and the campaign was viewed as a righteous one. Thousands of Americans—many of them newly arrived refugees—reported for duty, prepared to give their life in defense of the free world.

Jean and Julian did not hesitate to fight for their adopted country. The induction doctor accepted Julian but refused to admit Jean because of a leg injury suffered during his youth. When Julian set off for armed service in July 1942, Jean resumed his work at Chappell with the financial burden of the family once again largely on his shoulders.

Despite the pressure, Jean was living the American dream. Here he was in the greatest city in the world, safe and free. He was climbing the corporate ladder at America's greatest music publishing house surrounded by America's most respected composers and songwriters. In the plush offices of the RKO building, he was soaking up the street-savvy Tin Pan Alley rhetoric and immersing himself in creative works dense with American themes.

Initially Jean was engaged to find and sign new writers of theatrical musical shows. Either he would contact the show's producer or he would approach the show writers directly and induce them to have Chappell publish their music. Writers knew that they would obtain the same percentage guaranteed by law with any publisher. Therefore, to attract good talent the deal might include covering the expense of preparing all the orchestrations (the individual sheet music parts required for each orchestra instrument) needed for the show. For this, Chappell maintained a number of outstanding arrangers under exclusive contract to work with their show music. This was mutually advantageous, since the company would then also be entitled to publish the arrangements of the song, in addition to the original song itself, increasing their royalties.

For these reasons, and because of its global reach, a writer would take an offer from Chappell very seriously—even if the customary advance was not forthcoming. No other publisher had the global power and influence of Chappell because the company owned a majority share of Chappell & Co. in Great Britain. They also had powerful representatives or subsidiaries who could promote a writer's work in other major European countries.

Jean had studied the business carefully—and nowhere more carefully than at the bandstand's edge. It was the height of the era of sweet bands and soft crooners. Radio had increased the reach of popular music tremendously. Getting a respected bandleader like Guy Lombardo or a singer like Bing Crosby to perform a song on radio assured enormous returns. The odds were not favorable, however. A study of ASCAP performance records from 1938 revealed that out of the 15 million performances played on radio in 1938 almost half could be attributed to only 15 percent of the song pool.[1]

Until *Variety* gave it a name in October 1938 and ASCAP reminded its publisher members of New York State's laws on commercial bribery, there was no form of "payola" that would not be offered in return for a plug. Even the most ethical orchestra leader felt justified in accepting these rewards—be it money in their pocket, support for the band, discounted rehearsal space, or a "cut-in" where the leader would be listed as one of the composers on the copyright to share in the long term royalties should the song become a hit. Bandleaders felt justified because it was only through their band's performances that a song might gain popularity at all. They knew that if a song became an enormous hit, the author and composer could live comfortably, collecting royalties perhaps for their entire lifetime. What did these bandleaders have to look forward to? How comfortable would they be when they could no longer work? Unless they wrote and published hits themselves, they had no opportunity for such long-term security—even if they performed the song on a record that sold millions! Eventually, the pressing run for their record would be exhausted and their band's version would die. The song itself, however, would live on, perhaps covered by major performers for decades to come as a result of their efforts to first popularize it. And so these practices went on, despite scorching editorials in *Variety* bemoaning the evils of payola, and its deliberate circumvention of the Federal Trade Commission's code of ethical business practice.

Between 1935 and 1945, wages and the cost of living fluctuated wildly as international trade collapsed, domestic production faltered, and America prepared for war. Professional managers tightened their belts during the war years like every other American. To protect against spiraling inflation brought on by the shortage of goods, rationing was established for gasoline, sugar, coffee, shoes, fat, meat, and cheese as the war progressed. On April 1, 1943, President Roosevelt froze prices, wages, and salaries.[2]

Jean struggled throughout the war years at Chappell, his salary probably never topping $100 per week. At one point, everyone at Chappell was forced to take a fifty percent cut in pay. Nevertheless, payola was part of the game, and Jean knew he had to get with the program if he hoped to compete in this business. Needing grease for the wheel, he found himself dipping into his own meager resources. Sometimes he would wager as much as 20 percent of his own weekly take-home pay.

Even though his efforts consistently yielded results, these were rarely reflected in his paycheck. Max Dreyfus had not become a millionaire by being careless with his money, and although Chappell had practically unlimited resources, Max was careful to instruct his staff not to use them. He wanted results that cost him nothing and was delighted when they seemed to appear out of thin air. Fritz Spielman recalls Jean's complaint of never having received a bonus for placing the hit song "Symphonie" in a motion picture.

Jean was not much better off than anyone else in the business, all of whom faced the same challenges, but he seemed to have better luck than most others. This probably had more to do with his style than with money. He was refined, but at the same time very warm and personable, with natural charm that put people at ease. Jean genuinely liked people, and he liked what he was doing. It was this quality—probably above all else—that distinguished him. He succeeded more than others because his polish shone a little brighter, his handshake felt a little warmer, and his offer came through a little clearer than those of his competitors.

The fruits of these labors, however, served only to profit Max Dreyfus and Chappell Music. Jean did not come to America to work for someone else. He wanted something of his own, and having attained the level of professional manager responsible for one of Max's major divisions, he knew he had gone just about as high as he could in this company. Where Chappell Music was concerned, probably the only way up was out.

Jean had been watching his mentor over the years as if he were studying the moves of a master chess player. He learned the importance of nurturing new talent, but he also noticed that Max had no interest in long shots. Invariably, Max chose artists that had already proven themselves as dedicated, original, consistent, and prolific artists. He wanted catalogs, staff, works, and writers with proven track records. Anything less gave him heartburn.[3]

For instance, by the time George Gershwin came to Max, he had gained the admiration of singer Sophie Tucker and had already been published by Harry Von Tilzer, a famous publisher of earlier decades. Despite this recognition, Re-mick music publishing house hired him as a demonstration pianist rather than a composer, but this did not deter him. In 1915 Gershwin began making piano rolls of his own music for Standard Music Roll and Aeolian Companies, and produced them with remarkable regularity under a variety of assumed names. It was only after his excellent work as a rehearsal pianist for *Miss 1917* under the direction of Victor Herbert and Jerome Kern that Max was convinced of the young man's relentless drive, unlimited talent, and long-term potential. In 1918 Max hired Gershwin exclusively to write songs for his T. B. Harms firm.

Vincent Youmans followed a similar path, progressing from composing and playing works recorded to piano rolls and then preparing and rehearsing musi-cal shows for the armed forces during World War I under the direction of John Philip Sousa. He also worked as a demonstration pianist and song plugger for Remick and went on to assist Victor Herbert on *Oui Madame* in 1920. Only after these successes was Youmans invited into Chappell as a salaried songwriter.

Jean also had learned that even the world's greatest song would not sell itself. It was up to the music publisher to find—or even create—a place for the song on the contemporary music scene, because doing so could reap rewards beyond the song itself. Max Dreyfus himself worked the street to place Gersh-win and Youmans's works in popular musicals that would provide the best pos-sible exposure. His successes included placing Gershwin's "Some Wonderful Sort of Someone" in Nora Bayes's show *Ladies First* and inserting two George Gershwin-Irving Caesar songs into *Good Morning Judge*. These achievements encouraged Gershwin to start writing his own scores for Broadway musicals, thereby producing a more valuable type of music property for Max's firm.

A key ingredient to his success was the fact that Max specialized. He picked an area of music and proceeded to dominate it throughout his career. Even as the movies were stealing Broadway's promotional power, he continued to resist diversification. Broadway was his power position in the industry and, as long as Broadway remained the centerpiece of American popular music, he would remain at the top of the music pyramid.

Max and his brother Louis also took a systematic approach toward acquiring companies. They would begin by quietly buying up small chunks of stock, adding to these over time until they had acquired a major stock share. They were then poised to take over the company or exercise control over the board as their needs required. T. B. Harms, for instance, was originally acquired in this way, as was Britain's Chappell & Company. The Dreyfus brothers also held 50 percent of Remick, a company that, in a number of important cases, acted as Chappell's talent farm and over which they exercised their influence from time to time.

Finally Jean realized that the greatest investment Max ever made was to stand by ASCAP during its first tenuous decade. He came in on the ground floor as one of its early publishing members and, at that time, had nothing really to lose if it failed. But he understood that if it took off, the organization could grow to become the most powerful entity in the music industry. The gamble paid off, and the goodwill the organization showed him throughout the 1920s and 1930s was well worth those few tense years of peer criticism.

It also did not escape Jean that Max had a powerful asset in his brother. Louis was skilled, but in a different way from Max. Louis preferred financial management to the practical work of music publishing. He also preferred to live in London. It was through Louis's manipulations that the British firm of Chappell & Company came under the Dreyfus brothers' control. They collaborated on many such investments and complemented each other's strengths in almost exactly the same way that Jean and Julian brought different talents to their business ventures. Such parallels fascinated Jean, who knew that the Aberbach brothers could learn much from the Dreyfus brothers' success.

Through its own persistent arrogance, ASCAP had lost its monopolistic hold on the music industry. Several key publisher members had left to join another newly formed performing rights organization—this one aligned with radio broadcasters. Broadcast Music Incorporated (BMI) was created in protest of an exorbitant increase in the performance royalty imposed by the board of ASCAP in 1940, which doubled the cost of broadcasting any ASCAP work. When the broadcasters refused to pay, the members of ASCAP retracted their catalogs, expecting the broadcasters to give in to the outrageous demand. Much to their surprise, folk and country music, blues and jazz—songs that ASCAP had no interest in and no control over—began flooding the airways. Worse yet for them, the public reaction to the change was positive.

As the most powerful ASCAP board member, Max Dreyfus was among those publishers who had endorsed the rate increase. Max felt that a recent boom in record and sheet music sales and projected steady growth in the broadcast industry warranted a significant rate increase that would be enforced over the next five years. Radio executives, however, felt ASCAP failed to consider several constraining factors likely to slow radio's growth such as the war, audience loss to television, and the cost of retrofitting stations to leverage the new FM bandwidth.[4] Nevertheless, ASCAP persisted in its demands.

When the plan backfired and BMI emerged, Max and the other members of the ASCAP board summarily ignored it. BMI had been established with very little start-up capital, and although major networks had made pledges of partial support, they were slow to live up to their commitments. Moreover, broadcasters were wary of the crude, often amateur music that represented the bulk of BMI's start-up catalog. They had every reason to believe the new performance rights organization would simply fade away.

Max had no intention of according any credibility to the little upstart BMI organization, but all that changed in late 1940. Suddenly longtime ASCAP firms Peer International and E. B. Marks defected to BMI. This put a disturbing new spin on things. BMI had grown to a staff of 220 people over the course of the year, shipping about fourteen new popular songs and thirty-five arrangements of popular public domain tunes each week to approximately 150 radio stations around the country.[5] They had gone from doing no business to generating $1.8 million by the end of 1941. Despite these developments which proved beyond any doubt the public interest and profitability of folk, country, jazz, blues, and international music, Max still resisted adding these genres to his catalog or allowing ASCAP to consider handling them.

One could argue Max was simply out of step with the times, but from a strategic standpoint he did the most logical thing. Acknowledging the fledgling organization or embracing its crude content could have done nothing but undermine his own interests and devalue his copyrights. To the end he would remain staunchly against BMI and everything it stood for, and he probably expected the rest of his staff to do the same.

But working in the music trenches, Jean could hardly ignore the fact that BMI was boasting hit songs almost from the very start. Tucked in with their mainstream pop hits like "I Don't Want to Set the World on Fire" (words and music by Eddie Seiler, Sol Marcus, Bennie Benjamin, and Eddie Durham), which turned out to be the top song of 1941, and the Mills Brother's popular revival of Johnny S. Black's "Paper Doll" from 1915 were successful hillbilly tunes like the audience-participation hit "Deep in the Heart of Texas" (words and music by June Hershey and Don Swander), and "You Are My Sunshine" (by Charles Mitchell and Jimmy Davis, the latter of whom popularized it as a campaign song for his successful run for Louisiana governor). Worse yet, some of these songs were finding their way into the hands of major singers. Bing Crosby, for instance, made a hit with his Decca recording of Al Dexter's "Pistol Packin' Mama."[6]

The purveyors of so-called "serious" popular music suffered yet another setback in May 1942 when James Caesar Petrillo, Union leader of the powerful Chicago chapter of the American Federation of Musicians and the acknowledged king of its national board, ordered a strike by its national membership to protest loss of work from radio's replacement of live performances with records. Anticipating this, some record companies worked around the clock for months stockpiling recordings that would be released gradually over the time musicians were banned from setting foot in a studio. Others raided their back catalogs, unearthing and releasing sessions that had been shelved for one reason or another. A cappella singing (vocal music not accompanied by instruments) was revived, and producers experimented with nontraditional accompaniment, such as whistling and ensemble kazoos. The lack of new material, and the need for recorded music to entertain the American troops, further increased the popularity of hillbilly and race music both on disc and over the air.

Jean saw a tremendous window of opportunity opening before him. Though the industry was still a confusing mess, he could tell the difference between *an* opportunity and *the* opportunity: The former made money, whereas the latter made fortunes. This was no little shake-up. The entire industry was reorganizing itself. If he acted now, he could carve out his own place in it.

It was not as though Jean was a stranger to country, jazz, or blues music. After all, the first two important publishing companies to leave ASCAP for BMI were the very same two companies Jean had represented as an independent in Paris a few years before—Peer International and E. B. Marks. These two had somewhat different problems with ASCAP, but they shared the belief that ASCAP's distribution scheme was unfair. This tiered rating system assigned compensation rates for a song based on a variety of factors including frequency of play, market reach, and chart position. These distributions were not uniform for all publishers, but were adjusted based on factors including membership seniority. Longtime board members such as Max Dreyfus continued to control the guidelines for awarding ASCAP membership and assigning compensation rates. Senior board members also continued to receive the lion's share of ASCAP revenues, even when their firms showed declining performances.

E. B. Marks was one of the original Union Square Tin Pan Alley song pluggers who had built an impressive catalog of popular hits over almost forty years. Like several other firms, he had been fighting a decade-long battle to get his catalog upgraded to the highest distribution rate then monopolized by six publishing firms, two of which Max Dreyfus owned or had a substantial interest in (Harms and Remick). Marks, along with Sam Fox, G. Schirmer, and others, argued that the major portion of songs now included in films overwhelmingly belonged to them, and that since most of the money was now coming from the movie companies, they were entitled to proportional compensation—an upgrade to the highest distribution rate.[7]

Although a contemporary of Max Dreyfus, E. B. Marks was a very different kind of publisher. Marks came up from the street and had no highbrow illusions about either his talents or the public. Compared to Dreyfus, he was the P. T. Barnum of Tin Pan Alley, fashioning his first hit from a sensational newspaper story about a lost child who discovers that the policeman assisting her is really her long-lost father. "The Little Lost Child" became a music-hall hit in the 1890s, enabling the establishment of the Joseph W. Stern & Co. publishing house, which became the firm of E. B. Marks when his writing partner retired. Marks championed music of the people and for the people. He created the illustrated song slide, a series of action and sentimental pictures that assisted theater audiences in recalling lyrics for musical sing-a-longs.

Where Max Dreyfus looked for music of the highest quality that would appeal to the elite and trickle down to the masses, E. B. Marks looked for music that would appeal to the widest possible audience, the elite be damned. During the years Jean was representing him in Paris, Marks had several popular hits that underscored his dissident urge to buck highbrow tradition. While Max was publishing the Ira Gershwin-Vernon Duke classic "I Can't Get Started" and Noël Coward's "Mrs. Worthington (Don't Put Your Daughter on the Stage)," Marks was publishing "The Cockeyed Mayor of Kaunakakai," eventually popularized by comic artist Hilo Hattie.[8] He also published "Let's Dance," the raucous theme song of the Benny Goodman Orchestra, a band that ushered in the swing era and touched off jitterbug dancing frenzies that bordered on mass hysteria. Marks did not stop there, shaking the tree again with the haunting, controversial, and singularly powerful Billie Holiday antilynching song "Strange Fruit" by Abel Meeropol (a.k.a. Lewis Allan) in 1939. Marks also had several Spanish hits, including "(Allá en) El Rancho Grande," which became a bestselling record for Bing Crosby, "My Shawl (Ombo)," the theme song for the internationally renowned Xavier Cugat Orchestra, and "What a Diff'rence a Day Made" whose English lyric adaptation would eventually become an American standard, recorded by scores of popular artists.[9] By contrast, the closest Max Dreyfus seems to have come to publishing a Hispanic hit during this period was Richard Rodgers and Lorenz Hart's "All Dressed Up (Spic and Spanish)" from the 1939 musical *Too Many Girls*.

Another disgruntled ASCAP member was Ralph Peer. His ASCAP firm, Southern Music, was founded in 1928 and housed many popular tunes—including much of the catalog of Hoagy Carmichael. Victor Recording Company shared ownership until Victor sold outright to Peer in 1932. His other firm, Peer International, was probably formed to collect folk, blues, country, and international songs that ASCAP refused to handle.

In addition to controlling all the performance revenue in the industry, the ASCAP board seems to have believed it was their responsibility to uphold a certain "quality" standard in American music. Peer was directly affected by this. Writers of folk, blues, country, and international music were denied membership in ASCAP on the basis of the inferior artistic quality of their work, making it virtually impossible for them to collect any money for the public performances of their work. Ralph Peer could not collect performance royalties on the many songs he had worked to popularize, such as the hillbilly works of Jimmie Rodgers (the legendary "blue yodeler" now regarded as the "father of country music") and the Carter Family, whose renditions of Appalachian folk music became enormously popular.

That all modern American country and western music can be traced back to one of these two artists whom he recorded in Bristol, Tennessee, during the 1920s is testament to Peer's unique pioneering insight. Peer's copyrights were infused with a quintessential American spirit and, as his continental representative, Jean was exposed to all of them. He represented all of Peer's copyrights in Europe, including those original songs or arrangements of public domain tunes by writers denied ASCAP membership. Among the gems were numerous Jimmie Rodgers hits such as the 1932 "Gamblin' Polka Dot Blues," "Peach Picking Time Down in Georgia" (featuring his distinctive blue yodeling), and "Mother, Queen of My Heart" (written with Hoyt Bryant), the last two preserved on Victor recordings produced in 1933, the last year of his life.[10] The Carter Family contributed "I'm Thinking Tonight of My Blue Eyes," (1930), "Jimmie Brown, the Newsboy" (1931), "Amber Tresses Tied with Blue" (1932), and "Worried Man Blues" (1930).

There were other country numbers as well, including the popular "Roll Along, Kentucky Moon" (1932, Bill Halley), "Walk Right In" (1930, Gus Cannon and H. Woods), which enjoyed popularity with a new generation during the folk revival of the 1960s, as well as "When the Bloom Is on the Sage" (1930, Fred Howard and Nat Vincent), which became the theme song of "Tom Mix and His Straight Shooters" radio series.

Peer's ASCAP firm, Southern Music, included the blues inspired work of Hoagy Carmichael: "Georgia on My Mind" (1930, with Stuart Gorrell), "Lazy River" (1931, with Sidney Arodin, introduced by Mildred Bailey), "Lazybones" (1933, popularized by Rudy Vallee), and "Down t' Uncle Bill's," and "Fare-Thee-Well to Harlem," the last three of which were written with Johnny Mercer.

Peer's catalog included jazz as well. There was the jazz instrumental "South" (1930, Charles Carpenter, Bennie Moten—the pianist, not the bassist—and

Thamon Hayes), Louis Armstrong's hit "You Can Depend on Me" (1932, Charles Carpenter, Louis Dunlap, and Earl Hines), and "Business in F" (1931, Archie Bleyer), introduced by Fletcher Henderson's Orchestra.

Peer also collected international songs: "Green Eyes" (1931, Adolfo Utrera and Nilo Menendez, English lyrics by E. Rivera and Eddie Woods), a Cuban-flavored best-seller for the Jimmy Dorsey Orchestra a decade later; "Adios" (1931, Eddie Woods and Enric Madriguera), theme song of Madriguera's orchestra; and the quintessential Afro-Cuban piece, introduced by the fiery Xavier Cugat orchestra, "Babalú" (1941, Margarita Lecuona, English words by Bob Russell).[11]

That both of Peer's catalogs ended up with Jean Aberbach for continental representation early in Jean's career seemed like a matter of design rather than accident. This was music no one else would touch—much of which could not even be classified as valuable enough for representation in its own country of origin. Yet Jean gladly accepted the challenge. What attracted him to it? How could someone schooled in the fine arts and classical music have an appreciation for the raw, "primitive" folk, jazz, and blues songs that made up the Peer catalog and peppered that of Marks?

Jean had grown up in Vienna, where folk music was the springboard for many great composers. During the eighteenth century, Wolfgang Amadeus Mozart (1756–1791) composed pleasant, playful concertos that mirrored the rural simplicity of the countryside surrounding him there. In the nineteenth century, the German *Lieder* tradition flourished. These high art poems and stories were modeled after old English and Scottish ballads. In the hands of Franz Peter Schubert (1797–1828), these folk-inspired songs became revered concert music that still retained a quaint, folksy feel by recalling the sounds of nature or sketching picturesque rural scenes through its piano accompaniment and poetry. "Gretchen am Spinnrade" (1814), for instance, presents the courtship and musings of a peasant girl, much of which takes place above the whirring sound of her spinning wheel. A generation later Johannes Brahms (1833–1897) successfully merged Beethoven's classical ideals with Schubert's quaint romanticism, creating some of the most powerful orchestral music ever written. Where his songs were concerned Brahms also turned to the genuine simplicity of folk music. He regarded the folk tunes that surrounded him in Vienna as ideal models. Painting quaint, rural country scenes through music by using familiar folks tunes and retaining the folk-song form of verses alternating with chorus, Brahms anchored some of the most harmonically complex and technically demanding classical works of the period.

Therefore, growing up in Vienna Jean understood the value of folk music as the seed of—if not the model for—great works in the popular and art music traditions. As Peer's representative in Europe years before, he had had no problem promoting the unusual songs found in Peer's catalogs. Little did he know that this novelty American music would later become the key to his success.

Sometime in 1942 all the pieces fell together and he suddenly realized that he was in a unique position, given his familiarity with the music and intimate understanding of the copyright business, of these new music trends. Perhaps, he could convince Max to finance an independent BMI firm so that together they could compete with Peer and Marks. On the other hand, BMI was still in its shaky start-up phase and was looking for bright new publishing talent that would lend credibility to its operation. Perhaps he could leverage his reputation at Chappell for some start up money and establish his own company. Just as Max had done with ASCAP, he would be coming into BMI on the ground floor. He could specialize—but in hillbilly music and other popular song forms, rather than Broadway show tunes. Or maybe he would somehow buy into BMI existing companies—maybe even Peer International or E. B Marks.

By 1943 he was anxious to act, due in part to a real threat that was gathering: Fred Rose, an ASCAP songwriter and Nashville radio figure. Rose had suddenly appeared in town seeking ASCAP funding for his fledgling publishing firm, a coventure with top hillbilly artist Roy Acuff. He met with ASCAP general manager John Paine, proposing to sew up the commercial market for hillbilly music by capturing all its major songs and songwriters for ASCAP. In this way, ASCAP would not just steal the fire from BMI, it would extinguish it completely.[12]

Rose had been admitted to ASCAP as a songwriter in 1928 on the strength of three popular songs: "Honest and Truly," "'Deed I Do," and "Red Hot Mama," but these were the best he would ever produce. By 1934 he had achieved only a Class 4 ASCAP rating, which afforded only $200 a year in revenue. Settling down in Nashville, he mounted a radio program on Nashville's WSM, on which he displayed his expertise in songwriting by inviting callers to suggest topics and then composing a song on the spot.[13] The show quickly brought him in contact with all the top performers who frequented the *Grand Ole Opry,* one of the nation's top country music radio shows.

His experience with Tin Pan Alley publishing led to his co-venture with Roy Acuff—a suitable replacement for his former singing star partner Gene Autry, who had recently dissolved their relationship to go his own way. The publishing firm of Acuff-Rose took flight after Acuff had already proven a strong public interest in sheet music of his songs. After his engagement as a regular performer on WSM radio's *Grand Ole Opry* weekly program in 1938, Roy Acuff performed in a Hollywood film of the same name in 1940. Upon returning home to Nashville, he and his wife compiled a songbook containing many of his most successful songs. Before long he had professional printing plates made for a postcard-type foldout songbook called *Roy Acuff's Folio of Original Songs Featured over WSM Grand Ole Opry*, which he offered for 50 cents apiece. He promoted these on the *Grand Ole Opry* radio show and on his own regional *Roy Acuff Songbook Show*.

Roy Acuff and his family experienced the raw power and profitability of radio from their kitchen table. The first announcement on a program prompted several thousand orders, and the family spent the next several years employing friends and relatives to address envelopes to the devoted fans.[14] It was not a particularly novel idea. Bradley Kincaid had made similar fortunes selling songbooks on Chicago's WLS by then, but it was the first real money Acuff had seen and the first solid sign that his luck was turning after almost a decade of fiddling for sweat and starvation. Acuff's star rose fast, and before long he was considered an integral part of the *Grand Ole Opry* family and a significant factor in the program's national success. Eventually he would be named its master of ceremonies.

Through this experience, Acuff came to understand the value of his intellectual property and for a long time used the dubious postage-stamp method as the means of copyrighting his songs. He would transcribe them on postcards and mail them back to himself so that the date stamp might prove his ownership

Roy Acuff. Courtesy of the Grand Ole Opry Archives.

in a legal dispute. Fred Rose managed to win his confidence and convince him there was a better way to make money from his properties. Acuff lent his name along with some seed capital to the joint venture, leaving the general business administration, promotion, and any further funding to Rose.

Jean knew exactly who Fred Rose was. Together with Gene Autry he had been nominated for an Academy Award for the song "Be Honest with Me" from Autry's 1941 film *Ridin' on a Rainbow*. It lost to Jerome Kern and Oscar Hammerstein II's "Last Time I Saw Paris," but many were surprised that it was a serious contender. Suddenly Rose had put western music on the Tin Pan Alley map and the ASCAP membership was forced to sit up and take notice. Rose was in town now trying to leverage that political capital into ongoing cash support from the reluctant society. Having gained the confidence and friendship of most of the Nashville artists, Fred Rose could be unstoppable with the power and money of ASCAP behind him.

Jean felt the pressure of his closing window of opportunity. He had worked long enough for Max Dreyfus and felt it was time to strike out on his own. One day Jean discussed the matter with Dolfi, but his father forbade it. The family could not afford to lose Jean's Chappell salary at this time. Dolfi's decision was a setback, but Jean did not need to dwell on it. The Fred Rose issue was swiftly resolved by ASCAP, who declined the offer to fund him because syndicated performances of this type of music were rare and Rose could only guarantee non-network performances, for which ASCAP did not pay. Instead Acuff-Rose obtained a small advance from BMI and pledged membership there. Jean knew it would take Rose far longer to succeed with that fledgling organization.

CHAPTER 7

The Rebbe Sleeps

B y 1943, hillbilly music was no longer virgin territory. Jean knew that even if they started a firm that day, it would be a long, hard hill to climb. Peer and Marks had both demonstrated its commercial potential over the past decade and, in addition to Acuff-Rose, scores of small, inexperienced publishers were cropping up every day to handle this growing industry for the thousands of would-be songwriting stars. But if Max had taught him anything, it was not to waste his time except on mature, experienced talent. Unfortunately, anyone with a reputation and a string of hits behind him was surely already represented. It was going to take money to attract the best of them.

Jean already knew who the best of them were. He had been following them for years. The Sons of the Pioneers had been around for almost a decade doing supporting performances and bit parts in numerous Hollywood cowboy movies. They were recorded live every week at a local Los Angeles radio station as part of a distributed national radio series. Their close harmony and colorful, finely crafted cowboy tunes were unmatched, and from their ranks emerged one of the most beloved cowboy singers of all time as well as one of the genre's most influential songwriters. In a hot Los Angeles radio studio, songwriters Bob Nolan and Tim Spencer joined actor-singer Leonard Slye—soon to become Roy Rogers. As the Pioneer Trio, they introduced a trio yodeling style in 1934 that captured the spirit of the West and the heart of America.

The Pioneer Trio ushered in a cowboy mania that swept the nation. The American West lay dormant in the minds of most Americans east of the Rocky Mountains, until the Depression brought it to the forefront of the news. Uprooted from their prairie homes, thousands of families streamed out of America's heartland, traveling west in search of migrant work in the fertile regions of California. To transplanted New Yorkers working in the West Coast entertainment industry, they brought with them distinctive speech patterns, mannerisms, and a quaint, pragmatic code of conduct that had developed from a century of self-sufficiency and cultural isolation on the Great Plains and Southwest. Hollywood movie executives recognized in them a raw romanticism—especially in the lifestyle of the American cowboy. To sling a gun, ride the range, and sleep out under the stars personified ultimate freedom to most moviegoers, who knew nothing of the filth, hardship, and danger actually endured in the profession. Indeed, few cowboys would hire on for more than one cattle run in their lifetime if it could be avoided. Seen through the rose-colored lens of a Hollywood camera the life of a cowboy was glamorous and exciting. Their clothes—which never changed—were dusty, but never dirty. They could lasso a steed with one hand, drink a fifth of whisky with the other, shoot a rusty tin can from half a mile, and, oh yes, they could all sing in perfect homespun harmony.

Rodeos were commonplace at this time, where men competed in the dangerous skills of a fading era. Many buckaroos were more intent on attracting a talent scout than they were on winning a rodeo prize. Some of the best ropers and riders eventually found their way into the Hollywood stunt industry, although very rarely into leading Hollywood roles. Rex Allen and Bob Baker had some experience with ranching, but Gene Autry, Hollywood's biggest western screen star, was said to have been so bad at riding horses that the movie studio insisted on a year of riding lessons before they would use him in a feature film.[1]

The myth of the cowboy was created in song and movies by entertainers like the Pioneer Trio, who were distant enough from the lifestyle that their vision would not be marred by its harsh reality. Leonard Slye left his native Ohio for California, where he worked as a gravel-truck driver and migrant fruit picker; Missouri-born Tim Spencer had lived in Oklahoma and New Mexico before settling in Los Angeles, where he worked in a Safeway grocery warehouse; and Canadian-born Bob Nolan moved to Tucson, Arizona, in his teens before coming to California, where he worked as a hotel car hop and a Santa Monica beach lifeguard.[2] Whatever they knew of real cowboy life never interfered with their idealized vision of it. Hollywood soon embraced them as being both genuine and polished enough for its purposes.

The Pioneer Trio expanded, adding new members, and became known to the world as the Sons of the Pioneers. They got their big radio break in 1934, and Decca Records became interested and recorded them. Soon after, they were being included in Hollywood movie shorts and providing the music for Universal's *Oswald the Rabbit* cartoons. They started appearing in Hollywood features, performing their songs and acting in bit parts.

Their first feature, *The Old Homestead*, was followed by *Song of the Saddle* and *California Mail* with Dick Foran, *Gallant Defender*, *The Mysterious Avenger* with Charlie Starrett, and several films with western star Gene Autry. In 1936 they were included in the enormously successful *Rhythm on the Range* with America's biggest popular singing star and heartthrob Bing Crosby, during which he introduced Johnny Mercer's "I'm an Old Cowhand." As a result, their brand of western music took on a crossover popular appeal.

It was not clear back then to Jean or anyone else that the Sons of the Pioneers were a quintessential American institution that would go on to host numerous talented members and survive for several decades. The group was just simply enjoying their unexpected success, turning out unforgettable songs

Sons of the Pioneers. Courtesy of John Fullerton.

that captured the spirit and romance of cowboy life in the Wild West—songs like "Cool Water" and "Blue Prairie."

Although he spent his days plugging Gershwin show tunes around New York and promoting Rodgers and Hammerstein musicals around Hollywood, Jean appreciated these simple, evocative songs with much the same enthusiasm as the Karl May books he had read in his youth about the wild American West. But now he was in a position to judge them against the very best songs in the popular music industry that passed through his hands every day, and he was impressed. These were songs of admirable craft and quality, as professional as anything Tin Pan Alley had to offer.

Among them was the crown jewel of western songs, "Tumbling Tumbleweeds." Originally entitled "Tumbling Leaves," it had its birth as a poem in 1927. Bob Nolan reworked the words and added music to create the title song for Gene Autry's first feature film (*Tumbling Tumbleweeds*, 1935). Late in 1937, the Sons of the Pioneers signed a contract with Columbia Pictures to appear in Charlie Starrett's western film series, and the song was used in each film as the opening and closing theme. Then, in 1940, Bing Crosby released a version of it on Decca Records. "Tumbling Tumbleweeds" climbed the popular charts to become a bestselling hit. It would return again, sung by Roy Rogers in *Silver Spurs* (1943).[3]

"Tumbling Tumbleweeds" captured the essence of the American West as potently as the Charleston did the Roaring Twenties. Clearly here was an American classic in the making. It had remained persistently popular for several years and had transcended its genre roots, crossing over into the pop field. It was heard constantly on radio and in films, and the public never seemed to tire of it no matter how many versions they heard. Together the words and melody crystallized an image of a hot, dusty trail, and the loping gait of a mare meandering past prickly arms of towering saguaro cactus as twisted knots of Russian thistle weed gently roll by in the wind.

If nurtured and promoted properly, Jean knew that "Tumbling Tumbleweeds" would be remembered and played for decades more, reaping money for whoever owned its copyright long into the future. But he had not yet found a way to gain meaningful access to it. The Sons of the Pioneers were the busiest, most popular and respected cowboy singing group in the country, and his work for Chappell afforded no opportunity whatsoever to interact with them. Furthermore, the copyright to "Tumbling Tumbleweeds" was committed to Sam Fox Publishing Company, so there was no conceivable business opportunity to pursue. Despite these obstacles, Jean was certain that, given time, he could find his way to these talented songwriters and capture this valuable copyright.

In the meantime, Jean focused on simply finding a way to finance their business so that when Julian returned, they would be prepared to move. He began looking for business opportunities no one else had noticed—anything that might quickly generate the operating capital needed to launch a company.

There was no shortage of possibilities. Thanks to the war, there was an explosion of new popular music forms. Recognizing the value of using entertainment to sustain troop morale, the U.S. War Department sought music that would appeal to the broadest cross section of the armed forces. The music used for this purpose was 86 percent new material, of which 70 percent was split between classical, hillbilly, race music, and other types of specialized entertainment.[4] For the most part, United Service Organizations (USO) shows incorporated mostly light songs on frivolous or humorous subjects embedded in energetic music designed to lift the spirits of the troops. These tended toward simple themes with catchy melodies that were easy to remember—songs like "Chattanooga Choo-Choo" and "Don't Sit under the Apple Tree (with Anyone Else but Me)," "Boogie Woogie Bugle Boy of Company B," and "Praise the Lord and Pass the Ammunition." There were also many songs written in ways that would remind troops what they were fighting for—distinctly American songs on American themes about the places and people they had left behind like "Pennsylvania 6–5000" and "I'll Be with You in Apple Blossom Time."

Thousands of talented refugees were also streaming into the United States from all parts of Europe. Among them were seasoned performers and composers—like Fritz Spielman—who were unfamiliar with U.S. copyright law and needed representation and assistance in managing their worldwide copyrights. At the same time, their refugee communities were looking to them for familiar entertainment, giving rise to yet another popular trend—ethnic pop hits. The Yiddish "Bei Mir Bist Du Schön," an overnight smash hit by the Andrews Sisters in 1938, foreshadowed their overwhelming success with "Roll Out the Barrel," an Americanized version of the Czech melody "Beer Barrel Polka," which became World War II's most popular good-time tune.

In this musical melting pot Jean was searching for some exceptional business opportunity that would require a minimum of cash investment and staff and yet immediately generate enough revenue to nurture their fledgling venture. What profitable opportunity was waiting out there that no one else had seen?

Jean eventually recognized an obscure opportunity that offered BMI publishers additional revenue for performances of music resulting from live radio performances captured to disc that were subsequently reproduced and aired on other stations. This was part of BMI's initial business plan when they entered the business in 1940 and it provided a strong competitive advantage over their archrival, since ASCAP collected only for live—not recorded—performances on radio.

As the practice of airing recorded radio performances gained popularity, ASCAP publisher members were faced with a dilemma. Because membership in both organizations was prohibited, either they would have to collect royalties on these airplays themselves or else jump ship to BMI. ASCAP members who eventually joined BMI were attracted to the convenience of letting BMI handle this matter. They liked the idea of BMI collecting all their performance revenue—both live and recorded—rather than having to do any of it themselves.

Music publishers stood to benefit in many ways by joining BMI. They understood that BMI would pay additional revenue from the airplay of commercial recordings of the music they themselves might arrange with top bands or singers. Most of them also realized that they would be paid for radio performances of cover recordings of their hit tunes arranged and produced by others. What most did not completely understand was that they were entitled to performance royalties—in fact, and the same level of performance royalty—on any music they owned whether it was good or bad and whether the performer or song was known or not! Whatever form it took—even if it was created by studio musicians and featured unknown artists for use as syndicated background music to an advertisement or a dramatic radio piece, they would be paid!

Today we know it as "canned music" or "elevator music"—arrangements and performances of well-known songs by studio bands and unknown singers that could be recorded and reproduced cheaply and sold at budget prices to radio stations for use as background or fill music. The best-known of these companies was Muzak, a Warner company dating back to 1938. Initially, Muzak failed to obtain a license from the FCC to compete directly with network radio in the area of commercial music. It reorganized its plans to instead provide businesses with high-fidelity background music distributed electronically through telephone or power lines.

Wired radio like Muzak was actually part of a larger service industry called the transcription business whose practitioners provided exceptionally high fidelity programming not only distributed to commercial businesses like restaurants and department stores but to individual radio stations for rebroadcast as well. The transcription industry had been around for about twenty years, having developed from an interest in creating and distributing certain kinds of radio material—like advertisements with background music—across many markets.

Its importance became obvious when, during the 1920s, some famous radio singers—Fred Waring and Bing Crosby among them—began to hear their songs, captured *from the radio and recorded on disc,* being played on other radio stations. During the mid-1930s, the publishing industry moved to challenge radio stations that used these pirated performances, and they won injunctions forbidding their use without compensation. Thus, a legitimate offshoot industry arose, with several companies specializing in capturing live radio performances to disc with state-of-the-art recording equipment. These companies would then license their theatrical or song rights and reproduce and distribute the discs for rebroadcast on other radio stations. They also began creating special performances such as advertising spots with background music on behalf of commercial sponsors such as Wrigley's and the Ford Motor Company, who were looking to promote their brands nationally. Finally transcription companies expanded into creating studio recordings of unobtrusive original music that could be piped into restaurants and hotels.

By 1936 four services were contracted to provide transcriptions to at least 350 stations and were reaping more than $1 million a year for the sale of these programs and spots. The Music Publisher's Protective Association (MPPA), lobbying on behalf of most of the industry's music publishers, pushed through legislation that required the radio stations or advertisers to pay for each piece of music used, ranging from 25 to 50 cents per play, or else a blanket license of $15 per year enabling unlimited performances of up to 200 manufactured discs. In 1935 this reaped publishers an additional $200,000 in royalty revenue.[5]

BMI's entry into this area standardized payment collection and protected the publisher from retaliatory actions by stations and networks. Most were vehemently against paying for rebroadcasting these live radio performances. Few publishers would risk jeopardizing promotional opportunities for their newest commercial recording by demanding payment for recorded transcription performances of older works from a radio station—whether or not it was within their legal rights to do so. But BMI shielded a publisher from being singled out, and their legal counsel could be engaged if they were.

It rarely came to that. Spawned by the radio industry itself, BMI's rates were comprehensive, affordable, and understandable to the radio stations that licensed through it. Collection for the use of transcriptions was built into the overall BMI blanket licensing scheme. Thus, fees for these types of radio plays were hidden in the finer details of the blanket licensing agreements.

Beyond policing their own catalogs and monitoring their own commercial recordings, most publishers were unconcerned about transcription companies. They were minor players in their world, generally regarded as powerful promotional opportunities, but not profit centers. Publishers licensed the right of electrical transcription (the recording of live radio performances) to transcription companies for a nominal fee from time to time mainly because it provided additional radio exposure for their songs. Broadcast of a previously recorded live radio performance could boost sheet music sales and interest others to perform the song, advertisers to license it, or record companies to produce it.

Most performers also saw radio transcriptions as a promotional device. Only the highest-ranking performers who feared overexposure, tried to control the use of their recorded performances on radio. As for songwriters, they had little control over the exploitation of their songs through transcribed radio performances. The Standard Uniform Popular Songwriters' Contract, approved by

ASCAP and the MPPA and adopted industrywide on behalf of their members in 1932, regarded transcription royalty rights not as an intrinsic right but as a grant right that the publisher could withhold from the songwriter, and most often did. Therefore, if songwriters were aware of these rights at all, they probably valued the promotional potential of transcription radio plays far more than any share of the small royalty revenue that was generated.

Because transcription rights were a relatively minor part of their business, the licenses granted by publishers were usually generous and comprehensive. Even for publishers handling well-known songwriters whose works featured well-known singers or bandleaders, the relatively insubstantial royalties derived from recorded transcriptions used in syndication, background advertising or wired music, were rarely considered a deal breaker. In these arrangements, the transcription company assumed copyright ownership for the underlying arrangement as well as for the source master of the live radio performance recording, the original song copyright remaining with the publisher. In addition, the transcription company also captured the right to subsequent reproductions and rebroadcasts.[6]

When BMI inaugurated this new area of revenue collection, transcription companies were completely naïve about their hidden profit potential. Up until that time their profit was derived solely from the direct sale of their recordings to radio stations—not from the collection of performance royalty revenues. Under the existing copyright law, however, the transcription company was regarded as a kind of combined music publisher and record company that was, in fact, entitled to all the benefits afforded any other music publisher. Most transcription companies had no idea that they had acquired the right of performance and could collect performance royalties each time these transcription records were played.

Transcription companies also serviced advertisers who were often unwilling to pay for star singers performing hit tunes. Therefore, transcription companies often had original music created for specific interludes or to accompany advertising spots by paying competent, but unknown, composers and performers a flat fee in a work-for-hire arrangement. In these cases, the transcription companies obtained exclusive worldwide rights to these new compositions and were entitled to all the privileges afforded any other publisher. It had never occurred to them that the original—albeit largely mediocre—music they themselves were creating for special spots could also be generating extra money in the same way as a top forty commercial song performance, each time it was played on the air. Even mundane, transitional background music could be generating cash!

This was the obscure advantage that Jean recognized. Each electrical transcription license granting a radio station to rebroadcast a previously recorded live radio performance represented small money in and of itself, and so it was overlooked or ignored by other publishers. But the popularity of radio was growing along with the volume of station licenses, so that in the aggregate it represented a huge revenue opportunity. Transcription firms were making good money from the sale of their transcription discs to a large number of radio stations. They were unaware, however, of their right to also collect performance revenues each time those radio stations actually played those transcriptions discs. Much as he and his brother had done with SEMI, Jean knew that they needed only to find a willing transcription company to partner with, set themselves up as publishers and register transcription works with BMI to begin collecting money.

They would use the same strategy they had with SEMI. They would offer to register and track these copyrights for a percentage. The proceeds would be used to generate revenue for the Aberbachs' own fledgling firm. Julian could easily manage the work on his own and with little or no staff. He would simply monitor the royalty revenues that were being collected for each rebroadcast of a live radio performance that the transcription company recorded and distributed to other radio stations. This was the sort of work he had already done very successfully for Salabert in Paris. It was found money!

Most important, this was an area of business Chappell music could not care less about. Until their business could support the family, he could not leave Chappell, so the last thing Jean wanted to do was to alienate his mentor over a conflict of interest. He could not keep their new company a secret from Max Dreyfus and the rest of Chappell & Co. The music publishing community was too small for a profitable venture to remain hidden for very long. It could, however, be characterized as Julian's venture, and since it would be engaged in an area of the business Chappell had no interest in, there should not be a problem. As they had done in Paris, the most secure way of proceeding was for Jean to continue with Chappell while Julian got their new business under way.

While Jean waited for Julian to arrive back from the war, he continued to refine the plan. A lot depended on locating many unregistered copyrights that had good potential for reuse. Even under the best of circumstances their new firm would likely be short on cash the first year or two from the lag in time between play and pay. They would start collecting songwriters and copyrights as soon as possible, but even if they found a hit tune, it would be at least a year before any substantial revenue would be seen. A considerable bankroll would be needed to attract quality talent and copyrights to their firm now that others were actively harvesting the black and hillbilly scenes. What Jean needed was a partner—one with deep pockets—who shared his enthusiasm for hillbilly music and recognized its market potential.

As month after month wore on, Jean began to feel the pressure of his shrinking window of opportunity. The end of the war was nowhere in sight, making it impossible to know when Julian might arrive back to join him. He began to rethink his options, and there is some evidence that Jean aspired to own or share ownership in a division of Chappell. Not only would he have entered the industry with a powerful ally, he would have gained a small foothold in Chappell music—much in the same way as Max had begun his career by assuming an interest in T. B. Harms, the pregnant seed from which he germinated his sprawling corporate holdings. Jean thought there might still be a chance to interest Max in these new music genres—perhaps initiate a BMI division in which he might obtain a share. Surely, this would be the best possible solution to his problem.

But Max had absolutely no interest in polluting his catalog with hillbilly music. He stubbornly refused to embrace these genres. Some of his prize students, however—including Broadway composer Richard Rodgers—had no such prejudice. Rodgers had experienced the West for himself during his brief stint in Hollywood during the 1930s, though he did not write for the western movie market during that time. Only Cole Porter had ventured into the fray, writing "Don't Fence Me In" based on a poem acquired from a Montana man. Rodgers was certainly aware of the hundreds of mediocre films being churned out by Republic and Monogram film studios, and he certainly looked on with some fascination when Gene Autry and Fred Rose submitted "Be Honest with Me," from the motion picture *Ridin' on a Rainbow,* which challenged his own song for an Academy Award.[7]

Back in New York and working again for Max at Chappell, Rodgers found himself groping for fresh new ideas for Broadway musicals at the same time as western movies and radio shows were flooding the market. Hillbilly music enthusiasts such as Jean who walked the floors of Chappell at that time probably encouraged him. Even the venerable firm of Irving Berlin was, by this time, publishing western tunes. Berlin had sought out Bob Wills on the strength of his 1938 Vocalian recording of the instrumental "Spanish Two-Step," offering to publish it if words would be added to it. In its new form, it would become one of the most beloved western swing tunes of all time, "San Antonio Rose."[8] It was not long before western music and folksy themes began to feel less alien to Rodgers.

Relief came by way of the troubled New York Theater Guild, who solicited Rodgers to adapt the story of *Green Grow the Lilacs* to the Broadway stage. The guild had successfully produced the play in the 1930s featuring cowboy singer Tex Ritter, but since then had been slowly sinking into debt. They hoped to repeat the success that had swept another of their folk-themed plays, *Porgy,* to tremendous acclaim on the Broadway musical stage at the hands of George Gershwin almost a decade before. Despite a nearly plotless story, an unknown cast, and a little-known director and choreographer, in the hands of Richard Rodgers *Oklahoma!* became an overnight sensation and ultimately proved to be the biggest runaway hit Broadway had ever seen.[9]

Despite his New York–centric outlook, Max could not help but notice the effect that Hollywood was having on the music business. By 1939 approximately 65 percent of all ASCAP publishers' income was going to companies owned or at least partly controlled by the film industry and much of this income was being derived from songs written for and made popular by Hollywood films.[10] Jean's prior experience in the film music industry made him the natural choice to represent Chappell from time to time in Hollywood, promoting Chappell songs and theatrical rights to Hollywood film producers.

When *Oklahoma!* hit big in March 1943, Max was surprised and delighted. He sent Jean to peddle the work in Hollywood. Excited by this remarkable work Jean enthusiastically scouted the film rights for *Oklahoma!* in Hollywood where, because of the popular success of the work, it was not too difficult to find leads. At one point Paramount offered 100 percent performance profit back to the writers for the screen rights, confident they would make their money off the distribution rights. In the end, the writers chose to go with the experimental film company Todd-AO, whom they found through Arthur Hornblow—the Hollywood producer who had engaged Rodgers and Larry Hart to write the score for the Paramount musical *Mississippi* in 1934. The progressive firm offered the opportunity to employ an experimental panoramic film process using a new wide-angle camera, 65-mm film, and magnetic sound track equipment offering full stereophonic sound. Through it, the jumpy lines that separated the three panels of the inferior Cinerama process were gone, and the crisp, clear visuals and booming stereophonic sound brought the audience right into the action. No other offer could sway them.[11]

Despite its success *Oklahoma!* did not change Max's attitude toward the market potential of genuine hillbilly music or its appropriateness in his core Chappell catalog. While even the most reserved publishers like Irving Berlin, Inc., were climbing on the bandwagon, Max staunchly held his ground. Highly stylized Broadway versions like *Oklahoma!* were acceptable, but he had no interest in the "real" thing—the kind of off-key, nasal, twangy music he heard from time to time on the radio, or that could be found peppered throughout second-rate Saturday matinee adventure movies, like those being churned out by the bushel by Republic Pictures.

Established in 1935, Republic Pictures Corporation grew out of Herbert J. Yates Republic Film Laboratories. It filled the need for a second movie feature (called "B" pictures) to accompany major studio releases. Republic was able to churn out low-budget, fair-quality action adventure films. It established the western movie trend, producing 386 western films before its decline in the 1950s. Music was an important element and greatly contributed to the success of their films. It was responsible for building the popularity of the Sons of the

Pioneers and for creating cowboy singing stars Gene Autry and Roy Rogers, who greatly influenced the rise of the western music trend.

Even after Republic's movie songs took on a new, glamorous Broadway luster, Max Dreyfus could not be swayed. Pioneer Leonard Slye (stage name, Roy Rogers) notes that after Republic's founder returned from a New York business trip during which he had seen *Oklahoma!* on the Broadway stage, Yates issued a memorandum demanding that Republic western features would, from that point forward, be modeled on that of the celebrated Broadway musical. Thereafter, Rogers asserts, everything about the look, feel, and style of his movies changed. His wardrobe became more glamorous, the sets more lavish and unrealistic, and the situations less believable. In effect, the movies took on a Broadway fantasy quality. Where in the past songs would be interpolated into the action, it was now permissible for songs to interrupt the action of the film in thoroughly unbelievable ways. Before long, all his films were ending with a full-cast musical number after the action of the story line was finished, in familiar Broadway finale style.[12]

Already known for their generous use of music in their films, Republic now began turning out films with nearly continuous musical scores, although much of the sound material was still pieced together from stock inventory recordings. Out of this clutter, however, a hit song would emerge from time to time that would capture the popular interest and chart well. Even as some of these songs crossed over to the popular music charts and overtook their mainstream counterparts, Max still remained completely uninterested in country and western music for his catalog.

When Jean was a young boy, he used to take religious lessons from a teacher who would always sit on his hands in a white chair, and after a short time would promptly fall asleep. "Such a scholar I could have been had I not been afraid to wake up Rebbe Hirsh!" he would say. This is one lesson he never forgot. To avoid the same mistake, he had spent a lot of time trying to wake up Max to the fact that he could make a lot of money by embracing emerging music genres. He had done everything he could think of to prove not only the profit potential of western music to Max, but that he was more than capable of managing it. And where was Max? He was perched on a comfortable white chair, sitting on his hands, and drifting off to sleep. The old man was surrounded by opportunity and Jean was poised and eager to help him achieve it. How could he ignore such obvious signs? *This rebbe—he will not wake up!*

CHAPTER 8

Betting the Farm

O
ne day, quite unexpectedly, Jean received a call from Julian. He was convalescing at a veteran's hospital in Washington, D.C. His army career had come to an abrupt halt, and he was ready to come home.

Julian was thirty-three years old when he entered the army in 1942. He had been inducted into the Officer Candidates School at Fort Benning, Georgia, became an officer, and because of his excellent command of languages, he was selected for counterintelligence work. He adopted an alternate name, Jerome J. Brooks, and was put in charge of secretly training Free French refugees in the use of American weapons and tactics. Eventually he was approached to command an elite parachute unit that would be dropped behind enemy lines to conduct counterintelligence activities. Unfortunately, during the very first training jump, he had fallen and torn a cartilage in his knee. The operation confirmed that he would not be able to participate in the action, and so he was awarded a pension and dismissed from further duty.

Over the winter of 1943, Jean visited Walter Reed Hospital where Julian was recuperating. The service had not changed his brother a bit. Consistent with his clever nature, Julian had gravitated to the position of least effort and best advantage. He was afforded certain luxuries, among them time off to visit the fine art museums in and around Washington and to gain some exposure to local southern music. He shared Jean's assessment that there was potential in these fast-growing popular music trends. They could simply pick up where they had left off in Europe—using Jean's transcription idea as a springboard for their new company. The matter was discussed with Dolfi, who gave his blessing.

Standard Radio Electrical Transcriptions owners, Gerald King and Milton Blink, had offices in Chicago and Los Angeles. It was one of the country's largest transcription firms. It was generating substantial sales and had created a considerable amount of original material in the process. Their staff, though skilled in the creation and sale of such work, was not knowledgeable about the changing intricacies of the music publishing industry. The Aberbach brothers, Jean explained, could offer a valuable service to Mr. King and Mr. Blink in connection with their core catalog.

It was no accident that Jean focused on Standard Radio Electrical Transcriptions. The catalog featured a large number of western works.[1] Among the lesser known writers like Texas Jack Lewis and Rudy Sooter, who wrote "I'm a Real Buckaroo," and "Let Me Shake Your Old Cowhand," could be found fifteen works by Spade Cooley, mostly cowritten with lyricist Eugene "Smokey" Rogers. Cooley was an up-and-coming western swing bandleader making waves on the Venice Pier in Los Angeles. It was rumored that crowds as large as 4,000 would show up for his weekly barn dances.

Cooley took over as the king of western swing when Bob Wills was inducted into the armed services. A former member of Jimmy Wakely's band, by the end of 1942 Cooley commanded the largest western swing band in the country, and his reputation was spreading. He quickly became a star of radio and screen, appearing as a featured side man on Gene Autry's *Melody Ranch* radio shows and supporting him in the movie *Home in Wyomin'*. This was not Cooley's first appearance in film. He closely resembled Roy Rogers and was often used as a stunt double for him during the late 1930s. But there was an even more compelling reason Jean was attracted to this transcription catalog. Standard Radio Electrical Transcriptions provided direct access to the Sons of the Pioneers and, by extension, to the most valuable western copyright in the business, "Tumbling Tumbleweeds."

There is a curious link between Standard Radio and this coveted work. After adding music to the poem, writer Bob Nolan entered into an agreement with Sunset Music on April 3, 1934. Nolan and Sunset's owner Harry Walker rescinded the agreement a short time later and, joined by staff announcer Harry Hall of KFWB radio, entered into an agreement with Sam Fox Publishing Company on July 11, 1934. This was probably done to induce Walker to give up the publishing rights and possibly as a reward to Hall for bringing together a deal that held the promise of placing "Tumbling Tumbleweeds" in a 1935 Fox-owned Gene Autry film. The film, as it happened, already featured on-screen performances by the Sons of the Pioneers.

Hall had been an important figure in the Pioneers career from the start. He was responsible for their eventual name change from the Pioneer Trio to the Sons of the Pioneers (believing the men looked too young to be "pioneers" themselves, but that they were perfectly believable as "sons" of pioneers).[2] Hall was also present in the radio station sound booth the very first day the trio displayed their unique trio yodeling style. Station manager Gerald King—the same Gerald King who became co-owner of Standard Radio Electrical Transcription—used Hall to relay his approval to hire the group.

The radio station that King managed was KFWB, a flagship station in the fledgling Warner Brothers radio network. He was sold on the talent of the Pioneer Trio as soon as he heard them, but he did not offer them their own show until after their arrangement of "The Last Roundup" was favorably reviewed by a respected radio columnist in a major Los Angeles newspaper. On December 15, 1934, their song "Tumbling Tumbleweeds," recorded the previous August on Decca Records, hit number 13 on the music charts. Recognizing an interest in their music beyond his own radio station, King started his recording company. He began recording KFWB's musical radio programs to sell to other radio stations throughout the country. Realizing the opportunity available in the new transcription market, King left radio management entirely and hooked up with Blink to devote his full attention to developing their new business.[3]

Although Standard Radio itself did not own the copyright to "Tumbling Tumbleweeds," it had recorded many other works by Bob Nolan and his group. In fact, several hundred selections by the Sons of the Pioneers were recorded during 1935.[4] Jean abandoned research into any other firm. Here was a partner with deep pockets, who not only shared his enthusiasm for hillbilly music but brought a substantial number of hillbilly copyrights to the bargaining table. Standard Radio was the perfect opportunity.

Julian's return to New York in the spring of 1944 prompted the completion of a deal the details of which Jean had already put in place. An agreement in principle had been reached with King and Blink whereby the Aberbach brothers would organize and manage the royalty rights of Standard Radio's transcription catalog for a 50 percent share of the revenue. Each party would contribute substantially to the new firm. Standard Radio would turn over any song copyrights it owned or would obtain over the next ten years. For their part, Jean would secure funding by leveraging a company he and Dolfi had set up in January called Biltmore Music. While Jean secured a letter of commitment from BMI and arranged a lyric reprint deal to obtain advances to cover operating expenses, Julian went to Chicago to finalize the deal.

On April 29, 1944, Milton Blink, representing himself and his partner Gerald King, assigned all worldwide publishing rights of all Standard Radio song copyrights to a temporary joint holding company called Crown Music, Inc. in exchange for a 50 percent stock share in the company. This separated these properties from any other Standard business. The signing probably took place in Chicago and named Julian and Dolfi as equal co-owners with King and Blink. Because of his position at Chappell, Jean would act as an officer on the board, but not participate as a named owner. Instead, Dolfi would take his place and hold his stock shares until the business could support bringing him on full-time. Until they decided on a name and the permanent joint corporation took form, Biltmore would act as the service company. The following month, everyone except Dolfi committed to employment agreements. Julian became president and general manager of the corporation and was provided with a salary of $50 per week.

To raise cash for the venture, Jean had used his reputation, contacts, and influence. On January 21, 1944, he secured a deal with D. S. Publishing yielding $3,900 a year for lyric print rights. In March, he also secured a guarantee of $12,000 a year from BMI for performance royalties contingent on at least fifty radio plugs (performances) every six months. Since Biltmore itself had no substantial catalog holdings at this time, Jean must have secured these funds on the promise of access to songs contained in the Standard Radio catalog. Both contracts explicitly demanded Jean's direct involvement in the conduct of Biltmore's business. BMI went even further by demanding that Jean must "devote all of your time and efforts to the operation and management of this company, and that you will in fact be the owner of substantially one hundred percent of the corporation." By April, however, Jean had already removed himself from this position at Biltmore, turning over the presidency and the BMI contract to Julian, probably to avoid conflict of interest issues with Chappell.[5]

This was completely in keeping with the brothers' operational habits. Biltmore—like all their other ventures—was an Aberbach brothers equal coventure regardless of who conducted business or was named in official documents. For instance, Jean and Dolfi were named as directors and Julian as president for the purposes of opening bank accounts. But Julian was second signature to Jean on most internal documents and contractual arrangements between Biltmore and Standard Radio, which suggests that in official matters, Jean played the primary role. On the other hand, all the contracts with outsiders—such as songwriter agreements—were executed by Julian to protect Jean in his role as an employee of Chappell. Because of this, it is impossible to know exactly who was actually responsible for what deals. In the end, where the Aberbach brothers are concerned, such distinctions are superfluous. In most business matters, Jean and Julian's roles were extraordinarily interchangeable. Who did what was generally dictated by convenience and circumstance.

Biltmore Music, Inc., took up residence at the New York offices of Standard Radio Electrical Transcriptions, 1 East 54th St. Jean conducted these activities with the help of a part-time assistant, his first cousin on his mother's side, Frederick "Fritz" Kohn. Kohn was one of many relatives the Aberbachs would employ in their business over the years. In August 1946 he became a board member of Hill and Range, the future umbrella firm that would become the springboard for most Aberbach musical projects. Fritz probably manned the office part time during the day when Jean was at Chappell.

In the meantime, Julian spent most of his time in Chicago, working at Standard Radio's main offices. The Standard Radio catalog consisted of approximately 200 selections that included transcriptions of works by songwriters including Ozzie Nelson, Ray Noble, Cindy Walker, Spade Cooley, and Jimmy Wakely performed by top popular bands, among them those of Duke Ellington, Bob Crosby, Alvino Ray, and Jack Teagarden.

It also included public domain song arrangements. A public domain arrangement is the copyright of a new version of a song never or no longer protected by copyright. Works by nineteenth-century American folksong composer Stephen Foster, for example, can be performed and recorded freely without payment of royalties. If a new symphonic arrangement of "Oh! Susanna" is performed or recorded, however, the arranger is entitled to royalty compensation on the arrangement of the song.

Almost immediately, Jean began drafting documents that clarified Gerald King's percentage interest in the songs. Other documents secured each songwriter's official acknowledgment of Standard Radio's sole or partial interest in some or all of their songs. This contract cleanup process took about six months. In the meantime, Julian was in Chicago organizing the catalog and registering each song with BMI. As he had done with SEMI and Salabert years before, he began to calculate back royalties to which the company was entitled but which had never been paid. Perhaps to further deflect suspicion in the music community away from Jean, Julian continued using his assumed name when doing business—the one that he had acquired during his covert army work. From that point forward, Julian would be known to the music world as Jerome J. Brooks.

The original Standard Radio agreement signed in April clearly stipulated that within three months a new permanent joint corporation would be created and the other companies dissolved. It would absorb Standard Radio's transcription catalog now in Crown Music and Biltmore's D. S. Publishing and BMI deals would be transferred to it. The new firm was called Hill and Range Songs, Inc., the name chosen to emphasize the country and western copyrights that would be put into it. Any song other than country and western would get put into another firm called Normandy Music. Both parties contributed $2,500 each in start-up capital, none of which could be used for salaries. Hill and Range Songs, Inc. was incorporated on December 9, 1944.

At that time a number of songs—and songwriter relationships preexisting with Standard Radio—were transferred to Hill and Range Songs. Among these was the comprehensive acquisition of all Spade Cooley's works owned by Standard Radio, including his "Blue Mountain Waltz," "Yodeling Polka," and "Cowbell Polka." It also included fourteen other songs cowritten with Eugene "Smokey" Rogers, plus Rogers's solely written song "Forgive Me One More Time." In addition to song copyrights, the standard songwriter contracts with Rogers, Rudy Sooter, and Texas Jim Lewis were also transferred.[6]

Curiously, the several hundred transcriptions of songs by the Sons of the Pioneers that King had recorded in 1935 were not among the works found in the Standard Radio library, already having been absorbed into firms owned by publisher Sylvester L. Cross. Cross co-owned Cross Music Company and American Music, Inc., the latter of which contained most of the works of Bob Nolan. Nolan had signed with Cross and Winge of San Francisco in 1935, probably signing away the sheet music rights to his works outright for a small fee. This was a common practice. According to Julian, Tim Spencer also sold many of his works to Cross outright as well.[7]

The corporation elected officers: Gerald King as president, Milton M. Blink as vice-president, and Jerome J. Brooks as secretary. Jean J. Aberbach was named general manager. To reduce his regular workload, Jean renewed his ongoing relationship as U.S. representative for Éditions Salabert, adding Julian. He offered him half the revenue earned, except for an agreement with Lowes that he had previously secured.

During the time leading up to the incorporation, Julian persuaded the Standard Radio partners to let him set up a small office at their Los Angeles headquarters, which was under the direction of Gerald King. He probably arrived in the early fall 1944. When he arrived, Julian checked into the Hollywood Hotel, bought a secondhand Buick, and went to work. He began frequenting the local hillbilly performance scene, chief among them Foreman Phillips's famed *Country Barn Dance*. Located south of Santa Monica on the Venice Beach Pier, it attracted several thousand patrons on weekend nights. It had been operating since 1941 and had touched off a West Coast trend of ballroom barn dances featuring hillbilly swing music, taking its cue from live radio shows like Chicago's *National Barn Dance* and the shows that broadcast live from Nashville's Grand Ole Opry. During 1943, the Country Barn Dance had regularly featured Spade

Cooley, but after a showdown in October of that year between Cooley and Bob Wills over the coveted title "king of western swing," Cooley had moved his show seventy miles east of the beach, to the Riverside Rancho Ballroom.

On one of these occasions, Julian went to see what all the fuss over Spade Cooley was about. He was amazed at the size of the crowds the performer was drawing—the place was overflowing with thousands of patrons, and still more hopeful fans were lined up on the street. Julian heard Cooley perform a new song called "Shame on You." Something about it excited him, and he struck up a conversation with Cooley's manager. Driven by instinct, Julian impulsively committed fully half of Hill and Range's available capital at that time—$1,500—to secure the rights to this song as part of an exclusive songwriter contract with Cooley. He sent a copy of the song back to Jean in New York.

Jean took one look at the song, read the lyrics, and went right through the roof![8] At that time, Hill and Range was pitifully cash-poor, operating almost solely on the $3,000 quarterly advance from BMI. They had all deferred their salaries, and Jean had to use what he was earning at Chappell to subsidize expenses, because the arrangement with King and Blink specifically prohibited

Spade Cooley.
Courtesy of
Bettman/Corbis.

the use of investment capital for salaries.[9] He had been frugal with the use of their funds, carefully doling them out only when the return on investment was absolutely assured. Thus far they only had been used to induce well-known bandleaders who had regular performance spots on network radio to publish their music through them. Since they would perform these compositions on the air almost every week, there was no doubt whatsoever that BMI's royalty advance would be recouped. But he could not fathom how this song was going to make them money.

While popular in the dance halls, Spade Cooley had virtually no chart experience. Nor did he have a regular radio spot. He did have a record contract with OKeh, a division of Columbia, but that seemed to be going nowhere. Because of the wartime shellac shortage and other constraining factors, Columbia had released relatively few recordings during 1944, probably shuffling lesser artists and first-time hopefuls like Cooley to the bottom of the pile.

Although he was not in the habit of buying music by the pound, Jean also noticed that the song had only sixteen bars rather than the customary thirty-two. Being only half as long, twice as many verses would be needed for "Shame on You" to fill out the time of a typical radio song. This would make it more repetitious, and therefore potentially less attractive to radio DJs and record companies. But that was not the worst of it. Did Julian even *read* the lyrics to the song?

> Shame, shame on you. . . . Shame, shame on you. . . . Ran around with other guys, Tried to lie when I got wise. Foolish girl. . . . Shame on you. . . . Shame, shame on you. . . . Shame, shame on you. . . . Can you hold your head up high, Look your friends right in the eye? . . . No you can't. . . . Shame on you. . . .

Not only was the song too short, its sexually charged lyrics increased the difficulty of selling it. Had they really invested their life savings in half a song with questionable lyrics? He was sure his brother had lost his mind!

And then there was the artist himself, whose fate was sealed as soon as Bob Wills returned from his short stint in the armed services. Fiercely self-confident, Cooley had a fiery stage presence and formidable fiddling skills and had some successful forays into both radio and film. His band was first-rate and featured the smooth lead vocalist Tex Williams. They continued to attract tremendous crowds in California. The "battle of the bands" with Wills proved Cooley's band superior and the popular favorite. Most scholars and aficionados today agree that Cooley surpassed Wills in substance, style, and innovation, and that some of his music represents the pinnacle of the western swing style.[10] Even Wills himself admits that by 1944 he was past his creative prime.

Despite this impressive list of accomplishments, Cooley was destined to play the tragic foil for the dapper Wills. The problem was, in the eyes of the mainstream music industry, western swing was not so much a music form as it was a novelty. The sort of shows MCA had slated Wills to headline indicated they thought of him more as a circus ringleader than a respected entertainer. Through the winter of 1944 and 1945, the "Bob Wills and His Great Vaudeville Show" featured thirty-nine performers, only thirteen of which were in his band.[11] The money was phenomenal, but the schedule was brutal. Nevertheless, Wills possessed a calm perseverance that enabled him to endure under these conditions. With a volatile mix of Irish, Scots, and Cherokee blood, Cooley lacked the poise and finesse Wills possessed that enabled him to snag the MCA Talent Agency and toe the corporate line in exchange for being catapulted onto the national stage. Without such representation, Cooley remained only a regional California phenomenon.

Then there was the problem of the tune itself. What southern Christian would allow such a record in their home? With everything else going against it, religious bias was the last thing they needed. "Shame on You" was not a hopeless situation, but Jean expected and prepared for the worst. Julian, on the other hand, trusted his judgment and stood by his decision. He quickly pursued Columbia Records' veteran artist-and-repertoire man Art Satherley for a recording, dragging him down to one of Cooley's impressive shows.

The preexisting recording contract between Cooley and OKeh/Columbia had been signed September 30, 1943. Adding to the difficult wartime shellac shortage, powerful American Federation of Musicians Union leader James Caesar Petrillo called a musicians' strike in August 1943 prohibiting members from recording until a new contract with recording companies and broadcasters was struck. OKeh had signed Cooley probably as part of a union-busting maneuver. As a nonunion musician, Cooley was not restricted from recording.

Around the time Cooley was signed and should have recorded, the U.S. government eased shellac rationing. But the influx of new, startup record companies into the industry further strained the available pool of shellac. Nevertheless, Julian sold Satherley on Cooley's timely marketability.[12] Convinced, Satherley released the recording in January on the OKeh label and by March 31, 1945, "Shame on You" hit number 1 on the country chart—a new chart *Billboard* had introduced a little more than a year before. It slipped in and out of the top position for nine weeks. In all, it would remain on the country charts for almost eight months, even making a respectable dent in the pop charts, settling in at number 13.[13] It was concurrently released by Lawrence Welk, whose own recording featured another well-known western performer, Red Foley, and in April singer-actor Bill Boyd, who had his own radio show on WRR Dallas, released another version with his Cowboy Ramblers.[14]

"Shame on You" turned out to be a tremendous success by country music standards. It reaped good performance royalties. Unfortunately, these could not be collected for almost a year—nor would many records be sold. Owing to the shellac shortage, only 50,000 recordings were pressed.[15] Still, "Shame on You" was a shot of adrenaline for the Aberbach brothers. It confirmed the Hill and Range relationship with Art Satherley and established its reputation with the Los Angeles western songwriters and performers. It put an Aberbach brothers' property on the music charts and, therefore, Hill and Range on the music industry map.

There are few decisions in Jean's life that can be counted as complete errors. When his vast professional knowledge faltered, his instinct would usually point the way. But on this matter, both his experience and his instinct failed him. This, however, is why he and Julian worked so well together. They viewed the world in different ways that were most often complementary. What one missed, the other saw. Colleagues and staff never saw them argue. Their mutual trust and respect for one another far outweighed any personal frustrations they had with one another. In this case, that's what carried Jean past his fears and objections, to support Julian in this decision.

Years later Jean remembered this story in his memoir sketches:

> Gustav Rimmel was a big composer in the Operetta business. One day Rimmel visited me at our house in Hollywood. This was a big honor for me. Rimmel took a seat at the piano and began to play something in three-quarter time. He called it the Satellite or the Star of Venus Waltz. I immediately knew this song was not for me. I tried to say something so as not to insult him. Unfortunately, the only thing I could think of at the time was "Don't you have something . . . a little more down to earth . . . something not from outer space?"[16]

Risk and success go hand in hand. If it were easy to pick hit songs, everyone would be doing it. Like the "Star of Venus Waltz," Jean had been expecting something from his brother a little less brazen and controversial—something a little more down to earth. But sometimes it takes something from outer space to really put you into orbit.

CHAPTER 9

Hardy's Horsemeat

A s soon as the Hill and Range incorporation papers were prepared in December 1944, Jean and Julian switched places. Jean ventured west to California to finalize documents with Gerald King during part of a springtime trip for Chappell, leaving Julian in charge of the New York office. He was probably there from January through April 1945, during which time he also finalized the transfer paperwork for Spade Cooley's exclusive songwriter agreement in between his regular work of peddling Chappell songs to Hollywood producers.

Jean began frequenting the local western music hot spots, rooting out other potential hit songs. He struck up a relationship with Ted Daffan, then headlining weekly at Foreman Phillip's Country Barn Dance. Julian had written off the hard-drinking Daffan as too hard to handle, but Jean thought he was worth the risk. Hardly an unknown quantity, Daffan already had a string of recording hits on Decca and OKeh, his most memorable being "Born to Lose" from a Columbia session in which he cut twenty-four sides, the copyright of which Irving Berlin

Music picked up. It was an uphill battle, but Jean eventually won Daffan's confidence. The relationship would eventually yield several bestsellers.

Although he talked to many other artists as well, Jean devoted most of his attention to pursuing western music's biggest star, the legendary Bob Wills. Like "Tumbling Tumbleweeds," Bob Wills was a country and western prize. By the time Jean approached him, not only was Wills the top western music star, he was also one of the top-grossing performers in the country. Because of this acquiring Wills presented a formidable challenge for the Aberbach brothers and their fledgling enterprise.

Wills's career had been long and hard, rising from the Dust Bowl of West Texas during the late 1920s and 1930s. There he assimilated the distinctive rhythm and feel of the blues while working shoulder to shoulder with black cottonpickers during his destitute youth. His audiences, however, were predominantly Native Americans and Mexicans, and he found that no matter what song he played, the couples invariably fell into an unusual dance best described as resembling the hopping moves of a prairie chicken, apparently rooted in the traditions of the Southern Arizona Pima Indians. To accommodate them, he created the "Spanish Two-Step" and later updated this duple meter dance song with the jazzy rhythms he had learned from the black cotton pickers. The new version became his calling card, the famous "San Antonio Rose," and it introduced an exciting new music style that later would be dubbed western swing.[1]

During the hard years of the Depression, Wills was forced to think strategically about his future, and it was during this time that he first asserted his practical business sense. As the economy slowed down and the dance circuit faltered, Wills looked for a way to leverage the talents in his band for steady,

Bob Wills. Courtesy of Gertrude Wills Fowler.

full-time employment. In 1932, when jobs were perilously scarce, he managed to secure corporate sponsorship from a local flour mill for a radio series by pledging each of his band members to a forty-hour workweek at the mill—in addition to their performance work on the radio show! At a time when most other groups disbanded for lack of work, Bob Wills and his band were together, solvent, and gaining wide regional exposure through radio. The show quickly became the most popular, longest-running radio show in the Southwest.

Interest in Wills and his new musical style grew throughout the 1930s.[2] He began recording in 1929 with Brunswick, later moving to Vocalion, where he recorded almost constantly throughout the decade. Wills did seventy-seven sides for Vocalion, becoming its second-most-recorded artist after the Hoosier Hot Shots, who contributed eighty-eight. Art Satherley estimated that by the late 1930s Wills records were played on 300,000 jukeboxes and his songs were heard by millions in every sector of the country every day. But it was not until he recorded "San Antonio Rose" in 1938 that the mainstream music publishers began to take notice. He was flattered by encouragement from renowned jazz violinist Joe Venuti, and Irving Berlin Music approached him to publish it. With some 200 recordings already under his belt, Wills was secured by Art Satherley for his first Columbia recording session in July 1941.

The session was actually a by-product of Wills's film spots. Columbia had engaged him to appear and perform in a few of their western movies. The new medium worked well for Wills, who thrilled film audiences with his looks and colorful western attire. Their enthusiastic response led to more Hollywood work. While Tulsa remained his home, he and the band began spending long periods on the West Coast. He was signed to costar in eight Columbia pictures during 1942 and, while there, he played weekly dances, attracting 15,000 people to Venice Pier over one three-night weekend.[3]

The sound that attracted them—and Columbia Records—was not the precise, jazzy, horn driven big-band sound that Wills had been striving to attain over the past decade, but the energetic country fiddle sound exemplified by "San Antonio Rose." With his players at the height of their professional skills, Wills was thoroughly dismayed when Satherley reminded him that what he and his public wanted was his classic country fiddle swing sound. When his band members began to depart, one after another, for wartime service during the early 1940s, it became impossible for Wills to advance musically. Finally, he himself was inducted into the armed service in the fall of 1942, but out of shape and in his forties, he was excused after only a few months to tour the country for a national war bond drive. This tour secured the foundation for a strong national following, and his popularity grew.

Wills eventually moved from Tulsa to the San Fernando Valley in California in late September 1944. By this time, he was commanding $21,000 for two nights on Venice Beach, but he was not happy. When he wasn't on the road, he was making pictures in Hollywood. The work, the money, and the fame didn't seem to make him happy, and he was drinking heavily.

Although Wills desired to create a regional dance circuit in California similar to that which he had established in the Southwest, MCA, who now handled all his performance bookings, had him touring the entire country for most of that year, headlining a cast of thirty-nine in his large music and dance vaudeville show. It was a grueling schedule. Wills worked constantly, sometimes every night of the week. It paid off in wider national market exposure. Thousands around the country were abandoning famous swing orchestras to attend his dances, and he was outgrossing even the Tommy Dorsey and Benny Goodman bands. In several instances he broke attendance records, and people had to be turned away from his shows.[4]

Wills returned to Hollywood in late January 1945, coincidentally at the exact time Jean arrived to finalize the transfer of assets into Hill and Range with Gerald King. Wills had three Columbia recording sessions scheduled with Art Satherley in 1945, the first of which took place on January 24, 1945. He recorded "Hang Your Head in Shame," "Texas Playboy Rag," "Roly Poly," "Stay a Little Longer," and "Smoke on the Water," the latter predicting the defeat of the Axis powers in Europe. On April 20, 1945, he recorded "New Spanish Two Step"—the old fiddle tune with new lyrics—and two war songs, "Silver Dew on the Blue Grass Tonight" and, most important for Hill and Range, "Stars and Stripes on Iwo Jima."[5]

"Stars and Stripes on Iwo Jima" was composed between the time the island of Iwo Jima was taken on February 23 and the recording session a month later, during which time Jean became aware of it. He may have been aware that it would be used in an upcoming national war bond drive. Such exposure guaranteed large performance royalties. He aggressively pursued the publishing rights but was unable to secure them before departing on April 20. During a stopover in Chicago, however, he received confirmation that the deal went through. Colonel H. H. McGhee, apparently acting as Wills's manager, wired Jean in Chicago to inform him that the current copyright owner, Cactus Jack (aka cowriter Cliff Johnson), would release the publishing rights for $1,000.

Jean instructed the New York office to draft two checks, each in the amount of $500, for Bob Wills and Cliff Johnson to secure the deal. This implies that Johnson was the sole writer of the work and that Wills—not having contributed substantially to the creation of the work—was cut in as a cowriter, as was customary for the time. The follow-up paperwork was completed after Jean returned to New York and the song rushed to production for use in the Seventh War Loan Drive that opened on May 14. The contract was confirmed by "J. J. Aberbach" at the New York City corporate offices. As Julian was signing his name exclusively as Jerome J. Brooks on his contracts at this time, this initial contract with Bob Wills was both negotiated and secured by Jean.

When Jean arrived back in New York, Julian was released to return to California, where he followed up on Jean's work and became the point man for other transactions with Wills for the rest of 1945. This was typical for the Aberbach brothers, who were never territorial about their business deals. Whoever was on the scene or available at the time would take care of business, and follow up would be handed off between them as necessary.

In the Hill and Range contract, "Stars and Stripes on Iwo Jima" is identified by its first lyric line: "When the Yanks Raise the Flag on Iwo Jima." While it would be the first Wills song to generate money for Hill and Range, that money would not be generated by licensing the song to Columbia for the Wills recording. In fact, the contract rider with Wills specifically excluded Hill and Range from any royalties obtained on that recording, indicating it was probably arranged by Wills himself. Jean and Julian would make their money by licensing the song for recordings by other artists.

Jean secured the rights to this important song on April 25, 1945. It overtook the country charts, becoming the number 1 record during the week of July 7, 1945.[6] More important, it established a critical working relationship between fledgling Hill and Range and America's most influential western swing performer.

Up until this point, King and Blink had been the perfect partners—silent partners—too busy with their own work to bother much about their little investment. Jean and Julian had been operating quietly, probably sharing only as much information about their business dealing with Wills and other artists as they felt they had to. By the fall of 1945, however, the transcriptions were generating some money, and so were some of the more mainstream copyrights they had found and put into Normandy Music, for instance "Suspence," the theme song to notable band leader Tony Martell's orchestra.[7] Altogether it was enough to capture the attention of the senior partners.

Suddenly, King and Blink thought it was time to exert some executive power over their younger partners. In the late fall of 1945 they suggested that Hill and Range should put King's son Jack and Blink's wife Melva on the payroll.[8] The move was unexpected and seemed to betray ulterior motives for the venture— that it was their intentions all along to use this venture to subsidize their dependents. They followed up by transferring all their company share to them by January 1946. Suddenly the Aberbach brothers were no longer in partnership with seasoned professionals, but with amateurs who could contribute nothing to the operation and would only drain capital and drag the business down.

Jean and Julian agreed that their company would go nowhere if saddled with unproductive partners. But with only two chart hits under their belt, they were in a weak position to split from their rich and powerful partners. Worse yet, King and Blink were under the impression that any money secured from BMI on the strength of their catalog, credit, and reputation was, in essence, a loan to the Aberbachs and that they were entitled to 100 percent of the cash less any out-of-pocket expenses borne by the operation. Splitting from King and Blink probably meant not only buying back their corporate shares at an increased value, but also paying back the company's outstanding "loan" that effectively amounted to $12,000.[9]

Years earlier, while Jean and Julian were living in the Paris townhouse and working the SEMI deal, they took on a young man who lived with them and helped out with domestic chores. Hardy Rothschild turned out to be an excellent cook. His only fault was that he liked to eat lots of meat, which was scarce at that time. And because Julian was also a boss in the house, Hardy had to fight every night for his meat—and Julian won most of the time.

After a while, Hardy could stand it no longer, and plotted his revenge. One night when a cousin of theirs was visiting, his chance came. The meal was delicious, and Julian asked for more and more meat. As usual it came from Hardy's portion. But instead of complaining, Hardy served it with the utmost graciousness, and additional meat was also offered to the rest of them.

After the meal was finished Hardy asked "So, how did you like it?" Everybody complimented him on the meal—so much so, that Hardy brought the rest of the meat to the table. Julian ate as if it was his last supper. Then Hardy removed the dishes, rubbed his hands with delight, and said, "I am pleased to hear everyone liked it so well, and that I did not have to eat so much of it by myself. Because, you see, it was horsemeat!"[10]

That's how Jean & Julian felt about the sudden move by King and Blink. The beef had turned to horsemeat. They were not prepared to squander their business careers playing nursemaid to amateurs. They took a pragmatic view of the situation and resolved to focus their efforts on quickly accumulating business assets that would enable them to survive a prospective business split. In only a matter of months, Jean and Julian would be able to take some pleasure in dishing back some of what they had been served.

CHAPTER 10

A View from the Bridge

Over the course of 1945, Jean and Julian had captured the rights to two significant hits, "Shame on You," and "Stars and Stripes on Iwo Jima," but if these afforded substantial royalties, they had not yet yielded much more than would cover operating expenses. On the expansion front, they had secured international representation as well for "Shame on You" and "Kitchy-Kitchy Koo," but these were minor deals. They had also pursued relationships with other significant western artists and with individuals connected to the western movie industry. This included signing character actor Smiley Burnett, Gene Autry's sidekick, who had written "The Wind Sings a Cowboy Song." Burnett also cowrote three other tunes with Lee Penny that were secured by Hill and Range, but apparently none of these generated ready cash.[1] Whether because of BMI distribution delays or simply because they generated less than needed, taken together all these deals were not generating growth capital.

As far as King and Blink could tell, Hill and Range was just barely meeting expenses and seemed to be a risky business that could easily turn into a money

pit. This perception was good news for the Aberbach brothers, because keeping the company's potential obscure would ensure the lowest possible terms
for settlement with their partners. As long as they worked quickly and quietly,
they could dispose of King and Blink before anything else broke big enough to
raise suspicions and therefore raise the settlement price.

During his recent California trips, Jean had made fast inroads into the
major studios as a representative of Chappell Music. His quick wit, European
film music experience, and his professional manner put pressured directors and
producers at ease. He found the work both creatively challenging and personally
fulfilling.

Jean approached Max about moving to California and continuing his work
for Chappell as its Hollywood representative for film. He was completely open
and candid with Max about his intentions concerning Hill and Range. Concur-
rent with his Chappell work, he wanted to start helping his brother on the work
of Hill and Range.[2] While he had proven himself a formidable business manager
for the New York office, it was not too difficult to convince Max that his most
valuable work for the company had been achieved through placing songs in
Hollywood films. Apparently, Max gave his blessing. As he had no interest in
western music, there wasn't any reason to anticipate a conflict of interest, only
one of time. He allowed the arrangement probably with the proviso that Jean's
work on Hill and Range not interfere in any way with his obligations to Chappell Music. Once again, Jean had managed to successfully balance himself with
one foot in both worlds. He preserved his working relationship and salary with
Chappell, but he could now openly devote greater time to the day-to-day affairs
of Hill and Range.

Shortly after New Year's Day 1946, Jean arrived in California. Over the
holidays, he organized the Aberbach brothers' affairs in anticipation of the King
and Blink split. Together he and Julian secured a number of deals jointly that
were separate and apart from their work with the country and western music
for King and Blink. For instance, a three-way partnership with Ray Ventura and
his several international firms and with the Canadian Music Sales Corporation
was consummated, naming Jean as agent in June 1945.[3] Jean also drafted joint
ownership agreements that included Julian in all the deals he had been pursuing
outside Hill and Range. For instance, in January 1946, Jean assigned 50 percent
of his stake in certain dramatic plays to Julian. Later, in March, he would add
Julian to an arrangement connected to the motion pictures *Henry V* and *Duel in
the Sun*, a subcontract management deal Jean had struck with Chappell Music to
market souvenir books. This simply confirmed what had always been their understanding: The Aberbach brothers shared equally in all business ventures.

Jean mounted a relentless campaign to build up the Aberbach brothers'
resources. It was essential that he and Julian land some major business deals

before the split with King and Blink. Jean's energy was directed toward carefully chosen, highly lucrative targets, for it would be on these key deals that Hill and Range would have to depend after the split. Jean also realized that, to the fullest extent possible, they should leverage the backing and business connections of King and Blink while they still had them.

Time was of the essence, but was in maddeningly short supply. To make most efficient use of it Jean actively sought opportunities that might serve both Chappell and Hill and Range interests. Already there were a few good prospects of that sort in the works—and one spectacular deal was just about to be concluded.

Jean had finally forged a path to the Sons of the Pioneers and to their coveted song "Tumbling Tumbleweeds," probably with the help of Harry Hall, Gerald King's former radio associate. During the spring of 1945, around a breathless schedule that consisted of pursuing Hill and Range leads—including Bob Wills and Ted Daffan—and placing Chappell music in Hollywood films, Jean began to court the current custodian of the song, Sam Fox.

Sam Fox Publishing was among the firms that had lobbied and failed (along with E. B. Marks and Peer International) to obtain a rate increase from ASCAP for their catalogs during the 1930s. Unlike Peer and Marks, Sam Fox had built his entire business around the film industry, providing music services critically needed throughout the movie industry's nascent period. He began in 1913 by distributing piano arrangements of "mood music" that would accompany silent film. From such inauspicious beginnings Sam Fox Publishing would grow to become one of the most lucrative distributors in the business, placing millions of pieces of sheet music in national variety stores including Newberry's, one of the nation's largest "five and dime" store chains. Alert to changing music trends, Fox embraced hillbilly music during the 1930s when the industry surged into its western movie phase, and a few Fox songs even became popular hits.

Practically speaking, however, Fox had had little to do with the popularity of any of their songs, including "Tumbling Tumbleweeds." This was a utilitarian publishing firm—a stock sound house that provided a wide variety of services to the film industry. Generally, filmmakers who turned to it did not expect to find the best songwriters, but they counted on it to come up with serviceable music quickly, and at a fair price—whether theme music, featured songs, or background music to enhance their moving pictures. The firm employed some in-house composers, few of whom were notable, and acquired outside works from other writers only when necessary. There was usually little incentive for songwriters to exert pressure on the company to promote their work because most songs were acquired outright as works for hire, an arrangement wherein the author gives up royalty rights altogether in exchange for a flat fee payment up front. Such was the case with "Tumbling Tumbleweeds," whose writer, Bob Nolan, never received any royalties from Sam Fox.

Bob Nolan. Courtesy of John Fullerton.

Unaware there was any other means of making money from a song, Nolan probably gratefully accepted a onetime flat fee—probably $25—hungry for the immense promotional exposure its use as the theme song in Gene Autry's film would buy for the Sons of the Pioneers.[4] Most of Fox's copyrights simply lived and died with their associated movie projects. Most had an average market life-span of about a week—the span of time during which a typical film played in local theaters. With back-to-back production schedules, there was never any time for follow-up song promotion before Fox moved on to the next project.[5]

Tumbling Tumbleweeds was Gene Autry's first feature film and Joseph Kane's directorial debut. It was one of many western movie projects Sam Fox would work on that year. It is unlikely the publishing company paid any special attention to the film's remarkable theme song. The film was probably relegated to Republic Picture's lowest film budget category (their Jubilee line), which allotted only seven days for shooting and a budget of only $30,000.

Even if it fell into the Anniversary films group, which afforded a budget of up to $120,000 and fourteen days for production, it is still doubtful this song would have received much attention. Republic also differed from all other B movie companies and even most of the majors in that their pictures, including their serials, were equipped with nearly complete musical scores. The sheer volume of music that needed to be produced from week to week would have obscured the potential of any one piece.

Nevertheless, the song flourished. In addition to its constant inclusion in films throughout the 1930s, its popularity was further reinforced by the Sons of the Pioneers who performed it often on their weekly Los Angeles radio show, which was nationally syndicated. With so much going for it, "Tumbling Tumbleweeds" hardly needed Sam Fox's promotional efforts to become popular. By the time 1940 rolled around, it was already the industry's most familiar western song—a natural choice for Bing Crosby, who had worked with the boys in his film *Rhythm on the Range* in 1936. Whether he deserved it or not, "Tumbling Tumbleweeds" was making Sam Fox a lot of money.

In 1945, however, the firm was undergoing a severe cash crunch. Despite internal dissension over the fate of their prized copyright, by the time Jean arrived in California during early 1946, Sam Fox Publishing was willing at least to meet and see what Jean had to offer.[6] He arrived wearing his Chappell & Co. hat, rather than his Hill and Range hat—and for good reasons. Any potential for a deal rested solely on someone being able to do for Sam Fox better than he could do for himself. Chappell brought to the table promotional resources—both domestic and international—that Fox wanted, and Hill and Range simply did not have. Fox was looking for a substantial advance as well as for an increase on his current royalty rate. Chappell was in a strong position to do this, and Hill and Range was not. Furthermore, acquisition of so valuable a copyright would have significantly increased the value of Hill and Range assets further complicating a settlement with King and Blink.

Jean, however, had another more compelling reason to place the song with Chappell rather than make a bid for it himself. It came back to the confusing issue of performance rights. Money-making copyrights were the bread and butter of music publishing, and both ASCAP and BMI fought each other constantly to protect their relationships with writers and publishers so as to maintain control of their lucrative copyright properties. Before long, each was accusing the other organization of using insidious tactics to induce publishers and writers to switch affiliation. Because of this, it would have been difficult—perhaps even impossible in 1945—to transfer "Tumbling Tumbleweeds" to the Aberbachs' fledgling company, specifically because Hill and Range's affiliation was with BMI, whereas Sam Fox was an ASCAP firm.

Since Bob Nolan maintained no formal writer affiliation with either ASCAP or BMI at this time, "Tumbling Tumbleweeds," was, by association with Sam Fox Publishing, an ASCAP catalog copyright. It could not be transferred into Hill and Range Songs, Inc., which was a BMI affiliate, without great difficulty. The fact that Sam Fox was willing to part with only 50 percent of its interest in the song further complicated matters. A co-venture with Hill and Range would have meant that BMI and ASCAP would be co-administering the song, creating an unusual, highly controversial situation. These factors left no doubt in Jean's mind that "Tumbling Tumbleweeds" must be placed with Chappell.

The deal was consummated on January 28, 1946. Sam Fox conveyed 50 percent interest in the song, relinquishing all promotional responsibility as well. Curiously, the work did not end up in Max's core catalog, but in Williamson Music, the firm owned by Richard Rodgers and Oscar Hammerstein II that was closely associated with Chappell.

Williamson Music had been formed in 1944—named after Rodgers's and Hammerstein's fathers' first names. It served as the repository for their joint work, beginning with *Oklahoma!* At the close of 1945, Rodgers and Hammerstein's interest in folk and country themes was still strong. When Jerome Kern died during 1945, Irving Berlin took over and completed the score to *Annie Get Your Gun,* which the partners produced. That same year, they themselves created the score for the 20th Century–Fox musical remake of the bucolic film *State Fair* first produced in 1933, which had starred Will Rogers. It reaped them the popular hit "It Might as Well Be Spring," whose renditions by Sammy Kaye, Dick Haymes, and Paul Weston each peaked in the top ten on the pop charts during late 1945. Parking "Tumbling Tumbleweeds" in this repository probably seemed like the natural choice.

It is also likely that Jean found Max only lukewarm on the acquisition and simply called in a favor from the only Chappell associates he thought might be sympathetic. Williamson music was a publishing administration deal whereby the authors contracted Chappell staff to manage their copyrights using a Chappell subsidiary company called Crawford Music. So while Williamson was effectively a subsidiary of Chappell, it remained wholly owned by the writers.[7]

This firm almost exclusively housed Rodgers and Hammerstein's work. "Tumbling Tumbleweeds" was among only a handful of songs by other writers that found its way into this catalog. Sammy Fain and Irving Kahal's "I'll Be Seeing You," written in the 1930s, is notable. It was revived during the war years and became immensely popular. Why only these few songs, and no others, were accepted into the Williamson catalog remains a mystery.

Jean had leveraged "Tumbling Tumbleweeds" into a position that was just an arm's length from where he wanted it to be. Although the prize was out of his reach, as long as it was housed in Williamson music and was directly managed by Chappell, it was still safely under his control. Williamson's association with Chappell kept any other publishers away from the tune.

This deal also elevated the Aberbach brothers' profile in their chosen field. To the Sons of the Pioneers and other western songwriters, Jean and Julian were no longer just newcomers who had made a few lucky guesses. They were powerful publishers apparently with connections to the vast promotional resources of Chappell Music. Jean could leverage the "Tumbling Tumbleweeds" acquisition to attract other promising writers.

As soon as the "Tumbling Tumbleweeds" deal was concluded, Jean started work on promoting the song. In a telegram dated April 5, 1946, Jean reports from California on the Sons of the Pioneers' new recorded version, urging Max to obtain and review a test pressing in New York. Despite their numerous recordings of the tune, this RCA Victor recording from their March 15 session remains the definitive version. Based on an orchestration by Country Washburne, former bass player for the Ted Weems orchestra, it relied solely on group harmony with the addition of Ken Carson's whistling. Over the course of the spring, Jean reported that Gene Autry would definitely rerecord a new version featuring a large orchestra and chorus. Another telegram in May reports that it might be used as Roy Rogers's theme song for his upcoming national radio series, and that it was also under consideration for use in an upcoming Walt Disney film. In August Jean confirmed its continued use by the Sons of the Pioneers as the theme song to a new transcription series.

At the same time, Jean was not lax in his responsibilities as Chappell's West Coast representative for film music. In a telegram dated May 2, 1946, Jean assured Max that songs in the making by Jimmy McHugh and Harold Adamson for a new film were reserved for Chappell's catalog. He referred to offers made to Samuel Goldwyn for Chappell songs, confirms the adaptation of "Why Do You Pass Me By?" and Buddy De Sylva's "Another Kiss" for use in upcoming MGM films, and reports his success in placing "Among My Souvenirs" with a William Wyler production featuring top stars Myrna Loy and Frederick March. He also reported on his progress with writers on developing the film score for David O. Selznick's upcoming production of *Spellbound* and detailed his lobbying efforts to secure "Symphonie" as the theme song to the upcoming film *Arch of Triumph* that headlined Ingrid Bergman, Hollywood's biggest female star.

Jean had ambitious goals for each of these Chappell properties which he pursued with a vengeance. Once the goal was achieved, these properties were set aside. By contrast, Jean was tireless in his promotion of "Tumbling Tumbleweeds." He used his best efforts to convince Max of the mainstream potential of the song and the growing profitability of country and western music. With Max's lack of interest in the genre, what could he hope to gain?

What the Aberbach brothers needed right now was a way out of the King and Blink deal. Jean hoped that proving success with "Tumbling Tumbleweeds" might interest Max in providing the backing the Aberbach brothers needed to split from King and Blink. Perhaps they could create a co-owned country and western Chappell subsidiary? Now, with the biggest western prize in his pocket, maybe Max would see the potential of this growing popular music market. The magnificent 1947 orchestral version of the piece proved its broad and lasting popularity. But Max Dreyfus continued to regard "Tumbling Tumbleweeds" as nothing more than a passing novelty.

In his memoir drafts, Jean recounted an incident with the famous playwright Arthur Miller. One day he happened to see "A View from the Bridge" and contacted Miller's agent about turning it into a musical. An exclusive arrangement was made for two years under the condition that Hill and Range pay two composers chosen by Miller to compose the score. Convinced of the composers' talents and of Miller's own good faith in the partnership, Jean agreed.

Two years later they convened at Miller's apartment to hear the work. Miller pretended to be interested, but when the demonstration concluded, Miller said he thought that although the music would be good, he still would not like it. It turns out that Miller already promised these rights to a brother of the composer Rossini and had no intention of accepting the work of these two composers or any others. Jean took some comfort in the knowledge that when Rossini's brother's piece was finally presented in Italy, it was a failure.[8]

Like Arthur Miller, Max was driven by his own agenda. No matter how successful "Tumbling Tumbleweeds" might become, no matter how much money it made for Chappell, *although the music would be good, he still would not like it.* Hillbilly music would not become a mainstay of the Chappell Music catalog.

Standing on the bridge between tradition and progress, eager to move forward, Jean and his contemporaries could not see beyond the legend to the man himself. Max represented a generation as yet unwilling to yield to the next. Having done everything possible to interest him in these profitable new song forms, Jean could only hope that if Max would not embrace the future, then at least he would stay out of its way.

CHAPTER II

The Hired Band

J ean's involvement with "Tumbling Tumbleweeds" during 1945 established an important business relationship with its writer Bob Nolan and
with the Sons of the Pioneers. Extremely busy with radio, film, and personal appearances in addition to their RCA Victor contract, the Sons of
the Pioneers had had little contact with either Jean or Julian during the
previous year. "Stars and Stripes on Iwo Jima," recorded by them during their
August 8, 1945, RCA Victor session, appears to be their only Hill and Range
tune.[1] As current manager of their most prized song, however, Jean could now
command more of their attention.

His newly won status came none too soon. Fred Rose was successfully peddling his songs to country and western performers that were published through
Acuff-Rose, his coventure with performer Roy Acuff. The Sons of the Pioneers'
January 7, 1946, session featured four sides, three of which were country songs
by Rose. Afraid of losing these important songwriter-performers to his chief
competitor, Jean redoubled his efforts to win the publishing rights to their whole
catalog for Hill and Range.

It soon became clear that while Nolan might have written their most popular song, it was Tim Spencer who looked after the business of the group. A prolific songwriter himself, Spencer's contribution was no less important than Nolan's to the success of the group. With classic western songs like "The Timber Trail" and "Gold Star Mother with Silvery Hair," Spencer's songs were certainly considered valuable and were probably of interest to Acuff-Rose and others. But his value to the Aberbach brothers was far greater than his considerable songwriting talent.

Tim Spencer held a unique position on the Hollywood western social scene. Not only did he write for and manage its premier western music group, he was respected as a devout Christian and a leader in the local religious community. On weekends, he opened his home to friends and neighbors, who would visit and participate in hymn singing. When he discovered he could beat the new tax laws by registering as a nonprofit religious organization, Spencer incorporated his home as a Christian house of worship. The Hollywood Christian Group eventually included major luminaries, including the Reverend Billy Graham, George Beverly Shea, Mickey Cohen, and actress Rosalind Russell, all of whom Jean met through Tim Spencer.[2] As leader of this growing and powerful Los

Tim Spencer.
Courtesy of
John Fullerton.

Angeles social group, Spencer was beyond reproach. He was greatly trusted by his fellow artists and could prove very influential in engaging other songwriters for the firm if the Aberbach brothers could only bring him under their wing.

This notion may have crossed the minds of other publishers as well, but none so far had been successful at winning him for one simple reason: He was already spoken for. Like Bob Nolan, he had sold many of his songs outright to Sylvester Cross's American Music for a flat fee and was not enjoying any royalties at all on these past works. Moreover, Spencer had a long standing obligation to Cross for future works. By 1946, however, Tim Spencer had become aware of the new royalty opportunities BMI was making available to songwriters and was probably already contemplating what to do about it.

The partnership of Cross and Winge that created Cross Music Co. and American Music, Inc., operated out of San Francisco. It dominated the western and hillbilly music publishing west of the Rockies during the 1930s. Cross apparently provided a useful and satisfactory service to writers—probably in the form of sheet music printing—but by 1946 Cross's method of doing business had become obsolete. A printer turned music publisher, he failed to adapt to the changing times.

Some of his business practices came under government scrutiny. Until investigated, Cross would actually *charge* artists a fee to publish their songs—a practice that may have been reasonable in the early printing days but was completely unethical for a publisher who was not providing any other remuneration. Only after this did he begin paying a flat fee for songs, still avoiding collection and distribution of author-composer royalties as required by BMI. Cross was not alone in this practice. Many small music publishers did the same throughout the 1940s, feeling perfectly justified because of the unusually high risk associated with promoting fringe music genres while their markets were still being developed.

When informed artists began to challenge these practices, most publishers adapted. Cross, did not. He remained sorely out of step with the times.[3] If Tim Spencer and the others were aware of Cross's failure to meet his new obligations as a BMI music publisher, they did nothing about it, perhaps because of their longstanding, apparently cordial, business relationship.

With the changing business atmosphere, Jean and Julian recognized that considerable legal weight could be brought to bear on Sylvester Cross. It would not take much effort to convince Spencer that Cross's negligent business practices would render Spencer's existing exclusive contracts unenforceable. Jean and Julian felt that they would have little trouble recapturing all of Spencer's earlier works as well. There was only one problem with this plan. The power lay with Spencer, not Hill and Range. Once they explained the situation, nothing prohibited Spencer from simply going off and doing it on his own. At the top of his profession, and with only a handful of western artists and movie houses in the industry, who could Spencer not reach and influence on his own? At this stage of his career, even the top popular singing stars, movie studios, and record producers would not refuse a visit from the leader of western music's finest singing group.

Spencer could be courted for an exclusive songwriter's agreement, but even with a substantial cash advance, there was no reason to suppose an offer from the Aberbach brothers could be made more attractive than an offer from Acuff-Rose or anyone else. What could they offer that Spencer could not get for himself?

While Jean and his brother pondered this problem, they forged ahead in other areas. Details for several new recordings of Paul Westmoreland's "Detour" were confirmed—versions by Wesley Tuttle on Capitol, Elton Britt on Victor, and Spade Cooley on Columbia's OKeh label. The Tuttle and Britt recordings would shoot into the top ten on the charts, but Cooley's version would eclipse even these, becoming their second chart hit and among his biggest songs.

Foy Willing, who also recorded a version on Decca, signed with Hill and Range just five days before Jean secured the pivotal "Tumbling Tumbleweeds." Willing fronted the second-most-popular western music group in the country, the Riders of the Purple Sage. They could be found in most of the western movies that did not feature the Sons of the Pioneers. Pairing Tin Pan Alley songwriter Sid Robin with Willing yielded the bestselling Sons of the Pioneers hit "No One to Cry To." Jean also secured two hits by Ted Daffan, "Headin' down the Wrong Highway" and "Shut That Gate," cowritten with Dick James, in March 1946.[4]

During the early months of 1946, another crucial relationship was also coming together with the queen of western song, Cindy Walker. Jean had expressed an interest in meeting her to Don Allen (one of Standard Radio's producers).[5] By now she was a respected songwriter with strong links to some of the industry's top artists. She had created or cowritten numerous works for Gene Autry, Roy Rogers, and Dale Evans. She was also writing for musical comedy genius Spike Jones and His City Slickers, whose catalog would be acquired eventually by Hill and Range. More important, she had contributed thirty-nine songs to the industry's biggest star, Bob Wills, in connection with his eight Columbia film and recording sessions. Now a Decca recording artist in her own right, she was doing a series of transcriptions of her songs for Standard Radio.

This versatile young woman was an absolute original. Walker was supremely confident of her abilities and careful in business matters, turning only to her father from time to time for business advice. The little he offered, when paired with her strong talent and keen instincts, secured her a level of career independence as a songwriter that would be enviable even today. By the time Cindy Walker met Jean she knew—as did most everyone in the business—that she could write her own ticket.

Cindy Walker.
Courtesy of the Grand
Ole Opry Archives.

Try as he might, Jean could not convince Cindy to come on board under an exclusive contract. Cindy was absolutely clear in her convictions—she wrote songs for singers, not publishers. Remaining free of any exclusive publisher representation enabled her to shop her songs directly to the artists for whom she had written them. It sweetened the deal that the song could be placed with any publishing house the artist preferred.

By November 1945 Walker already had a relationship with Hill and Range by virtue of her collaboration with some of the artists Jean and Julian had signed. During that time she had written "Triflin' Gal" for Al Dexter (of "Pistol Packin' Mama" fame), which fast became one of his biggest hits. Dexter had placed "Triflin' Gal" with his own firm but turned the song over to Hill and Range for exploitation. By acquiring publishing in this way, eventually Hill and Range would handle eighty-seven of Walker's tunes. Aside from "Triflin' Gal," Hill and Range represented "New Broom Boogie," "Kokomo Island," and "Texas Waltz" (recorded by Al Dexter); "Watching the Bubbles in My Beer," "Don't Be Ashamed of Your Age," "How Can It Be Wrong," "Sugar Moon," and "The Warm Red Wine" (recorded by Bob Wills and the Texas Playboys); and later "Cherokee Maiden"—acquired by Hill and Range when they bought the original publisher, Santley, Joy. "Cherokee Maiden" achieved number 1 on the charts for Merle Haggard in 1976. Other Walker compositions in the Hill and Range catalog were "Take Me in Your Arms and Hold Me" (recorded by Les Paul and

Mary Ford and also by Eddy Arnold); "Loreli" and "Roses of Yesterday" (recorded by Elton Britt); and "The Gold Rush Is Over," "The Next Voice You Hear," and "Just Keep a-Movin'" (recorded by Hank Snow). And the great songs just kept coming: "Answer the Phone," "Two Glasses Joe," "Hey, Mister Bluebird," and "Texas vs. Kentucky" (recorded in various pairings by Ernest Tubb, with Loretta Lynn, Red Foley, and the Wilburn Brothers); and "How Sweet It Is to Know," "Christmas, Christmas," and "The Night Watch" (recorded by George Beverly Shea). "The Night Watch" was also recorded by Jo Stafford and Red Foley and in the 1990s by Mel Tillis.

But perhaps Walker's best-known work is "You Don't Know Me," a country classic first recorded by Eddy Arnold, who gave Walker the song's title. Jean and Julian were instrumental in landing seventy-eight recordings of the song by such artists as Ray Charles, Elvis Presley, Steve Lawrence and Edie Gormé, Vic Damone, Carmen McRae, Henry Mancini, Jam Howard, Jerry Vale, and Lenny Welch. It continues to be recorded every few years by a notable performer, more recently by Charlie Rich, Mickey Gilley (for whom it became a number 1 hit), and Emmylou Harris.

Walker would not be locked down by an exclusive agreement with Hill and Range. However, her father was impressed with Jean and Julian's enterprising skills. A cotton buyer, he was not very familiar with the entertainment business, but A. A. Walker was a genuine, down-to-earth man who believed in good business practice and the protection of contract law. He saw something special in Jean and Julian. He expressed to his daughter the opinion that the Aberbachs were very smart operators and that it would be in her best interest to give special attention to Hill and Range. They would become, he predicted, very, very big in the business.

Jean was particularly interested in Cindy's extensive work with Bob Wills. Columbia studios had hired her to write all the songs for Wills's eight movies. To date, they had managed to capture only one or two of Wills's songs. Jean was still working on a way to bring Wills under exclusive contract, but like Walker, Wills continued to resist. Since "Stars and Stripes on Iwo Jima" hit in the spring of 1945, they had secured only one other of his tunes: "There's a White Cross Tonight on Okinawa (And a Gold Star in Some Mother's Home)," written with Cliff Johnson and Cliff Sundin.[6] Wills was the kind of artist who could carry them successfully through the split with King and Blink. Jean struggled to rope him into an exclusive deal and capture all his works—past, present, and future—for Hill and Range, even though the model for doing so was crystal clear. This model had succeeded in keeping Biltmore solvent in the month leading up to the incorporation of Hill and Range.

One year earlier, in spring 1944, Jean had obtained the advance from BMI through Biltmore that made possible the coventure with King and Blink that

resulted in Hill and Range. Biltmore's obligations to BMI, however, were oner-
ous. For its initial contract, BMI expected at least ten major network plugs
(broadcasts of a Biltmore song on a syndicated radio station) a week to justify
the advance of $12,000 per year. Their advance depended on getting at least
ten plugs per week, otherwise their advance would be reduced. Unfortunately,
when the deal with BMI was consummated in March 1944, Biltmore's catalog
consisted only of "Kitchy-Kitchy Koo," a moderately successful copyright that
had become popular here and abroad thanks to Lawrence Welk's recording and
its use in a film called *On Community Sing*. They needed more songs in the
catalog to cover this quota.

To quickly add more properties, Jean and Julian set up co-owned partnership companies with several bandleaders who had regular spots on network
radio. This was a sure bet, since no bandleader could be faulted for performing
his own theme song at the beginning and end of each program, or as transition
interludes for promotional spots. They cut partnership deals with Vincent Lopez, Tony Lane, and Enric Madriguera in August 1944. Their brilliance was in
recognizing that bandleader's theme songs did not depend on public popularity
or chart success to generate royalties. Whether it was good or bad, whether it
hit the charts or not, whether it was memorable or forgettable, an amount of
money was generated for the Aberbachs every time the song was played.

The approach was not unheard of. Bandleaders became aware that extra
money could be made by performing their own music on radio during the 1930s.[7]
Increasingly, they began to write and use their own music. Some sought out
established publishing houses to oversee the administrative process of collecting airplay royalties on their works. For instance, bandleader Enric Madriguera
hooked up with Ralph Peer in 1931 to promote and manage the business of his
hit theme song "Adios."[8] Bandleaders regarded a coventure publishing company
as a step up in the business world—something they could call their own. Jean
and Julian saw them as cash cows. Some of these arrangements worked out. Others didn't. The corporation created in partnership with Vincent Lopez, Pianola
Music, was short-lived, but Airlane Music, a coventure with Tony Lane, and
Enric Madriguera's joint firm called Riviera Music appear to have endured.

Employing the concept of joint corporate ownership that he learned from
Max, Jean managed to preserve much of the BMI advance funds while at the
same time ensuring a small, steady, and predictable stream of revenue to keep
them going through 1944. Having tested the strategy with numerous bandleaders, it seemed natural to try it with Bob Wills.[9]

In June 1945 Wills moved to a ranch near Fresno in northern California with
his sixth and final wife, Betty. A few months later, he began recording a transcription series for Tiffany Music, Inc., in Oakland, California, which included more
than 220 selections that would compete for airplay with the relatively miserly

number of commercial recordings Columbia had been able to release for the artist over the previous few years.[10] The rights to these mechanical transcriptions were retained by Tiffany, Wills getting only the typical upfront fees. He did not participate in the copyright ownership of these transcription arrangements.

Wills's only experience with music publishing had been with Irving Berlin, for "San Antonio Rose." One group member claims Wills remained completely ignorant about song royalties and found out about them during the early 1940s by talking to other musicians. But for some reason, even Jean's business expertise could not win him over. It took a long time to win the respect and confidence of country and western's biggest star, but after a long year of prodding, Jean and Julian Aberbach finally discovered what made Bob Wills tick. They won him over by appealing more to his ego than to his pocket. They gave him his own company.

Wills was the biggest country and western star, and among the biggest popular stars in the country, reputed to be grossing $340,000 a year.[11] No advance fee they could offer would be attractive to such a wealthy artist. On the other hand, his talent management agency MCA, that booked all his tours, controlled almost every aspect of his professional life—except this one. Music publishing was among the few areas left where he could still assert himself in the business of his career.

The notion of owning a publishing company was appealing on a number of levels. First, it provided a better long-term rate of return on his copyrights. He would earn royalties as 50 percent publisher in addition to the money he would receive as author-composer. Second, some group members were already pressuring him to share song royalties, and the joint publishing company provided a business structure and administrative staff to manage such distributions. Finally, it acted as his pension fund. The publishing firm became the home of copyrights written by his group members where he, as part publishing owner, could participate in their royalty revenue while at the same time satisfying their requests to receive royalty money as author-composers. It was a win for everyone.

Bob Wills Music, Inc., publishing company glorified the name of Bob Wills and collected all of Wills's available songs under one roof. Not only did it render a sense of permanence to his legacy, but it made him feel that he had some hand in the preservation and promotion of that legacy. Jean engaged him in a fifty-fifty corporate partnership. He also engaged Wills in an exclusive songwriter's agreement. This arrangement made him feel as if he was working for himself as much as for anybody else. Working on an exclusive contract was perfectly palatable when arranged for a company that he himself half-owned and that bore his name.

Their arrangements were made on May 17, 1946. As if to bless the deal, the very next day the "New Spanish Two Step"—also known as "San Antonio

Rose"—grabbed the number 1 spot on the country charts and held it, on and off, over the next sixteen weeks.

When Bob Wills entered Columbia studios again on September 4, 1946, in addition to his writer's share he was entitled to half the publishing rights revenue to the new songs he was about to record. During that session he recorded "Cotton Eyed Joe," "Brain Cloudy Blues," "Virginia," "Punkin' Stomp," and "Bob Wills Boogie." For his final Columbia contract session in Chicago, October 15–16, 1947, he recorded "A Sweet Kind of Love," "Texarkana Baby," "New Texas Playboy Rag," and "Deep Water."

Over the next several years (well into the 1950s) Wills would contribute numerous hits to the firm he co-owned with the Aberbach brothers: "Fiddlin' Man" (1946); "Sugar Moon" and "Don't Be Ashamed of Your Age" (1948) with Cindy Walker; "Bubbles in My Beer" (1948) with Tommy Duncan; "Keeper of My Heart" (1948) with Jerry Irby; and "My Shoes Keep Walking Back to You" (1956) with Lee Ross. The Wills firm also handled a new arrangement of Wills's father's old time fiddle tune "Faded Love" (1951). Bob Wills Music would also represent works in which Wills did not participate as writer, but which he popularized through his performances and recordings: "I'm Gonna Be Boss" (1947) by Jess Ashlock, "Rag Mop" (1950), cowritten by his brother Johnnie Lee Wills and Deacon Anderson, and Cindy Walker's "Warm Red Wine" (1949) were among those that became top chart hits.

It was Max who had taught Jean the trick of partnership companies. Max used it to appease his accomplished Broadway songwriters when money no longer proved an effective incentive. Dreyfus realized that late in their careers, wealthy songwriters like Jerome Kern, Cole Porter, Richard Rodgers and Oscar Hammerstein II, and Lorenz "Larry" Hart could easily finance their own publishing organizations and hire away experienced talent to run it. So he appealed to their sense of vanity instead, offering them the prestige of owning and comanaging their own companies. In this way, he was able to keep his songwriter roster intact and fend off competitors who might have stolen them away.[12] Jean saw how such arrangements reflected favorably in the volume and quality of these artists' creative output and how little was ultimately sacrificed in the way of revenue for Chappell.

He applied the same concept to Wills, but it was the relationship the Aberbachs forged with Sons of the Pioneers leader Tim Spencer that ultimately proved to be pivotal in the story of Hill and Range. Jean aggressively pursued Spencer for the rights to his new song "Cowboy Camp Meetin'" that was slated for the Sons of the Pioneers March 15 recording session. Using the joint publishing device as leverage, Jean signed the song April 2, 1946, stipulating that it be automatically added to their joint publishing firm as soon as the company was in place. Tim Spencer Music, Inc., was formed by April 24, at which time Spencer also signed an exclusive songwriter's agreement with his new firm.[13]

The terms of this arrangement were a little unusual. The exclusive songwriter's agreement was longer than most—five years instead of the customary three—to match the initial term of the incorporation agreement. Also, responsibilities for the growth of the corporation as well as its profits would be equally divided among all its owner partners. Therefore, the contract demanded that each partner match the other in the number of copyrights added to, and number of records secured for, the company. To make his song quota, Spencer would have to target professional colleagues and friends for songs.

Eventually all the Sons of the Pioneers committed their available works and signed exclusive songwriter's agreements with Tim Spencer Music, Inc. On May 14 the elusive Bob Nolan transferred all his copyrights except "Tumbling Tumbleweeds" into this company. Following in Spencer's footsteps, he also signed a five-year exclusive songwriter's agreement with Tim Spencer Music, pledging also to assist in recapturing any properties held by Sylvester Cross and American Music. Others quickly followed, including Tim's brother Glenn, as well as Hugh and Karl Farr. Tim Spencer Music proved to be a powerful magnet for other artists: Fleming Allan and Sam Allen, Bob and Slim Newman all joined the ranks, as did Roy Rogers and Dale Evans who contributed "My Heart Went That-a-Way."

Fifty percent of something is far better than 100 percent of nothing. Giving up half their revenue was a small price to pay to ensure the Aberbach's fledgling venture would survive. Taken together, "Tumbling Tumbleweeds," and the Tim Spencer and Bob Wills joint ventures secured three substantial anchors that the Aberbach brothers could use to leverage cash, credit, and industry credibility. What had worked well with moderately successful network bandleaders back in New York a few years before proved irresistible to Tim Spencer and the otherwise intractable Bob Wills. Jean and Julian were able to retain most of their available cash and gamble little on these ventures except their own talents, in which they were completely confident.

The partnership firms with Tim Spencer and Bob Wills were created quietly. Both corporations were created with Jean and Julian personally—not with Hill and Range, and because of this Jean and Julian now had the resources they needed to split from King and Blink.

During May and June 1946, Jean visited Max back in New York and reaffirmed his ongoing employment with Chappell Music as division head and film music representative, while Julian arranged to lease offices at 7164 Melrose Place in Los Angeles. Everything was finally ready. Although it turned out to be very costly, at least the split with King and Blink was amicable. In a letter dated

August 5, 1946, Gerald King expresses, on behalf of his partner as well, their willingness to dissolve the partnership because they had realized nothing from any of its publishing activities. Jack King and Melva Blink would give up their shares in exchange for $10,000 paid to each of them in $250 weekly increments. Jean and Julian would walk away with the company name and all the copyrights but leave the right of electrical transcription on all these works with their senior partners. King and Blink were prohibited from engaging in country and western music publishing for a period of three years, and Hill and Range's BMI future royalties would be attached as collateral for the hefty settlement fee. Acting as general manager, Jean quickly prepared the papers, settling with Gerald King on August 30, 1946. The Aberbach brothers emerged from the split with their reputations intact and the company solvent.

Over the course of six months, Jean and Julian Aberbach had taken the Los Angeles western music scene by storm. They had captured western music's biggest star and its most influential singer-songwriters in exclusive business relationships. Bob Wills and his Texas Playboys as well as the Sons of the Pioneers were at their disposal to promote their co-owned copyrights. By December they would also conclude an exclusive distribution deal with Al Dexter, whose catalog boasted a parade of number 1 bestsellers such as "Pistol Packin' Mama," "Too Late to Worry, Too Blue to Cry," "It's Up to You," and "Wine, Women, and Song." Before long all the important western writers would be on board, thanks to Jean's work on "Tumbling Tumbleweeds" and their associations with Wills and Spencer, which greatly influenced songwriters' perception of the Aberbach brothers and their company.

Having exhausted the western talent pool in Los Angeles, the Aberbach brothers needed to broaden their horizons. Clearly the next challenge was Nashville. The Grand Ole Opry broadcast weekly from Ryman Auditorium in Nashville. It was fast becoming the Mecca of hillbilly music. Conceived as an appealing vehicle to sell insurance for the National Life and Accident Insurance Company, the live performance national radio show on WSM was attracting the best country singers, instrumentalists, and comedians in the country.

Established in 1925, going national on the NBC radio network in 1939, the Grand Ole Opry had become a longstanding southern institution and a source of fierce regional pride. Nashville's music scene was thriving, and many of its artists were the genuine article, not some movieland facsimile. But here the Aberbach brothers were completely unknown, and as for being Austrian Jews, they might as well have been from Mars.

This was also Acuff-Rose territory. As the Opry's most successful performing artist, Roy Acuff's joint publishing company with Fred Rose was growing quickly and threatened to dominate the country music industry. With the King and Blink buyout draining their resources, large upfront cash advances were not an option. Without the ability to make strong cash offers, it seemed they would make only a weak entry into the Nashville music business. The Aberbach brothers needed to find a way in, but how?

By January 1947 their plan of attack had already revealed itself in the deals made with Bob Wills and Tim Spencer. It suddenly occurred to them that the single largest impediment to their expansion—money—was not what the Aberbachs needed. In fact, in most cases, they wouldn't need it at all. What the Aberbachs needed were *partnerships—lots and lots of partnerships!* In the Bob Wills and Tim Spencer deals they had created a way to acquire copyrights assured of promotional exposure by top-selling artists with no money down. As partial owner-publishers, Bob Wills and Tim Spencer had an extra incentive to encourage their groups to perform works in the joint catalog because they would personally reap additional royalties as a result. There was no reason to assume that Nashville songwriter-performers—however big or small—would not warm up to the same opportunity.

Such arrangements provided an unprecedented competitive advantage over other publishers. There was nothing unethical, illegal, or wrong with the idea. In fact, the arrangement was much fairer to the partner artists, giving them more money and more control over their songs. Most traditional American music publishers resisted the notion because giving up 50 percent of their revenue seemed insane. Only a music publisher with courage and supreme confidence in his abilities to pick prolific talent and effectively motivate them to help promote their work would wager half his potential earnings!

But that was the problem with traditional Tin Pan Alley publishers. They had a code of unspoken rules by which everyone played. But this was a new world. Country and western music was virgin territory. There were no rules and few real players. Jean and Julian Aberbach were about to write their own rules. In fact, they were about to start a whole new game in Nashville that would shake the very foundations of the music business. In time, it would spawn a business trend that would redefine the relationship of talent to management. Jean and Julian had absolute confidence in their abilities as publishers and also understood that greed was a powerful motivator. They felt that any percentage they would give up in these partnerships would be offset by the extra efforts that performer-owners like Bob Wills and Tim Spencer would make in an effort to line their own pockets. The beauty of the plan was that it required very little capital. All they really needed was a phone call, a letter, or a lunch, and they could capture the attention of most of Nashville's songwriter-performers.

Things were looking up in the spring of 1946. Although the King and Blink settlement made them more cash-challenged than ever, the picture they managed to project to the music world was one of tremendously successful music publishers with infinitely deep pockets. How else could they have landed exclusive deals with western music's most prized artists other than by offering a better deal and executing it profitably for their partners?

Early in their youth, the brothers had learned that appearances can be a powerful thing. Jean recalls it this way in his memoir sketches:

> During our youth, Julian and I wanted everything, but much of it we could not afford. Every year there was a big party in Vienna at the Burg gardens behind the castle. The only problem was that we had no money to get in. I suggested to Julian that we go to the entrance anyway—that somehow we would manage to get in. When we arrived at the door I saw three taxi cabs arrive which were transporting the orchestra's instruments. Without hesitation, I opened the door of one and pulled out a drum. Julian understood immediately and selected another instrument. Carrying these instruments we both strolled past the entrance gate and entered the gardens without having to produce tickets. Everyone simply thought we were part of the hired band![14]

Jean and Julian Aberbach had overcome enormous obstacles to gain their business independence. They had finally cleared the last great rise, capturing almost all the western talent available in Los Angeles. From atop the Hollywood hills they could just hear the swells of country fiddle music far away in the distant hills and hollows of Tennessee. There was a party going on out there that they were not about to miss. With Bob Wills and Tim Spencer as their calling cards, they got up, brushed themselves off, and boldly marched toward Nashville.

CHAPTER 12

Nashville Steamroller

F lanked by Bob Wills and Tim Spencer, the Aberbach brothers quietly slipped in through the backdoor of Nashville. Certainly it would have raised eyebrows had two Austrian Jews just shown up one day, cruising the Nashville honky-tonks for hit tunes and talent, but lucky circumstance had already singled out a most appropriate target for them. Best of all, they could attain it without ever setting foot in Nashville. Los Angeles would remain their base of operation, and it was from there that the Aberbach brothers launched their assault on Music City. Almost overnight, their presence was felt—and it was something on the order of a moderate earthquake.

The lucky circumstance was American Music. Tim Spencer and Bob Nolan were not the only artists whose arrangements with Sylvester Cross begged to be challenged. Numerous other artists had turned to Cross during the 1930s, eager to print songbooks and sheet music folios that could be used for self-promotion and as an extra source of income. Indeed, greater public exposure was the only tangible reward that regional songwriters received from music publishing until BMI was formed in 1940. That purpose was apparently sufficient, for Sylvester Cross counted most of the top country and western stars as his exclusive clients.[1]

Ernest Tubb was among them. He had shown success on the charts over the previous two years with "Soldier's Last Letter" in 1944 and "It's Been So Long, Darling" in 1945, each of which held the number 1 position on the country charts for four weeks.[2] His immense popularity among small-town folk displaced to the urban centers during the war confirmed him as the biggest singing star in country music and among the most important regular cast members of the *Grand Ole Opry.*

Tubb hailed from Texas, where he got his start performing predawn singing spots on local radio and dollar sets in San Antonio cafés. Corporate sponsorship earned him the nickname "Texas troubadour" while doing small shows and selling beer from town to town for the Texas Brewing Company. He found overnight fame when his Decca recording of "Walking the Floor over You" was released in the fall of 1941 and sold 400,000 in the first year, later topping a million.[3]

But it had been a long, hard road to "overnight" success. In fact, he had been recording since 1936, when Jimmie Rodger's widow Carrie became impressed

Ernest Tubb and the Texas Troubadours. From left to right: Herbert "Tommy" "Butterball" Paige, Jimmie Short, Ernest Tubb, Johnny Sapp, and Leon Short. Courtesy of Thomas E. Andrews.

with the teenager's heartfelt renditions of her husband's songs and arranged a session with RCA records. But even the lucky charm of Jimmie's own guitar, which she lent to him for the session, did not convince RCA's producers that Tubb had star quality. Undaunted, Tubb convinced Mrs. Rodgers to intervene again some years later to arrange for a session with Decca under its cofounder and pioneering producer Dave Kapp. The use of electric instruments was fast becoming a matter of necessity, rather than an artistic choice. Increasingly, artists were turning to electrified instruments so that their music could be heard above the din of the noisy honky-tonks. The timing was right, and this recording put the electric guitar sound of West Texas honky-tonk on the map, quickly marking Tubb as among the most progressive of the country and western artists. After his *Grand Ole Opry* debut in January 1943, he moved to Nashville and became a regular on the show.[4]

Tubb's rags-to-riches career would eventually mark him as one of the founding fathers of modern country music. He would popularize the use of electric instruments, remove the term "hillbilly" from the genre and, along with Hank Snow, establish an annual celebration in honor of the fountainhead of country and western music, Jimmie Rodgers. These efforts would focus and energize the growing country music trend. Tubb would encourage Nashville's fledgling recording industry, promote the music nationwide through a vigorous record-store and mail-order business, and even bring the best of country and western music to New York's celebrated Carnegie Hall concert stage in 1947.[5] His career would culminate with his election as the sixth member of the Country Music Hall of Fame in 1965.

But it was really Tubb's personality—not his music—that made Tubb invaluable to the Aberbachs. As Tubb's songs would define the essence of progressive country music, so too would his honesty, generosity, and compassion define the essence of country gentility.[6] Characterized as probably the most decent, genuine, and trusting artist country music has ever known, Tubb valued honesty above all other virtues. Longtime personal manager James Garland "Hoot" Borden described Tubb's attitude: "Just don't ever lie to him, no matter how much it hurts—or steal from him. He'll forgive almost anything else. Ernest never really understood dishonesty. If a man tells him something—any man—it's the truth to Ernest."[7]

Tubb was fast gaining a reputation as one of the most generous and encouraging artists in Nashville. He was a tireless friend to up-and-coming Nashville performers and songwriters. Aspiring performers and songwriters regularly sought him out for career advice and help, and he never turned them away. Hank Snow, Hank Williams, Johnny Cash, and other artists would attribute a significant part of their early career success to his direct intervention.[8]

The parallels with Tim Spencer were striking. Ernest Tubb held the same social position and wielded the same professional influence in Nashville that Tim Spencer did in Los Angeles. Recognizing how quickly western songwriters fell in line as soon as they engaged Tim Spencer, the Aberbach brothers knew Ernest Tubb could be their ticket to the Nashville ball. By engaging Tubb in an exclusive partnership relationship, they would win his trust—and, by extension, the attention, respect, and trust of most of the established and emerging artists in Nashville.[9]

Tubb first recognized the cash potential of publishing while working the Memphis fairgrounds in 1942. There he saw Roy Acuff's phenomenal success selling his songbooks. Tubb was grateful when Cross agreed to take a chance on him and print his first songbook in 1941. Now apparently based in Los Angeles, Cross followed up this success with the *Ernest Tubb Song Folio of Sensational Successes* in 1942, after which he granted Tubb permission to market a new series of songbooks from Nashville via radio.[10]

From Tubb's perspective, Cross had done him a great favor by allowing him to finance, print, promote, and sell his own songbooks from Nashville, when, in fact, those are all the things a publisher is typically expected to do for an exclusively engaged songwriter! Adding to the absurdity, Tubb thanked him publicly for the privilege: "To my dear friend, Sylvester L. Cross, president of American Music, Inc. . . . I want to express my deep appreciation for permitting me to publish this Radio Songbook for my radio friends."[11] It is evident that Tubb had no idea what his BMI publisher was supposed to do for him, nor did he realize that Cross should have been paying him author royalties for the many public performances of his work. Jean and Julian knew it would not take much to convince Tubb that Sylvester Cross was not exactly being honest with him.

By December 11, 1946, a joint ownership arrangement was confirmed between Hill and Range Songs and Ernest Tubb that created a publishing company subsidiary called Ernest Tubb Music, Inc. Tubb, engaged to the company by an exclusive songwriter's agreement, began recruiting other artists for the firm in Nashville.[12] Ernest Tubb Music, Inc., signed not only works he cowrote with Rex Griffin, Zeb Turner, T. Texas Tyler, and Henry "Redd" Stewart, but also songs by Jimmie and Leon Short—two of the artists he took along to Carnegie Hall—and Guy and Vic Willis. A few years later he added the first works of his young son Justin.

Tubb opened his own record store in 1947, which quickly became a magnet for new songwriters and aspiring performers. The addition of the *Midnite Jamboree* weekly live radio broadcast from the store after the Saturday night Opry shows made the record shop a showcase for hopeful talent. Thanks to Ernest Tubb, Jean and Julian had direct access to Nashville's burgeoning talent farm, and they were prepared to take full advantage of it.

Initially, Cross may have taken a dim view of the Aberbach's raiding techniques, but, ever the Viennese diplomats, Jean and Julian appear to have maintained cordial business relations with the publisher. Keeping on Cross's good side made good sense. He still controlled some of Bob Nolan's most important works, including "Cool Water," "The Touch of God's Hand," and, most recently, "Blue Prairie," cowritten in 1946 with Tim Spencer. He also controlled many other valuable works from the 1930s by a host of other leading artists. Knowing that they were in a financially weak position to mount the numerous lawsuits it would take to wrest all these copyrights away from him, Jean and Julian instead appeared as a potential business partner and resource to Cross, offering to engage in mutually beneficial business arrangements that might eventually lead to valuable copyright acquisitions.[13]

Keenly aware that savvy players like the Aberbach brothers could easily facilitate his financial ruin by making his business improprieties public, Cross made little effort to keep his artists from joining up with Hill and Range. Instead, he welcomed Jean and Julian's business overtures and would sell songs to them from time to time—often contacting them directly when he happened to need money.[14]

For those works he refused to sell outright (among them the important hits by Nolan and Spencer), a mutually beneficial arrangement was created whereby Hill and Range acted as sole selling agent for American Music on many of these works. Jean and Julian thereby protected their interest in the songs from other fortune seekers, profiting from them to some extent while at the same time correcting Cross's injustice to the artists. In time, Hill and Range would redress past inequities as well.[15] It was relatively easy to keep Cross happy with periodic cash inducements while acquiring his artists and slowly absorbing his copyrights.

On April 7, 1947, a joint company was created with another Opry veteran, Bill Monroe. The exact date of incorporation of Bill Monroe Music, Inc., is not known, but a corporate resolution dated November 11, 1947, directs its creation.[16] Joining the radio show just two weeks after its national network debut in 1939, Monroe brought the exciting sound of Appalachian string-band music to the *Grand Ole Opry* stage. He and his Blue Grass Boys had transformed the scrappy hillbilly string-band style into a virtuoso art form marked by technical precision, heartfelt gospel spirit, and breakneck performance speed so dazzling that the controlling members of the Opry granted him a regular spot on the show for as long as he wanted.

A reserved and serious man, Monroe kept to himself and controlled every aspect of his group's performance, repertoire, and business. He first recorded for Victor during 1940 and 1941 at the insistence of Eli Oberstein, who had assumed all artist and repertoire (A&R) duties for the label—including those

Bill Monroe.
Courtesy of the
Grand Ole Opry
Archives.

connected with hillbilly music previously handled by Ralph Peer in the 1930s.
During the war years, however, Monroe had done no recording. During those
years, the audience for traditional bluegrass music was shrinking from the
mass migration of country folk to urban centers, where Ernest Tubb's electrified
honky-tonk music was rising in popularity. It might have faded away altogether
but for Monroe's efforts to mature the genre. He used this transition period to
experiment with personnel and instrumentation and to dissect and refine the
bluegrass song forms. He began recording again in 1945, this time for Columbia.[17] Adding Lester Flatt on guitar and Earl Scruggs's forceful three-finger banjo
the following year, Bill Monroe's sound and style finally coalesced. By the time
Bill Monroe Music was incorporated, the group's effortless delivery, dazzling
instrumental solos, and balanced, soulful harmonies set the standard for the
classic bluegrass sound—a sound that confirmed him as "Daddy Bluegrass."[18]

The notion of creating original repertoire for the bluegrass genre had never
been a priority for Monroe. He had sought only to refine and extend the bluegrass
style while preserving the purity that was directly embodied in its traditional
tunes. But in 1945, he and Flatt began creating new works for the group, probably
driven by a creative need to expand the traditional repertoire that they had all but

exhausted. When Jean and Julian Aberbach offered him an appealing new way to make money as a joint publishing partner, Monroe had even greater incentive to write original songs. Before long, he and Flatt had created a considerable body of strikingly original repertoire that redefined the bluegrass genre. Some of these songs would become popular favorites and beloved bluegrass standards, among them "Will You Be Loving Another Man," "Sweetheart You Done Me Wrong," and "Blue Moon of Kentucky"—a tune that would prove pivotal to Jean a decade later in the hands of a young singer named Elvis Presley.[19]

Jean and Julian Aberbach's presence in Nashville grew. They apparently signed Merle Travis as a songwriter, although it is unclear whether they had a partnership company with him or just acquired his works through an exclusive songwriter's agreement. "Divorce Me C.O.D." in 1946 and "So Round, So Firm, So Fully Packed" and "Smoke, Smoke, Smoke (That Cigarette)" in 1947 all became major country hits. At the same time Jean and Julian continued to pursue his early works held by Sylvester Cross, acquiring partial ownership of some of the copyrights.[20]

With ambassadors like Travis, Tubb, and Monroe—the latter two at least signing songs and talent to their own firms—Jean and Julian hardly needed to set foot into Nashville for their business to flourish. As if things were not going well enough, it was about this time that *Opry* master of ceremonies Roy Acuff chose to make a career change that would have significant impact on the Aberbach brothers' infiltration of Nashville.

At the time they were courting Bob Wills and Tim Spencer, Roy Acuff still reigned supreme as the top star of the *Grand Ole Opry* and lead partner in Nashville's only music publishing firm, Acuff-Rose. He held a coveted position in Nashville, having also stepped into the prestigious role as emcee of the "Prince Albert Show"—a full half-hour segment of the *Grand Ole Opry* sponsored by the R. J. Reynolds Tobacco Company. Fellow artists regarded him as a role model in business and those who wrote songs also looked to him as a potential vehicle for their own success. His performance of a new song on the national radio shows could launch careers and generate huge profits for songwriters. Thus, few artists, established or amateur, would not consider an offer by Acuff-Rose to publish their works because of the favor it would curry with the influential star. In this sense, Roy Acuff controlled songwriting success in Nashville as a gatekeeper does admittance to an exclusive party.[21]

After carrying a large measure of the success of the *Grand Ole Opry* on his shoulders for eight years, however, Acuff had grown restless. The radio show was the best possible opportunity for national promotion, but performances on radio paid little. By 1946, Acuff had built a tremendous national following that transcended the show itself, driven by a string of recording hits, his mail-order songbooks, and his starring roles in seven feature films.

Acuff had also toured extensively during World War II in morale-boosting shows for thousands of American G.I.'s. In fact, a poll of U.S. servicemen rated him far higher than Frank Sinatra in popularity, and a war correspondent reported that Japanese soldiers stormed American positions on Okinawa boosting their courage with the rallying cry "To hell with Roosevelt, Babe Ruth, and Roy Acuff." His fame had spread worldwide. Clearly the Opry needed Acuff more than Acuff needed the Opry. Rightly convinced he would advance his career by doing more movies and performance tours, Acuff left the Opry—and Nashville—in April 1946, coincidentally at the very moment the Aberbachs were just beginning their assault.[22]

Acuff's partner Fred Rose was left behind in Nashville to look after their joint publishing business. As the only game in town and with their BMI revenues growing comfortably, it seemed nothing could threaten their continued success. Thus, Rose took a relaxed attitude toward exclusive songwriter's contracts, relying more on gentlemanly understandings rather than airtight written contracts. This had the positive effect of preventing the firm from being saddled with encumbering relationships that demanded the caretaking, promotion, and publishing of numerous mediocre songs. There being no reason to presume talented writers could go elsewhere, Rose was left much free time to pursue what he knew best and loved most: writing songs.[23]

Rose was more interested in crafting pop than country songs, but having grown up in Evansville, Indiana (only 150 miles from Nashville), it was not hard for him to adapt his talent. Most of the early songs brought into the firm were either written by Rose, authored with him, or nurtured to maturity under his guidance. Rose himself contributed a number of songs, including "Blues on My Mind," recorded by Roy Acuff, and "Roly Poly," a popular Bob Wills tune. He also wrote "Texarkana Baby" with Cottonseed Clark and recorded by Eddy Arnold.[24]

Rose's attitude toward acquisitions was selective. He was most interested in finding or creating the great songs of country music—well-crafted songs that would endure as country standards. He spent his time working on particular songs or ideas that showed exceptional creative promise. This creative—rather than business—approach paid off in some respects but fell short in others. Soon the catalog would boast some of the most memorable and profitable country songs of the period. By cherry-picking only the most promising works for the catalog, however, Acuff-Rose would leave most of Nashville's talented songwriters susceptible to outside competition.[25]

No one knew better the value of an influential performer for a songwriter's career than Fred Rose. Had Gene Autry not enlisted in the Army Air Corps in midsummer 1942, the firm of Acuff-Rose might never have been born. During their close four-year association, Autry had recorded song after song by Rose, generating steady royalties and ultimately capturing an Academy Award nomination for "Be Honest with Me" in 1941. With Autry gone, Rose no longer had a premier outlet for his songs until he hooked up with Acuff shortly after returning to Nashville. He had come there specifically to forge another songwriter-performer alliance with a successful artist. He sought out Acuff, who insisted that Rose manage the business aspects of the publishing venture.[26]

Rose should have recognized that songwriters were attracted to the firm mostly because Roy Acuff could provide network exposure for their songs that would guarantee royalties and that Acuff might persuade other performers to perform and record them. This doesn't mean they felt Rose provided no value. His reputation for crafting award-winning songs was legendary. In their own minds, if not in truth, he was far less important to their careers than was Acuff.

By contrast, Hill and Range had created exclusive agreements with most of the top performers, whether they were songwriters or not. Fledgling songwriters knew that placing a song with Hill and Range gave it a better chance of being performed by one of any number of Hill and Range artists—perhaps Red Foley, Ernest Tubb, or Elton Britt—than by placing it with Acuff-Rose now that Acuff was no longer on the scene.

There were other, even more compelling business reasons that the Aberbach brothers' offers were vastly more attractive than the arrangements offered by Acuff-Rose. Some artists like Leon Payne were not comfortable with Rose tampering with their finished product.[27] Whereas Fred Rose felt the need to tinker with the tunes he obtained, Jean and Julian made a clear distinction between their jobs and those of their artists. Except for volunteering a few titles and concepts, Jean and his brother trusted the artists to produce valuable works, and instead put their full attention on promoting them. Also, Jean and Julian were willing to accommodate an artist's need for periodic draws against their anticipated income if needed, whereas Rose forced artists to wait a year or more to obtain their royalties as a lump sum, believing that draws "tended to make a writer too comfortable, reducing his incentive to produce."[28]

Acuff-Rose engagements mirrored that of a typical publishing house, retaining full ownership of their company and publishing rights. Hill and Range, on the other hand, was willing to launch publishing companies in an artist's name, sharing equal ownership with them, thus not only raising the artist's prestige in business circles, but providing an equity interest to the artist that could be used to build a retirement nest egg or leverage a bank loan.

It came down to a simple matter of dollars and cents. The Aberbach brothers were willing to wager more—in fact half again as much as Acuff-Rose—on artists that would sign up with them. This was not because they had Max Dreyfus as a backer, as some speculated, or because their checkbook was fat with advance money from BMI. The bottom line was that the Aberbach brothers were willing to gamble a substantially larger percentage—fully half their own potential earnings—on the confidence they had in the creative talents they signed and their ability to promote them to mutual success. In other words, on a $2.00 gross royalty, where the artist's author royalties represent $1.00 and the publisher's royalties represent $1.00, Acuff-Rose was willing to pay the artist only $1.00 for the author royalty, but the Aberbach brothers were willing to pay $1.50 (the author's share, plus half the publishing share).[29]

With Roy Acuff out of the way and Rose neither motivated nor equipped to fend off the attack, it was open season on Nashville. Hill and Range Songs swept in like a tornado, and Jean and Julian started creating music publishing companies by the bushel. They immediately targeted Clyde Julian "Red" Foley, the artist who had taken over emcee duties on the *Prince Albert Show* after Acuff had left. Foley had built a strong reputation before he joined the Opry as a showman on the WLS *Barn Dance* (and its successor *National Barn Dance*) in Chicago. It was the nation's most popular country music radio program, and he became as well known for his quick wit as for his music. Foley had had several early hits on Decca, including "Old Shep" in 1941—a sentimental ode to a German shepherd—and Zeke Clements's patriotic hit "Smoke on the Water" in 1944, which vowed revenge for the bombing of Pearl Harbor. Jean and Julian remembered him most for helping to make "Shame on You" their first chart success. Fronting Lawrence Welk's orchestra, his version hit number 1 on the country charts in November 1946. Since then he had had a hit with a version of the Cajun tune "New Jolie Blonde." Their joint firm, Home Folks Music, Inc., was created on September 11, 1947. Foley would remain emcee of the popular *Prince Albert Show* at the *Grand Ole Opry* for almost a decade, during which time he would contribute thirty-nine top ten hits to the charts, many of which ended up in the firm. Eventually, it would include works by Jenny Lou Carson, Sheb Wooley, Pee Wee King, and many others.[30]

Another occasional Opry guest, Elton Britt, also joined the Hill and Range ranks on June 30, 1948, forming Elton Britt Music, Inc. Widely regarded as the best yodeler of his day, Britt was a frequent collaborator with Ernest Tubb and was best known for "There's a Star-Spangled Banner Waving Somewhere," considered the most popular patriotic country music song of World War II.[31]

Jean and his brother didn't go after only the big fish. Virtually anyone who was writing songs in Nashville was on their list. Some writers naturally looked them up when, as cowriters with one of the joint partners, their works ended up in a Hill and Range partnership firm anyway. For the most part, however, the Aberbach brothers relied most heavily on the generous goodwill Ernest Tubb sent their way from the small performance stage behind the busy cashier's counter of his crowded record store.

Tubb got more pleasure out of helping someone else out than watching his own songs climb to number 1. While contributing tunes to his own firm like "Don't Look Now (But Your Broken Heart Is Showin')," he continued to recommend Hill and Range to other songwriters like Jerry Irby, whose "Drivin' Nails in My Coffin" he had recorded. When someone would ask for his advice on music publishing, invariably he would steer them to Jean and Julian. No one who knew Ernest would question his opinion. According to his son Justin, the feeling in Nashville was "if they were involved with Ernest, then they were straight up. . . . And he, I know, got a lot of writers to come with Hill and Range. Because people would come to him and say 'Where can I go? Who's honest?' And he would always steer them toward Julian and Jean."[32]

Tubb championed the Aberbachs not only because they had always treated him fairly, but also because he shared their progressive vision of the potential for country music. He realized that Jean and Julian were working to bring country music to a wider audience by bringing Tin Pan Alley professionalism to Nashville. This, in turn, would encourage major label interest in local talent. Moreover, he had a great respect for what the immigrant brothers had achieved. Therefore, it was easy for him to recommend the firm, and he sent many artists their way, including Hank Snow and Johnny Cash.[33]

Johnny Cash, performing at a DJ convention in the early 1960s. Courtesy of the Grand Ole Opry Archives.

Because of Ernest, and because of the chain-letter effect of their partnership firms, it was not long before every writer in Nashville knew about the straight-up opportunities offered by Hill and Range Songs. In fact, their presence was so pervasive that a joke started circulating around town that if you were a wannabe Nashville songwriter, then a surefire way to catch an Aberbach was to simply to leave your door unlocked at night. In the morning, you could open your bedroom closet door and out would pop Jean or Julian. "How do you do?" he would ask in a high-pitched Viennese accent. "I would like to sign you to a writer's contract!"[34]

The partnership relationship obliged both parties to pledge substantial participation in the joint venture. The artist was obliged to produce songs and to seek opportunities for performances and promotion. By the same token, Hill and Range had specific stated responsibilities, which often included the printing of folios or a certain number of copies of sheet music, or guaranteeing a minimum number of radio plugs, recordings, or film placements. If either party failed to fulfill its responsibilities, there were no insidious ramifications. When the three- or five-year contract termination date came around, it would simply not be renewed.

Aberbach deals stressed the mutual benefits of partnership, each party contributing its talents and expertise so that both parties could succeed. The brothers felt this form of incentive would be far more effective in motivating artists than tactics such as withholding a draw for the duration of a royalty period or only accepting certain copyrights they felt had promise, as did Acuff-Rose.

They were right, and history would bear this out. Except for 1953, when both companies produced twenty-one top ten hits, Hill and Range outpaced Acuff-Rose by anywhere from 23 percent to 75 percent in the number of top ten hits produced each year between 1945 and 1954. While a large number of Acuff-Rose's hits were those of Hank Williams, by contrast Hill and Range provided exposure to a wide range of well-known artists, as well as peripheral country songwriters. All in all, between 1948 and 1952, Hill and Range produced approximately 30 percent of all the top ten country and western chart songs, with 1949 as its best year, when it claimed 35 percent.[35]

Hits included properties in Hill and Range Songs, Alamo Music, Home Folks Music, Bob Wills Music, Brenner Music, Brazos Music, Valley Music, Ernest Tubb Music, Jenny Lou Carson Music, Texoma Music, Tim Spencer Music, Ark-La-Tex Music, and St. Louis Music. Hits from Acuff-Rose were from Acuff-Rose Publications and Rose's ASCAP firm, Milene music. American Music also fell within the top four firms with the greatest number of top ten hits during this period, but there is a significant downward trend starting in 1949, probably because of the gradual absorption of its catalog into Hill and Range.

Peer Music International ranks as the fourth company, but except for a spike in 1951 of sixteen, its hits ranged only from one to nine hits in any year.

In 1946, Jean and Julian Aberbach had slipped in the back door of Nashville, entirely changing the way business was done. One year later, the Aberbach brothers controlled most of Nashville's songwriters under strict exclusive agreements connected to their many joint partnerships. Free-floating songwriters more often than not ended up with the Aberbachs, whose checkbook—now fat with BMI credit against future earnings—usually won the day.

While Acuff-Rose was still publishing hits, its roster of artists had grown alarmingly short—Pee Wee King and his Golden West Cowboys partner Henry "Redd" Stewart, Paul Howard, Clyde Moody, Mel Foree, and Fred Rose's gifted girlfriend Jenny Lou Carson were among the few luminaries left.[36] In time, even some of these enduring relationships would fray. By the time Roy Acuff returned to Nashville in 1947, Jean and Julian Aberbach had all but taken over. These outsiders had stolen his fire—right out of his own backyard.

During their youth Jean and his brother were known for their pranks and cleverness. No matter the obstacles, if they set their sights on a goal and applied their wits, they would find a way to it: "Most of the time, I would have the ideas, but often it was Julian who executed the ideas. It was a convenient arrangement that began in our youth. On one occasion we managed to get into a social ball like that! Not having enough money to buy tickets, I had an idea. I made the suggestion to Julian, who agreed. While the doorman was momentarily distracted, we slipped slightly behind him. Then Julian politely tapped the doorman's shoulder and asked if we could leave the party for just ten minutes. When the doorman replied, 'No!' I responded, 'Well then, we'll just stay in!'"[37]

The approach was the same, whether for a Viennese ball or for a Nashville party. Jean and his brother had adeptly slipped behind Fred Rose when he wasn't looking, tapped him on the shoulder, and declared they would just stay in. Once inside, they steamrolled their way from one end of town to the other. After only a year on the road, Roy Acuff arrived back in Nashville to feel the aftershocks of a music publishing scene that had been picked clean by the Aberbach brothers. By the time the Nashville gatekeeper got back to his post, the Aberbach brothers no longer had to hide in closets. They pretty much had the run of the house.

CHAPTER 13

The Disappearing Act

J ean and Julian kept their main office in New York, where Dolfi and Anna still lived, slowly shifting emphasis to California as their business grew. To cover Nashville they sent a representative named Ben Sabia. This small Jewish fellow figured that "when in Rome, do as the Romans do," and so one day he showed up prowling backstage at the Opry all duded up in riding chaps, western boots, and a cowboy hat. It seems he had the notion that Nashville was a hopelessly backward little town devoid of any sophistication whatsoever, and that the stars all rode horses to the show! Everyone, including Ben, had a tremendous laugh over this and he was immediately adopted by the good-natured Opry artists. He was a good contact man and kept things moving along.[1]

Their conquest of Nashville hardly slowed Jean and his brother's work in other areas. While the most important country deals were being struck in Nashville, the work of Hill and Range continued without pause in New York and Los Angeles. Jean and Julian split up and divided their time between these locations, passing in transit on their way from coast to coast but touching base daily by telephone. It was no longer just the two of them. They were beginning to amass a small, loyal staff that oversaw office management, sheet music warehousing, and distribution. Nevertheless, Jean and Julian remained hands-on music publishers, handling financial management, song selection, and promotion themselves.

By the middle of 1947, country and western music—once considered unsuitable for the mainstream music public—was a force in the mainstream record industry. More and more ASCAP writers began writing country-styled tunes and peddling them to country singers. Cross-pollination was happening in the other direction as well, with a number of country singers trying their hand at covers of mainstream pop tunes. The lines between ASCAP and BMI began to blur as songwriter members of the competing camps began writing songs with one another.

Further encouraging this trend was the upcoming American Federation of Musicians union strike, slated for January 1948 when the five-year contract that union boss James "Caesar" Petrillo had struck with the broadcasting industry would expire. For all his efforts, Petrillo could not stop the inevitable march of technology, and over the previous four years records had taken over the airwaves, reducing the average musician's opportunities for paid live radio engagements to a minimum. The rest of the music industry, however, was booming, and 1947 would prove to be the industry's most profitable year, rivaling even the legendary gross revenues of 1921.[2]

The irony was that it was the musicians' own studio recordings that were crowding them out of live radio jobs and off the air. Petrillo once again threatened to prohibit musicians from making any more recordings until a contract that would correct this inequity was struck with the broadcasters. But it was a different world now, and this strategy would ultimately prove much less effective than it had during the musicians' ban he had imposed five years earlier.

While record companies scrambled to stockpile enough recordings to outlast the strike, as they had in 1943, musicians prepared to be benched until Petrillo negotiated a more favorable arrangement with the radio networks. Popular songwriters, on the other hand, were in a far better position than they had been five years earlier because hillbilly music was no longer novelty music. It was a popular and profitable genre. Most mainstream songwriters recognized that next year's livelihood would probably depend on recordings performed by nonunion musicians, and so they quickly began to craft tunes for country and western artists—by far the largest, most successful group of nonunion performers. The ASCAP Society Board was not pleased with this turn of events, nor was most of its affiliated publishers. Increasingly, ASCAP songwriters were trying to submit country and western–styled songs that might capture slots on the country music charts—the kind of music for which ASCAP was neither organized nor equipped to collect royalties.[3]

The murkier the ASCAP waters got, the happier Jean became. It was just what he had hoped would happen. In fact, in some ways, he had helped engineer it. Foy Willing's Hill and Range debut hit, "No One to Cry To" was cowritten with Sid Robin—a Tin Pan Alley writer with no western hits, best known for the pop standard "Undecided" (with Charlie Shavers, 1939), and the theme song for vibraphonist Lionel Hampton's band (with Benny Goodman). And hadn't their chief Nashville connection, Ernest Tubb, brought the *Grand Ole Opry* to New York's prestigious Carnegie Hall? The performances took place on September 18 and 19, 1947, and included Jimmie and Leon Short, Radio Dot and Smokey Swann, the Texas Troubadours, and Rosalie Allen—all of whom were writing songs for Hill and Range. The only other known participants were comedienne Minnie Pearl and master of ceremonies George Dewey Hay.[4]

Jean may not have instigated this event, but he had a strong interest in making sure it was successful. Bridging the gap between country music and mainstream pop represented a home run in music publishing, because it meant that audience appeal for a song had expanded to multiple markets. Still working at Chappell as its West Coast representative for film, Jean tried to leverage his mainstream contacts with Chappell at every opportunity in an attempt to wed these two worlds. Every time he managed to play a hillbilly demo to a mainstream filmmaker or record producer, the value of Hill and Range copyrights grew as did his reputation as a powerbroker between Tin Pan Alley and the majority of country performers with whom he now held some influence.

One of his mainstream contacts back in New York was Ed Nelson, a song-writer who had had success a generation earlier when he cowrote the World War I hit "When Yankee Doodle Learns to Parlez-Vouz Français," with William Hart. This was followed by "Auf Wiedersehen, My Dear," in the early 1930s, a hit for Bing Crosby's only real competitor, Russ Colombo.[5] Aside from enticing him and some of his veteran ASCAP cowriters to throw songs their way, Jean took on Nelson's sons Steve and Ed Junior, along with a raft of younger writers such as Cy Coben, Charlie Grean, Irving Melsher, Milton Leeds, Jay Glass, and Fred Wise. Although these young songwriters began their careers crafting pop tunes, they were soon encouraged to expand into the country and western field. Jay Glass, Steve Nelson, and Fred Wise, for instance, were hired in March 1947 to develop music for "Heroes of the Old West" starring Roy Rogers.[6]

Paying these songwriters would be complicated unless Hill and Range set up companies that were affiliated with ASCAP. On July 28, 1947, Jean set up Alamo Music to contain the songs of these and other promising ASCAP talents that were drifting their way.[7] Although BMI considered it a form of defection, Hill and Range Songs was fast becoming that organization's star publisher, generating new money from new country hits, rather than from Tin Pan Alley back catalog like E. B. Marks.[8]

The company's tremendous growth and increasing profitability gave it considerable leverage over the BMI organization. BMI maintained flexible policies where its star publishers were concerned, largely because the organization was still not doing very well in comparison with ASCAP. Only 10 percent of top-charting songs were those of BMI. In 1947, BMI licensed only four out of the thirty-five most played records of the year, and only five of the thirty-five best sellers.[9] While long-standing firms like E. B. Marks far outperformed them with classic copyrights, Hill and Range was generating new money from contemporary hits on which the organization's long-term future likely would depend, rather than the Tin Pan Alley back catalog.

Jean's professional relationship with key figures in the recording industry was as important as his relationship with country and western songwriter-performers. Up-and-coming RCA record producer Steve Sholes was, by far, the most important of these, and his early work in the music business would have a profound impact on the Aberbach brothers' success.[10]

Sholes had been around the New York music scene for a long time. He began his career as a messenger for RCA Victor in 1929 while pursuing a college degree at Rutgers University in New Jersey. He followed his father into the business, who had worked for the Victor Talking Machine Company during its early years. Professionally trained in clarinet and saxophone, Sholes did some session work as a staff instrumentalist. Artist and repertoire (A&R) chief Eli "Obie" Oberstein recognized his greater talent for record production management and by the late 1930s, he was coordinating landmark sessions with jazz innovators Jelly Roll Morton, Sidney Bechet, and Mezz Mezzrow.[11]

It was about this time that RCA recognized a growing hole in its music repertoire. Since the departure of Ralph Peer in 1932, RCA Victor had lost its pioneering edge in hillbilly music. In 1939, realizing that hillbilly music was again fashionable (and therefore profitable), RCA Victor's newest vice president, Frank Walker (formerly Ralph Peer's chief rival at Columbia Records), sent Sholes to coordinate hillbilly recording sessions in Atlanta.[12]

Steve was a company man through and through, and his sense of duty along with his inherent honesty and selflessness often left him ill equipped to manage interpersonal politics in anything but a diplomatic, compromising way. This would cause him some bitterness in later years, when other less senior, more aggressive staff members would supersede him on the corporate ladder.[13]

Sholes's easygoing management style made him one of the most effective and beloved record producers of all time, able to gently coax the best performances out of his artists and onto the records. Senior executives like Oberstein and Walker knew how to apply their available resources, and Sholes was proving to be both an innovator and a hit maker for hillbilly music and for African American jazz and blues, collectively referred to as race music. Moreover, he was a strategic thinker. Among his first marketing moves was to dig up, dust off, and reissue Ernest Tubb's very first recordings (RCA Victor sessions dating from 1936 that had been shelved), to capitalize on and compete with Decca's successful "Walking the Floor over You" in 1941.[14] Such calculated insights made Sholes an invaluable asset to the label and among the most important factors in its success.

As World War II got under way, a portly Steve Sholes was drafted into the service. He quickly found the U.S. Army's manual labor unsuitable for his ample girth. With the help of Tommy Dorsey's vocalist Jack Leonard (music manager at Fort Dix) instead he was assigned to the Office of War Information Special Services division to manage their morale-boosting "V-disk" project during 1943 and 1944.

The V-disk project was organized to record new music, integrate masters contributed by record and transcription companies, and capture to disc air checks—or rehearsals—of radio broadcasts by star performers such as Bing Crosby and Dinah Shore. More than 10,000 waterproof containers were distributed every month, each containing 100 record-player needles and twenty discs containing four hours of music. They were broadcast on the armed forces radio network and played at social functions. By the time the war ended, 4 million discs were being distributed annually. Seventy percent of the songs were popular music, but the rest was divided between classical, hillbilly, race, and other song forms.[15]

Sholes became one of only six men responsible for selecting and clearing all the songs for these discs. At the same time, he refined his live production skills, managing recording sessions with bandleader Hal Kemp and for the great blues pianist Fats Waller. When he left the service, he returned to RCA and continued his groundbreaking work in race and hillbilly music. His big break came in 1945, when Frank Walker left to establish MGM's record division, turning over the entire RCA Victor country and western division to Sholes.[16]

Jean probably first got to know Sholes during the early 1940s while Julian was still in the service and Jean was managing and promoting copyrights for Chappell music in New York. Although they were engaged in different areas of the music industry and working with different kinds of music, both men had achieved a comparably high stature in this still small business community. They probably first became acquaintances, then friends, over their shared enthusiasm for the emerging music trends. Close in age, doubtless Steve also found Jean's cultured background and diplomatic business style exceptionally compatible with his. For his own part, Jean recognized that Sholes was already far along in forging a path to exactly where he wanted to go. Indeed, it is entirely possible that Sholes's V-disk work tipped Jean off to the discovery of the King and Blink transcription opportunity that launched Hill and Range in the first place, since air checks were a large portion of the material used and transcription companies like King and Blink would have been among those mined for V-disk material. Whatever their initial connection, both men developed the same vision for the future of hillbilly and race music that became the foundation for an enduring lifetime friendship and business relationship.[17]

Under Sholes, RCA Victor signed the Sons of the Pioneers to a recording contract on December 28, 1944, only a few weeks after Hill and Range Songs was born. Because the group was in Los Angeles, the sessions were handled on the West Coast by RCA Victor producers Kuhl and Art Rush. Jean and Julian made little headway placing tunes through them for the early sessions, perhaps because they had little suitable material to offer during those early days. But their success rate got much better after Jean captured "Tumbling Tumbleweeds" for Williamson Music and the joint firm was created with Tim Spencer in the spring of 1946.

If the California producers had previously posed an impediment, Jean was now able to get past the stone wall with the weight of Chappell, Spencer, and Steve Sholes behind him. The March 15, 1946, session yielded not only the definitive, masterfully orchestrated version of "Tumbling Tumbleweeds," but also Foy Willing's collaboration with Tin Pan Alley's Sid Robin on "No One to Cry To." Along with Tim Spencer's "Cowboy Camp Meetin'" (also secured by Jean at the creation of Tim Spencer Music), this session was in radical contrast to the previous two RCA sessions controlled by the Rushes. Those sessions featured several songs by publishing rival Acuff-Rose, but only one by Hill and Range—"Stars and Stripes on Iwo Jima"—and that one may have come about without any Aberbach intervention.[18]

By September 1946 Sholes had taken over production of the Sons of the Pioneers Hollywood sessions, conducting them either with fellow V-disk producer Walt Heebner or with his production assistant Charlie Grean. From that point forward, most of the songs recorded by the Sons of the Pioneers were Hill and Range, housed in the jointly owned publishing firm of Tim Spencer Music. These sessions yielded recordings now regarded as probably the best, most characteristic work of the Sons of the Pioneers' long career. It was clear that the group's market potential could be achieved only if the music could be made palatable to the mainstream audience. Striving to deliberately commercialize their sound, production became more controlled and orchestrated—and consequently more acceptable to mainstream audience ears. The group's popularity soared as a result, which validated a marketing approach that served RCA and Hill and Range equally well. The success of these landmark sessions cemented Jean and Steve's working relationship. As a result Jean enjoyed unprecedented access to this most important producer, and Sholes welcomed his visits because invariably Jean brought him the best song material.[19]

In turn, Sholes often referred potential business opportunities to them. During the spring of 1947, while deep in the throes of the Pioneers sessions, a remarkable demonstration disk came to the RCA studios. It had been forwarded from a trusted booking agent at KWTO radio in Springfield, Missouri, and featured a young guitarist who had been recently working there. Charlie Grean, then working as Steve Sholes's assistant, music arranger, and control room technician, was also in charge of identifying the most promising talent from the scores of twelve-inch acetate demonstration discs that arrived at the studio every week. So impressed was he that Grean could not help playing the recording over and over again. He recognized Chet Atkins to be a true original.[20]

Sholes recognized the talent too—and he needed an answer to Capitol's Merle Travis, who was capturing public attention with his great guitar chops and tolerable singing. But marketing a solo guitarist was still risky. The guitar was only just coming into its own as a featured instrument. Historically used as part of the rhythm section, it was hard to hear over a backup band or orchestra. While great strides recently had been made by guitar innovator Les Paul, electronic amplification of it was still not yet perfected. Also, unlike fiddle or wind players, who could stand forward of the band to lead it, guitarists tended to play sitting—hunched over their instruments, head bowed and barely moving—a stance not at all conducive to projecting an audience-friendly personality. This factor could make or break an artist's image and marketability.

Apparently Sholes wasn't willing to take such a risk alone. He asked Jean to hunt down Chet Atkins, and if he would sign him to a publishing deal and assist in his promotion, then Sholes would be willing to offer him an RCA Victor recording contract as well. Impressed by the demo, Jean lost no time locating the remarkable guitarist and signing him.

Chet Atkins's remarkable career was launched with his simultaneous signing to RCA Victor and to Hill and Range. Atkins sold everything he had and moved to Chicago, where Steve and Jean met him in August 1947 for his first recording session. Chet was always grateful for the chance Steve Sholes gave him, and he acknowledges that Jean Aberbach was pivotal in that decision.[21]

This auspicious signing would eventually transform country music. Of the handful of individuals in Nashville who recognized the potential of mainstreaming country music, no one had as direct an impact on shaping the sound of commercial country music than did Chet Atkins. Through his innovative solo performances, and the arranging and producing work he would later do as manager of RCA's studios in Nashville, Atkins would define a slick new performing and production style that would come to be known as the Nashville sound. This new, modern country production style embodied a polished character that made country music palatable to the mainstream music-buying public.

This was not the only artist Sholes pushed Jean's way. At about the same time as the Sons of the Pioneers entered the studios in California for their first RCA Victor session, Sholes took over recording management of an up-and-coming Nashville singing star. Eddy Arnold's adaptable voice had been steadily growing in popularity since his Opry debut in 1940 as a sideman for Pee Wee King. The young Golden West Cowboy set off for a solo career when singled out by Opry executive Harry Stone, who gave him his own singing spot on the show and helped confirm the recording contract with RCA.[22]

Like Spade Cooley, Arnold had to wait out the musician's union strike in 1943, entering the WSM studios the following year for a landmark session in December 1944 that marked the very first commercial recording done in Nashville since 1928. By June 1945 he had recorded four songs: "Mother's Prayer" and "Mommy, Please Stay Home with Me, "Each Minute Seems a Million Years," and "Cattle Call." By Tex Owens, "Cattle Call" was the perfect vehicle to show off Arnold's talents, providing a lilting melody for his round, warm baritone through which he slid easily into chorus after chorus of gentle yodeling. But when the more mainstream flip-side tune "Each Minute" was listed on the folk chart and sold 125,000 records, it became apparent that his future was in pop music rather than cowboy tunes.

More impressive than his sales numbers, however, was Arnold's overwhelming affect on his audience. It was proven by the sale of a million dollars worth of war bonds over a twelve-hour period during his fifteen-minute radio spots on WMPS-Memphis in June 1945.[23] Not just his warm singing style, but his good looks and easygoing manner projected a comfortable "boy-next-door" honesty that was universally appealing. Young and old, southern sophisticate and country bumpkin—everyone seemed to like him.

Jean had spent his entire American publishing career urging hillbilly and mainstream music to meet at the middle. Suddenly through Steve Sholes, he had access to a young vocal artist who seemed to personify that merger. Arnold's voice could adapt to either pop or country songs and was the perfect vehicle for a crossover tune. With the right song there was a good chance he could expand past the country audience, embracing the much larger mainstream pop audience as well, thereby eclipsing even the reach of superstars Frank Sinatra and Bing Crosby who could dominate the pop scene but could not capture the more populous rural audience as well.

As soon as "Each Minute" hit, the Aberbach brothers moved to acquire Arnold's songs, but they succeeded only in gaining assignment of "Mommy, Please Stay Home with Me" from writer-performer Wally Fowler. Using their characteristic two-pronged attack, Jean peddled songs to Sholes in New York while Julian pursued the artist himself in Nashville. They had only fair results, and despite their close relationship with Sholes, it was proving difficult to get Arnold to pay much attention to Hill and Range.

Up to this point, Arnold's choice of songs had been inexorably linked to music publisher Fred Forster, who had first brought Arnold to RCA's attention and advised the young artist through the contract negotiations. Forster had had a clear agenda, and it was probably his promise of promotional support that convinced Sholes's predecessor, Frank Walker, to sign Arnold to RCA in the first place. This put Forster in the position of controlling most of the songs that Arnold recorded.[24]

Understandably, Arnold owed a debt to Forster, and he reciprocated by favoring Forster's songs for his first session, choosing three out of four from Forster's catalog. Thereafter, an unusually high percentage of songs Arnold recorded prior to November 1947—roughly one in every three—was supplied by or ended up in firms connected to Fred Forster. Apparently to appease the publisher but still preserve his freedom of choice, Arnold promised to refer any unpublished song he intended to record to Forster for representation. In this way, Arnold could choose any song that came to him, but as a large number of these were unpublished, Forster would still end up owning and promoting them. This was a comfortable arrangement for both parties and something the career-driven Arnold could live with.

On top of controlling a third of all the songs Arnold was recording, Fred Forster apparently also had a business relationship with rival publisher Fred Rose. Rose was also supplying a fair number of songs to Eddy Arnold—and a few of them had even ended up in Forster's firms. Although he was assigned no credit for the work, Rose is said to have doctored "Cattle Call," nearly a decade old, for Arnold's first session. Rose solely wrote "Easy Rockin' Chair" for his September 24, 1946, session.[25]

If Forster was not directly influencing Arnold's song choice, he nevertheless may still have been limiting the pool of songs that reached him. When Arnold burst onto the *Billboard* charts in 1947, it was with four major jukebox hits—chief among them "I'll Hold You in My Heart (till I Can Hold You in My Arms)," which tallied up twenty-one weeks in the number 1 spot. Less impressive although still respectable showings were made for "To My Sorrow," "What Is Life without Love," and "It's a Sin."[26] The first three were published by Forster's BMI company, Adams, Vee and Abbott, and the rights to the fourth were retained by Fred Rose.

The path around Forster to Arnold logically seemed to be Steve Sholes, who had taken over Arnold's recording sessions starting in July 1945. As A&R man, Sholes was specifically responsible for finding the right songs for his performer. Jean and Julian managed to place Paul Westmoreland's "Can't Win, Can't Place, Can't Show" for the March 20, 1946, session, as well as one or two other songs. Jean trusted Sholes to always give fair and equal consideration to all the songs they presented to him, but for some reason Arnold was recording more of Forster's songs than those of any other publisher.

As chief A&R man for the RCA Victor country and western music division, Sholes had absolute veto power over the songs his artists could record. In fact, few debut singers had any power over what they recorded because at that time the song was the star, not the performer. Most singers were simply viewed by record executives as a vehicle for a good song. If a song hit, then other labels scrambled to capitalize on its success by creating their own versions of the very same song featuring their own roster of performers. Very often, one could find five or six—if not more—versions of the same song by different performers on the charts at the same time! When it came to the choice of song, it was the record producer, not the artist, who typically had the last word. But Arnold was not just any artist. More to the point, Arnold's manager, Tom Parker, was not like any other personal manager.

Not long after Arnold left for his solo career, and while on the road with an Opry show touring Florida, Eddy Arnold came in contact with Tom Parker, who was warming up for his infamous role as "the Colonel" for Elvis Presley almost a decade later. Parker was not a real colonel (an honorary title bestowed on him by former singer, then Louisiana governor, Jimmie Davis), nor was he even American. While he perpetuated a number of myths about his past, he was, in fact, Andreas van Kuijk, born in Breda, Holland, who gained passage to the United States on an ocean liner—either as a deckhand or a stowaway—and simply never left.[27]

Arriving probably in the spring of 1929, Parker worked the carnival circuit during the early 1930s, which was a good "no questions asked" job for an illegal immigrant. He graduated to independent show promotion by the late 1930s, expertly handling advance local promotion for artists such as cowboy movie star Tom Mix and veteran singing star Gene Austin.

Famous for the hit "My Blue Heaven" a decade earlier, Austin was in the autumn of his career. He hired Parker as his booking agent and promotional manager in 1939. The tireless front man did a good job resuscitating the waning star's career on the rural Southeast performing circuit, admirably boosting his performance draw. Parker declined an invitation to move with Austin to Nashville. Before long he was doing local advance work for the Opry's top stars, including Ernest Tubb and Roy Acuff, declining yet another invitation to move to Nashville from the latter, discouraged that the star would not submit to full-time personal management. Parker waited until the genial Arnold came along, recognizing in him a young, malleable talent on his way up.[28]

By the fall of 1945, Tom Parker was acting as Arnold's personal manager, stepping up to bat when a two-year personal management arrangement with

WSM's Artists Service Bureau chief Dean Upson terminated.[29] The wait had paid off, and now, allied with the fast-rising star, Parker came to "Music City" on his own terms. Reinforcing Arnold's most appealing points, Parker took an aggressive grassroots approach, capitalizing on the artist's honest Tennessee plowboy image. He effectively worked advance promotion, setting up radio spots and plastering concert posters throughout the South where the artist was to appear. It took little effort to secure commercial sponsorship from Ralston Purina for an Opry segment and for half of another daily radio show on the strength of Arnold's immense talent and charisma.

Parker devoted virtually all his time to Arnold's business and exerted almost absolute control over almost every aspect of his career. By 1947 he was already pulling rank all around Arnold—placing his band on salary (rather than the customary shared percentage basis), adding his own name to Arnold's advertising, and even demanding a percentage of the Opry profits from the artist for his performances on the radio shows.

There was one area, however, in which Parker did not seem to interfere. Arnold's informal business arrangement with music publisher Fred Forster remained as much in force after Parker took over management as it was before. This was unusual for Parker, who was not known for his restraint around business opportunities. If he could make a buck, his hands were all over it. More likely, he was still learning the ins and outs of this confusing music publishing business and could not yet fathom how to profit by it.

Jean didn't want to battle Forster every time he placed a song with Arnold. He wanted a firmer relationship with the artist, if possible an exclusive one like the ones he held with Tim Spencer, Bob Wills, and others. This would secure precedence for Hill and Range over any other competitor. Breaking Forster's hold on Arnold would take more than just winning over the artist. It soon became clear that the power broker in this deal was not Arnold or Sholes, but Parker.

Tom Parker's hold over Eddy Arnold was challenging, but not insurmountable. By 1948 Hill and Range had secured for themselves an exclusive business arrangement with Eddy Arnold. The deal Jean forged with the artist was not the usual joint publishing firm, nor was it exclusive in the sense of restricting him from recording other publishers' works. Arnold would not be boxed into an exclusive arrangement with any music publisher, wanting nothing to restrain him from his central goal of finding suitable songs. He had absolute faith in his talents and believed that if the right songs could be found, he would not need the extra revenue and distractions that copyright ownership in songs would bring him. Jean instead negotiated a business agreement whereby the artist would simply convey any unpublished song he happened to come across to Hill and Range. It was the same arrangement he had had with Forster, but in this case, Hill and Range paid Arnold a yearly cash retainer.[30]

Eddy Arnold and Jean Aberbach, on the set of a public service photo shoot for the U.S. Forest Service, ca. 1947. Courtesy of Eddy Arnold.

This arrangement had the desired effect of removing Forster entirely from the picture as recipient of songs Arnold happened to find, but provided no assurance that the artist would pay greater attention to songs offered him by Jean or Julian. In fact, it specifically avoided this since Arnold refused the offer of a joint company. One virtue of the arrangement, however, is that it left open the possibility of assigning the half copyright ownership normally absorbed by a performer-partner elsewhere. Predictably, it was Tom Parker who ended up with this portion, and by creating a joint publishing company with him, instead of Arnold, Jean and Julian shifted the odds in their favor. In addition to co-owning any song Arnold brought into the company, Parker shared in the publishing revenues of any Hill and Range Song recorded by Eddy Arnold.[31]

Arnold was by no means naïve about the backroom dealings. He knew exactly what was going on and welcomed it. Arnold strongly believed that a singer was only as good as his songs. After Jean and Julian had brought him a few good songs, he quickly recognized them as uncommonly good judges of song quality. They had good ears and could recognize an "Eddy Arnold tune," bringing him, nine times out of ten, good songs. It was critically important to him that he have the right of first refusal of any good song the Aberbach brothers came across. He counted on the fact that by his having no claim on the copyright, they would be inclined to offer all their songs to him first before showing them to another big performer who would insist on absorbing part of their earnings. This self-interest would drive the Aberbach brothers and their partner Parker to bring him what he wanted and needed—indeed, what his entire career depended on—good songs.[32]

For Hill and Range, it was a win-win situation. What Jean and Julian had been unable to accomplish directly with Arnold through Sholes was now accomplished easily with the cooperation of his manager. The publishing percentage usually afforded their partner artist simply went to the artist's manager instead. They probably gave up no more than usual for the deal, and at the same time they secured a valuable professional ally.

While he continued to pick his own tunes, recording several by other publishers (including Forster) over the course of his career, Jean and Julian consistently brought Arnold so many great songs that were right for his voice that he ultimately required few from anybody else. Arnold was also able to effect a graceful change in his relationship when Forster brought him a song he did not like by repeating the publisher's own sage advice: "When you get a song, and it's a good song for you, you record it, even if it's written by your worst foe. If it's good for you—you record it."[33]

In the shadows stood the cigar-puffing Colonel, quietly presiding over the transactions that were making them all pleasantly wealthy. Parker thoroughly enjoyed the prestige his powerful, erudite partners brought him. The Aberbach brothers were the slickest music publishers he had ever met. They were a force not only in Nashville but on both coasts and were building a music-publishing empire with potentially global reach. Parker knew that while money was good, knowledge was power. If he could not beat the Aberbachs at their own game, he would at least soak up enough knowledge about music publishing to beat up most everybody else.

Jean continued to work for Chappell on salary as division chief and West Coast representative for film music. As the entire pop industry moved to embrace country and western music, there was increasing opportunity for conflict of interest in Jean's work. It was only a matter of time before some of these songs would cross over to the pop charts and hit Max Dreyfus's radar. They had already crossed swords in August 1947, when Max insisted they turn over a hit by Harlem-based songwriter Floyd Hunt, probably "Old Memories." While Julian resisted, Jean convinced him that his continuing position at Chappell, with its income, prestige, and resources, afforded the best possible means of growing their business.[34]

Knowing it was only a matter of time before another conflict arose with Max, Jean began preparing an escape plan. Reorganizing their operation under California law offered considerable tax advantages. They set up a California bank account and in December 1947 created Hill and Range Songs, Ltd., as a California firm in preparation for moving the entire operation out there when the time came.

Jean then turned his attention back to the task of developing song material for Eddy Arnold. The singer began recording hit after hit with songs from the Hill and Range repertoire. In all he would have five number 1 hits in 1948—all of which were Hill and Range tunes: "Heartful of Love (for a Handful of Kisses)" by Eddy Arnold, Steve Nelson, and Ray Soehnel; "Anytime" by Herbert Happy Lawson; "Just a Little Lovin' (Will Go a Long, Long Way)" by Zeke Clements and Eddy Arnold; and "I'll Hold You in My Heart (till I Can Hold You in My Arms)" by Eddy Arnold, Hal Horton, and Tommy Dilbeck.[35]

The tune that would prove pivotal for Hill and Range, and change the course of Jean's career, was a song they apparently acquired from Lou Levy's Leeds Music on April 24, 1947, called "Bouquet of Roses." Under Hill and Range it was polished into a hit by Steve Nelson and Bob Hilliard.[36]

Everyone, including Steve Sholes, was sure this would be a hit for Arnold. Jean simply went to the studio one day and handed the work to Steve, saying "Hey, this would be great for Eddy Arnold!" Steve looked it over and said, "You're right. It fits. Let's go!"[37] "Bouquet of Roses" shot up the country charts to number 1, hitting the week of June 5, 1948, and it remained on the charts for nineteen weeks, giving Arnold and Hill and Range their first gold record. It remained in the top one hundred for fifty-four weeks, crossing over to the pop charts and climbing to the number 13 position, where it remained as a pop bestseller for twenty-seven weeks.

There was no way Max would not notice it. Months earlier Jean had tried to interest Max in the tune, believing it was best placed with Chappell since Julian was not organized to promote a standard pop tune, but Max had repeatedly turned down the offer. Now that it had charted much higher than any Chappell song, Max and his brother Louis insisted the copyright be turned over to Chappell Music. "Jean, my brother and I want to talk to your brother and tell him to turn the song over to us on the terms we suggested a couple of months ago." Jean said, "Mr. Dreyfus, at that time it was a speculative situation. Now the song is fast becoming a big hit, and I would really have to advise my brother not to turn this song over to you, particularly since he had given you the chance several times and since you turned it down, and since the song had come as far as it had by his own efforts." Max did not for one moment believe the success of the song rested solely on the work of Julian Aberbach, and in this case he was right. The song had been placed with Sholes by Jean, not Julian. Jean and Julian had already given up the Floyd Hunt song. How were they to build up their company if every time they got a hit, they had to turn it over to Max Dreyfus? "Jean, I think Chappell and Company is too small for the both of us. I think it would be better if you would go your own way, and I would continue to take care of my own business." With that, Jean's career with Max Dreyfus was over.[38]

Jean had worked for Max for ten years and there seemed to be no way to satisfy his mentor without sacrificing his own ambition. The whole industry was finally embracing country songs and country stars, and he had done a lot to make that happen. Why shouldn't he now reap the benefits? *Max had never shown any interest in this music before, but now that it is making money, he is suddenly claiming it!*

Jean owed Max a lot—but he did not owe him their future. True, the man had effectively launched his American career, but Jean had repaid that debt time and again with his devotion to his duties and money-generating deals he brought in that reaped tremendous benefits for Chappell. Jean had even looked the other way when promised bonuses had not been forthcoming.

Upon relaying Julian's decision, Max was livid. "Max Dreyfus told my brother to turn the song over to him, or else don't come to work anymore," recalls Julian.[39]

Sadly, Jean had no choice but to oblige. Now it was time to wipe the slate clean and move on, for he could think of no way to pacify both Max and Julian, and despite his affection for Max, his future clearly lay with his brother.

CHAPTER 14

Waltzing to the Brink

A fter his split from Chappell Music, Jean traded places with Julian, who had been working in California. He located a large house on Hollywood Boulevard. A rich, mahogany-paneled poolroom on the ground floor would be converted to their office, and there was plenty of space to accommodate their living quarters, as well as those of Anna and Dolfi. In time, they would acquire adjacent properties, knocking down three houses in all to create four acres of gardens surrounding the house. Avocado, fig, and tangerine trees speckled the landscape, which overlooked a breathtaking view of the sprawling Los Angeles metropolis.[1]

They were heavily leveraged and, for the first time since they had begun their adventure five years earlier, Jean was no longer supplementing the development of Hill and Range with his Chappell income. Instead, he was drawing an income from it. To ensure they had enough money to cover expenses, Jean negotiated a new agreement with BMI in March 1949, against which they were able to borrow $10,000 and would borrow another $20,000 the following year.[2]

If Jean felt charmed and a bit cocky, he certainly had reason to be. The path from King and Blink to rivaling the top country and western music publishers took less than twelve months. How neatly things had fallen into place! Sylvester Cross's American Music had conveniently provided valuable relationships with country and western music's top stars. Those strategic relationships—especially the one they forged with Tim Spencer—had presaged their Nashville triumph through Ernest Tubb. All this had taken place while Roy Acuff, Nashville's most powerful force, was conveniently absent from the city. This remarkable succession of events had weakened their chief competitor significantly.

Over the past two years, Jean and Julian had seriously eroded the Acuff-Rose roster and the prevailing business publishing atmosphere in Nashville grew tense. Fred Rose's son Wesley now working for Acuff-Rose was among those that felt the Aberbachs were little more than big city robber barons out to chip away at their profit margin. Bitterness toward the Aberbach brothers was about to reach new heights. One of Acuff-Rose's most important writers was about to jump ship, and it would be both a personal and a professional blow to the company.

Red Foley's sister-in-law, Jenny Lou Carson, was a brilliant songwriter, but a shy, deeply troubled young woman who regularly turned to alcohol. Like Cindy

Jean, accepting a BMI award for Eddy Arnold's hit "Anytime." Courtesy of Susan Aberbach.

Walker, she had moved from a singing career to one of songwriting, probably refining her craft under the experienced guidance of Fred Rose. She was one of its first songwriters, contributing "Jealous Heart" in 1944 to the fledgling Acuff-Rose publishing firm. It became their first popular hit. Her professional relationship with Rose turned personal, then turbulent, possibly exacerbated by the fact that Rose himself was a recovering alcoholic. She had contacted the Hill and Range New York office in 1946, announcing that she had just broken up with Rose and was seeking independent representation for her works.[3]

Having failed in securing Cindy Walker for an exclusive songwriter's contract, Jean and Julian cast hopeful eyes her way and were delighted by what they found. Hailing from bustling, cosmopolitan Chicago, Carson was not strictly a country writer. In fact, her clever songs, endowed with rich, contemporary metaphors, straddled the fertile valley between country and pop. Steve Sholes already recognized the progressive quality of her work, using "Many Tears Ago" for Eddy Arnold's second Nashville session in July 1945.[4]

The Aberbach brothers jumped at the opportunity of working with this talented songwriter. "Chained to a Memory" was secured for Eddy Arnold's March 20, 1946, Chicago session and two versions of "A Penny for Your Thoughts" had been offered to the Sons of the Pioneers the following September. By 1949, after several years of successful ad hoc representation, Jean finally confirmed an exclusive songwriter's agreement with Carson in 1949, and a joint firm was created with her.[5]

Even though it was Carson who originally sought them out, this move sealed the bitter breach that had long been brewing between Acuff-Rose and Hill and Range. Jenny Lou Carson was just one more star-quality songwriter with whom Acuff-Rose had failed to follow through. She came to the Aberbachs, they believed, because Acuff-Rose had not aggressively promoted her works, just as they had not promoted the works of other artists who were quick to sign with Hill and Range. Both "Jealous Heart" and Red Foley's hit "Chattanoogie Shoe Shine Boy" have both been called "hits by happenstance" that had little to do with Acuff-Rose in-house promotion. Nor did the firm bother to build on the momentum of these hits.[6]

Other important members on the Acuff-Rose roster also had slipped away, such as Henry "Redd" Stewart, who Jean exclusively signed to Ernest Tubb's partnership company on June 1, 1947.[7] A strong relationship preexisted between Ernest Tubb and Redd Stewart. Both had been members of Pee Wee King's Golden West Cowboys, and Tubb had recorded Stewart's "Soldier's Last Letter." The song enjoyed tremendous success, remaining on the charts for twenty-nine weeks—four of them in the number 1 spot. On the strength of this smash hit, and a few other successes provided by local songwriters—most notably Johnny Bond for "Tomorrow Never Comes"—Tubb saw both the artistic value and the profit potential of signing good songwriters to his new Hill and Range publishing company. With Tubb now turning out sales of between 300,000 and 400,000 copies per single release, Stewart was more than happy to sign up, take the advance against projected earnings, and begin crafting songs with Ernest Tubb in mind. This collaboration resulted in another chart topper that year, "Two Wrongs Don't Make a Right," as well as "It's a Lonely World," which would have similar success when a new version was released in 1955.[8]

Pee Wee King's loyalty to Acuff-Rose probably wore out at about the same time. An accomplished accordionist, Frankie "Pee Wee" King (born Julius Frank Anthony Kuczynski) originally put together the Golden West Cowboys in Kentucky a decade before. With Stewart then on board as fiddler and lead vocalist, they became Grand Ole Opry regulars after their debut on June 5, 1937, bringing a strong sense of professionalism—along with smart, flashy western costumes—to the Opry stage. The Golden West Cowboys toured aggressively and were a popular dance band, frequenting both coasts and appearing in several western movies and broadcast radio shows. But with the exception of "Bonaparte's Retreat," cowriters Stewart and King had had little commercial success with either songwriting or recording. Acuff-Rose had the job of popularizing Stewart and King's work, but they were apparently not working very hard at it.[9]

There was good potential here, and Jean knew it. On June 26, 1947, Kentucky Music, Inc. was created, which was probably a joint firm with one or both of the artists. As soon as King and Stewart were each secured with exclusive songwriter agreements, Hill and Range began aggressively promoting their works. For instance they included mention of their works on the backside of sheet music for Johnny Tyler's "Oakie Boogie" dated 1947. A listing for "Pee Wee King's Folio of Waltzes, Square Dances and Polkas," "Red Foley's Sacred Album," and "Bob Nolan's Sons of the Pioneers' Cowboy Songs" can be found there.[10]

One of the waltzes in "Pee Wee King's Folio" was a popular tune that had long been the Golden West Cowboys theme song. A lilting and delicate melody, the instrumental had once been known only as the "No Name Waltz." Then one day, while driving back to Nashville from Texarkana, regional pride took hold, and inspired by Bill Monroe's radio rendition of the popular "Kentucky Waltz," King and Stewart forged the timeless lyrics of "Tennessee Waltz."[11]

The song languished for almost two years before RCA took an interest in recording it. With Stewart singing lead, the Golden West Cowboys version hit the country charts on April 3, 1948, and stayed there for thirty weeks, topping out in the number 3 spot. Lloyd "Cowboy" Copas (another former Golden West Cowboy) jumped King's own debut with a version that climbed to the number 3 spot and stayed on the charts for seventeen weeks, and the Short Brothers also contributed a rendition on Decca.[12] Most important, the song crossed over to the pop chart, with King's original version making a respectable showing there at number 30.

"Tennessee Waltz" became what was known in the business as a "sleeper." While it made only a fair showing on the popular charts, it remained on them, selling steadily throughout the year to become a quiet popular hit that continued to be revisited. Erskine Hawkins and his orchestra, for instance, followed up in 1950 with a version on Coral Records. Jean was certain they had found an enduring crossover hit—perhaps one that could even rival that of "Tumbling Tumbleweeds." There was only one problem. Technically speaking, it wasn't his.

Typical Hill and Range agreements called for the conveyance of "all rights to compositions" created by its artists, in whole or part; "arrangements of public domain tunes" for the purpose of public performance and exploitation worldwide; and "rights to changes and derivative works." Not all of King and Stewart's small body of original works, however, were unencumbered. By the time the writers were signed to Hill and Range, "Tennessee Waltz" already appears to have been conveyed to their chief competitor, Acuff-Rose.

As soon as they had arrived back in Nashville from their Texarkana road trip around Christmas 1946, Stewart and King had given the new lyrics over to Fred Rose. Despite the fact that Fred Rose himself offered a few critical lyric changes, little effort was made to record or promote the song, and for years it remained buried among the manuscript files, a scribbled set of lyrics written in the dim light of a truck cab on the inverted side of a matchbox cover.[13]

Stewart and probably King were both under Hill and Range exclusive contract for at least a year before they had the opportunity to record it. Since King had no recording history with the label, Steve Sholes was inclined to trust his instincts rather than the artist's where choosing songs was concerned. It was risky to introduce a new artist with unknown tunes, so when recording a waltz was discussed for the first session, Sholes chose the then popular "Kentucky Waltz" over King's own song. But once the commitment to record "Tennessee Waltz" finally was made in 1948, a heavy industry buzz developed over the song strong enough to convince Syd Nathan (owner of King Records in Cincinnati) to scoop its public debut from RCA with his own version by Cowboy Copas. There was even a version by rival Roy Acuff, which achieved number 12 on the national hit parade.[14]

A copyright filed with the federal registry is consummate proof of ownership and the key to protecting a songwriter's property. Administering the filing of songs for copyright is the most fundamental responsibility of a music publisher. Up to this point, so little attention was paid to the song by Acuff-Rose that it was never filed.[15] It was not until promotional efforts by Hill and Range began to pay off that somebody over at Acuff-Rose perked up, retrieved the scribbled matchbox cover and—after a year and a half of inaction—proceeded to file its copyright. Meanwhile, Jean continued to promote the song apparently believing it was written while under exclusive contract to Hill and Range. Neither company probably had any idea the other thought it was their property.

Although the details may never be confirmed, the root of this misunderstanding was probably the writers themselves. The fact that Rose had never filed a copyright for the work or done anything to promote it may have led the writers to believe that it was theirs to take back when they left the Acuff-Rose for Hill and Range. Further complicating matters, Stewart pledged future song royalties against a loan from Ernest Tubb so that he could make a down payment on a house.[16] Establishing an agreement whereby song royalties from BMI would be diverted personally to Tubb or to Tubb's Hill and Range partnership firm only reinforced the impression that the work was owned and controlled by Hill and Range.

Jean had no idea Acuff-Rose would claim the song. He believed he owned at least half—if not all—the publishing rights to "Tennessee Waltz" when it was first recorded in 1948. Such ownership would have given him the right to authorize derivative works and new arrangements. He pursued every opportunity to promote the work and managed to place the song with Mercury's most daring producer, Mitch Miller.

Miller had taken over as director of the label in October 1947. A trained classical oboist, he came with open ears and a boundless sense of adventure. No genre or song was too challenging, and no record got anything less than his full creative attention. Miller brought a new sense of precision to the pop music world. His recordings were meticulously constructed and flawlessly arranged, reflecting a broad aural palette that mirrored the sonic and tonal experimentation of the last half century of symphonic music. He exploited sound effects and new recording techniques to create novelty and atmosphere in his recordings. He experimented with microphone placement, giving added depth to recordings long before the concept of stereo recordings was perfected. With Frankie Laine, a pop singer best known for his 1946 hit debut remake of the dated 1931 Carroll Loveday and Helmy Kresa tune "That's My Desire," he turned out the Academy Award nominee "Mule Train" (by Johnny Lange, Hy Heath, and Fred Glickman, 1950), memorable for its snapping horsewhip effect.[17]

Miller was particularly captivated with the multitrack recording method developed by guitarist innovator Les Paul. Paul's breathtaking guitar technique was augmented to almost unbelievable heights in his 1948 Capitol recording of "Brazil." By this time, his finger dexterity was beyond amazing, and his new overdubbing technique gave the astonishing impression that six Les Pauls were improvising together.[18]

Excited by this new technique, Miller began experimenting with overdubbing. Looking for a tune to pair on the flip side of Patti Page's scheduled Christmas song release "Boogie Woogie Santa Claus," her manager Jack Rael brought "Tennessee Waltz" to Miller's attention. The Erskine Hawkins orchestra version had been passed on to him by Jerry Wexler, a *Billboard* record reviewer. Believing the unusual overdubbing technique might help generate some press for the disc, Miller recorded three versions, with Page singing solo, duet, and trio harmony with herself.

By Christmas 1950, the long-term sales potential of this song and the enormous royalties at stake were obvious. As soon as the Patti Page version was released, it left the Christmas tune on the flip side in the dust, jumping to number 1 on the pop charts, where it was unchallenged for the next thirteen weeks. The longer it stayed on the bestseller list, the more other performers scrambled to record the tune. Guy Lombardo, Jo Stafford, the Fontane Sisters, the duo of Les Paul and Mary Ford, and Anita Day followed up with their own versions. It was also lampooned by musical satirist Spike Jones and even motivated the rerelease of Pee Wee King's original version. But it was Page's honey-sweet version that stood head and shoulders above them. Destined to achieve unprecedented postwar sales in excess of $6 million, it became one of the most profitable tunes of the twentieth century.[19]

The overwhelming success of the Patti Page version came as a pleasant surprise to everyone, including its writers, who were savoring the prospect of enormous royalties. The first sign of trouble seems to have appeared a year after the first recordings came out, when BMI finally got around to accounting and disbursing substantial royalties for it. At that time BMI probably discovered there were two BMI affiliates claiming royalties for this work, Acuff-Rose and Hill and Range.

Acuff-Rose filed a lawsuit in Nashville, probably in early 1950. By the end of the year they had mounted a separate action in New York, where Mercury Records was withholding its record royalties pending the settlement. The stakes were not small. "Tennessee Waltz" was not just a hit. It was a historic musical milestone with seemingly limitless profit potential. It was generating astronomical revenue and there was no end in sight. By May 1951, 4,800,000 records and 1,100,000 copies of sheet music had been sold, probably representing $175,000 in revenues. Whether the parties believed they had a strong or a weak case, this was a copyright worth fighting for. But the distribution of this money was stalled for months by the messy copyright litigation. Before long, it didn't matter to Pee Wee King who owned the publishing rights to the work, as long as he got his money.[20]

King was also upset because Hill and Range was publishing an arrangement of the tune by the Short Brothers. It was not uncommon for artists to misunderstand that the typical arrangement made with a publisher entitled them to make new arrangements of tunes without consulting them. To King, who was ignorant of the publishing nuances, the promotional advertisement for the Short Brothers' arrangement made it appear as though the duo was claiming to be the original composers and that, by extension, Hill and Range was taking advantage of him. He had nothing but bitterness for the Aberbach brothers, who appeared to be letting others claim his work and standing between him and his royalties.[21]

But Jean was not in this game to win approval from his songwriters. Acuff-Rose had never done anything to promote this song, nor to promote the works of many other songwriters whose careers had taken a turn for the better as soon as they had signed up with Hill and Range. Since they had switched alliances, Stewart had been paired up with Ernest Tubb and was turning out promising tunes (one of which became a hit); a folio of King's work had been printed and was being promoted; and a record contract had been confirmed with RCA. Any expense and energy for the success of King and Stewart and for their beautiful tune had been contributed by Hill and Range. That Acuff-Rose should now walk away with all the rewards seemed completely unfair. Having lost "Tumbling Tumbleweeds" to Chappell, Jean was not going to let this one go without a fierce fight. Apparently there was enough merit to the claims on both sides to keep the case moving along for many months. It threatened to drag on forever unless something could be found to tip the balance one way or another.

Jean found it in a claim Chappell Music had pending against Acuff-Rose. It was a legal action against Acuff-Rose Chappell had chosen not to pursue. If pressed, it would burden Acuff-Rose enough to reduce their ability to pursue the "Tennessee Waltz" claim. They might have to give up the lawsuit.

Chappell Music? Just because Jean no longer worked *for* Max didn't mean he would not work *with* him. Whatever terms the two men left on, relations seem to have normalized not too long after. According to the 1949 BMI agreement, special provision was made for Jean to continue representing Chappell Music on commission despite the fact that any deals relating to Chappell would be ASCAP matters. The agreement also cited a number of copyright properties excluded from BMI control—including their Eddy Arnold hit "Bouquet of Roses," whose international rights had been licensed to Chappell Music. This may have been the *quid pro quo* for assigning another property to Jean that he could use to press a claim against Acuff-Rose.[22] The threat of a countersuit put Acuff-Rose at a severe disadvantage, stretching their legal staff and draining their resources. Suddenly they were poised to lose the "Tennessee Waltz" case because they could no longer afford it.

Their attorney in New York, Harold Orenstein, referred the matter to Gang, Kopp & Tyre, one of the oldest, most respected legal firms in California. It was fast becoming known for this new area of copyright law. Recently the firm had taken on a young, ambitious attorney named Milton Rudin, who was being groomed to take over all courtroom litigation. The case was being handled by a senior attorney, Bob Kopp. Kopp believed that Hill and Range had no right to acquire a property, solely for the purpose of burdening a competitor on another lawsuit. Rudin doggedly searched through volumes of legal briefs, turning up only a remote 1880 statute that had never since been used. Much to his amazement, the judge ruled that, in accordance with the New York statute, one corporation cannot take assignment from another solely for the purpose of suing a third party.

Jean was stunned. Until this obscure statute came to light, he and his attorney, Ben Starr, thought they were within their legal rights to use this approach. The outcome returned them to their old tug of war with Acuff-Rose. Dismissal of the counterclaim, King's mounting bitterness over the Short Brothers affair, and hold up on the royalties tipped the scales in favor of Acuff-Rose. Without the songwriter's support, Jean knew their case was doomed. Probably sometime in late 1952, Jean abandoned the claim in exchange for Acuff-Rose dropping its suit, each party apparently absorbing its own legal expense. He dissolved the exclusive contract with King the following year.

The out-of-pocket cost to Hill and Range was high. By the time Acuff-Rose mounted the lawsuit, Hill and Range had already produced a costly folio arrangement by the Short Brothers, and was actively promoting the recordings. They were forced to absorb the loss of promoting a song to enormous success that would end up directly benefiting their chief competitor.[23] Ironically, Acuff-Rose had fallen victim to the same problem just a few years earlier. Failing to fully investigate Hank Williams's most famous tune, Fred Rose believed Acuff-Rose fully owned the rights to "Lovesick Blues" and promoted it accordingly. Around 1949, Mills Music stepped forward with proof that the tune had been copyrighted by its firm in 1922 by Irving Mill and Cliff Friend. While they demanded all royalties be turned over, Mills Music graciously afforded relief to Acuff-Rose so that it could recoup its promotional investments. No such courtesy was extended to Hill and Range, despite the fact that the enormous popular success of the tune could be traced exclusively to their extensive promotional activities and investment.

It had been their first major setback, and while Jean was not happy about it, he was still more than a little impressed. The firm of Gang, Kopp & Tyre had won the case for their client using an obscure legal statute few others would have imagined existed. Their perseverance had completely destroyed not just the counterclaim, but ultimately the entire Hill and Range case. While he did not like it, Jean could still respect them for it. He had been taught a great lesson: *in business, the value of exceptional legal advice cannot be underestimated.* Because he had been taught the hard way, this was a lesson Jean would not forget.

CHAPTER 15

Keyhole Logic

Despite the enormous sums that had been at stake, the net effect of "Tennessee Waltz" had more to do with reputation than with money. The full impact did not become clear until Hill and Range legal counsel Ben Starr put in a call to Jean probably in late 1951, announcing that Tim Spencer wanted to take a look at the books.[1]

Tim Spencer was unlike any other co-owner they had. Shortly after they created his publishing company, Spencer had eased out of his performing career, devoting himself almost entirely to the business of songwriting. He was getting more and more interested in learning about how things got done at Hill and Range.

Tim Spencer's inquiries could not have come at a worse time. They were implementing a new accounting system that was supposed to help organize print inventory and simplify accounting and distributions. But the transition period was painful, and at times the system proved more confusing than helpful.[2] Further complicating matters, BMI had gone through a number of policy changes over the years. Where that money came from and where it was supposed to go was a matter of broad interpretation and had been for some time as the fledgling BMI struggled to stabilize its own accounting and distribution practices.

Unlike ASCAP, who distributed the author-composer share of royalties (as opposed to the publisher's share) directly to songwriters, BMI left this task in the hands of its publisher members. Some had abused the privilege. To be sure he was being paid fairly, Tim Spencer engaged an energetic property rights lawyer named Edythe Jacobs, who recommended they take a closer look at how Hill and Range was managing these funds.[3]

As co-owner of his corporation, Tim Spencer had every right to take a look at the books. But Jean suspected that doing so would end up generating more questions than it would answer, because BMI's fluid rate structures seemed to change as often as the wind. Inevitably this would invite even more scrutiny from the rest of their co-owners. Before long, the press would be focused on picking through their private business affairs.

Jean often told a story about his times in Paris working for Jacques Rosenberg of Campbell, Connelly. There were young girls who would come by from time to time, believing Rosenberg was the owner of a film company. They would want to give an audition and would ask for a microphone. The staff would always tease them and say, "The keyhole is the microphone!" Without a second thought—and much to the delight of the gentlemen onlookers—the girls would bend over very far and begin singing into the keyhole![4]

Don't ever be caught singing through the keyhole, while the rest of the world is looking up your skirt! Clearly, this was one of those "keyhole" moments. Events over the past two years had been enormously distracting. Between the split from Chappell, the "Tennessee Waltz" lawsuit, fluctuating BMI policies, the office improvements, and the overwhelming pressures of managing an international business that had grown into a multimillion-dollar enterprise in a few short years, he had no doubt some essential details had been overlooked. Pondering Tim Spencer's request, Jean could feel the hem of their skirt begin to rise behind them.

Jean never let pride get in the way of good judgment. There is no better way to ensure your advantage than to purchase the advantage of your opponent. He also understood that it was always better to have a winner on your side, regardless of the cost, and was always willing to pay top dollar for the best legal talent.

Jean immediately phoned Norman Tyre of Gang, Kopp & Tyre—the firm that had defeated them in the "Tennessee Waltz" case. Tyre assumed Jean was steamed about the case and wanted to discuss it with him, but instead was surprised when Jean said "Anyone who could beat me in that case, I want him to be our lawyer. We never should have lost that case. I have to hand it to you guys. You stayed above board and won that case as a matter of law—and I'd like to hire you as our lawyers."[5]

Business, like marriage, is a two-way street. Each party brings talents and ambitions to the venture. But inevitably, some compromise is required from both parties to make the relationship work. If the parties respect their roles, maintain a comfortable working relationship and stay focused on mutual goals, their conjugal accomplishments can far outshine those they might have achieved individually.

By forging a new business model that resulted in joint companies, the Aberbach brothers were "married" to many of their songwriter-performers. The role distinctions between artist-creator and promoter-accountant remained clear in most cases. Co-owners like Bob Wills, Elton Britt, and Ernest Tubb and songwriters like Jenny Lou Carson were focused exclusively on their careers and left accounting and business details entirely to Aberbachs. But Tim Spencer was different. He had gone into semiretirement from the Sons of the Pioneers in 1947 and began paying more attention to his personal finances, a large part of which were being generated by Tim Spencer Music. Then, in 1949 Jean moved to separate Bob Nolan's catalog from Tim Spencer Music. Suddenly Spencer became keenly focused on his Hill and Range business affairs. Just what exactly was going on here?[6]

It was far less insidious than it perhaps appeared. Sylvester Cross still held many of Nolan's copyrights in his American Music company. While the Aberbach brothers' intervention had forced Cross to confront the issue of royalty distribution to his writers, nevertheless Cross's relationship with those writers continued to strain. Because Nolan himself desired independence, and also because litigation might have to be mounted to recapture these works, it was decided to transfer Nolan's songs to a new, jointly held corporation called Bob Nolan Music, Inc. Indeed, to have done otherwise would have placed Tim Spencer Music at needless risk.

The terms for separating Nolan's from Spencer's work were outlined in a letter of agreement naming Edward Gray as Nolan's attorney-in-fact in June 1949. It was witnessed by several parties, including Spencer. It transferred Nolan's exclusive songwriter agreement, as well as his copyrights, to his new corporation, Bob Nolan Music, and reconfirmed his willingness to cooperate in the recapture of outstanding copyrights. Nolan would benefit not only from the streamlined songwriter royalty distribution, but also as recipient of half the publisher royalties as partner in his own company, should any outstanding works from any third party source be recaptured.[7]

This was not the only reason Jean pursued this restructuring. Nolan was one of many a songwriter caught in the snare of changing business practices at that time. A writer's ability to collect money for the public performances of his songs depended either on his membership in ASCAP as an individual songwriter or—since BMI did not yet allow individual songwriter members—

his association with a BMI member publisher. Since both organizations were now demanding exclusivity to lock up profitable copyrights in long-term royalty collection agreements, a songwriter could affiliate with one or the other, but not both, organizations.[8]

By association with American Music, and with Tim Spencer Music, and now as joint-owner of a subsidiary Hill and Range firm, Bob Nolan was indisputably a BMI writer. Unfortunately, his most profitable song was not in a BMI firm at all. Indeed, Bob Nolan was personally losing volumes of "Tumbling Tumbleweeds" performance money that were rightfully due him every year because it was half owned by Sam Fox Music and half owned by Chappell's Williamson music, both of which were ASCAP affiliates. Because he was an exclusive BMI member, Nolan could not collect songwriter royalties on his most lucrative work from ASCAP.

Bob Nolan's problems with "Tumbling Tumbleweeds" remain on public display in a most unusual venue even today. Wall, South Dakota, is the home of the famous Wall Drug, whose intriguing signs pepper Interstate highway 90 for hundreds of miles. The now-sprawling complex of quaint shops, kiddie rides, and unique western memorabilia began in 1931 as a rundown little drugstore. After five years of struggle, the owner and his wife hit on a simple advertising device to draw thirsty travelers to their establishment—free ice water. Over the years they collected hundreds of photographs from passing patrons, who read the signs and stopped for ice water, some of them famous. On the wall next to a life-size animatronics display of a western band that plays cowboys songs for a dollar is a framed piece of sheet music for "Tumbling Tumbleweeds." It references "Williamson Music by special arrangement with Sam Fox publishing company" above a framed copy of the 45-rpm disc. The following inscription by Nolan indicates his rocky history with this famous western song: "This is a copy of my second song written in 1932—it has been both bad and good to me.—Bob Nolan."[9]

Jean had not known Nolan at the time he moved to acquire "Tumbling Tumbleweeds" from Sam Fox for Chappell's Williamson Music. Since Nolan was not a member of either ASCAP or BMI at the time and had not been collecting performance royalties from American Music or from anyone else, the issue of his membership in either organization had no bearing whatsoever on the deal. Sam Fox was an ASCAP company and that made "Tumbling Tumbleweeds" an ASCAP copyright.

Since then, a lot had happened. Tim Spencer Music (a BMI company) had been created and Nolan's other copyrights collected in it. For the first time ever, Nolan began to be paid songwriter royalties on the public performances of his works through BMI. Unfortunately, because of the prevailing industry policies, if Nolan now wanted to collect money on "Tumbling Tumbleweeds," it appeared he would have to renounce his BMI affiliation and apply for membership in ASCAP, in effect giving up all the songwriter royalties he was now collecting on all his other songs through BMI.[10] Nolan fell victim to a classic industry catch-22—an enigma that writers who came after him avoided by illegally taking pseudonyms so they could discreetly register and collect from both organizations.

When Jean maneuvered the song into Chappell's Williamson music, he could not have known how important BMI would become to Nolan's financial future. It seemed the only clear-cut way to resolve the situation now, was not only to challenge American Music for its Nolan copyrights, but to eventually challenge Sam Fox and Williamson Music for ownership of "Tumbling Tumbleweeds" so that all Nolan songs would end up with BMI.

The first step in this process was to position Nolan as a principal in his own corporation, which would carry psychological weight in a legal case—the wronged songwriter, acting on his own behalf to protect his own welfare and that of his family. If they succeeded, Nolan would eventually be paid all his royalties through a single source, BMI. Naturally, the Aberbach brothers would also benefit with half the recovered and future publishing proceeds.

While documents show that Tim Spencer approved splitting Nolan's work off from his own, around this time he began to scrutinize his business relationship with the Aberbach brothers more closely.[11] His was the first company created with a major songwriter-performer. Being no novice to business management, Spencer made sure he got exactly what he wanted. Each party would contribute equally—tit for tat—in finding and assigning songs to the catalog. They would also match each other in placing these works with major labels for recordings. The contract stipulated an equal share of the gross. Hill and Range could deduct manufacturing fees, reasonable copyright fees, and advances to writers and artists, but otherwise would have to absorb all other operating expenses. Royalties would be distributed every six months, and Spencer would have equal access to the accounting books for verification.

Jean was a man of his word. He engaged in contracts with the utmost gravity and sincerity. Contracts were meant to clarify—not to obscure the truth. There was, however, a problem inherent in every contract Hill and Range had ever made. It was a problem not unique to Hill and Range, but one that would prove more troublesome to this company than to most. The central problem was that there were always more than just two parties involved in a Hill and Range contract. The problem was that Hill and Range had a silent partner—it was called BMI.

As gross revenue provider, BMI was the de facto third party to all these ventures. Although it operated in the background, the organization was still the kingpin in these contracts, distributing the collected royalties by complex formulas to their affiliated publishers who were expected to share those distributions with the writers. Apparently, there was enough different about Tim Spencer's partnership corporation to avoid its inclusion in the 1949 BMI blanket agreement with Hill and Range, an agreement that had provided advances against the earnings of Hill and Range and all other affiliated companies including Bob Wills Music, Ernest Tubb Music, St. Louis Music Corporation, Elton Britt Music, Bill Monroe Music, and Home Folks Music. Apparently, Tim Spencer Music required a separate, less standard, and probably more complex accounting.

Jean's concerns were not over whether he had kept his own books well enough, but that he did not keep those of BMI. Hill and Range was deeply affected by the transitory nature of BMI policies as that organization struggled to grow and compete. Reinventing itself at every impasse, the organization was still less than a decade old, and it had grown almost too fast to manage. From a rented office, with a temporary staff of four in January 1940, the organization undertook a breathless expansion during its first year and was forced to diversify quickly in order to survive. In addition to its core business of tracking and collecting royalties for concert and radio performances, it was also forced to become a lyric print publisher, funding promotional sheet music magazines in competition with *The Hit Parader* and *Song Hits*. BMI had also weathered a grand-jury action taken after only one year of service that nearly destroyed it. The desperate rush to develop a loyal user base resulted in a confusing array of payment options that included blanket, per-program, and per-use access to BMI music for broadcast.[12]

While the diverse licensing plans were attractive to music venues and radio stations, it was an absolute nightmare for the BMI accounting department. Blanket BMI agreements at this time were necessarily riddled with exceptions, deferrals, income caps, and contingencies as the organization struggled to anticipate the growth of the company, as well as the growth of the music industry, in relation to its own. BMI dues were based on percentages, and percentages were adjusted according to station revenues that could change radically from quarter to quarter. Special promotions and exceptions were often used to attract new radio station members. This further complicated accounting. But it was the slippery deals it had struck with the networks (its biggest money generators) that caused the most confusion and ambiguity, because the rates were calculated as a percentage of a station's advertising budget. This meant that the networks themselves could control how much they paid out to BMI simply by controlling how much gross advertising funds they allotted to each of their subsidiary stations.[13]

Collecting the money at the prevailing rate of the moment was only half the problem. How to divvy up the proceeds was even more difficult. BMI generated $1.8 million in its first year and would bring in nearly $2 million during its second. Nearly a quarter of the first fiscal year's earnings were earmarked for the E. B. Marks catalog—despite the fact that 5,000 to 6,000 of its copyrights were under dispute by ASCAP writers. BMI had also set up its own subsidiary publishing house, Radiotunes, and began paying out subsidies to encourage the formation of new companies owned by film studios. At the same time it began providing supplemental revenue to companies like Hill and Range who maintained fully staffed offices in more than one geographic region. Finally, to engage and keep new publishing firms with them, BMI offered guaranteed advances against expected revenue a company might earn. These were based on complex calculations derived from how well a catalog had done in the past. All this made working with BMI flexible and attractive, especially for the innumerable start-up firms founded by bandleaders, songwriters, talent agents, and film companies—but it was the recipe for a heart attack for any reasonably diligent fiscal accountant.

BMI's organizers decided early on that if it could not always limit the complexity of its fiscal affairs, it could at least limit the number of members it was accountable to. It did so by resolving that it would not distribute funds directly to author-composers as did ASCAP. Instead, it would distribute both author-composer and publisher money to its member publishers, who in turn were expected to distribute the author-composer royalties to their affiliated writers.[14]

In a perfect world, where all the policies were clearly set and stayed stable to the completion of term periods, where all the licensees were paid in full and on time, where all the distributions made sense and were fair, and where all the accounting books were in good order, this policy might have worked. Instead, BMI set the stage for disaster, leaving volumes of money very often in the hands of small, inexperienced publishers. Some were incapable of fiscal management. Others were convinced that they were entitled to all royalties—including those of the author-composer—on the copyrights they controlled and published and simply never distributed anything to their writers.

Jean was not one of them. He had worked too long as a business manager at Chappell Music to neglect the inherent trust that provided the basis of songwriter–publisher relations. While it had been a struggle, he stayed abreast of the BMI policy changes and their responsibilities to their member songwriters. Everyone else seemed satisfied with the administrative services of Hill and Range except Tim Spencer. But because Spencer was a co-owner rather than just a contract songwriter, he could demand that Hill and Range justify every penny he thought Hill and Range should have paid out to him.

There is no doubt some creative accounting had been done to manage BMI's confusing distributions. Attorney Milton Rudin remarked, "They were getting reports, as I recall, from BMI accounting on the basis of one cent for local, two cents for network, and another report would come along on the basis of three cents and six cents, and then in another." If this case ever went to trial it would be disastrous. The publicity from it could infect their relationships with every other songwriter-performer they were working with. It could engage the Aberbach brothers in litigation that could cripple, if not destroy, the company.

Right or wrong, Jean could not let that happen. He requested a meeting with Rudin to discuss their options. The best course of action was to quickly reconfirm their relationships with every other artist and to ratify all existing copyright registrations. Only then could Jean be sure that the case would proceed on the strength of its own merits, and not disrupt relations with other artists.[15]

Stalling the progress of the case until this was done proved easier than they had expected. Tim Spencer's attorney was very enthusiastic, but she was not a very careful lawyer. Edythe Jacobs's first mistake was to forget to allege that Tim Spencer was, in fact, a shareholder in the corporation. When confronted with the motion to dismiss on these grounds, she laughed, told Rudin it was a "stupid motion," and proceeded to file an amendment correcting the oversight. In her zeal, however, she also filed a Special Demerit to the Complaint, which raised questions on a number of other things she had also not pleaded properly. It was a simple matter for Rudin to prolong the case while Hill and Range put its house in order, because he continued to find errors in Jacobs's work that continued to set her back. Before long the initial filing period ran out—another thing she objected to but could do nothing about, and the judge set back the case accordingly. She was forced to start over from ground zero. Instead of pleading less, she pleaded more and more until, by about the fourth amendment, she was completely frustrated. In the meantime, Jean and the staff worked furiously to ratify all their copyrights and reconfirm their business relationships with all their songwriter-performers, thus ensuring that no one else would feel inclined to join this suit against them.[16]

By the middle of December, Edythe Jacobs was completely frustrated and humiliated.[17] Rudin had used the laws to his best advantage, and although the case was progressing in her direction, it was moving along only at a snail's pace. She was angry enough at the progress that it was not enough to simply win the case for her client. If at the same time she could also embarrass and harass the Aberbach brothers, so much the better. When she got wind of their intentions to move, she knew exactly what to do. She was determined to make things as costly and cumbersome as possible for them.

For some time, the Aberbach brothers had been contemplating moving headquarters back to New York. They had long since exhausted the western talent in Los Angeles and new musical frontiers were opening up, with roots in gospel and secular blues music east of the Rockies. They planned do the majority of the move over the 1953 Christmas holiday weekend, leaving only a skeleton office staff behind to maintain a business presence on the West Coast.

Edythe Jacobs had gotten wind of this, and to disrupt the move she had chosen to serve subpoenas for their depositions on the day and date that would most impede their plans. Jean, Julian, and a few other staff members were required by law to be available in California when they were all supposed to be in New York receiving the moving trucks and setting up their new offices. To add insult to injury, she had also attached a requirement for the production of documents—but was purposely vague about which ones she might want. Very likely, it would be impossible to produce the necessary papers when required, since everything was already boxed up. The difficulty of locating them and transporting them to the proceedings from the other side of the continent was probably impossible.

Jean asked Rudin what he thought they should do. Rudin wracked his brains for a solution based in jurisprudence. When he came up empty, he started looking for any other way around the problem. Half jokingly, he suggested a scenario that might at least stall the inevitable. "The court is going to give her the position that she is entitled to something, but we won't know until Wednesday, Thursday, or Friday what you have to keep back. We could offer to pay her expenses to New York. The court might grant that relief, but I have no way of knowing what the judge will do. Therefore I suggest that you pack everything up, but put the oldest files that you need the least in one truck. And fill that truck, a moving van, up with those old files." Jean couldn't help but crack a smile.

Edythe Jacobs was not a wealthy lawyer. She had an office—not much larger than a closet in a crowded building, which she shared with another attorney. At about 7:30 in the morning, the truck backed up to the building. Rudin had ordered them to bring along extra people, and this team of movers began crowding up the cramped lobby of the old Occidental Petroleum building with file boxes, carting them upstairs in the structure's only elevator. Once upstairs, they began piling the boxes in the hallway, seriously obstructing access, since Jacob's office was not yet open. Before long no one could get upstairs, or around in the lobby or hallways, and the management was called. They in turn called the police.

Rudin had anticipated all this and was waiting in his office for the call. The police said a complaint had been made and they were going to have to stop any further moving. "They have with them," Rudin explained, "a subpoena *duces tecum*—that's an order of the court. You, Mr. Policeman, will be interfering with an order of the court. You ought to call the city attorney, or call headquarters, before you make that move." They did so, and received instructions from their headquarters not to interfere.

Rudin arrived a few hours later along with Jean, Julian, office manager Grelun Landon, and Hill and Range counsel Ben Starr. What they found was a delightful mess. Boxes were everywhere. They also brought along not one, but three, court reporters, as Jacobs (in yet another oversight), had failed to convey to Rudin (as was customary) that the depositions slated for the same date and time would be taken in succession rather than concurrently.

The building supervisor was angry, building residents were miffed, and poor Edythe Jacobs was just short of hysterical. The thousands of files were everywhere, and as soon as Jacobs opened her office, movers began moving boxes into that cramped space as well. When it became clear they would not all fit, the building supervisor stepped forward and grudgingly agreed to open two empty offices to house the documents. By this time, the party got even larger, because Tim Spencer had arrived, along with his wife.

When it came time to take the depositions, Jacobs suggested she would take Jean's first. But Rudin held her to the letter of the law, insisting that all three would be taken at the time specified in the court order, and that if she didn't have the space or resources to do so, then Julian and Grelun would have to be recalled at another time. That was the last straw for Edythe Jacobs. She began arguing, then screaming at the counselor. Rudin waited for a break in the tirade, and then reminded her that "the law requires a deposition be conducted in a quiet proper atmosphere, and this doesn't afford that. You noticed three depositions. There isn't enough room for the witness, myself, your lawyers, and the court reporter to stand, let alone sit! We're leaving," he said with finality. Beaten, Jacobs pleaded for a settlement to the entire lawsuit, which was drafted immediately.

BMI's confusing distribution schemas that precipitated the ugly Tim Spencer case affected other companies as well. There was a growing discontent among BMI author-composers over BMI's fluid rate structures and their inability to collect directly from the organization. The problem had been brewing for years, but it came to a head in 1949 as BMI watched many of their big writers leave to join ASCAP. Finally, the organization began admitting individual author-composers, which was probably vital to its survival as a rights administration group. In August 1949, it began paying royalties directly to authors and composers for logged performances, rather than trusting they would be paid appropriately by their publisher affiliates.[18]

This was good for writers, but very bad for publishers because it diluted their influence over the organization and reduced overall royalty revenues, affecting cash flow. But these problems were minor compared to the growing fear that BMI was posturing to go into the publishing business itself. Unlike the nonprofit ASCAP society, BMI was not prohibited from setting up itself as a publishing house. The Aberbachs were among those who believed that once individual writers were admitted, BMI would move to acquire rights and interests in writer's copyrights as well, going into competition with its own publisher members. In one swift, canny move BMI could monopolize the market, and even large publishers like Hill and Range would be powerless against them.

Jean had a close relationship with the brilliant president of BMI, Sidney Kaye, who was a principal founder and the organization's driving force. Jean knew Kaye's high regard of him, but he probably never knew that the man who substantially built BMI during those early years regarded Jean as the most knowledgeable music businessman in the United States at that time.[19] What impressed him most was that Jean landed in this country as an immigrant outsider with few resources or influential ties, and that he used prevailing American law and a careful, systematic approach to business to excel past every other publisher in their field. Kaye believed that hard work and initiative should be rewarded, and when the Aberbach brothers needed help to start their business, he had given it by designating Hill and Range only one of three companies that was guaranteed large advances against their catalogs. Risking his relationship with Kaye was almost as painful as walking out on Max only a few years earlier. Nevertheless, softening ties with BMI was strategically smart. It was time to start playing both sides of the fence.

It's hard to let some dreams go—but even harder to have outlived them. Jean entered the 1950s with hopeful anticipation, but also with some regret. Some of the friendships that had launched their business were now gone or fading. With them went some of the joyous sense of wonder for the music he had dreamed about since his youth.

The easiest years were over. Jean and Julian now had a burgeoning multinational conglomerate to manage. No longer would their successes be unrivaled. They would need to work even more aggressively to stay competitive and keep the success they had worked so hard to earn. Country and western music would remain the dominant force in their catalog, but they had overstayed their welcome in Los Angeles, and their star was beginning to fall in Nashville as well. There were new, exciting trends to pursue elsewhere—in Chicago and Shreveport, in New York and Memphis that hinted of the same excitement that had brought them to country and western music in the first place.

How would they be remembered? A story Jean sketched in his notes was about his old boss in Paris, Jacques Rosenberg. In addition to being a publisher, Rosenberg had been a composer, and after he died of kidney disease, the crematory wanted to have one of his works played at his funeral. Unfortunately, the musicians did not know any and played a piece by well known classical composer Franz Schubert instead, the eulogist explaining that it might as well have been Rosenberg's.[20]

What would their swan song be? An accurate rendering of who they were, or some vague approximation that merely seemed to fit the occasion? Would they be remembered for paying some artists their first royalties ever, or be lumped in with the many unscrupulous publishers who never paid a dime? Would their tireless work to popularize country music be applauded, or would it be construed as exploitative greed by a couple of Nashville outsiders? Would they be remembered for giving up fully half their earnings so artists could share in the ownership of their own work, and in the control over their livelihoods and careers, or for the bitter Tim Spencer divorce? Jean could only hope that the song would be their own, and not some convenient substitute, the tune of which was out of step with the world as it had actually unfolded.

CHAPTER 16

Johnny Taps

B y the time the Tim Spencer affair concluded in 1953, the music
publishing industry was in chaos. The pressure to admit writer
members to BMI came about, in part, because of the efforts of the
longstanding Songwriter's Protective Association (SPA). Founded
by Fred Ahlert, Roy Turk, Sigmund Romberg, Harry Warren, and Billy Rose
in the late 1920s, it was a fraternal, lobbying organization formally introduced
in 1931. Its objective was to bring songwriting copyright law in line with other
entertainment law so that songwriters could enjoy the same control over their
intellectual property as did dramatists and authors. Among the rights they pursued was the ability of songwriters to retain ownership of works in their own
name for two twenty-eight-year terms of protection, and to control the *small*
rights (those of publication, mechanical reproduction—i.e., "recording"—and
public performance, which were considered distinct from *grand* rights, which
had do with theatrical works).

The SPA's most visible contribution was to establish a standardized songwriter contract across the industry during the early 1930s. In 1941, it renegoti-

ated with ASCAP and the Music Publishers Protective Association (MPPA) and won the establishment of equal distribution between writers and publishers, of revenues obtained from mechanical, synchronization (for film), and foreign publishing. It gave writers a say in how their music would be merchandised, required their approval for licensing to televisions and certain film rights, and obligated publishers to issue quarterly statements.

By 1946, the SPA had grown powerful, and was interposing itself in judicial affairs. One of its leaders pleaded for a reversal in the *Alden-Rochelle v. ASCAP* case, which denied ASCAP the right to collect per-seat fees for songs that appeared in motion pictures presented at independent movie theaters. They suggested that if reversal were not granted, the rights to license for film should revert back to the writer, not the publisher. While ASCAP was finally permitted to collect royalties for film (from the movie production companies rather than movie theater owners) the SPA suggestion that writers should be able to negotiate their own deals for film underscored the organization's long-term agenda to secure an interest in their copyrights that would allow songwriters to administer the licensing of their own works.

This prospect of negotiating individually with each songwriter for the use of their songs in film, for sheet music, on television, and on records shot panic throughout an industry that depended on an organized licensing schema. Although SPA was not successful, writers began to recognize the possibility of gaining more control over their creative properties. Over the next decade the SPA continued to grow in power, increasing the influence songwriters could assert over their publishers.[1]

While it was battling its writers on the licensing and ownership front, ASCAP was under siege for its distribution policies. Younger songwriter members were demanding a complete restructuring of the revenue distribution policies. They were somewhat successful, but despite sweeping reforms developed under the scrutiny of the U.S. Justice Department, in the end the changes did little to wrest a larger share of revenue from the veteran old-guard publishers like Max Dreyfus. While it appeared that some concessions had been made in a revised ASCAP distribution plan in 1951, veteran songwriters like Irving Berlin, Cole Porter, Richard Rodgers, Otto Harbach, Oscar Hammerstein, and George and Ira Gershwin—whose works were controlled by the senior publishing houses like Harms, Witmark, and Chappell—ended up with even more earnings under the new plan. No number of song plays would allow new publishers to move more quickly into the higher-paying seniority class. After all the legal wrangling, the net effect was that checks going to new, young publishing houses promoting new, younger songwriters turned out to be less revenue, not more.[2]

Completely frustrated, there was a general feeling among ASCAP songwriters that the organization was no longer acting in their best interest. Many felt it was distributing funds unfairly. They also felt it was preventing songwriters from exercising creativity in the popular music field, where the bulk of the revenue generating opportunities was now coming from. By opening individual writer membership in BMI and pledging support for developing a serious contemporary concert music repertoire, BMI snatched away some of ASCAP's most progressive young writers, among them William Schuman, Norman Dello Joio, Roger Sessions, Walter Piston, and the American Composers Alliance, which boasted Aaron Copland as its shining star. By 1952 BMI was actively promoting "serious" American music, thus enabling its songwriters to work in any field of music they wished without restriction.[3]

It was only the most self-confident ASCAP members who left. Unsure of their prospects and confused by the politics, the rank-and-file ASCAP members began to consider ways of quietly circumventing the problems of exclusive membership in ASCAP. Many ASCAP writers were not bold enough to openly jump ship and move existing ASCAP-licensed works to BMI, choosing instead to license new works with BMI under discreet pseudonyms. This allowed them to reap benefits from BMI while still protecting their official ASCAP membership, so they could continue to get revenue generated by the copyrights they'd previously registered through it.

When Jean and Julian considered their options, expanding their publishing company to include ASCAP publisher membership made sense for a number of reasons. First, Jean knew that as long as Max was in control of the ASCAP board, publisher interests in ASCAP would be protected, whereas the future as a BMI member was less clear. Second, the sheet music slump of 1947 caused an abrupt shift away from sheet music and toward records. Publishers could lose opportunities to sign songwriters who preferred affiliation with a particular rights organization if they were not affiliated with both ASCAP and BMI. Publishers were also at a disadvantage when promoting songs to record producers, who might see affiliation with one or the other organization as preferable.

Record producers were gaining importance in the industry. Individuals representing record companies—not publishers—now called the shots when it came to releasing a record, where the most profit could be made. Recognizing this, songwriters began to put more energy into promoting to artist & repertoire (A&R) men at record companies rather than publishers, partly because publishing could be used as a bargaining chip in these negotiations. Writers knew they could get a better publishing deal if a record contract was assured. They also knew that some A&R men favored certain publishers, because of quiet financial arrangements between them— kickbacks were everywhere. Like Cindy Walker, most songwriters now believed that leaving open the publishing placement of a song was in their best interest because the record deal might be contingent on placing their song with a specific publisher favored by the record producer. If

RCA wanted to record a song, but the songwriter was an ASCAP affiliate, Hill and Range (a BMI publisher), could not compete for the property.[4]

Finally, many ASCAP writers unwilling to change their affiliation to BMI on the basis of a popular experiment were coming to Hill and Range with their properties because Jean held a pivotal position between Broadway and the buckaroos. The perception—if not the truth—was that the Aberbach brothers exerted control over not only most of the writers of country and western music, but most of its performers as well. Mainstream ASCAP songwriters who wanted covers by the Sons of the Pioneers, the Riders of the Purple Sage, Ernest Tubb, or Merle Travis were compelled—by courtesy, if not by contract—to go through Jean and Julian Aberbach with their songs. Most of these songs ended up in Hill and Range's first ASCAP firm, Alamo Music.[5]

Alamo Music was originally set up July 28, 1947. Over the next few years, it accumulated ASCAP writers, some of whom had an interest in interacting with country and western writers and performers. For instance, they paired Jay Milton with Spade Cooley to create "Red Hair and Green Eyes". Other ASCAP writers signed were Irving Melsher and Lou Shelly, as well as Paul Secon and Remus Harris, who contributed songs like "Ham 'n' Eggs," "Sierra Sarah," and "Oh, How You Lied."[6]

Alamo, and other companies like it, challenged not only current conventions, but the very exclusionary foundations on which ASCAP had been built. Alamo was regarded with suspicion by ASCAP, fearing it would be used to pollute its catalog with low-quality music and subvert its membership to join BMI. ASCAP responded by increasing pressure on its songwriter members to remain loyal to the society. To broaden their popular music opportunities without jeopardizing their ASCAP affiliation, some ASCAP writers began cowriting for country and western performers and registering their works with BMI publishers under pseudonyms.

Rumbalero Music also appears to have been used as a BMI repository to accommodate moonlighting ASCAP writers operating under pseudonyms, or to manage split copyrights that resulted when an ASCAP songwriter openly collaborated with one from BMI. Rumbalero was set up on October 29, 1948, just after Jean left Chappell. Originally, the company was to be used to engage some of the best-known Cuban songwriters. Its headquarters were in the Radio Central building in Havana, under the management of Ernest Rocca, and a subsidiary partnership company was set up in New York with popular Cuban songwriter Osvaldo Farres. After discovering that most of their songwriters were six feet under, and Rocca was pilfering their royalties, Jean closed the Havana firm, transferring it into the Hill and Range conglomerate on April 21, 1950. Thereafter, it was used to house numerous country songs, some of which were written by Lefty Frizzell, Leon Payne, Jenny Lou Carson, and Don Robertson.

Some of the songs were of the split membership type. Others were BMI tunes for North America but were represented by ASCAP elsewhere.[7]

The renewal contract between Hill and Range Songs and BMI clearly places Rumbalero in a contingency category separate and apart from other Hill and Range BMI subsidiaries, suggesting that although it was a BMI corporation, it was somehow different. They may have used it to house their more difficult copyrights that would require greater care in accounting. For instance, it contained "I Really Don't Want to Know," which was cowritten by Howard Barnes and Don Robertson, the latter of whom was an ASCAP member.

Another famous song that skirted the rules was "Let Me Go, Lover," which was cowritten by Jenny Lou Carson (who was a BMI writer) and "Al Hill." The latter was a pseudonym for a well-known trio of ASCAP writers—Fred Wise, Kay Twomey, and Ben Weisman.[8]

Charlie Grean, Steve Sholes's studio assistant and a bass player who played on many Eddy Arnold and Hank Snow recordings, also was an ASCAP moonlighter. He recalls, "Yes, I published a couple of songs through [Hill and Range]. . . . I was with Steve [Sholes]—working for Steve, and he showed it to me [something that Jean had brought in] and said, there's something wrong with it . . . called "The Girl Who Invented Kissing." And I looked at it—I loved the idea. And I looked at it and said, I know what's wrong with it, and fixed it up. And Steve said, "Look, I'll get you a piece of it. We'll talk to the Aberbachs about it, find out who wrote it, and cut you in on it. It was a BMI song, and I was with ASCAP, [so they did not list my name]. I still got paid for it, though."[9]

Such backroom arrangements were rampant throughout the industry. As the bitter war over membership heated up between the ASCAP and BMI, conspicuous affiliation notices began to appear on published works. "There's No Wings on My Angel," for instance, cowritten in 1949 by Eddy Arnold and Irving Melsher, clearly lists the latter as an ASCAP affiliated writer, and a number of works by Cy Coben from that period also prominently bear the society's name.

With provisions in BMI's Hill and Range agreement already allowing Jean considerable latitude to represent Max in certain Chappell dealings on ASCAP administered properties, and having tested the waters with Alamo, Jean and Julian went on to create numerous other ASCAP companies including Shenandoah Music and Louisiana Music. Despite some reservations and restrictions, all these were acknowledged by BMI. The 1949 contract with BMI allowed the Aberbach brothers to operate ASCAP firms but prohibited them from promoting songs published through ASCAP. This restriction was ludicrous and unenforceable, especially where split copyrights were concerned, and the brothers tended to ignore it.[10]

Feeling comfortable with his BMI country and western portfolio, Jean started building up the ASCAP repertoire, hunting for copyrights of more mainstream music. In December 1952, an agreement was logged with the Theodore Presser Company for the representation of all John Phillip Sousa marching band songs in the French speaking territories, and for Italy and all its colonies. An arrangement was also made with the Lewis Music Publishing Company for most of the European territories. It included big-band works such as "Tuxedo Junction" (one of Glenn Miller's biggest hits) and "Jersey Bounce," made famous by Benny Goodman.[11]

By January 1953 Jean and Julian had transferred 100 percent of their personal interests in Alamo to Hill and Range Songs, Ltd. (U.K.), and were continuing to build their ASCAP repertoire.[12] As newcomer publishers dealing in new popular songs, Jean and Julian were caught in the same snare as all the young, progressive ASCAP members. Lacking ASCAP seniority, they were relegated to a minor position in the revenue distribution pecking order. Unwilling to suffer the status quo, Jean began looking for ways to boost their ASCAP standing. If he could not change the rules, was there a way to change the game?

Jean could not age his ASCAP companies into seniority. He could, however, populate them with seasoned copyrights that demanded revenue at the preferred seniority rate. But how? All the rights to proven standards were already tied up in airtight contracts with veteran publishing houses. What possible incentive could Hill and Range offer to cause the author-composers who owned these copyrights to break faith with their current publishers and switch to Hill and Range?

For many years there had been a common understanding that the original publisher had first preference on a copyright renewal for the publisher's share of the second twenty-eight year term of copyright protection. This was a gentleman's agreement ripe for challenge. When the first term of protection expired, all publishing rights reverted to the author-composer, affording them an opportunity to assign those rights anywhere they liked for the second term. If Jean could anticipate the copyright renewal, contact the author-composer, and convince him or her the Aberbach brothers could do a better job promoting their songs than their current publisher, Hill and Range might secure the contract for the second term.

As early as 1948, Jean was playing the copyright renewal game for Hill and Range. He acquired Herbert Happy Lawson's "Any Time" by courting and winning the rights to this song two years before it came due for renewal. Jean also obtained the premature renewal of "Wagon Wheels" by Billy Hill and Peter De Rose four years before it came due. This resulted in split copyright management, one half of the publishers share administered by Hill and Range (a BMI affiliate) and the other half by ASCAP, much to the dismay of ASCAP affiliated Shapiro, Bernstein, & Company—the original copyright owner who had published it exclusively since 1934.[13]

Early success with this copyright renewal strategy caused the Aberbach brothers to accelerate their efforts to acquire the second terms of seasoned copyrights. Doing so ensured a preferential rate through ASCAP that far exceeded what they could hope to obtain by gambling all their investments on promising new songs, no matter how successful those might turn out to be. But it was difficult work. Much arduous research was involved. You had to stay on top of which copyrights were coming due and then carefully contact the writer-composer who might or might not be open to the opportunity. In the meantime, you risked the possibility of alienating fellow publishers who expected the second term to automatically go to them. There was also never any guarantee that the owner would sway your way, even if you offered twice the advance they knew they could get from their current publisher. Songwriters were unpredictable that way, often sacrificing a better business deal to stay with the devil they knew.

Building an ASCAP revenue stream using this method was bound to be a long and arduous process, and while some publishers considered the risk-to-reward ratio acceptable, Jean Aberbach did not. It was not the Aberbach brothers' style to claw their way to the top, when a little thought and cleverness would transport them there in the blink of an eye. Jean went fishing for a pregnant opportunity, which ultimately revealed itself in the form of an ASCAP firm called Ross Jungnickel.

The Ross Jungnickel catalog was one of the oldest and most respected of the ASCAP firms. Its founder was the noted penman of "Just a Little Street Where Old Friends Meet," a homey little song that gained popularity in 1933. Jungnickel's catalog of Depression-era standards had been acquired by Lee Eastman, an outstanding music business attorney who would later become the father-in-law of Beatle Paul McCartney. During the 1950s, he represented the Current Writers Group and introduced actions that successfully limited ASCAP's monopolistic tendencies.[14]

Jean was attracted to Eastman's willingness to challenge ASCAP's status quo. He proposed a deal that would exploit a flaw in the ASCAP distribution rules, benefiting himself and Eastman handsomely, while also supporting Eastman's crusade to get ASCAP to change its unfair policies. By December 1952 all necessary arrangements were in place.[15] For a price, Eastman transferred all the seasoned copyrights out of the Ross Jungnickel firm, most probably to another company he owned of equal ASCAP standing. He then sold the shell company of Ross Jungnickel to Jean Aberbach. In this way, Eastman made money in the sale, without sacrificing the revenue standing of the Jungnickel copyrights in ASCAP, and Jean acquired a company—with no contents or copyright value whatsoever—except that it held a seniority position in ASCAP! Now all he and Julian had to do was begin populating this firm with acquired works that would automatically benefit from being a part of an ASCAP catalog that enjoyed seniority standing![16]

Jean and Julian continued enhancing their ASCAP position by obtaining partial ownership in respected catalogs. They wrested free the renewal rights from original publishers through back-door negotiations with the writer-composers or with families who inherited their legacy. While they were not the only publishers doing this, it was their remarkable effectiveness in sealing deals that most infuriated their fellow publishers. Jean and Julian were successful because they knew the system, worked the system, and left no stone unturned.[17] They looked in places ignored by less imaginative and thorough publishers.

One such place was Warner Music, which had been accumulating valuable music publishing catalogs for several decades to build a music library for Warner Brothers films. It bought Max's Harms catalog as well as his valuable De Sylva, Brown & Henderson catalog. In May 1930, the Justice Department determined Warner had grown too powerful and filed an antitrust action that would eventually unravel initiatives like Warner's that sought to control the means of creation, production, and distribution of music across multiple media markets. At the same time Warner was also burdened by a stockholder action prompted by that year's unexpected $8 million loss in revenue. It was caused by the Warner brothers themselves, who were caught with their hands in the cookie jar—pocketing $7 million in insider trading deals and passing this amount on, plus an additional $1 million in losses, to Warner stockholders.[18] These pressures, along with spiraling music production costs and a weak economy caused them to turn the catalogs back over to Max Dreyfus.

Buddy De Sylva, Lew Brown, and Ray Henderson were among the talents clamoring for fairness in ASCAP distributions. They had enjoyed a sensational rise to popularity, beginning with an unexpected hit for Al Jolson in *The Singing Fool* called "Sonny Boy" that sold over a million sheet music copies. By New Year's Day, 1929, they had four comedies and a musical revue running on Broadway. They cowrote a stunning climax for the show *Birth of the Blues,* in which W. C. Handy's blues served as counterpoint to Robert Schumann's classical works, the cacophony eventually resolving into Gershwin's "Rhapsody in Blue." Shortly thereafter, they were whisked to Hollywood under exclusive contract with a film company. They quickly turned out four hits for Fox's early talkie, *Sunny Side Up.*[19] These remarkable successes impelled Warner Brothers to acquire their catalog, and it is what kept Max as Warner's consultant, keenly focused on the caretaking of their copyrights. These were moneymakers that would continue accruing in value every year that passed. The songs could be repackaged for nostalgia albums. They were suitable for television and radio commercials, and could also set the tone for historical films. These were keepers.

Not long after the songwriting team disbanded, De Sylva abandoned lyric writing for a career in film production. He quickly became a powerhouse in Hollywood film as an executive film producer for Paramount. Never fully abandoning his musical roots, he applied some of the same promotional logic he'd learned in the music business to enhance his films. For instance, he introduced the notion that getting leading actors and singing stars to plug new films on late night television a few weeks before a release could build significant excitement for a film.

De Sylva never missed a good opportunity. By 1942 he was partnering with Johnny Mercer and Glenn Wallichs in a new label called Capitol Records. It would forge the path for the new up and coming independent record companies that would service niche markets. De Sylva provided executive guidance and bankrolled the venture to the tune of $25,000. Under his direction, Capitol Records became the first label to regularly service DJs with free promotional records, giving the fledgling company the edge it needed to compete against the giant record companies who limited their free promos to print reviewers. Under Johnny Mercer's creative direction, Capitol debuted with two respectable releases, Mercer's "Strip Polka" and Ella Mae Morse's "Cow Cow Boogie." By 1946 Capitol was dipping into the Aberbach catalogs to produce Tex Williams's "Smoke, Smoke, Smoke That Cigarette," along with two other big hits, a parody torch song called "Tim-Tay-Shun," and the black saloon-hall-inspired "Hurry on Down."[20]

Although De Sylva was no longer writing lyrics for songs, his copyrights remained popular over time, gaining value. These were the kind of copyrights Jean needed for his new ASCAP company, highly valued American standards that had been around for decades. De Sylva had collaborated with almost every important composer, performer, and dramatist of his time to create some of the most valuable American standards of all time. Aside from his collaborations with Brown and Henderson, his earliest works included collaborations with George Gershwin for "Stairway to Paradise," the lyrics for George White's long-running *Scandals,* and for Blossom Seeley's signature song "Somebody Loves Me" (with Ballard MacDonald and George Gershwin). He worked with Irving Caesar on "The Yankee Doodle Blues," with Jerome Kern for "Look for the Silver Lining" (from Kern's *Sally*), with Cole Porter (collaborating with Herbert Fields on the book for *Du Barry Was a Lady*), and with Victor Herbert for "A Kiss in the Dark."

De Sylva also had many smash hits with Al Jolson. Aside from "Sonny Boy," he was responsible for "Yoo Hoo" (with Jolson), "It All Depends on You" from the 1925 show *Big Boy,* and "California, Here I Come" (with Jolson and Joseph Meyer) and wrote "By the Honeysuckle Vine" and "Chloe" for the 1918 *Sinbad.* (While Jolson introduced "If You Knew Susie" in *Big Boy,* it only became a smash hit when sung by Eddie Cantor.)

De Sylva wrote the 1939 Academy Award nominee "Wishing," which was introduced by Irene Dunne in the film *Love Affair,* and "April Showers" (with Lewis Silvers, made famous by Louis Armstrong). Collaborations with Brown and Henderson from their many stage works yielded some of the era's most upbeat, clever, and memorable tunes, including "The Varsity Drag" and "The Best Things in Life Are Free" (1927), "Button Up Your Overcoat" (1927), and "You're the Cream in My Coffee" (1928). Kidnapped by Hollywood, the trio continued turning out hit tunes, this time for film rather than stage musicals. Some of their best-known works are "Keep Your Sunny Side Up," "If I Had a Talking Picture of You," and "I'm a Dreamer." These remain among America's most loved standards.[21]

Capturing any of these songs for the Jungnickel catalog would reap enormous benefits for Hill and Range and reinforce its seniority position in ASCAP. Sadly, by the time Jean turned his attention to the catalog, De Sylva was nowhere to be found. He had died prematurely in 1950 at the relatively young age of fifty-five. When the first twenty-eight year term in his copyrights expired, his widow authorized that Chappell Music, the original publisher, could renew for the second term.

Game over? Not so fast. Rumor had it that B. G. De Sylva had had a tryst at one time with one Marie Ballentine. Marie became pregnant, and while it was never clear whether the boy was his or some errant sailor's, De Sylva resolved to do the "right thing" and claimed paternity, filing papers in the local court acknowledging that the boy was his. This fact was conveniently buried at the time of the estate settlement, but somehow Jean got wind of it and posed the question to his attorney, "Does the kid have any rights?"[22]

Before answering, Milton Rudin set off to research the problem, taking the same approach as he had when representing Acuff-Rose against Hill and Range in the "Tennessee Waltz" case: *when in doubt, read the statutes.* What constitutes the law often morphs over time into interpretations that suit the prevailing culture. It was to Jean's benefit that Rudin was not a specialist in music publishing—he simply read the words. Summarized, the statute read that there would be a right of renewal in the twenty-eighth year of the original copyright that could be claimed by the author, if living; if the author be not living, then by the widow, widower, or children; if there be no widow, widower, or children, then by the author's executor; and in the absence of a will, to the author's next of kin.

By the time Jean got to it, the child's claim had already been tried and rejected in the Southern District Court. Apparently the court acknowledged that there was a son, but held that he wasn't entitled to a share, taking the prevailing view that De Sylva's surviving widow, Marie, was not required to share it with this illegitimate child.

That didn't sit right with Rudin. It came down to the grammatical structure of the sentence, which could be interpreted in more than one way. And the way most people were interpreting it made assumptions that simply weren't in the spirit of the clause, and Rudin felt he could prove it. He brought this opinion back to Jean and Julian, who thought that it was worth a shot. They recognized that this was not a simple court case. They would be appealing to the Supreme Court of the United States in Washington, D.C., but they believed they had a chance. Jean contacted Marie Ballentine and gained her consent to go forward on behalf of her son.

Indeed, on August 25, 1955, the Ninth Circuit Court came down entirely in their favor, reversing the earlier decision. In this new, radical interpretation, the court held that the rights of a child could stand independent of the presence of a widow or widower. Therefore, Marie De Sylva was obliged to share her husband's estate with Stephen Ballentine, despite the fact that Marie Ballentine could not rightfully be called a widow since she and De Sylva had never married. This was a complete shock to the publishing industry. It not only proved that copyright ownership could be won on the basis of questionable paternity, but the ruling had broader implications. It opened the floodgates for any child of any deceased writer to seek a share in the second renewal period, whether the surviving parent welcomed it or not. People like Max feared the worst, and saw hoards of bastards and malcontents coming out of the woodwork. Such entanglements would create an administrative nightmare![23]

Most music publishers watched in awe as the Aberbach brothers challenged and reinterpreted copyright law, earning them the right to sit among the ASCAP privileged. Even though Jean had simply used the law to their advantage, the perception was that they had stretched the law to fit their motives. Even those who believed this were not prepared for what came next.

A new challenge presented itself in the form of another "roses" song. "Moonlight and Roses Bring Mem'ries of You," was written by Tin Pan Alley tunesmiths Ben Black and Neil Moret, the latter name a pseudonym of ragtime songwriter Charles N. Daniels during the 1920s. It was a popular adaptation of the classical organ piece by Edwin H. Lemare called "Andantino in D-Flat." This case turned out to be even more challenging than De Sylva's because not only was there no widow, there were no children either!

Ben Black had died a bachelor before the second renewal period. Prior to this, however, the original publisher, Mills Music, confirmed a claim on the copyright by getting Black to sign over his second term well in advance of the onset of the second period. Hill and Range attorney Ben Starr recognized a problem. A signed statement was valid only if the author were living at the time the rights vested. If the author was not living, then the assignment was null and void, and the statutory scheme applied instead.

When the renewal period came up, Mills Music assumed it owned the next twenty-eight years on the basis of the agreement but never confirmed it with Black's survivors. Ben Black's three brothers had distributed all other parts of his estate to his nieces and nephews but had not yet distributed any of the copyrights. There was the loophole. Jean and Julian had already acquired Neil Moret's interest, and was administering it through the Charles N. Daniels company they had acquired. The Black brothers were happy to reopen the estate and assign Ben Black's interest to his nieces and nephews, who in turn made a deal with the Aberbachs for the second twenty-eight year term of copyright protection. In this way, Jean added Ben Black's half of "Moonlight and Roses Bring Mem'ries of You" to the Charles N. Daniels catalog operating under the Hill and Range umbrella, in exchange for a fee and the promise of continuing royalties. They no longer shared management with Mills music, but they controlled 100 percent of the publisher's share, both the Neil Moret and Ben Black interest.[24]

Capturing the De Sylva catalog was masterful, and adding the enduring copyright "Moonlight and Roses" to their Ross Jungnickel publishing company was even more clever. They acquired other senior works as well, including those of Ernest R. Ball, best known as coauthor of the familiar early twentieth century ballad "When Irish Eyes Are Smiling," ultimately building out the Jungnickel catalog with seasoned moneymakers.

The ASCAP board was thoroughly irritated.[25] Until they changed their policies, ASCAP would get nothing but grief from Jean Aberbach. He had found a legitimate way to obtain seniority in the organization by using creative work-arounds to capture and populate a shell company that already held seniority status, with some of American's favorite standards, by finding loopholes not only in ASCAP policies—but in U.S. copyright law itself. At the same time as advancing his own aims, Jean helped further the progressive efforts of people like Lee Eastman, who were also challenging the ASCAP board to treat all its members fairly. Even publisher colleagues who suffered by his success could not help but admire Jean for his clear-sighted cleverness.

One story Jean liked to tell was about a song plugger he knew while at Chappell Music. His name was Johnny Taps, and he worked for a competing company called Shapiro, Bernstein. Like Jean, he would go to the bandleaders with song drafts, but he had an annoying habit of holding people by the lapel while he was talking to them to make them listen. Particularly bothered by this, one bandleader in New York got an idea and had two suits made—one that was properly tailored, and the other which was not. During a rehearsal, Taps grabbed the bandleader by the lapel to get his attention. When the bandleader took one step back, not only did the lapel tear off, but the entire sleeve as well! "I'll never, ever play any of your songs again!" shouted the bandleader at the stunned song plugger. Apparently, this cured Johnny Taps of this habit forever and he was never again seen grabbing at people's clothing.[26]

For years, ASCAP had been grabbing publishers and songwriters by their lapels and force marching them down a road that had been paved with ASCAP rules. They prevented new publishers from obtaining their fair share of the ASCAP royalty pool because of seniority rules, discouraged songwriters from writing nontraditional songs or collaborating with non-ASCAP songwriters, discouraged the emergence of new media opportunities such as radio, and affected the ability of some writers and publishers to make a living in their chosen profession. Focused on maintaining the status quo, rather than changing with the times, its leadership felt it had the power to push, pull, and shove its membership as it pleased. This benefited only a few of its senior members, but no one knew exactly what could be done about it. Jean did. *He had an extra suit made.*

The Aberbach brothers took their place among the elite ranks of the senior ASCAP publishers by beating ASCAP at its own game. The Aberbach brothers deliberately paired ASCAP writers with those of BMI to produce popular hits, created ASCAP companies so ASCAP writers could be paid, and actively promoted their songs through new media such as radio. They also challenged and changed U.S. copyright law, clarifying statutes that ensured more fairness in estate settlements. None of these, however, were magnanimous gestures. Jean was a businessman and he had a plan. That plan was to achieve seniority status in ASCAP so the Aberbach brothers would obtain the highest level of distribution possible from ASCAP. All the activities—even the two Supreme Court cases—directly served that goal.

By acquiring and populating the shell of the Jungnickel company with copyrights from respected early twentieth-century songwriters Ben Black and Buddy De Sylva, Jean had built the false sleeve of their second, poorly tailored suit. The next time ASCAP began tugging on his lapel, all he had to do to expose their hypocrisy was to simply take one step back. ASCAP's stunned leadership was left holding the sleeve. They could not prevent Jean and Julian from taking their place alongside the senior ASCAP publishers and sharing in the richer distribution pot, because they now had a company with repertoire that met the seniority rules. It took two Supreme Court cases, but Jean finally beat ASCAP at its own game. The society was ultimately forced to reform its distribution scheme, not because it was fundamentally unfair to younger publishers and songwriters, but because Jean had proven it could be defeated.[27]

CHAPTER 17

Mr. Brums

The rumpled, blustering, cigar-puffing Tom Parker had figured prominently in their business over the past five years. Their arrangement with Eddy Arnold had created a working relationship between them, and while Parker could be difficult, Jean had found the relationship productive and mutually beneficial. Parker was a hard worker, something Jean could appreciate. He held up his end of the bargain, promoting the artist to ever greater career heights, along with the many Hill and Range songs they funneled his way. All parties got what they wanted. Arnold got great tunes from Hill and Range and reciprocated by sending on good tunes that came his way to Hill and Range; Parker got great material for his artist's vocal talent and apparently participated in the publisher's profit share, and Jean had a direct channel to the top crossover singing star of the time. Add Steve Sholes into the mix, and you had a pretty complete package—booking, tour promotion, publishing, artist management, recording, and distribution. It was the perfect recipe for success—for a while.

Parker's flamboyant style made a sizable and lasting impression on Nashville, and not everyone liked it. To this day, he is rarely described in anything but the superlative—the best, the crudest, the loudest, most inflexible, the cheapest, toughest, most egotistical—and most effective—popular music promoter the world has ever known. In the space of only three years, he had transformed the "Tennessee plowboy" into a country crossover superstar. On the strength of Arnold's five Hill and Range hits in 1948, Parker convinced him to leave his comfortable spot on the *Grand Ole Opry*. Within two years Parker had arranged movie deals, created a relationship with top talent agency William Morris, booked him on the popular Milton Berle television show *Variety,* and arranged for personal appearances in Las Vegas. Even those who did not like Parker had to respect what he had managed to accomplish for the young artist he had taken under his wing.[1]

Arnold enjoyed several years of superstardom while working with Parker, but it came with a steep price. Despite these achievements, any list of Parker's personal flaws still falls short in depicting the megalomania that drove the man to control almost every aspect of his artist's career and life. After working together for almost a decade, Arnold had had enough of Parker's overbearing management style, embarrassing promotional displays, and petty greediness. There were also insufferable intrusions into his personal life that sometimes had Parker, his wife, and their accompanying entourage invading the small Arnold home for extended stays. Each new encounter simply added to Arnold's discontent. In August 1953, Arnold formally terminated the relationship.[2]

The pivotal blowup took place in May 1953 at the Sahara Hotel in Las Vegas during Arnold's two-week engagement there. Parker was moonlighting on Arnold's dime—booking other competing artists on the sly while Arnold was picking up the expense tab. Arnold accidentally took a call meant for Parker's assistant, Tom Diskin, which accidentally informed him the Colonel was booking Hank Snow on the side. This infuriated Arnold who was paying Parker an exorbitant 25 percent of his earnings, reasonably expecting it bought him the exclusivity of Parker's services in return. This was the last straw in a series of interpersonal problems between the men that brought the relationship to a close. Discovering that he was secretly promoting Hank Snow, the up and coming Opry star who was directly competing with Arnold for top chart spots—sealed the breach between them.[3]

How Parker became engaged with Snow is no mystery. By this time, Snow was already under exclusive contract with Hill and Range, and he had a regular spot on the Opry and several chart-topping hits to his credit. Originally from Nova Scotia, Canada, Clarence Eugene Snow got his musical inspiration from his mother, a talented pianist who played for silent movies. She was a fan of country music's first real star, Vernon Dalhart, and expanded Snow's musical horizons

"Colonel" Tom
Parker. Courtesy of
Susan Aberbach.

by presenting him with a mail-order guitar that included a fifty-two-week lesson plan. With these implements, Hank's musical tinkering began. When his
mother interrupted his practicing with a record of a new singing star, Jimmie
Rodgers, Hank resolved to make a career in music his lifetime pursuit.[4]

The goal would be delayed by several years. His parents separated, and the
children were dispersed, with Hank ending up with his grandparents. Not willing to be away from his mother, he ran away to join her, only to be forced to flee
from home at the age of twelve to escape a cruel and abusive stepfather. Hank
took refuge at sea, working for four years as a cabin boy. Now a young, worldly
man of sixteen, he was ready to launch his career. As with many young, hopeful
male singers of his time, he emulated his idol Jimmie Rodgers, perfecting his
"blue yodeling" technique, which quickly earned him the moniker of "Canada's
Yodeling Ranger."[5] He landed a radio show in Halifax on CHNS and obtained
a record contract with RCA Record's Canadian division in 1936.

After marrying that same year, Hank and his wife Min struggled to make
ends meet. Min had absolute faith in Hank and supported her husband by
designing his outfits, adding a modest bit of embellishment to his workday
pants or a colorful bandana to his costume. She often did advance promotion

work—arranging the halls, putting up posters and selling tickets to Hank's little shows. Through radio, live performances, and record promotions, his popularity in Canada grew. His recordings found their way to record shops as far away as Europe. By this time, his voice had changed, deepening to a rich, full baritone that ended his yodeling career. Now billed as "Canada's Singing Ranger," Hank's own style began to coalesce along with his plans for career success. He would not feel truly successful until he gained the stamp of approval from the country that had spawned his idol, Jimmie Rodgers.

Snow's recordings and reputation were beginning to gain notice among country music fans and aficionados in the United States. One such fan and promoter, Jack Howard, arranged for a two-week engagement in Philadelphia during 1944, also introducing him to Big Slim, "The Lone Cowboy," a popular entertainer on WWVA in Wheeling, West Virginia. At Slim's invitation, Snow returned with his family later that year, settling in Wheeling to host two shows a day at the radio station.

But Snow craved the professional success that only Hollywood had to offer at that time. On a scouting trip there, he became friendly with Spade Cooley and did a guest spot on his weekly show on the Santa Monica pier. Happy Perryman extended the same courtesy during his show at the Painted Post. Snow also met several of the Sons of the Pioneers including Tim Spencer (all of whom were, coincidentally, in the process of being engaged by Hill and Range), and rubbed elbows with stars including Roy Rogers, Jane Powell, and Lon Chaney. Everything seemed to be encouraging him to return to California with his family.

While in Wheeling, Big Slim had taught Snow stunt riding. Snow outfitted his newly acquired horse, Shawnee, in silver-studded regalia, bought a trailer, and after an elaborate road show in Canada with Big Slim was complete, loaded up the family and headed west. He was never quite sure why he did it. He had starved in Philadelphia but had made good progress in Wheeling and it seemed he had good prospects at making a fair living on the East Coast, where fans appreciated him. He knew his diminutive stature and unexceptional looks placed him low on the list of prospective western film talent. Nevertheless, Snow was drawn to Los Angeles, the place where western music was thriving, and he was determined to be a part of it.

Once there, he engaged a good promoter who arranged a series of dates through the Pacific Northwest states, but Hank was bled dry for promotional money. The tour dates brought a fair wage, but between the tour costs and promotional expenses he returned to Los Angeles nearly broke.

He needed money and so he began making the rounds of the publishing houses in search of a deal offering a royalty advance. His first stop was Ralph Peer's Southern Music, on Hollywood Boulevard, but the manager there reported that the $300 advance he sought would need to be cleared through the

New York Office, which could take days or weeks—if it could be arranged at all. Discouraged, he remembered Hill and Range. He wasn't sure of the address, but confirmed it with a friend and pulled his Cadillac up in front of the small office then on Melrose, his small frame, fancy cowboy clothes, and horse trailer distracting Julian's attention from his meeting with Spade Cooley.

When Julian finished his conference with Cooley, he invited the young man in. Snow introduced himself and explained his serious situation to this total stranger. "Now my RCA Victor records are not selling here now, but by all appearances they are going to sell here," began Snow awkwardly. "What I am trying to say, is that I really am desperate, and I would surely appreciate it if you could see your way clear to let me have $300."

Julian didn't know anything about the artist and insisted on first listening to a tape of his music. Convinced the artist had merit, he then consulted on the phone with Jean who blessed the deal. "Well, how about $1,000?" Julian queried.

"God! I almost dropped dead!" Snow recalls. "And I said, 'Well, you don't know what you are doing for me.' They didn't ask me to sign . . . anything."

It is plausible that no signatures were traded during their first meeting. Contracts between reputable men were sometimes initially sealed by a handshake, and Snow was clearly not some kid off the streets. He came with plenty of respectable show and tell—tour fliers, proof of recordings in the form of tapes, radio posters, Canadian record reviews—as well as high-level references. These included Hugh Joseph, his Canadian RCA producer, the station manager of WWVA, and Ernest Tubb, who had become his longtime pen pal earlier in the 1940s over a shared enthusiasm for Jimmie Rodgers.

Jean was probably no more familiar than his brother with Snow's music either, but he knew they were not making a frivolous business decision. Echoing the Max Dreyfus style, he knew that signing a new, untried songwriter was a serious risk, but where a proven artist came across their path, they should jump on it. Snow had a strong track record and already had discs ready to move in the United States. Approving the immediate advance was a way of assuring that the artist would look no further for U.S. publishing representation. It bound them to him until the appropriate papers could be drawn up. Snow returned a few weeks after that first meeting with Julian to sign an exclusive songwriting contract with Hill and Range beginning in 1948. The Aberbachs captured all his popular Canadian songs for the U.S. market.[6] Only then did Snow begin making a real dent in the U.S. market.

Having invested advance sums to obtain exclusive publishing representation for Snow's Canadian hits, Hill and Range stood to gain the most by the distribution of Snow's records in the States and getting Sholes to record new discs by the artist. Now backed by the most powerful country and western publishing firm, Sholes seemed much more willing to put attention to the artist, a circum-

Julian Aberbach, Hank Snow, and Jean Aberbach. Courtesy of Susan Aberbach.

stance strongly reminiscent of Steve Sholes's arrangement with Jean over Chet Atkins. Sholes agreed to proceed with Snow's first U.S. session probably based on a combination factors: Snow's good showing of "Brand on My Heart" on the KRLD playlist; the successful sales of Canadian releases in that market; his successful guest spot on Ernest Tubb's Fort Worth Northside Coliseum show on February 2, 1949; and his new publishing association with Hill and Range. A recording session was set for March 1949, which yielded a Hill and Range hit—"Marriage Vow," a Jenny Lou Carson song that appeared on the flip side of Snow's own song "(I Wished upon) My Little Golden Horseshoe."[7]

Shortly after Snow arrived in Dallas in late 1948, he received an enticing offer to participate in a show in Fort Worth, Texas, called the Cowtown Jamboree, scheduled for February 2, 1949. Snow jumped at the chance to finally meet his fellow Jimmie Rodgers enthusiast Ernest Tubb, who would be headlining the show. The spot bolstered Snow's growing Texas reputation, Tubb further adding steam to his career later that year by making a hit of Snow's "My Filipino Rose," now also being promoted by Hill and Range.[8]

Eventually Tubb convinced Jim Denny to give Snow a spot on the *Grand Ole Opry*. He appeared January 7, 1950, but suffered only lukewarm reception on the show until his signature song, "I'm Movin' On," was recorded on March 28, 1950, hitting the charts on July 1. It won him a permanent spot at the *Grand Ole Opry* and in the hearts of country music fans. Snow's star was quickly rising. Aside from "I'm Movin' On," that session included two songs from Jean's New York songwriting protégés, Jack Rollins, Steve Nelson, and Ed Nelson Jr.: "With This Ring I Thee Wed" and "Paving the Highway with Tears."[9]

The *Grand Ole Opry* was the premier vehicle for keeping a country artist alive in the minds of the record-buying public, but it did not pay well. Artists supplemented their income by participating in traveling shows sponsored by WSM radio station. Snow participated in many of these tours, where he shared the bill with other Opry luminaries, including Hank Williams.

Most Opry artists, however, did not rely exclusively on these tours, and worked with booking agents to fill in the dates between tours. Because of this, it would not have been at all unusual for Snow or his booking agent to have accepted occasional opportunities that came through Tom Parker to fill in the date gaps left by the Opry tours.

Parker's booking agency was Jamboree Attractions. The company was started by Tom Diskin in Chicago. Diskin was already working for Parker, assisting in road management for Eddy Arnold. It was the clandestine vehicle Parker used to expand his opportunities on the sly beginning as early as 1952 while he was exclusively managing Eddy Arnold. Tom Diskin was the perfect shill for this game. Already assisting Parker in Arnold road shows, ultimately he was relegated for his entire career to a category best described as "secretary" to the Colonel. He was quiet, loyal, and likable. He was the type of person more comfortable taking rather than giving direction, and someone the abrasive Parker could trust to be a dutiful and effective middleman. He was also someone not likely to buck the tide, rock the boat, or otherwise play any kind of a divisive role in their work, at least none that was visible to outsiders. Parker used Diskin to shield him from potentially uncomfortable encounters with Arnold, funneling business through him, while in fact managing these arrangements at an arm's length. Snow was one of those artists Parker was booking on the side while still working for Arnold.[10]

By the time of their breakup in 1953, Parker and Arnold had already agreed to begin scaling back their relationship anyway, working out an amicable separation agreement that would have kept Parker booking dates for Arnold, but no longer managing his career.[11] Arnold wanted to slow down his career and pursue other opportunities, and Parker knew that meant less money in the long run. Parker had signed his new, young protégé Tommy Sands to Jamboree Attractions in 1952 as a way of getting around the exclusivity he supposedly had with Arnold. To capitalize on his relationship with Arnold while he still had it, Parker injected Sands into Arnold's tours whenever possible.

It was inevitable that Parker's sideline business dealings would eventually become visible to Arnold. Most accounts say that Arnold's embarrassing termination of him in 1953 took Parker by complete surprise.[12] On the other hand, Parker—always thinking two steps ahead—was also prone to inviting the future from time to time when it served his best interests. This might have been one of those times, since in the end he turned out to be completely prepared for the event.

Jean had run across characters like the Parker before—smart, resourceful people who sometimes went to extremes to arrange the world to their best advantage. He met one of them years ago in Paris during the time he was working for Campbell, Connelly and he recorded the encounter in his memoir sketches:

There are a lot of charming swindlers in this world. One can meet those kinds of people every day. There are some that can be useful and, therefore, some of whom you will willingly forgive. And that is why you have to be aware your whole lifetime, to recognize who you can trust and who you cannot. One morning, when I was working in Paris, a man named Mr. Brums arrived at my place of work and asked to speak with me. I sensed that this encounter would be extraordinary and invited him in. Mr. Brums entered holding a huge cigar in his hand which covered him in a thick cloud of smoke. "Why have you come to see me? I asked. "Mr. Aberbach," he replied. "I have come to make a rich man out of you!" "That is great!" I replied. "That is something you like to hear when you are only 19 years old! So tell me . . . how will you do it?" "It is very simple," he began. "I will die, and you will be the one to inherit all my assets! Look at my cigar," Mr. Brums said. "If a doctor sees a man who smokes such cigars in such amounts he will never examine the lungs and therefore never find out that I am suffering from terminal and rampant tuberculosis, which will take me to my grave within half a year." "That is very interesting," I said. "But please explain to me why you would want me for this honor?" "The money will come from insurance," he said. "I will take out an insurance policy naming you as beneficiary. Of course, you must pay me about a quarter of this insurance premium as an advance, because unlike me, you can wait for the money." "That's fair!" I said. "But why do you want money from me? What would you do with it?" "I am not looking for profit," he said. "Some will cover my expenses while I travel to the lung sanitarium in Davos." "You are a fraud!" I replied. "Why would a man dying of a terminal illness choose to spend the last of his time and money on a hospital that could not possibly make him well! You only want to cheat people! I don't ever want to see you here again!" So he left. The very next day, I was walking down the Champs-Élysées. I could hardly believe it, there was Brums! He had crutches, and was wearing a thick plaster cast down one leg from his hip to his toe. "Mr. Brums!" I asked. "What happened to you?" "Well," he began slowly, "Yesterday, when I left the publishing house, I went to the Folies Bergères. There I patiently waited for a Rolls-Royce to drive by—a rich one that had not one, but two chauffeurs. And when the car went by, I put one of my feet under the wheel. And, well, you can see the result!" he said, pitifully. "But what you cannot see is the lifetime of money I will get from this wealthy person when the lawsuit is settled!" Brums continued, ecstatic. "This thing turned out even better than the insurance scam, don't you think!?"[13]

Brums was a charming swindler who profited through creative design. Parker was cast in the same mold. He may not have deliberately stuck his foot under the limo, but when Arnold terminated his contract, Parker was prepared. He ambled back, sporting a smoldering cigar and an insurance policy under his arm that was grounds for a lucrative lawsuit. The contract he presented to Arnold's counselor Bill Carpenter was the seven-year arrangement Parker had made with RCA Victor that provided the artist with five cents per record and guaranteed that no artist on the label would be paid more than Arnold. There was only one problem: This contact was made between RCA and Tom Parker, not between RCA and Eddy Arnold. This meant that Parker, not Arnold, had a contract for recording with RCA and if Arnold wanted that contract to be turned over to him, it would cost money. When Parker suggested a settlement of $50,000 up front to buy him out of the contract and his 25 percent revenue stake, Arnold had no choice but to take it to make sure he would not be involved with the Colonel ever again, except at his own choosing.

Parker's cleverness yielded some nice seed capital to pursue other opportunities but things did not go quite as smoothly as he had planned. Jamboree Attractions had sunk considerable investment during 1954 into Tommy Sands, but no one was biting. The Parker-Arnold split had destabilized the productive Parker-Aberbach-Sholes triumvirate, but it had not affected Arnold's relationship with the Aberbachs or with his record producer, Steve Sholes. With Arnold now firmly in Steve Sholes's pocket, it was payback time for the Colonel, who was treated, as Gabe Tucker (another talent manager) recalls, "like a flea-bitten alley dog."[14] Jean feared that the longer the Colonel was bereft of focus, the more probable it was that their unpredictable associate would go off in some troublesome, complicating direction.

Relief may have come in the form of an RCA Victor Country Caravan Tour that was due on the road in late 1954. The caravan was going to showcase plenty of Hill and Range songs and artists, headlining Hank Snow. Parker managed to take over the entire tour management and $50,000 promotional budget from its originator Bob McCluskey, then head of RCA country and western promotional division. Shortly after the tour was concluded, Hank Snow began looking for a personal manager and Parker offered his services.[15]

Snow's name alone should have sufficed as his contribution to the venture, but the Colonel had a knack for extracting cash from any situation. When he saw an easy mark, he latched on. Cash poor by the end of 1954, Parker convinced Snow to fork over start-up cash to get their relationship going, formalizing an exclusive representation contract that would kick off on January 1, 1955. But Parker needed even more money. In December 1954 he suggested Snow also assume a 50 percent stake in Jamboree Attractions, whose value was then estimated at $5,000 (approximately $33,000 in today's money). After settling with Diskin over his 25 percent share, Hank Snow (then among country music's hottest singing stars) bought the privilege of lending his name, his reputation, his talent and goodwill, and his bank account to Tom Parker's reorganized booking company, Hank Snow Enterprises-Jamboree Attractions.[16] It was Mr. Brums incarnate! Parker had managed to turn his luck around by latching onto the right limousine. Hank Snow's reputation and checkbook was exactly what the Colonel needed for getting back in the game.

CHAPTER 18

Diamond in the Rough

J ean learned at a very early age that value could be found by keeping your eyes open and your wits about you. Among the millions of grains of sand beneath your feet, a diamond could be hiding. If he did not find it himself, he would be satisfied with a percentage if someone else did. After all, they had done well enough with Eddy Arnold.

Unfortunately, that train ride had come to an end. Tom Parker had tried to make Eddy Arnold into his lifetime meal ticket but had failed because Arnold—neither the person nor the artist—would not be kept perpetually immature. Arnold had been a gift of happenstance. Young and hungry, he had been the right blend of ambition, smarts, focus, persistence, and talent. Arnold always knew what he wanted, what he was best at doing, and what was best done by somebody else. Parker understood that finding another artist as talented and easygoing as Arnold would take luck and patience. Most other artists willing to submit to his style of management would rarely be as smart and well balanced. Most would take real work.

Hank Williams was a textbook example of a difficult artist. During his short career spanning only a few years, Williams had been about the only thing that gave Jean a run for his money where Acuff-Rose publishing was concerned. Fred Rose had been grooming this artist since late 1946, even though Williams was, in every way, a musical anachronism. He represented the genuine, raw, unglamorous hillbilly music of yesteryear. Rose had trouble marketing the artist at first, because Williams was simply not progressive enough for an urban market moving swiftly toward country-pop crossover. Rose, however, had little choice. As more and more artists defected to Hill and Range, and the sales of Roy Acuff and the remaining Acuff-Rose artists trailed off, Rose put the bulk of his attention on Williams. After a few surprising hits it became clear that Williams's music tapped a latent nostalgia in the hearts of rural country fans who yearned for simplicity and homespun values after the turbulent war years.

"Move It on Over" was Williams's first hit, entering the *Billboard* charts in August 1947—and not a moment too soon. Acuff-Rose's top ten activity on the *Billboard* charts had dropped sharply in 1946. The company charted only five tunes against Hill and Range's twenty, and 1947 had not shaped up any better. Had Williams not entered the picture at this precise time, the history of Acuff-Rose Publishing might read very differently today.

However, it took extraordinary effort to obtain hit material from the erratic artist. Rose worked hard to capture the right sound for Williams's voice, polishing the songs himself, and filling in with some tunes of his own when Williams came up short. The sides were promising, but the artist wasn't. Williams went on bender after bender, his wife and colleagues frequently bailing him out of jail or collecting him from one or another sanatorium throughout 1948. Rose himself, a recovered alcoholic, had to exercise tough love from time to time to keep the artist in line. When Williams split from his wife, Rose split from Williams until he sobered up and reconciled.

Eventually, however, the stars lined up for Hank Williams. In May 1949 he released "Lovesick Blues," a hokey tune that seemed more suitable to the 1920s than the 1950s record market. It hit fast, selling more than 48,000 copies in seventeen days, climbing to the top of the *Billboard* country charts. This success was followed only a week later by "Wedding Bells," which peaked at number 2. This double chart punch gave him the ammunition he needed to land a spot on the *Grand Ole Opry*. He soon becoming a regular and sometimes even filling in for Red Foley as emcee.

During his Opry period, his most enduring creative juices flowed. He was naïve about music publishing and sometimes used existing titles, ideas, or melodies. "I'm So Lonesome I Could Cry" was lifted from an MGM release schedule that was used as a film title. He also claimed "Lovesick Blues" was a public domain piece, but it turned out it was written by Cliff Friend and publisher Irving Mills and was still in the first twenty-eight year copyright protection under Mills Music. But Williams brought his own unique style to these songs, and audiences loved it.

The close working relationship between Rose and Williams brought Williams the fame he craved and Rose the hits he needed to stay in the running as one of the top four country song publishing houses (Acuff-Rose always trailed Hill and Range as second or third ranking for hits). Williams buoyed Acuff-Rose throughout this period when interest in their other artists was declining. He competed head to head with Eddy Arnold on the country charts, getting eight top ten hits in 1949 compared to seven by Arnold. The following year yielded the same spread of victory for Acuff-Rose, and Williams succeeded in overtaking Arnold again in 1952, his six top ten hits to Arnold's five.

Sadly, Williams's career was short-lived. The booze, pills, and a tempestuous marriage finally caught up with him on New Year's Day, 1953, when he was found dead in the back of a limousine on his way to a performance in Canton, Ohio.[1]

Jean and Julian were certainly aware of Williams early in his career. The Hill and Range firm Ark-La-Tex was set up to mine talents like Webb Pierce, who were active on KWKH and Shreveport's Louisiana Hayride during the exact time when Williams was building a reputation there. Organized by their manager-friend Oscar Davis, Williams spent time on numerous Opry tours that included Ernest Tubb, Red Foley, and Cowboy Copas—all artists connected to Hill and Range who were singing the company's praises. Despite this, Williams remained loyal to Fred Rose to the end.

Throughout 1953, Williams was at the top of his game—Acuff-Rose trailing Hill and Range in overall hits, but still besting them consistently with Williams's tunes in the country music top ten. But above all else, it was Williams's skill to reach down and touch the soul of music fans that Jean, Julian, Tom Parker, and Steve Sholes were on the lookout for, although they preferred it come to them in a less volatile and short-lived package.

The Colonel thought he had such a package in Tommy Sands. Publicly performing since the age of eight, Sands was a country music child prodigy. He debuted on Shreveport's Louisiana Hayride on September 3, 1949. Occasionally, Sands shared the stage with luminaries such as Harmie Smith and Tex Williams—and even Hank Williams. He became known in the Houston market for touting Sun Down Ice Cream on KPRC-TV's "Hoedown Corner," landing a three-hour weekly radio show as a DJ on Houston's KNUZ.

Coming from a musical family, Tommy spent much of his youth bouncing between Chicago and Louisiana, soaking up Chicago's South Side blues sounds and the emerging rockabilly in the South. Sands was fifteen years old when Parker latched onto him. He seemed perfect—hungry, young, handsome, accomplished, and focused completely on his professional career. Parker's $50,000 management dissolution settlement with Eddy Arnold at the end of 1953 probably provided the seed capital to push Sands's career, and throughout 1954 he is noted more frequently in the trades. In June he was voted thirteenth-most-promising male vocalist in *Cashbox*'s folk and western poll. On the strength of this, Parker obtained a record deal with Steve Sholes at RCA, but the records got only a lukewarm reception. Dangerously out of step with the trends, Parker was trying to transform the "West's Wonder Boy" into the next Roy Rogers. The down-home, milquetoast personae, however, was neither where the artist or the record label wanted to go. Also, Sands's voice was at that awkward stage—no longer a child and not quite an adult, which presented a marketing problem. Sholes canceled the contract later that year.[2]

Sands's failure was a huge blow to the Colonel. By the end of 1954, it seems he'd gambled pretty much all he had on the boy, and he turned to Opry headliner Hank Snow to bail him out. The Hank Snow Enterprises-Jamboree Attractions booking venture was Tom Parker's way of moving himself forward and leaving the Sands mess behind. Parker knew there were other prospects out there, and co-owning a booking agency with a top name artist put him in a good position to attract them.

One such prospect appeared on the horizon—a young hipster originally from Tupelo, Mississippi, quickly gaining media attention. Born January 8, 1935, Elvis Aron Presley was drawn to music from an early age, obtaining a cheap guitar and seeking guidance from relatives and church members. The family moved to Memphis in 1948, a town that was fast becoming a southern hotbed for emerging blues music. There he soaked up the sounds of boogie and blues DJ Dewey Phillips spun on his WREC radio program.

Presley performed at every possible opportunity, and by age sixteen, his growing self-confidence began to show in his longer hair, trendy sideburns, and flashy clothes. He graduated from high school on June 3, 1953, punctuating this with a performance that evening for friends. A month later he stepped into the small Sun Records recording studio owned by race music enthusiast Sam Phillips to cut an acetate recording at his own expense as a present for his mother, but probably also to try to interest the record producer in signing him. Phillips didn't.

Elvis was drawn back, time and again, to Sam Phillips's studio, attracted by Phillips's unabashed zeal for recording black artists like Rufus Thomas, Joe Hill Louis, Herman "Little Junior" Parker, and James Cotton. Eventually Elvis won over Phillips's secretary Marian Keisker, who convinced the reticent Phillips to give the polite boy a try on a cover record. While the recording went nowhere, it presented an opportunity the following month to join the Starlight Wranglers as lead singer. During an otherwise discouraging second session, Elvis broke into an energetic vamp of Arthur "Big Boy" Crudup's "That's Alright" and Phillips was stunned. Here was a white boy, who could belt out a blues tune without any inhibitions. His vocal inflections and suggestive body moves flowed from him like water flows from an open tap.

Phillips immediately knew he had something and took the recording downtown to DJ Dewey Phillips, who played it a few nights later. Radio listeners were astonished that the singer was a white boy from their own Humes High School. That night, July 8, 1954, marked the launch of Elvis Presley's popularity.[3]

Phillips quickly recorded a B side for the record, an upbeat version of Bill Monroe's "Blue Moon of Kentucky." Phillips and guitarist Scotty Moore scrambled to squeeze mileage out of their unexpected celebrity booking performances at local high schools, clubs, and shopping centers—anywhere they could expose the new sound. They persuaded WMPS DJ Bob Neal to add Elvis to his package show planned for the Overton Park Shell in Memphis. This event marks the first time Elvis exhibited the jumpy, ecstatic moves that would become his hallmark performance style.

By August 7, Elvis Presley's local fame was beginning to hit the trades, with the Spotlight section of *Billboard* noting the singer as a "strong new talent" able to "sock over a tune for either the country or the rhythm and blues markets."[4] A few weeks later, "Blue Moon of Kentucky" charted at number 3 on the Memphis regional country and western chart.

By the time Elvis, Bill, and Scotty split off from the other Starlight Wranglers, recording and management deals with Elvis were already in place. Phillips forged an exclusive recording contract with him, and Moore obtained an exclusive management agreement with radio personality and promoter Bob Neal. The group performed locally at the Eagle's Nest over the next several months as "Blue Moon of Kentucky" gained market momentum, eventually slipping onto the *Billboard* mid-South regional country and western chart.

Phillips used this leverage to shoehorn Elvis onto the *Grand Ole Opry,* emceed by Hank Snow, on October 2, 1954. Garnering only a lukewarm response and no offer to return, the crestfallen artist was still encouraged by Ernest Tubb after his performance on Tubb's *Midnite Jamboree* radio program.

While it's not completely clear what country listeners thought of the young artist that night, it was probably becoming clear to Tubb and other artists that the growing interest in rhythm and blues was changing the music scene. Mainstream country artists were going to be compelled to either embrace this progressive trend or be left in the dust. They weren't the only ones who knew this. Since the Tim Spencer lawsuit had wrapped up, Jean was keenly focused on the next emerging crossover opportunity—race music.

Hill and Range's St. Louis Music subsidiary became the repository for the long shots in this genre. These were the songs Jean and Julian were betting to beat the odds. Lucky for them, the increasing popularity of black gospel, southern country blues, and the hot, electrified derivative already popular in northern cities, proved that the odds were turning in their favor.

The Aberbach brothers' foray into race music had been by way of white gospel. By 1950, Eddy Arnold had demonstrated the mainstream popular appeal of sacred songs with successful renditions of "When Jesus Beckons Me Home" (Gene Arnold), "Open Thy Merciful Arms" (Don Whiston), and "May the Good Lord Bless and Keep You" (Meredith Willson). By 1952 Hill and Range was printing Sacred Octavos (small songbooks). They were even printing, publishing, and vending sacred greeting cards and postcards. By this time their catalog included gospel greats like "Precious Memories," "Touch Me, Lord Jesus," "Jesus Gave Me Water," "Swing Low, Sweet Chariot," and "Go Down Jordan." They had a number of gospel songwriters under exclusive contract and had also made arrangements with a number of respected gospel publishers, including the largest, Stamps-Baxter.[5]

Stamps-Baxter became the launching pad for collecting white gospel repertoire. Hill and Range established a general agreement with the company on June 27, 1952. This led to the creation of an umbrella company, Affiliated Music Enterprises, Inc., a BMI firm incorporated on October 14, 1953. In less than three years Jean and Julian would assemble the largest gospel publishing house in the world.

The speed of this success suspiciously resembles their conquest of the country and western fields—and no wonder: the problems were the same. Gospel songwriters were just as uninformed about song royalties as their country and western cousins. Since they had not registered with BMI as songwriters, they weren't collecting any author royalties on their songs when they were performed publicly or used on records. They lost out to smart independent record labels that would form their own publishing companies, pay them a flat fee, and retain both the writer and publisher share for themselves. Many gospel publishers were no better informed. Naïve about royalty rights, they earned profit only from the sale of their sheet music. In fact, Stamps-Baxter (the largest of them all) had never registered itself with any performing rights organization and therefore wasn't collecting performance royalties of any kind on its vast catalog.[6]

Seeing this opportunity, Jean and Julian applied the same model that had worked so well for them in country and western music. By simply offering the standard terms to writers, guiding them through the song registration process, and actually paying out the royalties, they quickly gained the trust of the songwriter community.

A business relationship with Hill and Range proved equally attractive for the gospel publishers. To Stamps-Baxter, performance royalties were found money they were willing to share with Hill and Range, in exchange for accounting services and the increase in market visibility they would get from being connected to a large, respected, and growing international publishing firm. It was a win for everyone.

While romancing the white-owned Stamps-Baxter company, the brothers became aware of the enormously prolific black writer Thomas A. Dorsey, some of whose works had made it into the Stamps-Baxter catalog. Now recognized as the "father of gospel music," Dorsey had recorded extensively as a blues artist under the pseudonym of Georgia Tom between 1928 and 1932, when he accompanied some well-known performers like Big Bill Broonzy and Memphis Minnie. His piano accompaniment style was influential, and he became known for a smutty, double-meaning song called "It's Tight like That."

Sometime in the 1930s he had renounced secular music and began writing sacred music exclusively, founding the Gospel Choral Union with Sallie Martin. Dorsey responded cautiously to the Aberbachs' offer of representation, but by February 1951, Dorsey confirmed his willingness to let Hill and Range promote and administer three of his top catalog songs: "How about You," "Want to Go to Heaven When I Die," and "Precious Lord (Take My Hand)." Jean used the latter to produce a huge Eddy Arnold hit later that year. The royalties were reportedly the first Dorsey had ever seen in his entire career. Having gained this influential songwriter's trust, they quickly acquired the renewal rights to these and many other works for the second twenty-eight-year copyright term, including Dorsey's classic "(There'll Be) Peace in the Valley."[7]

Revenue from black gospel music was assured because it serviced a vast, well-organized churchgoing audience. The secular side of race music was a much more complex beast, and for a long time the profit potential in it wasn't very apparent. Part of the problem was that the market was fragmented into regional styles. The chasm between someone who would buy rural country blues and one who would buy the urban electric version remained deep. Marketing problems persisted until *Billboard* introduced a combined rhythm and blues chart starting in 1949 that encompassed both. It was a clear signal that the market had coalesced.[8]

As regional styles came together under the rhythm and blues banner, a new market force also began to reveal itself. Because of advances in affordable radio electronics and a postwar prosperity that made cars affordable, teenagers were beginning to represent a lucrative marketing target. Hordes of high school kids congregated after school at the local drive-in hamburger restaurant, blasting their favorite DJ's picks from their cars long into the night. They weren't just playing the songs on their radios. They were buying the records and taking them home. It was their dollars that were fueling interest in this new music trend. Suddenly race recordings began doing brisk business, and popular black artists could demand top dollar from audiences that were increasingly mixed.

Entry into the rhythm and blues publishing arena proved challenging. Jean faced competition from record companies who were also smart enough to incorporate as their own publishers. People like Syd Nathan of King Records had been nurturing this market since the mid-1940s. They held tightly onto their copyrights, sensing the pop crossover floodgates would soon open.

Hill and Range had no equivalent of Eddy Arnold in the rhythm and blues field. Without a top-performing artist in their pocket, Hill and Range could not attract songwriters or smaller publishers to hand over their songs by guaranteeing performances by well-known artists that would enhance their revenue. They needed such a vehicle if they were ever going to get an edge on this market.

The Aberbach brothers already had a tenuous connection to Elvis. The flipside of Sun 209 featuring "That's Alright" was Bill Monroe's bluegrass classic "Blue Moon of Kentucky." Bill Monroe was exclusively signed to Hill and Range by this time, but that tune had been written before their agreement was made. Hill and Range would collect no publishing royalties from this Monroe song. Instead, it would all go to Peer International, who owned the publishing rights for the first term.[9]

As New Year's Day 1955 approached, Steve Sholes at RCA also became keenly aware that Elvis records were flying off record store shelves. Elvis's limited repertoire was generating considerable revenue through weekly airplay by enthusiastic DJs, through radio performances on the Louisiana Hayride, from brisk record sales numbering in the tens of thousands, and through live performances at clubs and dancehalls throughout the South. While the venues were not large, Elvis was selling them out and being held over by popular demand.

Sholes was not happy about Sam Phillips's upstart little Sun Label seriously challenging RCA sales in the South. With powerful southern DJs like Biff Collie, Dewey Philips, and Bob Neal singing Elvis's praises, not to mention the excitement reported from southern RCA distributors, Sholes was probably following Elvis's progress closely going into 1955.[10]

This was true for Tom Parker as well. On January 1, 1955, when his booking deal with Hank Snow officially kicked in, Parker was actively hunting up additional talent to round out the series of tour dates he was finalizing for Snow in mid-February. Around this time he was also actively pursuing the Louisiana Hayride management to allow him to set up an artist bureau. Parker's relentless focus on hunting up talent makes it hard to imagine that he was unaware of the *Billboard* notice about the Elvis's burgeoning success in both personal appearances and radio play throughout East Texas. Nor would review of the new single have escaped his attention. Of "Milkcow Blues Boogie," *Billboard* wrote "Presley continues to impress" and reviewers complimented "You're a Heartbreaker" for its "slick country-style reading."[11]

WMPS DJ Bob Neal had been booking Elvis and other performers around the region since November, but Neal knew his promotional reach was limited to the southern region. Oscar Davis was doing advance promotional work for the Colonel on an Eddy Arnold show, and Neal invited him to Elvis's Eagle's Nest show in Memphis. Davis returned the favor, inviting Elvis backstage to meet Eddy Arnold and the Jordanaires at his Ellis Auditorium date two days later.

Parker's approach to Elvis was reminiscent of his stalking of Eddy Arnold. Always holding his cards close to his chest, Parker studied Arnold, never letting anyone know that the artist had captured his attention, until he was sure he had a better than even chance of capturing him. When Oscar Davis brought news of Presley's phenomenal performances back to him, some accounts suggest the Colonel projected indifference but then secretly pursued him.[12]

Elvis was already within arm's reach. On New Year's Day 1955, he shared the bill with Tommy Sands on Biff Collie's Grand Prize Saturday Night Jamboree that took place at Eagles Hall in Houston. Three days later, Jean met Parker for lunch. We do not know what was discussed at that meeting, but given the industry buzz, it's hard to imagine Elvis Presley was not among the topics of conversation. "Blue Moon of Kentucky" was quickly rising on the Memphis local charts and would attain the number 3 position, crossing over to the mid-South country and western chart only ten days later. Elvis had performed the tune on the *Grand Ole Opry*, October 2, 1954, hosted by Hank Snow, where he also chatted with its creator Bill Monroe. After the gig, he had played the *Midnite Jamboree*, and was consoled by Ernest Tubb for his lukewarm Opry reception.[13] Texas DJ Biff Collie had attended the annual country music DJ convention in Nashville after having seen Elvis perform in Memphis on November 17, 1954. His enthusiasm for Elvis may have turned into a last-minute invitation to play the Palladium a week later (November 25). It certainly sealed Collie's invitation to feature Elvis on a Louisiana Hayride bill at Cook's Hoedown Club on November 28, 1954, and on the New Year's Day 1955 radio show with Tommy Sands at Eagles Hall in Houston.

With so many interactions with Hill and Range luminaries, his direct involvement in Parker's events and his lightning rise up the charts, it's hard to believe that when they met on January 4, Jean and the Colonel would have talked about much of anything else. Elvis was beginning to participate in large shows—one the very next day in San Angelo, Texas, with an audience capacity of more than 1,800. Over lunch, and probably again over dinner, they undoubtedly talked about this Elvis fellow.

Whatever they discussed January 4, when Jean and Parker left the table that day, each man embarked on his own mission—Parker to secure control over Elvis, and Jean to secure control over his repertoire. Parker caught up with Elvis a week and half later at his January 15 Louisiana Hayride show. Two days later, Neal announced that Parker would take over bookings and on January 22, 1955, Parker wrote to confirm that Elvis was booked on the Hank Snow tour taking place between February 14 and 18.[14]

Not five days later, the Parker-Diskin promotional machine was in full swing. Seeking opportunities even beyond just the concert stage, Diskin wrote a booking agent in Chicago to try to arrange a spot for Elvis on television. Meanwhile, Parker courted Harry Kalcheim at the William Morris Agency, the nation's largest artist management firm. Kalcheim could help open doors to motion picture opportunities. Parker also convinced Snow that Elvis would be a lucrative addition to their fledgling partnership and suggested Snow casually urge the artist to sign up with them for management.

With Jean on board, Snow stepping up as his mouthpiece, Neal set up to be marginalized, and Harry Kalcheim on the line, Parker probably felt the odds had shifted sufficiently in his favor. It was time to address the real stumbling block that stood between him and Elvis Presley. On February 6, Parker met with Sam Phillips and Bob Neal, declaring Elvis would go nowhere on a puny label like Sun, and that Phillips should step aside and let him arrange a deal with RCA.[15]

Jean was no less productive. According to his daybook, he traveled to Chicago to meet with "colored publishers."[16] We have no way of knowing exactly what business he conducted there, but it's a pretty good bet what was motivating him. Less than one month later, on February 22, 1955, Hill and Range acquired the entire catalog of Lester Melrose's Wabash Music, a Chicago-based music publishing company whose catalog included songs by Sonny Boy Williamson, Roosevelt Sykes, Big Maceo, Mildred White, Eddie Boyd, and Big Joe Williams. These copyrights represented a good, solid start for a rhythm and blues catalog, but there was one gem hidden inside that was almost certainly the main reason for the purchase. The catalog included all the works of Arthur Crudup—including Elvis Presley's breakout hit, "That's Alright."

Negotiations went quickly, probably because Wabash music posed no greater challenge than the many other naïve publishers Jean had dealt with in the past. It turns out Wabash's owner, Lester Melrose, was the Sylvester Cross of rhythm and blues music. He had been swindling black artists out of their due for years, much in the same way Cross had done with country and western artists. He would buy songs for a flat rate, keeping all the royalties, including the writer's share. Jean offered Melrose the same general bailout deal as he had with Cross: Sell your catalog to Hill and Range before the lawyers come calling, and Hill and Range will straighten out your books, expand your reach internationally, and cut you in for a hefty royalty. Always short on cash, it was an offer Lester Melrose wasn't inclined to refuse.[17]

Elvis and Sam

Sam Phillips and
Elvis Presley.
Courtesy of
Elvis Presley
Enterprises, Ltd.

With "That's Alright" firmly in hand, Jean immediately turned his attention to promoting his new-found copyright. He contacted Bill Randle, the influential DJ for Cleveland's WERE who had the number 1 program in the Midwest and the number 1 nationally syndicated radio show out of New York every Saturday. Jean's interest in Randle was probably larger than just "That's Alright." Any Hill and Range song he could get the DJ to play on his WCBS syndicated radio show meant royalties of a size that dwarfed regional radio exposure. But this savvy, erudite DJ was far too smart to be swayed if the material wasn't really there. Randle's ability to predict chart activity was legendary. He exhibited an uncanny ability to tap into the pop culture psyche and pull out discs he knew would be winners with his listeners. Randle had been exposed to Presley's music by fellow WERE DJ Tommy Edwards, who had been hyping "Blue Moon of Kentucky" on his show over the last several months. Two days before Jean met with Parker for lunch, Randle had given one of Elvis's tunes a spin on the New York show, but the tune didn't seem to impress him. Apparently, Jean aimed to change that. "Saturday, February 19—Bill Randle—5pm," Jean recorded in his daybook. Whatever the subject of Jean's meeting with him, when Randle returned to Cleveland after his New York radio show on February 26, he went directly to the Circle Theater, where Edwards was hosting the Circle Theater Jamboree that included Elvis. After the show, Edwards introduced Bob Neal and Elvis to Randle, who requested an interview, and they took off for the studio. The interview showcased three of Elvis's tunes, including "That's Alright."

Hill and Range was moving in on Elvis in other ways as well. Hank Snow and Ernest Tubb organized a memorial for the godfather of country music, Jimmie Rodgers, in Meridian Mississippi on May 25. Elvis was there, performing later that night at one of the celebration shows. He also participated in the parade along with Tubb, Snow, Faron Young, Slim Whitman, and many others the following day. Standing in for Hill and Range was Grelun Landon from the California office. Landon returned to California from the event with the idea that, while they did not own all the songs in Elvis's repertoire, maybe Hill and Range could obtain print rights from other publishers and put out an Elvis sheet music folio. Julian liked the idea and, after running it by Jean, they began to investigate the properties.[18]

Parker, apparently overseeing some Snow performances, arrived in New York on June 5, 1955, and had dinner with Jean. No doubt Elvis was a topic of discussion, because correspondence with Julian at about this time seems to indicate Parker was fishing for the Aberbach brothers to pitch into the Sun record buyout deal. But Hill and Range was in the business of investing in songs, not talent, and investing in a record deal would prove complicating.[19]

Nevertheless, Jean's interest in the artist had to be growing. Five years earlier, he had traded stock with Ahmet Ertegun and Herb Abramson for a fifty percent interest in Progressive Music, a publishing firm connected with Atlantic Records, then only two years old. Aside from reaping royalties from "That's Alright," now owned by Hill and Range, Elvis was also experimenting with covers of Atlantic Records tunes that were housed in that co-owned publishing firm, notably "Fool, Fool, Fool," "Shake, Rattle, and Roll," Ray Charles's "I Got a Woman," and "Tweedle Dee."[20]

As Elvis's repertoire was growing, so was his popularity. Most dates, Elvis stole the show. He could no longer arrive at concert halls unescorted for fear of being mobbed by adoring women who would rip the clothes right off him. Other artists—including Hank Snow himself—could no longer follow Presley on stage. His ability to overwhelm an audience left little enthusiasm (or even audience) for anyone else. About the only artist capable of stirring crowds like that was legendary heart-throb Frank Sinatra—and the money that followed that artist was enormous.[21]

But not all the news was good. *The Arthur Godfrey Show* auditioned Elvis but turned him down, feeling he was unprepared and unprofessional. Complaints were also circulating about lewd remarks made on stage, and about Presley not always arriving to shows on time. Parker was increasingly frustrated by Bob Neal. Neal's inability to control the artist was undercutting Parker's efforts to get a major label interested. What could be done about this?

A few days after Jean and Parker's June 5 dinner meeting, Phillips and Neal suddenly began to field inquiries from record companies interested in purchasing the recording contract. It is believed Parker himself may have started the rumor that the contract was for sale. If so, it appears it had at least one desirable outcome. Within days, Neal agreed to turn over complete control of booking and long-term planning to Parker. He also vowed to actively work to convince Elvis to leave Sun for a record company of the Colonel's choosing—perhaps fearing that a deal with any other company would likely threaten his personal interest in the artist.[22]

If Parker was the source of the rumor and the objective was to raise industry interest in the artist, then it was a risky strategy—unless he was already confident that whatever offer might be tendered would be countered by one from a company that put him in control. Parker's relationship with Steve Sholes at RCA was always tenuous, but his relationship with the Aberbach brothers was not. He knew that on several occasions, Sholes went along with deals if the Aberbach brothers were on board—Chet Atkins being a case in point. While Jean and his brother were not willing to pitch in cold cash, it cost them nothing to endorse a record deal for an artist that was already making them money. Parker may have felt that this was enough insurance to move forward. With industry interest mounting, Parker contacted Steve Sholes on June 21 and invited him to make an offer.

Perhaps because nothing was coming back his way from Sholes, Parker showed up again in New York, meeting with Jean on July 6 and 7. That evening Jean spent time with Sholes and his family, celebrating Steve's wife's birthday. Generally uninterested up to this point, Sholes suddenly softened and began putting together a deal. Two weeks later he offered a flat fee of $12,000 or else a bonus of $5,000 to Elvis with $20,000 recoupable in royalties. At this point, the chief stumbling block to this deal was Elvis himself, who was not yet willing to abandon Phillips and Sun Records. The deal languished over the next two weeks while Neal continued trying to convince Elvis to move off Sun to a major label.[23]

Meantime, Jean headed to the West Coast, arriving in Los Angeles on July 31. The print folio idea was moving forward nicely at the California office. Grelun was hunting down the various songs now made popular by Elvis. Since several of them were owned by Sun Records itself, Jean sent Phillips a proposal on July 13 to pay a flat fee of $25 per song for the print rights. These would be collected and bound with a cover featuring Elvis's picture.

Jean met with Parker a few days later, but the outcome of that meeting was stormy. Since Parker was not Elvis's manager, the brothers had been working directly with Phillips, Neal, and Elvis on the folio and probably felt no obligation to keep Parker informed. Parker was stunned to find out a folio was in the works and angry at Neal for not consulting with him.[24]

Parker's discontent had little impact on Jean. Besides, by now it was beginning to look like the Colonel might never pull off this deal with RCA. Maybe it was time to hedge their bets. On August 9, Jean notes Elvis for the first time in his daybook. There is only one name directly adjacent to it—Sam Clark.

Boston record distributor Sam Clark had been hired by ABC-Paramount to create marketing channels for records connected to their new television syndicate. They had been talking to him since July 14, the day after they'd sent the folio terms to Sam Phillips. Clark's first endeavor was to create the Mickey Mouse record chain to exploit music opportunities connected to feature television shows like *Zorro*. It was a difficult task for Clark until he hit on a winning idea—tapping into the independent record companies. He expanded his business to market records from small record labels, charging them a low fee to cover financing and promotion, while allowing them to retain their own identity. This venture had begun only in June, but by July 14, the day after the folio proposal was sent to Phillips, Jean met with Clark. While there's no evidence about what was discussed, struggling Sun records would have been among the independents that would have benefited directly from a relationship with Clark. From a publishing perspective, it didn't matter what record company Elvis ended up on, as long as it was one that saw Hill and Range as a helpful partner. In this way, even if the Colonel failed to secure a deal for Elvis, Sun might survive—and, therefore, so would this Hill and Range opportunity. But it appears nothing significant came of the Clark meeting.[25]

When Jean met with Parker again on September 16, 1955, in Beverly Hills, the Colonel's efforts to secure a record deal were not going well, and he was entirely frustrated with Neal's amateur handling of the artist. Whatever was discussed, the very next day Parker precipitated an argument that resulted in Neal pulling away from their joint booking arrangement. Thereafter, Parker quietly circumvented Neal and started dealing directly with Elvis's father, Vernon. In short order he obtained a three-year exclusive representation arrangement with Elvis due to kick in when Neal's arrangement expired at the end of the year.[26]

By early October, all the threads seemed to be coming together, and Jean kicked into high gear. He began meeting with counselor Ben Starr on October 15 to draft a publishing offer that would create co-owned subsidiary companies with Elvis. He made a note for attorney Lew Dreyer to make sure the proper authorization was in place with Bill Randle and the William Morris Agency to

Tom Parker,
Gladys Presley,
Elvis Presley,
and Vernon
Presley. Courtesy
of Elvis Presley
Enterprises, Ltd.

credit them in print. And he told Grelun to put a rush on an E. B. Marks song they were trying to arrange for the "Pressley" folio.[27]

On October 24, Jean met once again with Parker at the Warwick Hotel in New York, and later that day, Parker contacted Phillips. Parker informed him that he had secured exclusive rights from Elvis's parents, Gladys and Vernon, to negotiate a record deal. He asked Phillips to name his price. Backed into a corner, the headstrong Phillips suggested an outrageous number he was sure nobody in their right mind would meet. Undaunted, Parker delivered a down payment of $5,000 on October 30 which ultimately turned into a nonrefundable bonus, and agreed to deliver $35,000 by November 15.[28] This was a complete leap of faith, and over the next three weeks Parker had to wear down RCA to meet this extraordinary asking price.

Hill and Range attorney Ben Starr was quickly dispatched to Memphis to finalize acquiring Phillips's Hi-Lo Music Publishing catalog. While it supported the folio deal already in place, Phillips Hi-Lo catalog was insignificant from a publishing perspective. Instead, the gesture was probably meant to inspire confidence that the artist would be immediately equipped with the kind of song repertoire Sholes himself could not obtain.

Starr remained in Memphis as point man over the next several weeks, meeting with Parker in the days just after RCA committed to the asking price. He finalized the publishing structure with Parker, Gladys, and Vernon that created two new Hill and Range companies—Elvis Presley Music (a BMI company) and Gladys Music (an ASCAP company). Jean and Julian together would act as joint general managers, Jean in the role of secretary, and Julian as treasurer, with Elvis named as president, and his father, Vernon, as vice president. The stockholders retained the right of first refusal before stock shares could be offered for sale to outsiders. Like other Hill and Range partnership companies, these would be co-owned 50/50 between Elvis Presley and Hill and Range Songs, Inc. They created a standard three year-general partnership agreement dated November 21, 1955, that covered all properties created, co-created, or conceived by Elvis Presley and included the right to use his image and likeness for promotional purposes.[29]

The Colonel, however, struck a hard bargain. Clause 7, establishing automatic renewal for an additional three years, was removed from the contract and placed in a conditional rider; Clause 12, requiring the songwriter to provide a minimum of one song per month, was also removed—Elvis would be under no

Steve Sholes, Tom Parker, Elvis Presley, and RCA's Frank Folsam. Courtesy of Elvis Presley Enterprises, Ltd.

obligation to find or write songs. Hill and Range won the right to keep the folio separate but was obliged to print 3,000 extra folios (for a total of 5,000) and give them to Elvis at no charge. The first revenue Elvis would ever see from publishing was $625.35 from Hill and Range, sent to him on June 30, 1956, for his interest in the folio. They had pressed about 12,500 copies, with Elvis getting five cents per copy for the first pressing and three cents per copy on subsequent runs.[30]

For decades, there has been speculation about what part the Aberbach brothers played in bringing the "deal of the century" to fruition that shifted Elvis from Sun Records to RCA. A long-standing rumor persists that they cut a backdoor deal with Sholes, guaranteeing any shortfall on RCA's investment in exchange for the promise of securing the B side of every Elvis record for Hill and Range songs. Mitch Miller recounts, "He [Parker] had an offer from RCA—I don't know exactly what it was—but it was bigger than anyone else's. And RCA was a little worried about whether they could fulfill it. And Jean came in and said if they could have—I know this is true because he told me about it—if they could have one side of every Presley record they would guarantee his contract. So that took a big burden off RCA."[31]

The contract evidence, however, proves otherwise. Clause 19 explicitly asserts that Elvis was not restricted from using music by other publishers, except under very specific conditions. He was free to make any deal he wanted with any other publisher, provided he did not write the song, was not credited with writing the song as a cut-in, and that his name or likeness would not appear in promotional materials for the song.[32] "Elvis Presley was free to record anything he wanted. He had jointly owned music publishing companies, but he was under no obligation to record the songs that were presented to him that were a part of Elvis Presley or Gladys Music," Julian Aberbach remembers. "We made it our business to try to gather together teams of songwriters that we felt would be qualified to write songs for Elvis Presley. . . . We had at least fifteen teams of songwriters that were working to supply Elvis with the music that was needed. The choice of what he was going to record in singing or motion picture sessions was always entirely his own."[33]

Hill and Range Songs are found on at least one side of most Elvis Presley recordings not because of some backdoor deal, but because it was in Elvis's own best interest. Mitch Miller explains: "Then he [Jean] went further, because he was very smart. So to be the publisher, and have one side of every Presley record, so what does he do? He makes Presley the partner with him in the company. Therefore, the songs that they would have to put on the other side not only would have Presley's OK, but then he would also profit from them."[34] As co-owner of the publishing companies, Elvis would benefit directly by obtaining half the publisher's share in any song he performed or recorded that would be placed in his Elvis Presley and Gladys Music catalogs, whereas he would get none if he recorded a song contributed by any other publisher. He enjoyed fifty percent of the publishing revenues on any song he helped popularize that was placed into these companies.

This does not mean that Elvis picked his songs solely on the basis of whether or not they could be put in his publishing companies. Elvis was a consummate performing artist, and like Eddy Arnold wanted songs that were right for his voice. He exercised his right to record songs by other publishers from time to time when he found ones that he liked. But the practical outcome of his personal publishing interest was that, more often than not, Elvis chose to record songs that he could put in his publishing companies because he liked them well enough and they made him money.

Some accounts suggest the Aberbach brothers contributed cash to the RCA deal. Most of this confusion stems from an unsubstantiated assertion made by author Arnold Shaw. Shaw (not to be confused with the man who acted as vice president and general manager of Hill and Range during the early 1950s) said that Hill and Range "ostensibly" contributed $15,000 to the $40,000 conveyed by RCA. It has since been refuted by Norman Racusin, then chief financial officer of RCA, who actually authorized the amount. He confirms that RCA conveyed the full $40,000. This is consistent with Hill and Range corporate records. There is no mention whatsoever of any proposed or authorized disbursements of funds to RCA, nor any mention of involvement in the deal in Jean's daybooks, nor are there any large disbursements from bank accounts authorized during this period that cannot be accounted for.[35] Hill and Range did not contribute any money at all to the RCA–Sun Records buyout deal. The only money that came from the Aberbach brothers was connected to the creation of the co-owned Elvis Presley publishing companies.[36]

The publishing deals were signed in Memphis on November 21, 1955, the same day as the record deal. The investment was—relative to the RCA deal—insignificant. Rider A, Clause 22, of the general agreement engaging Elvis Presley shows Hill and Range offered only a total of $2,500—none of which would be recoupable against royalties. This fee would be broken out into three staggered payments, and $1,000 of it would be conditional on recording a copyright held in Elvis Presley Music.[37]

So the Aberbach brothers did not require that Elvis record only Hill and Range repertoire, Sholes to guarantee record sides, nor did they contribute cash for the record buyout. Instead, it was probably Jean's and Julian's publishing experience, Parker's proven promotional skill, and confidence in his own record management abilities that convinced Sholes to gamble his career and plop down the unprecedented sum to buy out Phillips's record contract. Why shouldn't he trust the same formula that had caused them to make a killing with Eddy Arnold? Why couldn't lightning strike twice when the very same gods were brewing up the atmosphere? By the time Sholes signed off on the deal, he probably just plain believed he'd make back the money.

But the rumor mill was dead-on right when it surmised Hill and Range was pivotal in bringing the deal of the century to fruition. Tracing back over Jean's activities that year, specific daybook entries show that at every critical juncture, before every pivotal move, Tom Parker consulted with Jean Aberbach. Was this mere coincidence?

Parker sought Jean out a few days after New Year's Day, the result being that in little more than a week, Parker had control of Neal's bookings and Hill and Range made a bid for the Wabash catalog including Elvis's hit "That's Alright." Parker approached Phillips to let Elvis move to a major record label in early February, but not until three days after Parker met with Jean in June did Phillips begin to field inquiries about the record contract being for sale. Sholes was invited to make a bid, but stalled. Only after Parker met with Jean three weeks later and Jean shared a casual dinner at Sholes's home did Sholes make a bid—albeit a weak one—in late July. Parker sought Jean out again on September 16 and the very next day he had a falling out with Neal, entirely taking over Elvis's management. And finally, he had left Jean only a few hours earlier on the very same day Parker forced Phillips to name his price.

That's a lot of coincidence, considering the fact that Jean interacted with Parker at almost no other time during this period. If Parker actively sought his counsel, it would have been in keeping with Jean's advisory role in the triumvirate. Steve Sholes, too, looked to Jean as the bellwether of good business sense. Hill and Range's involvement raised Sholes's confidence level to the extent that finally made the deal palatable. We may never know Jean's exact role in this complex play, but we can say with certainty that Jean was physically present on the scene, meeting with Parker and Sholes immediately before each and every significant event that moved this deal to its ultimate conclusion.

The essence of a diamond is nothing more than coal forged under great pressure. When Jean was growing up they would spend one month every summer in the posh spa resort town of Baden and nearby St. Helen's Valley—the Helental. One year he was walking along the beach and a bright flash caught his eye. He looked around, and among the sand and rocks he found a marvelous diamond ring! "I brought it to the police station, and the officer contacted the owner who had reported it missing. The woman was very wealthy and stunningly beautiful, and rewarded me handsomely . . . with 10 percent of the value of the ring—and with a kiss!!"[38]

Had Jean not had his eyes open and his wits about him, he would have missed that gem. Eventually it would have been washed out to sea or picked up by someone with sharper eyes. The glint of Elvis's potential was just enough to attract and keep the attention of the four people who could propel him to success. His talent was just bright enough to warrant unprecedented investment in an artist whose experience and repertoire was meager compared to other more seasoned artists. But sometimes, when the light is just right, the eye will catch something out of place—rare, and unusual. They had found their diamond in the rough.

CHAPTER 19

Under Pressure

Before Elvis became more than a blip on the radar, business expansion was the theme of 1955, and for the first half of the year that's where Jean put most of his attention. Changes to BMI policies for guarantee advances, government investigation of bribery practices known as payola, and antitrust actions mounted by ASCAP against BMI, all served to constrain their current Hill and Range business.[1] There was also drag on the business from the litigations they had completed or were in the process of mounting—*De Sylva v. Ballentine,* and *Miller v. Daniels*—the "Moonlight and Roses" case. While the music world was sorting itself out, Jean turned his attention to protecting what they had built, expanding their business worldwide, and preparing the groundwork that would enable them to jump forward, as soon as the new music trend revealed itself.

Though he kept out of the limelight, nevertheless Jean was a potent force on industry committees. The National Music Publishers Association (NMPA) board meetings focused on discussion of copyright revision. Publisher colleague Leo Feist was impressed with Jean's ability to provide a fresh perspective. Where other publishers were focused on the present, Jean was always probing the future—pushing the committee to project the impact of actions taken today on their collective future.

"Jean was a great asset to the NMPA board. One thing that completely impressed me was his unique ability to take the issue one step further. We would discuss an idea, and it was always Jean who would urge us to [follow it out, theoretically, to understand the result]. I don't think he was so much interested in the hypothetical concepts, as he was in evaluating the profit potential of these ideas, most specifically as to how they would benefit Hill and Range. . . . That was his concern—as it was the concern of all other publishers involved."[2] Such activities kept Jean in the middle of industry decision making and therefore informed on industry progress and opportunity.

In the months leading up to the Elvis Presley deal that was sealed in November 1955, Jean was already mining rhythm and blues songwriting talent and tunes for the Hill and Range catalog, possibly with that artist in mind. He visited rhythm and blues kingpin Syd Nathan in July on the same trip during which he leveled with Parker about the folio. Founder of King and Queen Records in Cincinnati, Syd Nathan had been cross-pollinating white and black genres since 1945 and had collected an impressive catalog of songs. His first recordings, targeted at circumventing the Musicians' Union ban of 1945, featured the "a cappella" black gospel sounds of the legendary Swan Silvertones and the Fairfield Four. White audiences, however, weren't ready yet to embrace black sacred music. Over the next few years he began mining the vibrant local club scene across the river in Covington, Kentucky, for secular black music, recording Bull Moose Jackson, Wynonie Harris, Ivory Joe Hunter, Lonnie Johnson, and Little Willie John. He would often have black musicians back up white singers, and vice versa, trying to find that magical blend that would appeal to racially mixed audiences. In 1950 he bought up the rights to Roy Brown's song catalog from DeLuxe records. Among the gems could be found "Good Rockin' Tonight," a tune that was a huge independent hit in late 1948 and 1949.[3]

Jean was also establishing a relationship with Mercury Records. Mercury had distinguished itself as being able to bridge the color gap in pop music by cutting black hits by white performers that served the wider pop market. Before long, Mercury was a compelling force in the mainstream pop music arena, and a clear challenge to the major record companies. Mercury had been formed in 1945 by a booking agent and son of a plastics manufacturer. It was well funded. It had enough resources to absorb the fledgling Majestic label and its 2,000 acetates. Its studios, a pressing plant, and thousands of backlog masters were purchased from Eli Oberstein's defunct Hit and Classic labels. These assets helped get Mercury off the ground. The label was also uncharacteristically aggressive in promotion.

It underwrote Frankie Laine's Midwest concert tour, cosponsoring dates with local retailers and probably partnering promotion with Hill and Range.[4]

Jean's relationship with Mercury was strong having given them Frankie Laine's first hit in 1947 "That's My Desire." Producer Mitch Miller was responsible for that hit—and for every other major hit the label had between 1948 and 1950 before he moved to Columbia, taking a few key artists along with him, including Frankie Laine.[5] With the color barrier being chipped away a little more every day, Mercury signed the Penguins away from the DooTone label, at the same time picking up the Platters, a group that would eventually be recognized as the most popular doo-wop group of the period. At the top of 1955, though, Mercury's problems were less about star performers than about getting good songs. Like many larger record companies, they saw their profits being drained away by even smaller upstart independent labels releasing great tunes by lesser-known black artists. Mercury fought back, turning out covers by white performers that outsold the smaller labels simply by virtue of having much wider distribution. The Crew Cuts covered the Chords' "Sh-Boom," the Diamonds covered the Gladiolas' "Little Darlin'," and Georgia Gibbs had a pop hit with "The Wallflower" (a.k.a."Walk with Me, Henry").[6]

In fact, some of their covers were outright plagiarism. Georgia Gibbs was about to make a huge hit on the label with "Tweedle Dee," a direct ripoff of LaVern Baker's Atlantic Records disc. This was no ordinary ripoff. The cover copied the vocal style, the arrangement, and the orchestration. Mercury even went so far as to try to get Atlantic's producer Tom Dowd, who had directed Baker's original version, to moonlight for them so the sound would be exactly the same. Baker's version hit on January 15, charting at number 4 on the rhythm and blues charts and number 14 on the pop; Gibbs's version hit the charts just two weeks later, coming in at number 2, thus proving that imitation is not only the best form of flattery, but is also the most profitable.[7] This had to have concerned Ahmet Ertegun and Herb Abramson, co-owners of Atlantic Records. They didn't have nearly as wide a distribution as Mercury. Lucky for them, what they would lose on the records they'd probably make back in publishing royalties, because by this time, their Progressive Music firm was half owned by Hill and Range Songs.

Jean's relationship with Atlantic cofounders Ahmet Ertegun and Herb Abramson was close. He saw the small Atlantic venture as an opportunity for nurturing rhythm and blues in the New York market. The son of a Turkish ambassador, Ahmet and his brother Nesuhi chose to stay in America after their father died. Moving from Washington, D. C. to New York, Ahmet hooked up with small-time producer Herb Abramson. After collaborating on a few sessions for Quality and Jubilee Records, Ertegun borrowed $10,000 from a family friend and they launched the Atlantic label, signing talent that most notably included Tiny Grimes. They experimented with various gospel acts, considered theatrical recordings, and sniffed around hillbilly music, finally landing their first hit in 1949 with the novelty tune "Drinkin' Wine Spo-Dee-O-Dee" by "Sticks" McGhee (with blues man brother Brownie McGhee on guitar), a cover tune originally put out by Harlem Records. Based on that hit, Jean probably took greater notice of the fledgling outfit and underwrote them in 1950 for a half interest in Progressive Music.[8]

Mercury's Georgia Gibbs version of "Tweedle Dee," was scheduled to be released at the same time as the original version by Atlantic's LaVern Baker. When Jean took his trip to Chicago to seek out "colored publishers" in late January 1955—the visit in which he picked up the Wabash catalog—he also visited Mercury Records. It is possible that he stopped by to lobby Mercury to hold releasing the Gibbs version for a few weeks because more royalty revenue from publishing could be had by staggering record releases of the same song rather than having the records compete with one another for record-buying dollars and radio airplay. But for Mercury, this was a blood sport. They released the record on January 29, going head to head for the same market that was pulling in money for Baker's Atlantic release.[9]

By April 1955, Jean was actively promoting the co-owned tunes in Atlantic's Progressive catalog, arranging the use of several by Atlantic artists such as T-Bone Walker and Ivory Joe Hunter for cover records on Capitol.[10] Of course, Jean had had dealings with Capitol from way back. Together with Julian, he had placed Tex Williams's "Smoke, Smoke, Smoke That Cigarette," "Tim-Tay-Shun," and "Hurry on Down" with the label.

Jean's business interactions were clearly more with Capitol than with RCA up through the middle of 1955. He touched base with producer Dave Dexter at Capitol at least once a month beginning in June. Staying close to Capitol made good business sense. By the mid-1950s, EMI was looking to gain a foothold in the U.S. market, but it had succeeded only in creating distribution deals with MGM Records and Syd Nathan's King records. The company was eager to become the first European enterprise to tap into the exploding American popular music scene and had its sights on acquiring Capitol. By the time EMI purchased the company for $8.5 million, Jean had accumulated a considerable amount of EMI stock. If Capitol was successful, not only would Jean's EMI stock shares increase in value, but the recordings he got with Capitol would have unparalleled distribution in the European market.[11]

It wasn't hard for Jean to come up with the money to buy EMI stock. The fact was, by 1955 they were swimming in it. In just eleven years, Jean and his brother had built a formidable American music empire. Over 1955 they used that wealth to acquire not only Wabash music, but Reg Connelly's impressive catalog of British standards. Together with their country and western revenue, the net result was that by the end of 1955 Hill and Range music was the fastest-growing ASCAP member and the seventh-highest-paid BMI publisher affiliate.[12]

But there was great uncertainty in the fickle music business. Jean needed to protect their profits and expand their reach in Europe. Investing in a well-established, respected company like EMI made sense. Even so, neither he nor Julian was comfortable putting all their eggs in one basket. They wanted other ways to ensure the family would be secure over the long term.

When Jean departed for his whirlwind tour of Europe in March 1955, it was to explore a new way to preserve their hard-earned wealth—the fine arts. Early in 1952, Julian had taken a trip back to Europe (his first since the war) and returned sporting two paintings—a clown by Georges Rouault and a flower piece by Moise Kisling. Both early twentieth century artists, Georges Rouault's intensely Christian themes tended to be powerful representations of the torment of Christ, metaphorically capturing the despair and suffering of humanity wrought by World War I. Far tamer, the neorealist Kisling enjoyed painting flowers, a favorite subject of the brothers. Jean was skeptical of the investments at first, until they turned around and sold the Kisling for double the money.[13]

Almost half Jean's European trip in early 1955 was devoted to exploring European art. Bouncing between London, Paris, Berlin, Hamburg, Milan, and Rome, he explored the museums and private galleries. He was particularly attracted to highly provocative modern art and was especially excited about the naïve, enigmatic paintings of the German-Swiss painter Paul Klee and also with Gen Paul, now considered the last great painter of the Montmartre School, which had also included Pablo Picasso and Henri de Toulouse-Lautrec.

Jean was also taken by the young, up and coming "Miserabilist" Bernard Buffet, who had won the Prix de la Critique in 1948. While in Paris, Jean must have seen Buffet's exhibition at the Drouant-David gallery, which exhibited his shocking *Horreur de la guerre,* a representation of wartime concentration camps. While critics were mystified by Buffet's often cruel themes, Jean immediately understood this pessimistic realism, and he returned home with a work completed in 1948. Buffet was young, proven, and just breaking big. Jean viewed this as an opportunity, but he also understood that, like any other endeavor the brothers had undertaken, making their investments pay off would require work.

When he returned to the United States on May 17, 1955, Jean began looking up other Buffet enthusiasts who might be interested in a group show and remained in constant touch with Emmanuel David, Buffet's preferred dealer in Europe. Already Jean was strategizing how to boost Buffet's visibility in the States, thus increasing the value of his investment. Over the next few years, Buffet and other younger artists such as Friedrich Hundertwasser would become an active sideline for Jean.

This creative escape came just in the nick of time. The intense pressures of the music business had turned him from a publisher to a banker.[14] While he might be coaching songwriters like Steve Nelson and Bob Hilliard, planning music promotions, or plugging songs to record companies, Jean was managing money. He was investing in talent and applying their assets to ventures that promised profit in the future. Modern art provided a pleasant escape.

Jean wasn't the only music professional with an interest in art. Producer Mitch Miller had been an avid fan of art collecting for many years. Jean and he would talk about art, Miller himself being in the process of amassing an admirable collection.[15] Coincidentally, they would have many opportunities to chat about it over the upcoming months because Jean had recently taken a keen interest in the songwriting team of Jerry Leiber and Mike Stoller. Jean wanted Miller to produce some of their songs.

Leiber and Stoller were two white West Coast teenagers who were avid fans of rhythm and blues music. They burst on the scene in 1952, giving Charles Brown his hit song "Hard Times." Promoter Johnny Otis took them under his wing, funneling their tunes to several of his artists, including Willie Mae ("Big Mama") Thornton, who had a hit with their song "Hound Dog." This raucous blues tune overtook the rhythm and blues charts for seven weeks in 1953. That same year, the boys formed a record label called Spark with Lester Sill and engaged the Robins (the backup vocal group for Little Esther) to feature their tunes.[16]

Leiber and Stoller's continuing chart success with tunes such as "Riot in Cell Block No. 9," "Framed," and "Smokey Joe's Café," were garnering public attention. One day Mike Stoller lifted the ringing phone to hear Jean's high-pitched Viennese voice proclaim, "I understand that you and your partner have written a song about a motorcycle. My brother and I have always loved motorcycles. When we were boys we wished we had a motorcycle, and so we are especially interested in your song about a motorcycle." "Black Denim Trousers and Motorcycle Boots," about to come out as Capitol 3219 performed by the Cheers, was still a closely guarded secret. Stoller wondered how Jean knew about it and concluded that a powerful publisher like Jean Aberbach probably had spies in every record company.[17]

In truth, Jean didn't need spies. From June through August 1955, Jean was pouring attention on Capitol because it was about to produce a session for Tennessee Ernie Ford. Two tunes were submitted to Dave Dexter for the September 17 session date but he passed on both. According to Jean's daybook, these were "I'd Be a Fool to Let You Go," and "I Won't Be Ashamed to Pray."[18]

Ford had done Hill and Range tunes in the past, because some of Merle Travis's songs were particularly well suited to his voice. By then, Merle Travis had been under contract with Hill and Range for several years, his songs having been picked up through the American Music catalog acquisition. Ford's deep, rich baritone lent itself nicely to some work songs Travis had written and shelved a few years earlier. The unearthed "Mule Train" by Ford had become an enormous hit for Hill and Range in 1949, and Jean had other ones just like it tucked away, including one called "Sixteen Tons." Struggling to find a B side for "You Don't Have to Be a Baby to Cry," producer Cliffie Stone convinced label head Lee Gillette to let him use the unusual tune. When it was released on October 17, the DJs barely noticed the A side tune. Eleven days after it shipped, "Sixteen Tons" had racked up 400,000 units in sales. By the twenty-fourth day it had hit the one million mark, becoming the fastest-selling single in Capitol's history. It was so successful that the company had to gear up all its pressing plants to meet the demand. By December 15, less than two months after its release, it hit two million, making it the most successful single ever recorded up to that date.[19]

So deeply engaged with Capitol was Jean at that time, it's not surprising he caught wind of the buzz surrounding Leiber and Stoller's motorcycle song. It straddled the line between rhythm and blues and pure pop. Leiber and Stoller were already familiar with the Aberbach brothers. The boys had visited Jean and Julian's Hollywood home around 1954, probably to discuss a business relationship, but nothing had come of it. When Jean contacted the boys, Stoller was uneasy that news of the impending "Black Denim" recording had leaked. But Jean insisted he could get a cover, and that was enough to get discussions going.[20]

Jean's agenda was far bigger than he let on. Only his daybook provides the slightest hint of where he was going with all this. On August 9, 1955, the same day he first notes Elvis Presley and Sam Clark in his daybook, is also the first mention of Leiber and Stoller, and their Quintet publishing arm. Those names are situated immediately above the "Elvis Pressley" entry in the daybook. Was this just coincidence? Or was it the day Jean began strategizing long-term about Elvis Presley, and how possibly he might arrange a collaboration with Leiber & Stoller?

It was a match made in heaven—successful white songwriters, writing black tunes that appealed to both white and black audiences, for a dynamic, handsome white performer who could pull off black music. Wow! Notations made in his daybook on that date, and those that followed over the next few weeks, show that Jean was keenly focused on roping in these prolific songwriters with at least the tentative notion of eventually bringing them together with this new vocal talent.[21]

Jean wasn't inclined to divulge any of this to the songwriters at that time. Young, smart, and headstrong, Jerry Leiber and Mike Stoller personified a generation of rebellious postwar American teens bent on bucking the system. Corporate types like Jean represented that system and were to be avoided. The boys were doing more than well enough on their own, writing and placing songs with people like Jimmy Witherspoon, Floyd Dixon, and Charles Brown—black performers they idolized. They were wary of young, white punks like Elvis who were trying to emulate them. This would be a delicate dance for Jean, if it was going to work at all. He needed to gain their confidence. But how?

"Wouldn't you like someone else to handle your publishing?" Nope. They already had a publishing firm called Quintet Music and were doing well enough plugging their own songs, thank you very much. Undaunted, Jean used "Black Denim Trousers" as a pretense to pour it on over the days that followed. Through Lester Sill, a meeting was set up for August 12, and he lunched with the boys, meeting them again on August 16 to bring them together with Mitch Miller, who would produce the Columbia cover of "Black Denim Trousers" with French chanteuse Édith Piaf. The studio date was set for September 29.[22]

But despite Jean's efforts, the boys managed to retain all the mechanical income from the original record and all performance income from the tune. No doubt this was frustrating for Jean, and he nearly gave up on the obstinate pair saying, "I don't want any part of anything in which I do not participate in doing, and helping, and working." But he recognized that not pushing the issue would help him gain Leiber and Stoller's confidence, giving him the leverage for the more important opportunity he was about to present.[23]

Throughout these discussions, Jean continued to probe them. Shouldn't they be with a bigger record company? Jean could provide entrée to one of several large East Coast labels. Jean had managed to approach them at the exact moment they were just beginning to falter under the weight of their success. Songwriting, producing, plugging, and promotional responsibilities for their little label were becoming overwhelming. Their interest was piqued, but not enough to give up their independence.

Leiber and Stoller were actively producing at Capitol, and Jean met with Lee Gillette and Leiber on August 30, attending the session on September 1 that included recordings of "If You Don't Come Back," "I Can't Go On," and "Lovebug." Jean followed up with yet another meeting with them the next day. Atlantic was interested, he told them. In fact, in an unprecedented move, Atlantic was willing to buy out their Spark record catalog and take the team on as independent producers, giving them full creative control over their sessions. Atlantic would step aside and let these creative talents—rather than Atlantic's own A&R men—drive product creation. There was a catch, though. As part of the deal they would give up 50 percent of the publishing rights to their songs currently held by Quintet Music to the Hill and Range–Atlantic co-venture publishing arm, Progressive Music.[24]

To simplify administration, this co-venture would eventually be recast as Tiger Music. "When Atlantic signed Jerry and me to what we were told was the first independent record production deal, to make records for Atlantic . . . [we would have to] give up a label that we had here with our mentor Lester Sill at Spark Records. [Sill] liked our records a lot, and we were very successful in Los Angeles, but we were underfinanced and could not promote outside of our local territory here at that time. And so [Jean and the Ertegun brothers] convinced us. They said, 'We'll give you a royalty for making the records.' And they also indicated that in doing this, we should have a joint publishing situation on the songs that we wrote and produced for them."[25]

By September 19, 1955, they had a deal, and Jean instructed attorney Mickey Rudin to draw up the paperwork that would solidify the relationship between Hill and Range and Quintet Music in connection with Progressive. He looked over these papers and approved them on September 27, just days before Atlantic officially acquired Spark. In all, it took Jean less than eight weeks to get this exciting new songwriting duo under his watchful eye. It was the first step in steering them toward Elvis Presley, who would be engaged in partnership with Hill and Range just eight weeks later.[26]

But easing these songwriters into Elvis's world would take time. As soon as the Elvis deal was completed on November 21, 1955, Jean departed for another trip to Europe. He arrived home on January 30, 1956, the very same day Elvis had entered the RCA studios for his second recording session. Jean found himself immediately engulfed in chaos and forced to take on a frantic song hunt.

Jean did not expect Elvis Presley to be a major priority upon his return. Julian was to depart for the coast in just a few days and they needed time to debrief each other. There were also many loose ends to tie up from the trip, and he was also being pressured to prepare himself for the grueling testimony for the Cellar committee hearings that charged BMI publishers with unfair trade practices against ASCAP. But dealing with the Elvis situation was unavoidable. Steve Sholes was going nuts.

Over the two months Jean had been away, the luster of the Elvis honeymoon had worn off and the magnitude of the deal Sholes had made for RCA was beginning to sink in. The pressure to make back the unprecedented investment he had paid for the Elvis contract weighed heavily on Sholes. Parker had Elvis booked for back-to-back live performance dates. The artist was crisscrossing the Mid-Atlantic and Southern states sometimes daily. He had also arranged for some television performances on CBS's *Stage Show,* a variety show produced by Jackie Gleason and hosted by orchestra leaders Jimmy and Tommy Dorsey. All this meant progress for the artist, but it did Sholes no good at all unless he had recordings ready to go. If he couldn't produce and sell records, RCA's $40,000 investment would be wasted.[27]

Sholes was having a difficult time fitting sessions into Elvis's enormously demanding performing schedule. When he did get them, he was at a loss what to do with them. Elvis was unlike any artist Sholes had ever worked with. Elvis represented an emerging genre Sholes neither understood nor particularly liked. Lagging behind the independents, the stash of songs Sholes had at his disposal didn't appeal to this new young market. The first session in Nashville on January 10 and 11, 1956, yielded two cover tunes, one of Ray Charles's "I Got a Woman" from the co-owned Progressive Music catalog and one originally done by the Drifters, "Money Honey." Hill and Range had contributed two ballads from the Ross Jungnickel ASCAP catalog "I Was the One" (Schroeder, Demetrius, Blair, Peppers) and "I'm Counting on You" (Don Robertson), the latter said to be one of Elvis's proudest recording moments.[28]

The only really original-sounding tune was "Heartbreak Hotel" (Mae Boren Axton, with Tommy Durden), and Sholes was truly mystified over what to do with it. Written by a former publicity aide to the Colonel, the song was as unlikely a pop tune as he could imagine. With a tune like that, there was no middle ground—it was either going to be a runaway hit or a total failure. They had burned up nine hours of studio time (almost twice what he'd expected), and while the tracks were professional, they lacked the raw edginess Sam Phillips had been able to squeeze out of the tiny Sun studio. As a whole, the material didn't hang well together, and he was having trouble figuring out how to package it in a way that would use the material to its best advantage (for instance, which sides would be A or B, whether to release 45s or EPs). He was stumped.

His fears about "Heartbreak Hotel" only increased with Elvis's first few television performances. While it should have been the featured song on his *Stage Show* appearance on January 28, "Heartbreak Hotel" was put aside, the Dorsey orchestra having trouble backing the artist up on the tune. Instead, Elvis performed "I Got a Woman," "Shake, Rattle, and Roll," and "Flip, Flop, and Fly." Elvis's new single got no promotional airplay.

Sholes knew he could mine some of the tunes Phillips had not released, but that would take him only so far. Without new hit material for the artist, this deal would be dead in the water—and so would Sholes's professional career. In a panic, he called Sam Phillips, negotiating limited use of Carl Perkins's "Blue Suede Shoes" as a cover option, remarking that maybe he'd picked up the wrong boy.[29]

After two days of difficult sessions, the band took a day off, and on February 1 Jean met with Sholes and Parker for lunch to catch up after his trip. Elvis had recorded several tunes, including Arthur Crudup's "My Baby Left Me" and "So Glad You're Mine"—half of whose copyright has been transferred to Elvis's new Hill and Range co-owned BMI publishing company, Elvis Presley Music. However, Elvis warmed up to only one of the six songs handpicked by Sholes himself—Bill Campbell's "One-Sided Love Affair." Elvis himself suggested covers of Joe Thomas's "I'm Gonna Sit Right Down and Cry (over You)," and Little Richard Penniman's "Tutti Frutti." Beyond that they were pretty much scraping thc bottom of the barrel. For lack of suitable material, Sholes was compelled to exercise his option with Phillips to record a cover of "Blue Suede Shoes."[30]

RCA had people all across the country hyping the artist. Sholes had better have product to deliver fast. They had one more session coming in two days and he had no idea what it would be used for. He needed new material for Elvis—specifically written for Elvis—not covers of someone else's tunes, if this venture was ever going to pay off.

While Jean was as concerned as the other two men, he was not in a much better position to respond. Out of the loop for two months and back home for only two days, he was still reorienting himself from the trip. He'd not yet even seen the artist perform. Nevertheless, he dove right into the fray. While Parker departed that afternoon for Nashville, Jean met with Sholes the following day to get a feel for what the boy needed. On such short notice, Jean wasn't able to deliver new tunes for the February 3 session, so Sholes fell back to cover recordings of Lloyd Price's "Lawdy, Miss Clawdy," and Charles Calhoun's "Shake, Rattle, and Roll," the latter of which was from the Progressive catalog Hill and Range jointly owned with Atlantic Records.

Having just acquired Sam Phillips's Hi-Lo catalog, Hill and Range benefited directly from any performance done of "Mystery Train" (written by Little Junior Parker), Stan Kesler's "I'm Left, You're Right, She's Gone," and Jack Salee's "You're a Heartbreaker," as well as Charles Singleton and Rose Marie McCoy's "Trying to Get to You," which also ended up in the Hill and Range catalog.[31]

But it did not participate in several other songs Elvis recorded. "Good Rockin' Tonight," or Otis Williams and the Charms' "Hearts of Stone"—both firmly controlled by Syd Nathan's publishing companies connected to King and Queen Records.[32] Likewise Mack David's "I Don't Care If the Sun Don't Shine" (a peppy little tune, originally written for Disney's *Cinderella* movie, but ultimately recorded by Dean Martin in 1950) and Arthur Gunter's "Baby, Let's Play House" also remained in the hands of other publishers, as did Kokomo Arnold's "Milkcow Blues Boogie," which was owned by Lou Levy's Leeds Music.[33] Neither Elvis nor Hill and Range would enjoy any publishing royalties from these songs.

Luckily Elvis took a liking to songs in the Progressive Music catalog. Hill and Range stood to participate in mechanical royalties from his recordings of Ray Charles's "I Got a Woman," and if he recorded covers like Charles Calhoun's "Shake, Rattle, and Roll," and "Fool, Fool, Fool," written by "Nugetre" (which was Ertegun spelled backwards!). But Jean fully appreciated Sholes's dilemma. If this artist was going to break big, it would be with original tunes tailor made for him—not covers made popular by other artists.

Jean had a strong stable of writers he could engage to craft custom-made music for Elvis. Both Hal Blair and Don Robertson had already contributed ballads to Elvis's first RCA recording session. Maurice Mysels and Ira Kosloff gave him "I Want You, I Need You, I Love You" for the third. But these were stock catalog offerings the writers had submitted without any knowledge of what artist might record them. Instead, Jean needed to generate songs that spoke directly to the teenage audience, and for that he needed to hand off the project to someone with better ears for that sort of music than he had. And he knew just the person.

Cousin Freddy Bienstock had come onto Hill and Range full-time around the time Elvis was signed. On the evening of January 31, 1956, the night after he had returned from Europe, Jean met with Freddy for a debriefing. How things were going with the Elvis venture was probably a key topic of discussion.[34]

Jean knew that their success depended on maintaining close relations with the artist, keeping an eye on his changing tastes and maturing style, and steering the most appealing tunes his way. It was best to put Elvis in the hands of someone closer to his age, and more in tune with his musical tastes. While Jean continued to meet regularly with Sholes to review demos and plan promotions over the next few months, such as arranging rack orders for "Blue Suede Shoes" sheet music, responsibility for much of Elvis's day-to-day affairs was transferred to Freddy, who enthusiastically accepted the assignment. He would be in charge

Freddy Bienstock.
Courtesy of Freddy
Bienstock.

of soliciting and selecting the pool of demos that would be presented to this dynamic artist. Freddy did so well that Jean recommended a raise when Julian arrived back from Los Angeles on April 5, 1956.[35]

As Elvis wrapped up a two-week performance in Las Vegas, Jean once again boarded the Superchief train to Los Angeles, probably arriving there on May 10. He met with Capitol, CBS, Lester Sill, and Paramount Pictures executives, probably to solidify the working process of supplying tunes for the seven-picture deal the Colonel had confirmed with producer Hal Wallis on April 2. Like the Colonel, Jean knew that making Elvis a screen star was the best promotional strategy imaginable from a publishing perspective. Aside from putting a fire under their record sales, it would increase the artist's attractiveness for television appearances in which Hill and Range songs would be featured, thus providing a lucrative additional revenue stream from song performances on television called synchronization royalties.[36]

There was a high likelihood that Elvis would do well in film. Wallis and his partner Joe Hazen were seasoned producers with several notable popular films to their credit, among them Jerry Lewis and Dean Martin comedies and Humphrey Bogart's *Casablanca*. Elvis had done remarkably well in his March 26 screen test but even if he had not, a good looking, controversial personality with national name recognition was a bankable commodity. They were interested.[37]

Elvis's reputation, both positive and negative, was growing fast. "Heartbreak Hotel" hit big, earning the Triple Crown award (for achieving the top spot for sales, DJ plays, and jukebox plays simultaneously), and his first album shot to the number 1 spot and remained there for ten weeks. RCA was ecstatic, Elvis Presley representing fully 50 percent of its total pop sales for the month of May. The release of "I Want You, I Need You, I Love You" paired with "My Baby Left Me" broke RCA preorder records—300,000 orders for 45-rpm singles nationwide.[38]

Confident that Freddy could continue to manage Elvis, and hopeful that Wallis would require a steady stream of Hill and Range music for his films, Jean left for another eight-week trip to Europe on June 26, 1956. Administrative duties were left in the hands of Julian until he joined Jean in Paris a few weeks later, with family in tow. On June 5, 1956, Julian had sent the proceeds from a BMI advance royalty check to the Colonel for Elvis. His fast-growing success was beginning to reflect in his publishing revenue. Only six months into his Hill and Range contract, and already this check was more than three times the size of the first Elvis had received. He split $4,000 with Jean and Julian for royalty advances projected on "I Want You, I Need You, I Love You" and "My Baby Left Me." His share would be the equivalent of a little more than $15,000 in early twenty-first century money.[39]

When Jean returned to New York on September 11, 1956, he stepped into another chaotic Elvis whirlwind. This time they weren't scrambling to keep afloat, but instead struggling to keep from drowning in success. Just two days earlier, Elvis had achieved the stamp of national legitimacy by playing Ed Sullivan's nationally syndicated variety show *Toast of the Town* for the first time. Also, while he had been away, Paramount had passed on producing Elvis's first film, and instead 20th Century–Fox had picked up the option, sealing a deal for a picture called *The Reno Brothers*. While there were few opportunities for songs in the film, they still managed to get director Ken Darby to agree on giving up half the publishing rights to those few public domain tunes adapted for the film. Among them was a lyric adaptation of the beautiful traditional folk tune "Aura Lee." The title of the film was quickly changed to reflect the title of this new derivative work, "Love Me Tender." But where Leiber and Stoller were concerned, Jean was in for an even bigger surprise.[40]

It had been more than a year since Jean had inscribed the names of Leiber and Stoller next to that of "Elvis Pressley" in his daybook. While he might have hoped to put these talents together immediately, the timing had not been right. Signed to Atlantic, the duo had been intensely busy with producing. They had their first hit with the Coasters called "Down in Mexico" back in January, and from there it had been a straight shot to the top. They were doing so well by the summer that Mike Stoller decided to take some time off.

Stoller used his first big Atlantic royalty check to finance a long vacation in Europe. When he and his young wife Meryl stepped back onto the pier at New York harbor on July 25, 1956, they were more than a little distracted. They had just endured a terrifying six-hour ordeal as passengers on the ill-fated *Andrea Doria*, an Italian ocean liner that was rammed broadside by another ship 45 miles off the coast of Nantucket Island, Massachusetts, and had sunk at sea.

Only five minutes after the bow of the Stockholm sliced eighty feet into the midship cabins, the boat had taken on enough water to be listing starboard at twenty-five degrees—far enough to capsize it. Stoller and his wife spent three terrifying hours aboard the wounded, tilting ship before climbing down rope ladders into lifeboats dispatched by a passing freighter. The *Cape Anne* docked at New York harbor with its frightened passengers only a few hours before the *Andrea Doria* finally rolled on its side and dropped below the surface, ultimately having claimed forty-six lives.

Jerry Leiber was there to meet Stoller and his wife at the pier. Stoller remembers the conversation:

> Jerry: "Mike, man—you okay?"
> Mike: "Yeah, I guess so."
> Jerry: "We've got a smash hit!"
> Mike: "You're kidding."
> Jerry: "I'm not kidding. 'Hound Dog' is number one on the charts!"

Mike: "Big Mama Thornton?"

Jerry: "No, some white kid named Elvis Presley."

Mike (confused, and probably still in shock): "Elvis who?"[41]

Abroad for three months, Stoller hadn't been following the trades that detailed Elvis's meteoric rise. He was just stepping out when the Colonel got Elvis the two-week booking at the New Frontier Hotel in Las Vegas from April 23, 1956. While there, Elvis enjoyed the exciting club scene, catching Freddie Bell and the Bellboys performance of "Hound Dog." It had been a number 1 rhythm and blues hit by "Big Mama" Thornton in 1953, and Freddy Bell's rendition bowled Elvis over. He immediately added it to his repertoire as a show-stopper closing number, performing it to a wide television audience on the Milton Berle and Steve Allen shows. The reaction to his bump-and-grind ending (framed from the waist up to satisfy television censors) was still electrifying, and on July 2 he entered the RCA studios and recorded it. Elvis's rendition was released on July 13, astounding RCA executives as it shot to number 2 on the charts in just a few weeks. It would sell more than a million copies before being overtaken by its B side, "Don't Be Cruel," written by Otis Blackwell. This double-sided hit was unprecedented and would sell almost four million copies by the end of the year.[42]

Elvis had thrown Jean a curveball by warming up to a Leiber and Stoller song all on his own. It took considerable effort to convince the boys to give up a portion of the "Hound Dog" copyright to the Elvis's Hill and Range publishing company. The royalties the song would generate, however, dwarfed anything they had ever received.

Freddy began prodding them for more material. Jerry remembered a tune called "Love Me" that the boys had recorded with a former gospel duo called Willie and Ruth. It was written almost tongue in cheek as a parody of country music. Nevertheless, Elvis loved it, and recorded it at the September 1–3 session at RCA Radio Recorders studio in Hollywood along with many other tunes whose copyrights had been arranged to be half-owned by Elvis Presley Music. These included Enotris Johnson's "Long Tall Sally," Robert Blackwell's "Rip It Up," and two by Otis Blackwell, "Paralyzed" and "Reddy Teddy.[43]

Elvis also chose songs for this session from other publishers—Tannen Music, Westpar Music, and Cedarwood Music—proof positive that he felt free to exercise his right to record whatever work he liked. But the bulk of what he chose to record for this session and many others were Hill and Range songs. Why was that?

Any songwriter could submit a song to Hill and Range to be considered for Elvis's recordings, but to do so was costly. The expectation was that you would come in bearing a full-blown professional demo you'd financed with your own money, whereas if you were a Hill and Range staff writer, the company would pick up the tab. This made sure that the demos coming from the company were polished and professional. Because of this extra effort, Hill and Range tunes tended to be the ones that were most attractive to Elvis. Freddy invariably came prepared to sessions with hordes of polished demos customized to specifically suit Elvis's voice and style. The works presented by Freddy on behalf of Hill and Range simply tended to dwarf all other submissions in number, in quality, and in their ability to capture Elvis's attention through careful orchestration and often by vocal imitation. In the end, Hill and Range demos were the ones Elvis could most easily see himself doing.[44]

Freddy quickly won the trust and respect of the artist when he attended his very first Elvis session on July 2. Sholes was struggling to find suitable material, and they had just exhausted the available list. Freddy, however, had brought along a demo of Otis Blackwell's tune "Don't Be Cruel" and played it for the artist during a break. Already a fan of the songwriter, Elvis immediately recorded it, and it became the successful flip side of "Hound Dog." From that point forward, Elvis trusted Freddy to bring him good material.[45]

As September 1956 melted away, it was clear there were other hits to come. By late October, Leiber and Stoller's "Love Me" was released as part of Elvis's first album, climbing to number 6 on the charts. Steve Sholes reported that he had almost a million preorders on the song "Love Me Tender," likely the result of Elvis having performed it nationwide on the Ed Sullivan Show on September 9. It would sell 2.5 million records by Christmas. Elvis's popularity had already grown to the point that he was playing venues as large as the 80,000-seat Cotton Bowl in Dallas, Texas, and filling about a third of it. His second appearance on Sullivan's *Toast of the Town* on October 28 captured 80.6 percent of the national television viewing audience. He had sold more than 10 million singles—two-thirds of all RCA singles sales for that year. The revenue potential from this artist seemed limitless.[46]

While this was good for business, the Colonel was already concerned about overexposure. Elvis was showing up everywhere, and there was a chance people would quickly tire of him. It was time to scale back and build anticipation. They would concentrate on the films.

Film music was where Jean had started, way back with Meisel in Berlin. He knew that putting the right music to film was much different than writing songs for hit records. Film songwriters had to submit to the storyline, rather than letting their creative muse run wild. Some songwriters couldn't do that. Others, who thought their songs were the star, wouldn't do that. But Leiber and Stoller had already shown a natural flair for colorful storytelling in songs like "Smokey Joe's Café" and the humorous "Down in Mexico." Their songs already had a decidedly theatrical flavor. Jean knew they had the talent to do this, but would they?

As far as the boys were concerned, "Hound Dog" had been a fluke and "Love Me" was a hillbilly throwaway parody. Now they were being asked by Jean to write for uninspired storylines and give up all production control over their work—in addition to giving up half their copyrights! Somehow, Jean convinced them to contribute four songs to the seven-song score for the first Paramount movie—including the title tune and variations, "Loving You."[47]

But Leiber and Stoller were not the only songwriters Hill and Range engaged. Jean cast his net far and wide, distributing the script among a number of talented writing teams. Kal Mann and Bernie Lowe contributed "(Let Me Be Your) Teddy Bear," Aaron Schroeder and Ben Weisman provided "Got a Lot o' Livin' to Do," and Sid Tepper and Roy C. Bennett (who had had a hit a few years earlier with a novelty song called "Nuttin' for Christmas"), submitted "Lonesome Cowboy." Meantime Freddy got Claude Demetrius to create "Mean Woman Blues," which displaced one of Leiber and Stoller's tunes for the film.

Except for two stray tunes from other publishers, "One Night of Sin" by Bartholomew/King from Travis Music and "Blueberry Hill" by A. Lewis/L. Stock/V. Rose, from Chappell and Company, all other songs were Hill and Range. Hill and Range worked hard to bring the best, most polished material to the table, and typically it satisfied the need, thereby eliminating the search for anything else. That didn't stop Elvis from selecting tunes from other publishers from time to time, causing Freddy to scramble to negotiate rights with the current copyright holder, if it could be arranged. Sometimes he got those rights, and sometimes he didn't.[48]

From time to time, Freddy would come up short on material for sessions, and Jean would dip down into the catalog trying to come up with suitable material. Such was the case for the RCA Radio Recorders Studio session on January 19, 1957, when Jean brought two Jimmy Wakely songs ("I Love You So Much It Hurts Me" and "One Has My Name (The Other Has My Heart)"), as well as a few Gene Autry hits, including "Have I Told You Lately That I Love You." Faron Young's "Is It So Strange" stands as testament to Elvis's right to choose. He was determined to record this song whether or not Young would agree to give up half the copyright to his publishing company. Freddy was obliged by contract to make every effort to arrange this, and he managed to do so.[49]

Luckily, Jean was not necessarily bound to the country and western catalog when he went fishing for Elvis material. It probably came as a huge surprise at first that Elvis was a gospel enthusiast. Even during the early recording days with Sam Phillips, Elvis expressed an interest in doing a gospel album, but Phillips refused. By early 1957, however, the time was right to do a gospel disc.

The Colonel knew that much of the negative publicity generated by Elvis's controversial performance style could be countered by presenting him as a devoted, God-fearing Christian. Rumor has it that the network asked Elvis to perform "(There'll Be) Peace in the Valley" on his third Ed Sullivan show appearance on January 6, 1957, but that would have been a highly unusual request. Like records and film, television was expected to be repertoire neutral. Television executives could quickly find themselves in trouble with the performing rights societies if they were caught dictating repertoire to guest performers. Nor would the Colonel have allowed it, had it not been his idea in the first place. No, the buttons were being pushed by the Colonel, and behind him, probably by Freddy and Jean. After all, the tune was written by Thomas A. Dorsey and was part of the Hill and Range Music catalog.

Elvis was ripe to perform a heartfelt gospel tune, having spent a day in early December in an impromptu jam session at Sun Studios with Carl Perkins, Jerry Lee Lewis, and Johnny Cash (together they are referred to as the "Million Dollar Quartet"). Over several hours, Sam Phillips caught some thirty-six performances on tape, a significant portion of which were gospel tunes, ranging from "Blessed Jesus (Hold My Hand)" to "When the Saints Go Marching In," and Dorsey's "(There'll Be) Peace in the Valley."[50] Elvis recorded this song, along with another Dorsey tune, "Take My Hand, Precious Lord," and "I Believe" an inspirational pop tune written by Ervin Drake, Irvin Graham, Jimmy Shirl, and Al Stillman (from the Cromwell Music Catalog, not connected with Hill and Range) in his January 12–13 session. He rounded out his four-song gospel extended-play disc with a recording of Stuart Hamblen's "It Is No Secret (What God Can Do)," another non-Hill and Range song from Lou Levy's Duchess Music catalog. The disc was a hit, selling more than half a million copies.[51]

On February 25, 1957, Colonel Parker sealed the deal with MGM for Elvis's third film, *The Rock*. The script detailed a story about a young kid who gets in trouble with the law, spends some time in jail, and ultimately sings his way out. Jean lost no time distributing the script to his stable of songwriters. Competing against one another, he was sure he'd come up with winning material. But Jean was counting the most on Leiber and Stoller, who had proven themselves with key contributions to Elvis's last film, *Loving You*. Jean expected no less from their contribution for *The Rock*.

Jerry and Mike planned to be in New York pursuing a Broadway musical project. After they arrived, Jean invited them to the Hill and Range offices and presented them with a script for the movie. He expected to hear back from them a few days later, but the boys rarely got to town and were having the time of their lives dropping in at various nightclubs, and talking to people about Broadway shows and other ventures.

Jerry and Mike had rented a suite at the Gorham Hotel. They had also rented an upright piano for the living room in case they were inspired to write. Their excitement about being in New York was so consuming, however, that they had tossed the script in the corner with the pile of magazines provided by the hotel.

One Saturday morning, Jean knocked on the door, walked in, and said, "Well boys, where are my songs?" "Don't worry, Jean. You'll have them," they replied.

"Yes, I know I will," Jean replied. He glanced around the room, walked over to a big overstuffed chair, and pushed it in front of the door. Then he plopped his tall frame down in it and said, "I'm going to take a nap now . . . and you're not leaving until I have songs for the movie." The boys were flabbergasted, but imprisoned as they were in a hotel room with a piano and eager to get out they opened the script. As Jean dozed off in the chair they penned four songs in about five hours—including the title tune "Jailhouse Rock."[52]

Jean's motivational techniques with other songwriters were usually less extreme, but his stable of songwriters quickly came to learn that above all, Jean Aberbach valued professionalism. If you were talented, creative, flexible, and prompt, you could work with him. Otherwise, beware.

Freddy Bienstock tells a story that provides insight into Jean's personality. Just before stepping out to dinner one night, Jean got a call from one of their song pluggers in California. "'It's that crazy guy in California,' Jean said. And he takes his hat off and the last thing I heard him say is, 'I want you to come to New York immediately for a re-indoctrination course,'" recalls Bienstock.

It turns out this fellow was in charge of promotion. He was eager to please, but apparently a little too ambitious. Hill and Range had acquired a song called "Whither Thou Goest" and got Les Paul and Mary Ford to record it, but not before the original publisher put their recording out. Theirs was charting well, and the Hill and Range recording was trailing. But this guy figured out that if he could just induce disc jockeys to list the Hill and Range recording instead, then theirs would be number 1 on the charts.

This flagrant attempt at payola quickly got back to the original publisher, their record company, and the writers, who all threatened to sue the Aberbachs. A few days later, Freddy got the fellow on the phone and was shocked to learn the song plugger had quit. When asked why, the man likened a "reindoctrination course" with Jean Aberbach to being interrogated by the KGB. Thinking he'd not likely escape with his life, it was preferable to simply quit![53]

Jean could be implacable about things like timeline, budget, and professionalism, but he never interfered with the creative process. Mostly Jean supported his staff by providing challenging problems for those writers who were suited to particular assignments. He gave these creative talents the time to sit and study an artist until they understood his style and capabilities.

After witnessing Elvis's performance firsthand at the *Stage Show* rehearsal on January 18, 1956, Jean called up one of his staff songwriters, Ben Weisman. "Ben, we have just signed a new artist called Elvis Presley. He's playing on Tommy Dorsey's show. I want you to watch him . . . watch him very carefully, because I need you to write songs for him."

Because of his promptness and versatility, Jean looked to Weisman as one strategy in solving the lack of material for Elvis Presley. A good lieutenant with a passion to please, Weisman found himself glued to the television the night of February 18, 1956, carefully listening to Elvis's *Stage Show* performance—his voice, the background, the style, the harmony, and the lyrics.[54]

Weisman's relationship with Jean was closer than that of most of his other songwriters. He had been writing songs on and off for Jean since 1950 with partners Kay Twomey and Fred Wise. They were the first team signed to Hill and Range's Alamo Music company, which was connected to ASCAP. Typically, Kay came up with the ideas, Fred did the lyrics, and Ben handled the music. But Jean could be difficult to work for, and he showed impatience in the first few days after they'd been signed.

One day in 1950, Jean called them all to the office. "Well, I'm signing you up. And Ben, I want you to call me on Sunday and the rest of you I'll see Monday in my office." Jean gave Weisman his private home number and on the appointed day Ben dutifully put in the call. "Who is this?!" Jean demanded. "Jean, this is Ben Weisman," the songwriter replied. "See me in the office!"—BOOM! Jean slammed down the phone. Weisman was aghast, but assumed there'd been some misunderstanding.

When he walked into the office with his partners on Monday, he caught Jean in a foul mood. Jean shot the songwriter a piecing glare and yelled "Weisman! Don't EVER call me at HOME!!" Ben could feel the color coming to his face as he was dressed down in front of an office of total strangers. His partners shrank into the background, fearing for their jobs. "My God—what is this?!" Weisman thought. "Well, that's it. I'm quitting!"

Steaming for the rest of the day, the songwriter arrived back at closing time to give notice. By this time, however, the day's frustrations had worked themselves out and Ben found Jean in a remarkably lighthearted mood. He emerged from the office with a huge, warm smile: "Weisman! Come! We'll share a cab home," he invited. Still angry and resolved, Weisman endured the eleven-flight walk down the stairs, as was Jean's habit. As they got into a cab, Jean expressed concern: "So, why so quiet?" And Weisman declared, "Jean, I'm quitting!" "You're quitting?" Jean said, surprised. "Yeah. Jean, my parents don't yell at me as much as you've yelled at me over the past two days!" Jean was stupefied: "Well you called me at home." "Jean," Weisman interrupted, "how could I have gotten your private number? How could I have called you?" Suddenly it dawned on him that he'd given Weisman the number and directed him to call. Jean was devastated. "Oh my God! You're right! How could I have forgotten?" Jean reached an arm around to embrace him and Ben's anger melted away.[55]

That encounter set the tone for their relationship. Jean respected a man who wasn't afraid to stand up for himself. They became close friends and colleagues, even going out on double dates, visiting museums and occasionally taking trips together. Ben often visited Jean in California, staying at the house. Weisman would go off to pursue outside work from time to time, but their relationship always remained cordial. He was always a part of Jean's orbit.

This was true for other artists as well. Jean never held a songwriter back from success. In the case of Otis Blackwell and Winfield Scott, who wrote several hit tunes for Elvis, the exclusive songwriting agreement stipulated obligations on the part of both the publishers and the writers. If Hill and Range didn't feel that a tune was right for Elvis or any artist they were working with, the writers were free to take the tune to anyone they liked, even if it meant Hill and Range giving up all or part of the publishing rights. At least where Blackwell and Scott were concerned, exclusivity on their songs was limited to "right of first refusal."[56]

The songwriters who worked with Jean loved him because he was a fair professional and a man of his word. In one instance, a song by Winfield Scott was recorded by Elvis before Scott and Jean had concluded a contract. Jean knew that the songwriter could have taken the song anywhere he liked at that point, but Scott did not hesitate to sign the song over to Hill and Range.

"What had happened [was] Elvis had recorded the song, and the Aberbachs did not have a contract from me on the song, which put them in a very precarious situation. Here I am, with a song by Elvis and they don't have a contract! Now, there was no question about what I was going to do. I was going to sign the contract, because that had just been an oversight on everyone's part. But strangely enough, through all of this, Jean was very calm about it. And when we did get together he said, 'Well look,' he said, 'I have the contract papers here.' He said, 'Will you sign them?' I said. 'Of course.' And he said, 'You know, I never had any doubt that you wouldn't.' To me, that said a lot about the man. . . . He was a prince."[57]

Jean's genius was in recognizing the capabilities of individuals and tailoring assignments that challenged them to produce their best work. Weisman was a remarkably versatile writer who could craft songs in almost any genre. Above all, this was the characteristic Jean sought. He wanted writers who could write good songs on demand for any artist. Jean would urge his songwriters to fit a song to an artist like a tailor fits a suit to a man—custom made.

If Jean contributed to the creative process at all, it was usually only in a general way. His contribution was often a theme or an idea. The profitability of songs that tied in with popular culture merchandizing probably hit him during 1949, when Eddy Arnold recorded a novelty song called "Smokey the Bear" by Jack Rollins and Steve Nelson, as a public service for the United States Park Service.[58] They followed up with the tremendously successful promotion and merchandizing of "Peter Cottontail," recorded by Gene Autry in 1950.

Then, in 1951, Jean came back to the staff writers one day with another proposition: "Make me a song about a snowman!"[59] From this suggestion the beloved holiday song "Frosty the Snowman" was born. The following year saw the endearing snowman gracing the front cover of the annual Montgomery Ward mail-order catalog that reached millions of homes. It was the anchor for a huge, coordinated merchandizing blitz connected to the popular tune. Since then the song has been recorded by almost 140 major artists ranging from the Brady Bunch to Harry Connick Jr., and it continues to be among the most popular songs of all time.

In general, though, Jean left the creative work to the skilled people he and his brother had hired, raising a flag only when something didn't seem quite right. Very often the suggestions improved the final product. Like a good editor, Jean's talent wasn't to dictate to his songwriters, but to support their talents and encourage them to rethink the work in ways that might improve the final product.[60]

Jean also didn't need to hear a full demo to decide whether a tune had potential. On one occasion there was an opportunity to place a tune with Frank Chacksfield, a famous British orchestra leader. On a Friday, Jean called Ben Weisman into the office. "Weisman, I want something strings. . . . violin, something . . .," Jean told Ben. "I need it by Monday!" But Jean . . ." the songwriter pleaded. "I need it by Monday, Monday, MONDAY!" he pounded the desk.

Weisman went home in a panic. He worked all day Saturday, but the creative juices just didn't flow. He slept fitfully that night, the hundred or so discarded themes of the day floating around in his head. Suddenly he awoke and sat bolt upright with the memory of a theme composed in his sleep beginning to fade. He shot to the piano stark naked and scribed the tune.

On Monday, he arrived late in the day, and Jean and he exited the Brill Building. "Okay, Weisman, what have you got for me?" As they plodded along through the crowd, Weisman sang the tune to him "Dee, da daa, da daa, . . ." Jean listened carefully, their walk assuming the pace and rhythm of the proposed tune as they made their way up the thirty blocks to Jean's apartment on Central Park West. After Ben was done, Jean nodded. "All right. I think it has a chance. Go in the studio, get four violins and then give me the demo." A few days later Jean dropped by Weisman's place and listened to the demo "Fine! Let's hope Frank Chacksfield likes it," he said, scooping up the disc. For a month Ben sweated, waiting for the verdict. Finally, a telegram arrived from England and Jean called Ben with the good news. "You've got the next single, Frank Chacksfield . . . The Golden Violins! You see, I knew it in the first place!" he said with delight.[61]

Weisman's greatest success however, came from doctoring "Let Me Go, Devil" into "Let Me Go, Lover." The song had been written by Fred Rose's ex-girlfriend, Jenny Lou Carson. She had written it to express her painful struggle with alcohol. Feeling the song had potential in the pop field as well, Jean shopped it to Columbia producer Mitch Miller, but he declined.[62] "First the gambling . . . then the drinking . . . bottles of rye whiskey . . . Jean! Who's going to listen to this song? Alcoholics?? And if they are reformed they don't want to hear it!" said the producer. "Now, the tune's not too busy, so it might do as background music, but if what you want is a song hit with me, you're going to have to change the subject," Miller declared. Jean took the song back to the office, and got Jenny Lou on the phone. "Look—change the lyrics! Miller loves the song, but make it about a different subject!" The song, however, was a personal expression of her troubled life, and she flatly refused.[63]

As is, it got placed that year with country singer Johnny Bond in August 1953 for Columbia's OKeh label, and also with Sholes as a B side for Wade Ray's September 1953 session. Ultimately it became a turntable hit in the country field. People were buying it despite the fact that it wasn't getting much airplay.

Miller kicked himself for not jumping on the tune, but he kept it in mind as he worked his way into 1954 as the music director for the popular dramatic CBS-TV series called *Studio One*. Sometime after the interest in the tune as a country song died down, Miller came across an opportunity to insert a song as a dramatic interlude in the television show story, and he remembered the tune. He called Jean and said, "Look, I can use this here, as long as you can get the words changed to fit the story."

Operating under a pseudonym to protect their exclusive ASCAP affiliation necessary at that time, the trio of Twomey, Wise, and Weisman birthed the cowriter "Al Hill." In a half hour, Jean was back on the phone with Miller, assuring him they'd have a demo for him to listen to in a few days. While the trio scrambled to write new lyrics, Julian was dispatched from Los Angeles by train with demo in hand to the wilds of Enumclaw, Washington, in the dead of winter. His job was to convince Jenny Lou to let them release the work with new lyrics despite her personal feelings about the song. Everyone — including Jenny Lou — would profit enormously from this. Finally, a deal was struck, and Miller featured the tune using eighteen-year-old screen starlet Joan Weber.

Reaction to the tune was phenomenal. Millions of people had watched the television drama that featured the song and record orders poured into the Columbia switchboard throughout the next day. Miller scrambled to put every pressing machine he could get his hands on into action to meet the million preorders. This was the first record to prove the power of marketing music through the new medium of television, and it personified the phrase "overnight hit." It came about because of Jean's quick reaction to the problem of Miller's need to adapt the song for his television series, and Weisman's quick, creative response to the challenge.

Weisman output for Elvis is astounding. This is most remarkable because he wasn't a rock 'n' roll songwriter. Julliard trained, he acted as musical director of the U.S. Air Force Band during World War II. The session on September 1–3, 1956, included "First in Line," a song cowritten with lyricist Aaron Schroeder from the ASCAP Ross Jungnickel catalog. The session on January 12–13, 1957, yielded a hit that has become a standard of the era, "Got a Lot o' Livin' to Do," which was published through Gladys Music. Ultimately, he would contribute twenty-six songs to the Elvis legacy—mostly ballads, connected to his films.[64]

Elvis's films were the perfect vehicle for Ben Weisman's talent. But the films created challenges for others. Sholes and Parker were constantly at odds over scheduling. The problem was that Sholes was looking for perfect pop hits, whereas Parker and producers Wallis and Hazen were looking for incidental music that was not supposed to steal the show. Recording sessions that attempted to serve both purposes were never completely successful.

Elvis was beginning to exert his own influence over the sessions as well, demanding perfection in his own performances that caused take after costly retake. For instance, during the New York session of July 2, 1956, "Hound Dog" had required thirty-one takes to achieve Elvis's satisfaction. "Don't Be Cruel" required more than two dozen takes to complete.[65] Adding to the stress, friction increased between Sholes and the Colonel when the latter moved to separate the movie from the record sessions, effectively reducing RCA session time.

Some of the edge was taken off when Leiber and Stoller showed up to the *Jailhouse Rock* sessions at MGM Studios in Hollywood over April and May 1957. Apparently their curiosity had gotten the better of them, and they needed to see for themselves whether this artist was the real thing or just a good imitation of some of the black performers they'd worked with. What they found was a smart, polite, talented young singer whose enthusiasm for obscure black tunes and singers approached their own. He won them over, both as a person and as a creative artist.

Driven by their instincts, the boys quickly jumped in and began providing much-needed direction both in the control room and on the studio floor. Their contribution was significant and was appreciated by both the RCA staff and the artist himself. These exhilarating sessions yielded several versions of "Jailhouse Rock." It also yielded new Leiber and Stoller songs "I Want to Be Free," and "(You're So Square) Baby I Don't Care," as well as recordings of Abner Silver and Aaron Schroeder's "Young and Beautiful" and Schroeder and Ben Weisman's "Don't Leave Me Now." The boys were finally sold on Elvis's talents, and the artist was sold on Leiber and Stoller's producing ability.[66]

It was a winning combination, and one that consummated the hopeful juxtaposition of their names in Jean's daybook more than a year before. Typical of Jean's style, he quietly and deliberately worked the chess pieces from the shadows, moving the players closer together until things clicked. Jean may not have been the right person to choose hot pop material for Elvis, but he had remarkable instincts that guided him to plug the right people into the Elvis machine.

Like diamonds, talent is forged under great pressure. Conspiring together, Sholes, Parker, and the Aberbachs had taken this lean, hungry artist to the top of the music industry in less than two years. Elvis was as transparent as a raindrop. He was talented and malleable. Working together, they diligently chipped away at this rough stone until they hit that "sweet spot"—the perfect mix of pressure and support that focused this remarkably talented vocal artist on his audience with laserlike precision. What tumbled out was a perfect crystal that captured the light and spirit of its time in a way that still blinds us today.

CHAPTER 20

Restless Giant

As early as March 1957, Elvis's popularity had grown to the point that almost all his personal performances took on near-riot proportions. A local Michigan paper reported that "the only trouble with going to see Elvis Presley is that you're liable to get killed."[1] A show in Vancouver, British Columbia, a few months later was stopped twice as the crowd of 26,500 surged to the stage, and finally turned it over as Elvis exited the arena.

To guard against media overexposure, the Colonel began scaling back Elvis's public performances. Elvis's appearances went to the highest bidder, that being whoever was willing to top the Colonel's last price. Television appearances would go for $75,000, and he promptly turned down offers even from top industry personalities, including Dean Martin, when he would not meet the price.[2]

Elvis performed commercially at only a handful of locations. Nevertheless, he made numerous appearances throughout the year for charity fundraisers and benefits, which helped defuse his public image as a renegade youth. He stopped by Danny Thomas's "Shower of Stars" benefit for St. Jude's Children's

Jean Aberbach,
c. 1960. Courtesy
of Susan Aberbach.

Hospital, pitched in to send students from his high school to a football game, and performed at the Mississippi-Alabama Fair to raise funds for a youth center to be built behind his boyhood home in Tupelo, Mississippi.[3]

With his "golden goose" in hand, the Colonel began pulling rank on Wallis and Sholes. Their film and record contracts were renegotiated, which was always a losing game when the Colonel was on the other side of the table. To get Elvis to star in his first Paramount film, Wallis was forced to match the $100,000 Twentieth Century–Fox had paid for *Love Me Tender*. Parker also attached extra costs for the use of Elvis's photographs for RCA promotions, giving himself a twenty-five percent kickback.

But for Sholes, this was just the beginning. Maybe it was payback time for being kicked around when he was down and out in 1954, but Parker refused to allow RCA's top performer to headline for RCA's "Galaxy of Stars" television special that took place on April 29, 1957.[4] Worse yet, he told Sholes that Elvis should release no more than four singles a year, his contract ensuring this by a clause stipulating the songs chosen must be "mutually agreeable." He had only to say that all but four songs were disagreeable to force Sholes into submission. Increasingly Sholes was marginalized at the sessions, to the point that he couldn't very well call himself an A&R man, given how little control over song selection, recording, production, and final approval he had.[5]

On the other hand, there were two people the Colonel couldn't control, and their influence over Elvis was growing. Leiber and Stoller hit it off with Elvis, and they continued exchanges with the artist after the *Jailhouse Rock* recording wrapped up on May 9, 1957. A few weeks later, on May 22, Elvis informed the Colonel he would like to see their "Treat Me Nice" show up as the B side to "Jailhouse Rock," probably raising Parker's suspicions that the boys were getting too close.[6]

Having done so well assisting with the *Jailhouse Rock* sessions, Leiber and Stoller were back in the studio with him on September 7, with Elvis recording their song "Don't." The session was also devoted to completing a Christmas album. Nine of twelve songs were connected to Hill and Range. Still one song short of a full album, however, Leiber and Stoller had dashed off "Santa Claus Is Back in Town," which Elvis recorded on the spot, further building the trust between them.[7]

Understanding that his own personal battle with the Colonel was lost, Sholes did the next best thing he could think of to work around Parker's restrictions:

Mike Stoller, Elvis Presley, and Jerry Leiber. Courtesy of Elvis Presley Enterprises, Ltd.

He hired Leiber and Stoller as independent producers. They had proven themselves able to produce hit records and to write new tunes Elvis liked to record. Sholes probably hoped that this would entice Elvis to spend more time in the recording studio, since he enjoyed working with Leiber and Stoller.[8]

Soundtrack work on the film *King Creole* began in January 1958. Virtually every song recorded was placed in Elvis Presley Music or his new ASCAP firm, Gladys Music. As with *Jailhouse Rock,* the script for the Paramount film had circulated among several Hill and Range songwriting teams, with the best material from the pool being chosen. Claude DeMetrius, Tepper and Bennet, Wise and Weisman, Schroeder and Martin Kalmanoff, and Sid Wayne and Abner Silver all contributed to the score, along with Leiber and Stoller, who themselves provided five tunes.

The story, based on Harold Robbins's *A Stone for Danny Fisher,* begged for a title song that rocked, and Fred Wise and Ben Weisman's contribution of "Danny" fell short. Leiber and Stoller lobbied for their tune "King Creole" as the title song, and also as the name for the film. Sholes couldn't have been happier when the decision was made to add an extra session to beef up the tune. Hiring Leiber and Stoller just might be the ticket to getting hit tunes out of the film sessions. While these were the property of Paramount, having been produced by Thorne Nogar at Radio Recorders studio, it was still cheaper to negotiate their release on RCA than try to support entirely separate studio dates—if the Colonel would allow them at all. So well did the January 16, 1958, session go that Elvis insisted Leiber and Stoller be at his next recording session on February 1. Unfortunately, Leiber was down with pneumonia in New York on that date, and the resulting session attempted without him was disappointing.[9]

It was clear that Elvis looked to Leiber and Stoller both for studio guidance and for great tunes. What Sholes didn't count on was that the songwriter-producers' youthful exuberance would cause them to cross swords with the Colonel one too many times. They had already raised his rancor when they had submitted lead sheets for "Don't" and "I'm a Hog for You" directly to Elvis back in June 1957, rather than going through the normal process of song submission through Freddy. Parker got his opportunity to pounce when the boys pitched the idea of having Elvis star in a film adaptation of *A Walk on the Wild Side* to Jean and Julian in 1960.[10]

The split between Leiber and Stoller and Parker was unpleasant, and no amount of goodwill between the songwriters and Elvis could mend it. The boys were fed up with the Colonel's lack of imagination with the artist, and Parker, feeling they were exerting too much influence on Elvis, was happy to be rid of them. Disappointed at the outcome, Jean felt a compromise could have taken place, but Parker would not be moved. To rub it in, a few years later Parker would pull the two songs submitted by the songwriters from the soundtrack of

G.I. Blues, thus sealing the breach between them, and squashing what some believe was among the most important and productive recording collaborations in rock 'n' roll history.[11]

Parker, Sholes, and the Aberbach brothers had already endured many ups and downs over the eighteen months that saw Elvis Presley rise from a footnote in the trades to the most sought after, highly paid performing artist in the industry. Just when it seemed as if things had leveled out, Elvis received his induction papers. He entered the U.S. Army on March 20, 1958.

Over the next year, Jean worked closely with Parker and Sholes to keep public interest in the artist alive. Parker's insistence to restrict Elvis's recording output left Sholes empty-handed, with no viable backlog of recordings to draw on during his absence. RCA was forced to release a compilation disk of Elvis's bestsellers called *Elvis's Golden Records*. Sholes managed to catch the artist for a one-night session in Nashville just before he left, backed up by the strong talents of Chet Atkins and Hank Garland on guitar and Bob Moore on bass. They recorded five more Hill and Range tunes, including "Ain't That Loving You, Baby" by Clyde Otis and Ivory Joe Hunter.[12]

Freddy Bienstock was made vice president of Hill and Range on November 5, 1956, in recognition of his vast contribution to their success with Elvis. Freddy didn't always have the latitude to steer Elvis to the tunes he thought would work best for him. The Colonel's exclusive focus on film was frustrating. The scripts delivered to Hill and Range might make Elvis a star on screen, but it was not the best use of his vocal talent. Storylines were almost always mediocre and forgettable, making the challenge of finding suitable material that much harder. They were all stuck with the Colonel's vision for Elvis, and since the artist didn't seem to mind, Freddy did the best that he could under the constraints.

Typically, after the scripts were distributed, appointments would be made with the various songwriting teams to review their work. If he liked a song, Freddy would authorize the team to have a professional demo made. Very often these would be made with up-and-coming performers. Several demos, for instance, were made by Bobby Darin. Once he had a stock of recordings he felt comfortable with, he'd make a trip to wherever Elvis was, sometimes first running them by other members of Elvis's entourage to weed them out further. Finally he'd play the final picks for Elvis, and it would be up to Elvis to pick the tunes he most wanted to use.[13]

Freddy often looked to the seasoned writers Otis Blackwell and Winfield Scott for good material. Blackwell had given him his first hit tune with Elvis's "Don't Be Cruel" and the follow-up hit "All Shook Up," and his writing partner Winfield Scott had written "Tweedle Dee." Their material was consistently superior.

Blackwell and Scott had worked together on and off for years, first for Roosevelt Music, and then for Shalimar Music, before signing up with Hill and Range. Together they wrote for a wide range of rhythm and blues artists including Clyde McPhatter, Ruth Brown, and LaVern Baker. To make a living as songwriters, however, it soon became clear that they needed to expand their reach into the pop and country fields. They began writing for Conway Twitty, Carl Perkins, Connie Francis, Johnny Ray, and others.

Blackwell and Scott were versatile, but as black writers coming from the rhythm and blues field where creative expression was unbridled, they approached writing for Elvis's films in a different way. Most other writing pairs would take direction from the script and try to fit their work neatly into the storyline. Blackwell and Scott tended to ignore the script and just focus on writing good tunes for Elvis. Very often the songs were so good that Wallis found a place for them in script whether or not they fit the storyline. "Return to Sender," is the most famous of them.

Winfield Scott elaborates on their songwriting method: "The only direction we got [from Hill and Range] was we would get a script—a movie script. And in the movie script they would suggest different titles . . . they would suggest different spots for a song, and different types of songs. Everyone pretty much adhered to that—except us! We didn't adhere to that. We felt the best thing to do was to write the song—write the song!—which is what we did with "Return to Sender." We looked at the script, we saw where there were spots for songs, and they even suggested titles. And everyone would go and write for the titles. So therefore sometimes you would have eight or nine—or sometimes ten songs with the same title, in the same spot, with the same type of music. We didn't do that. We said, 'Hey, let's just go write a great song.' So that's what we did with 'Return to Sender.' And Hal Wallis came into town and heard us do it personally on piano. And he liked the song. And they made a spot for it in the movie! And not only that, they made the single, and it became the hit! So we learned a valuable lesson. [And the lesson was: Write a great song—and they'll find someplace to put it?] That's right!"[14]

For the most part, Freddy took care of monitoring the Elvis project while the artist was away in the service, but on a rare occasion Jean would get involved. Elvis's army unit was stationed in Friedberg, Germany. He had brought along his father, grandmother, and friends Lamar Fike and Red West, putting them up in a spa hotel close by the military base (his mother Gladys, had since passed on). While there, he participated in several promotional events put together by the Colonel back in the States. During June 1959, Elvis was granted a two-week furlough, and for this Parker went all out. At his request, Jean flew over with Freddy to orchestrate a press conference and to generally make sure Elvis would stay out of trouble.

There was good reason for concern. Elvis was prone to wilding from time to time. Parker feared Elvis would need supervision, and Jean was one of the few people that might be able to exercise some control over him. Aside from the press conference, Jean set up tours of the Louvre and other cultural points of interest for the artist, but it soon became apparent after Elvis arrived that the only cultural interest he had was in loose French women. Elvis struck out for the club district almost immediately, ducking into risqué clubs like Lido, Moulin Rouge, the Folies Bergères, and Bantu. Nevertheless, Elvis returned to Germany without incident, much to Jean and the Colonel's relief.[15]

Just under a year later, Elvis arrived at McGuire Air Force Base near Fort Dix, New Jersey, on March 5, 1960. Jean was there to meet him, along with Colonel Parker and several RCA representatives. Aside from these activities, Jean had little further direct interaction with the artist. With Freddy in charge, Jean turned his attention back to other matters.[16]

With the onset of the 1960s came fundamental changes in the music business that increasingly minimized the role of the music publisher as a driving force. Empowered by the very model Jean and Julian had encouraged (part ownership in their publishing rights), more and more songwriters began to recognize the profit potential of owning and controlling all of their publishing. A cult following for American folk music was also starting to grow, which didn't require huge production or marketing support. Artists like Pete Seeger and the Weavers, the Kingston Trio, and the Chad Mitchell Trio could make cult hits out of public domain tunes. An era of social suspicion was also brewing around the notion that politics and big business were repressing genuine American culture. Music publishers began to feel the pinch.

Hill and Range weathered the transition much more easily than other firms, in part because the Aberbach brothers stayed true to their mission. Well into the

Jean Aberbach
and Elvis Presley,
signing Playbills
outside the
Folies Bergères,
Paris. Courtesy
of Elvis Presley
Enterprises, Ltd.

1960s, and long after most publishers had given the model up, Hill and Range maintained a traditional publishing house, signing songwriters exclusively to create winning tunes. They maintained small studios at their penthouse offices in the Brill Building that were actively used by songwriters like Winfield Scott, Bennie Benjamin, and the prolific songwriting team of Doc Pomus and Mort Shuman.[17] They wrote almost 300 tunes, many of which are considered rock 'n' roll classics. By 1961 they were the most commercially successful songwriting team on the planet, contributing thirteen pop songs to the charts that year.

Pomus began as a white blues singer in the 1940s—a remarkable rarity at that time. He turned to songwriting full time after he got married. He took on the younger Mort Shuman, a piano player, grooming him as his musical counterpart. Together they started a label called R&B Records.[18] They chanced upon the Five Crowns, a vocal group including singer Ben E. King. This group morphed into the "new" Drifters, to honor performance obligations made by the manager of Clyde McPhatter's original Drifters group when it disbanded in 1958.[19]

Pomus and Shuman aligned with Atlantic Records and came under the wing of Leiber and Stoller, who produced "There Goes My Baby," "Dance with Me," and Pomus and Shuman's "If You Cry, True Love, True Love," in 1959 for the Drifters. Pomus was also collaborating on songs with Leiber and Stoller by this time, writing "Youngblood" with them for the Coasters, as the flip side to their high-charting "Searchin'" in 1957.

Pomus and Shuman fell naturally into the Hill and Range orbit, by way of the Leiber and Stoller/Atlantic-Progressive Music connection. They wrote "This Magic Moment" and "Save the Last Dance for Me," the following year, the latter regarded as one of the twenty-five most popular songs ever recorded. Presley alone ended up recording more than twenty of their songs throughout his career, including "Mess of Blues."[20]

Jean provided a studio space at the Hill and Range offices for Pomus and Shuman, but it was rarely used. Doc—crippled from polio as a child, sporting crutches and heavy metal braces on his legs, and growing progressively obese by the year—found it increasingly difficult to come on site. He rented a room at the nearby Hotel Forrest. "Little Sister," "Suspicion," "Can't Get Used to Losing You," "Surrender," and "Viva Las Vegas" were probably written from this hotel bed.[21]

The Brill Building studios remained busy during the early 1960s, under the capable direction of Paul Case, who was another Chappell alumnus. Jean brought Case in as general professional manager. Case proved himself early on by managing Johnny Mathis's partnership firms, Johnny Mathis Music and Noma Publishing, during the artist's most successful period. So successful was he that the company voted him a large bonus in 1959.[22]

Case was an excellent front man. By all accounts, he got along with everyone, had a good eye for talent, and was a natural "song doctor," often contributing

Doc Pomus and Mort Shuman, at their Hill and Range rehearsal space. Courtesy of Sharyn Felder.

ideas and sketches that made songs better. Aside from managing the inherited talents of writers such as Doc Pomus, Mort Shuman, Ben Weisman, Otis Blackwell, and Winfield Scott, Case signed new writing talents.

Beverly Ross was among the new talents he signed. She gave the Chordettes the 1958 hit "Lollipop," Bill Haley and the Comets' "Dim, Dim the Lights," and Roy Orbison's "Candy Man."[23] Case put Ross together with songwriter and aspiring producer Phil Spector. Lester Sill had convinced Leiber and Stoller to take Spector on as an apprentice, and they had sent him a plane ticket to join them in New York. He began working out of Leiber and Stoller's small one room production studio at 40 West 57th Street. Case also paired Spector with Doc Pomus, which yielded some hits: "Ecstasy," "First Taste of Love," "Laugh Right in My Face," "What Am I to Do?" and "Young Boy Blues."[24] Spector also collaborated with Atlantic founder Ahmet Ertegun on a novelty tune, "You Can Get Him, Frankenstein," and with Leiber on the enormous hit "Spanish Harlem."[25]

By late 1959, Leiber and Stoller were in great demand. They were booked solid, tied up producing things like Ben E. King's signature song, "Stand by Me," when Hill and Range called asking for them to do production work for singer Ray Peterson, who'd recently had a huge hit with Jeff Barry's "Tell Laura I Love Her" in 1960. Instead, the production duo threw the project to Spector. He chose an unlikely Joe Turner blues tune called "Corrina, Corrina." It came out on Peterson's Dunes Records the following year and was a good success, coming in at number 62 on the *Billboard* Top 100 songs for that year.[26]

Spector undoubtedly showed talent, but the pace of progress was too slow for his taste, and any measure of success went completely to his head. When he tried to circumvent his mentors and maneuver himself and Trio Music cowriter Terry Philips as contributors to Elvis's "Blue Hawaii," the axe came down. Neither Jerry nor Mike wanted (nor could Hill and Range afford) another fiasco with the Colonel, and that's just exactly what such a circumstance would have precipitated. Freddy stepped in and put the brakes on hard. Chances are Spector wasn't privy to all the painful history behind this at the time, but knowledge of it likely would not have deterred the willful songwriter anyway. Already he was bristling at walking in Leiber and Stoller's shadow and was plotting his escape.[27]

From time to time, Jean liked to tell a story about his first meeting with Hardy Rothschild, their Paris cook, whose horsemeat meal they would never forget. Hardy was clever in other ways as well, and offered other services to the Aberbach brothers:

> During our time in Paris, when Julian and I were launching our first SEMI business, a young man came to see me named Hardy Rothschild. He had a likeable appearance, presented himself well, and looked to be maybe twenty or twenty-two years old. I thanked him for coming but said that we had no use for an employee at that time. But Hardy quickly responded, "Then I have something different in mind. This will be very interesting for you. While I might look older, I am really not yet eighteen years old. I could sign contracts for you. And if the contracts should not turn out well, you could refuse to honor them because I was too young to sign them!" "Mr. Hardy!" I replied. "We are not interested. This kind of business is not our style. However, if you are really interested in working, you could work for us in our villa. We have a huge fireplace which needs to be tended constantly. Are you a good driver?" Hardy said that he could also cook pretty well. Hardy accepted the post immediately and turned out to be a first-class chef, heating attendant, and chauffeur.[28]

After his run at Atlantic Records, it seems Phil Spector tried to "pull a Hardy Rothschild," claiming that the agreement he had signed with Leiber and Stoller was null and void since he had been under twenty-one at the time he signed it! Because of this, he tried to disavow his contract and walk away, taking the proceeds from his work with him and cutting his mentors out of any publishing interest in his work going forward. Had he been working in California, he would have had the law on his side, but New York State law recognized him as an adult at age eighteen. Spector lost that battle but won in the end since around this time, the binding contract between them conveniently went missing from Leiber and Stoller's files. When Spector finally went back to California, Leiber and Stoller were happy to be rid of him.[29]

This did not bode well for Hill and Range. In the late 1950s they had incorporated a record company called Big Top.[30] Cousin Johnny Bienstock (Freddy's brother), who had gained experience as a record buyer and store manager for the Maxi Waxy chain, was brought in to oversee it. At the time Spector walked out, he had already spent weeks rehearsing the talented Crystals in the Hill and Range Brill Building studios for a Big Top recording. When he left, he took them with him. Back in Los Angeles, he launched Philles Records in partnership with his mentor Lester Sill, signing the group to it. This deprived Big Top of the Crystals' first Top 20 hit "There's No Other (Like My Baby)" and subsequent hits that included "Uptown," "He's a Rebel," and their enormous chart hit "Da Doo Ron Ron (When He Walked Me Home)."[31] Philles Records would become the most powerful force in the emerging street music trend, turning out some of the most memorable songs of the early 1960s. The label became known for its creative use of controlled echo and reverb to provide depth to recordings and for pushing the limits of the technology just short of distortion, giving the recordings a distinctive "wall of sound" production style. Songs like "You've Lost That Loving Feeling" by the Righteous Brothers are immediately recognizable as a Philles recording.

Hill and Range still continued to use Spector as a producer from time to time for Ray Peterson's Dunes Records and for Big Top, for instance replacing Burt Bacharach as producer for Arlene Smith's recording of "He Knows I Love Him Too Much."[32] And when Spector tired of working with the songwriting team of Jeff Barry and Ellie Greenwich, who gave him hits like "Da Do Ron Ron" and "Be My Baby," Case sold him a 50 percent stake in the songwriting team of Vinnie Poncia and Pete Andreoli. Together with Spector they produced the hits "The Best Part of Breakin' Up (Is Makin' Up)" and "Do I Love You?" to the benefit of both Philles and Hill and Range.[33]

As long as Case managed to keep Spector's nonsense in check, Hill and Range got itself an excellent driver, heating attendant, and pretty good cook. This strange but enormously creative little man would drive performers to near exhaustion, set fire to simple songs, and cook up soundscapes so dense and rich that they smoldered the charts and still take your breath away today.

Despite its early successes, Big Top record company remained relatively unprofitable. Considering the effort and expense, the returns on making records simply couldn't compare with the profit that could be had through music publishing. Nevertheless, Jean had authorized the company, and was willing to go along with the venture as long as it didn't distract from their core business. When

Tom Parker proposed to use the company as leverage in a renegotiation with RCA for Elvis's contract—a kind of fallback position if the deal fell through—Jean went ballistic and promptly shut it down. Competing in the record space presented a conflict of interest that could prove enormously damaging to their core business. Doors would close quickly if record executives thought Hill and Range was positioning to compete with them directly in their own business. Big Top was dissolved around 1963.[34]

Hill and Range was fast becoming one of the largest privately owned music publishing companies in the world. Expanding their reach across the globe, international Hill and Range affiliates and subsidiaries were promoting their catalog, which now offered a full range of popular genres—country, gospel, rhythm and blues, and pop. Between 1954 and 1966, Hill and Range contributed at least 208 songs to the *Billboard* top forty pop chart, half of which made the top ten, of which almost a quarter made number 1. Among their winners were gospel, foreign, folk, and motion picture hits.[35]

Hill and Range had had its best year in 1959, with twenty-seven songs hitting the top forty pop chart during that calendar year—a year during which Elvis wasn't even on the scene, still serving his stint in the army. The hits ran the gamut of styles and included the Coasters' wacky hits "Charlie Brown" and "Poison Ivy," Eddie Cochran's teenage rage "C'mon, Everybody," Johnny Cash's "Don't Take Your Guns to Town," Marty Robbins's "El Paso," the Drifters' "There Goes My Baby" and their Latin-inspired "Dance with Me," Fabian's "I'm a Man," America's sweetheart Connie Francis's "Lipstick on Your Collar," the foreign instrumental "Petite Fleur," and Ray Charles's ecstatic gospel-tinged "What'd I Say."[36] Considering the total accumulation of weeks their songs were on the *Billboard* top forty, on average the company contributed three of the forty hits for any given week between 1954 and 1966!

Hill and Range distinguished itself within the performing rights organizations as well. By 1963 the company had produced 240 BMI hit songs and this did not count the many comparable successes from their ASCAP firms. The little company Jean and Julian had launched had grown to 121 domestic companies and 129 international subsidiaries promoting American popular music in eighteen countries.[37]

Despite these successes, Jean was beginning to feel the wear of fifteen tumultuous years in the music business. Parker continued to be a difficult partner, Jean complaining "that man will give me a heart attack someday!" But it was Steve Sholes who turned out to be the unlucky recipient. Getting kicked upstairs and out of the direct Elvis loop at RCA probably won him a few extra years on his all-too-short life. He died of a heart attack only a few years later. Elvis, meanwhile, was getting warped by isolation and drugs. Already labeled the "King of Rock and Roll," he began to believe it, his naturally fragile emotions frayed by the painfully cool reception of the string of mediocre movies he was obliged to finish.[38]

Closer to home, Jean could not mend the rift between Parker and Leiber and Stoller, the talented boys' own stubborn ambitions unable to accommodate the Colonel's massive ego. And it was as though the young, impressionable Phil Spector sopped up the greatness and foibles of all these characters into one unstable package, turning his own frustrations into vicious outbursts against anyone who had anything to do with his early success. Struggling in his own psychological prison, Spector discounted the many opportunities given to him by his mentors, as well as by Hill and Range and its numerous talented associates, all of whom helped launch his career.[39]

Now into his second decade in this business, and with some remarkable successes behind him, Jean was beginning to understand that fighting even the ablest adversary in the music business couldn't hold a candle to the challenge of fighting one's self. As far as music was concerned, the Aberbachs' time was over. Beautiful, well-crafted melodies like "Bouquet of Roses," "Arrivederci, Roma," and "Room Full of Roses" were falling quickly out of fashion. He was not comfortable in a world where novelty tunes like "Louie, Louie," "Wooly Bully," and the ear-assaulting "(I Can't Get No) Satisfaction," could best beautiful tunes like Pomus and Shuman's "I Can't Get Used to Losing You," and Arti Glenn's "Crying in the Chapel."

While it still required most of his waking attention, the music empire he and Julian had built together could pretty much run on its own. Maintaining and promoting their enormous catalog, collecting and distributing revenue, and quietly absorbing proven tunes when the opportunity arose, was preferable to getting on top of a popular music wave that held little interest for him. Jean and his brother began to look for other opportunities and challenges beyond the music business.

The eleventh floor of the Brill Building where Hill and Range had its offices had a very substantial setback, resulting in two large terraces. Legend has it that from time to time kites were flown from there, one time getting tangled around a radio tower on one of the skyscrapers in midtown Manhattan![40] It took real skill to avoid getting tangled up on some part of the Manhattan skyline, and to avoid plummeting to the ground like a stone in an unexpected downdraft. But they probably thought it was worth the chance to clear Time Square, breeze over Tin Pan Alley, and shoot off beyond the East River to fly free. Their work here was done. It was time to let the wind catch their sail and spirit them off to some other adventure.

CHAPTER 21

The Art of Life

By the early 1960s the Hill and Range conglomerate was thriving. Owing in part to strong investment in office automation, the company managed well with only a small loyal staff. It expanded to include office administrator Pearl Ames, who kept their thousands of contracts in order, and counselors Lew Dreyer and Tom Levy.[1]

The staff also included a pretty young woman from the Bronx named Susan Clumpus, who had been an assistant to music publisher Howie Richmond. She joined Hill and Range during a time when Jean was absent for several months. Finally, one day Jean walked into the office and introduced himself. She found him unnerving, a bit frightening, but still very intriguing—somebody she would like to get to know better. So the first chance she got, she found some small excuse that needed a principal's signature. She knocked on his office door and opened it to find Jean in his boxer shorts propped up on his shoulders doing yoga. He shot her a huge grin and waved as best he could from his position while she, weak-kneed, backed herself out of the room! Over the next several months, she had many more encounters with Jean's weird wonderfulness.[2]

Jean and Susan eloped in the spring of 1964. It was a short event—barely an afternoon squeezed into an otherwise frantic business day. Now in his mid fifties, with Susan some thirty years younger, the marriage shocked everyone who knew him, most especially his brother. Nevertheless, Jean and Susan's love for one another never wavered, and over the next twenty-eight years they built a life and bore a loving family, daughter Anne-Rachel first, followed by sons David and Jason.

Marriage changed Jean. He began to redesign his life around building and caring for his family. They moved to Sands Point, Long Island, which was a location more suitable than New York City for raising children. His commitment to his family also refreshed his Jewish faith. Raised as a practicing Jew, Jean was dismayed to find a lack of facilities in the area to support Jewish religious studies. A nearby Jewish day school was about to close its doors, and Jean threw himself into rescuing it. He funded the school's deficit and applied his business management skills to guiding the institution back to profitability. The Solomon Schechter Day School of Nassau County eventually became a thriving Jewish studies institution, educating some 700 students per year. Jean acted as its president from 1977 to 1981, and remained as Chairman of the Board until 1992.[3]

Around 1967, Hill and Range vacated their posh Brill Building location, buying a building on West 72nd St. It had four floors, and they occupied all

Jean and Susan Aberbach, ca. 1966–67. Courtesy Susan Aberbach.

of them. All copyright materials were kept on the first floor, arranged in bins and shelves connected to a conveyor belt. Whenever anyone wanted to review something, they would press a button and it would come to them automatically. This was progressive for the time.[4]

The music business continued to be a source of both joy and exasperation. Despite the fact that almost all Elvis recordings produced between 1960 and 1965 serviced the needs of mediocre films, typically at least one song from a session charted high and sold well. Compilations such as *Elvis Is Back,* and the soundtracks albums *G.I. Blues* and *Blue Hawaii* (which remains Elvis's best-selling album ever) also did very well. As a result, by 1965 Hill and Range was making at least $400,000 a year in revenues on this single performer.[5]

In the mid-1960s, however, it became clear that Hill and Range's powerful position as a behind-the-curtains architect of popular music was waning. Although the company had amassed 240 BMI hit songs by 1963 (on average, twelve hits per year, some fifty of which sold greater than a million records), a year to year decline can be plotted from 1959 forward. After 1966 the company produced only 5 or fewer chart hits a year.

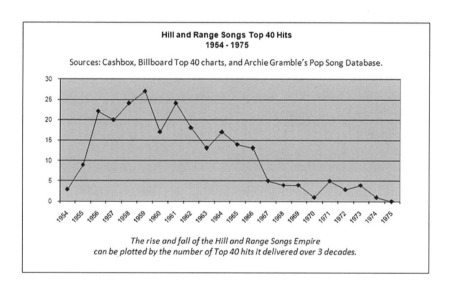

Hill and Range Songs Top 40 Hits
1954 - 1975

Sources: Cashbox, Billboard Top 40 charts, and Archie Gramble's Pop Song Database.

*The rise and fall of the Hill and Range Songs Empire
can be plotted by the number of Top 40 hits it delivered over 3 decades.*

Jean tried to offset the steady business decline with other ventures. In 1966 he acquired the coveted Joy Music catalog in an overnight deal for a hefty $2 million which may have helped along a deal the company had going for a joint music publishing firm with NBC-TV. Two years later he made significant investment in Nashville real estate, probably in partnership with Eddy Arnold.[6]

Hill and Range began downsizing in 1960, when it resolved to divest itself of its foreign affiliates. The large number of subsidiaries (129 in all) were the result of performing rights organizations in these territories requiring that international publishers establish a domestic presence. The subsidiaries had been organized to make foreign placement and the collection of royalties in those regions more efficient. As the decade progressed, however, Julian reported that anti-American sentiment was growing in Europe. Eventually, the advantages of doing business abroad were overtaken by the limitations on the number of U.S. corporations that could become members of foreign performing-rights agencies, and by restrictions on how funds earned in the foreign territory could be exported. It made sense to sell off these companies if they could. As these holdings were sold off, Hill and Range began consolidating its domestic holdings to position the company for sale. In 1970 Hill and Range acquired a major direct interest in Leiber and Stoller's Quintet Music to increase overall value of the company.[7]

The most likely buyer was PolyGram, a German-based record conglomerate. Its pop music division, Polydor, was very interested in cashing in on the American popular music trend. Polydor began distributing Big Top records throughout Europe, and although the experiment was short-lived, it established a working relationship between the companies.[8]

Polydor International had never had a publishing division. In 1966, however, the company decided to pursue such a venture, and got wind that Jean and Julian had decided to sell their international divisions. Polydor put together a deal that acquired most of the Aberbach European companies in 1967, purchasing all but the London and Italian firms. Considered one of the most valuable catalogs in the world, Hill and Range gave Polydor the seed catalog to immediately compete in the worldwide music publishing market.

The London subsidiary, however, went to Freddy Bienstock. Their cousin had been responsible for coming up with forty to fifty songs a year for Elvis. These not only had to fit the various storylines, but have some chance at becoming pop-chart hits. Among those that achieved success were "Stuck on You" (Aaron Schroeder/S. Leslie McFarland) with its flip side "Fame and Fortune" (Fred Wise/Ben Weisman) and "It's Now or Never" (Aaron Schroeder/Wally Gold). The pace was exhausting. By 1965, Freddy was looking to expand his own horizons. He saw opportunity in acquiring and running his own foreign firm. Therefore, he convinced Jean to sell him Belinda Music, their U.K. subsidiary. He renamed it Carlin Music.[9] The transition from Hill and Range staff member to entrepreneur over the next four years proved difficult, as Freddy began building his own music empire. He left for good in 1969, the split generating bad feelings on both sides.[10]

Despite his ups and downs, Elvis continued to be Hill and Range's cash cow throughout this period. Marrying longtime sweetheart Priscilla Beaulieu in April of 1967 seemed to suggest Elvis has passed through his reckless phase.

Almost nine months later to the day, daughter Lisa Marie was born, which, along with completion of his MGM film series of commitments, stabilized the artist even further. A sixty-minute NBC television Christmas special kept Elvis in the public's eye, encouraging the sale of a compilation release that consisted of mostly Hill and Range songs from his past repertoire.

The following years, however, proved difficult. The Colonel insisted on continuity in their business despite the cousin's unpleasant parting, so Freddy remained in charge of selecting songs for Elvis as a subcontractor to Hill and Range. Unfortunately, Elvis remained musically unfocused where new pop material was concerned as he spiraled down into depression. Despite the box-office success of the 1972 national tour, some reviewers considered it a failure, calling Elvis no longer a leader but a follower of music trends. The tour kicked off at New York's Madison Square Garden on June 9, 1972. Roger Hilburn, writing for the *Los Angeles Times*, however, pointed out the tour was top-heavy with covers of other artists' hits, including Hoyt Axton's "Never Been to Spain" and Marty Robbins's "You Gave Me a Mountain." Elvis also resorted to traditional folk material, including renditions of "Dixie" and "Battle Hymn of the Republic." A massive worldwide broadcast from Hawaii was planned for late in the year, but his home life was falling apart, with Priscilla moving out and filing for divorce.[11]

As Elvis was dismantling his life, Jean began dismantling Elvis Presley and Gladys Music, seeking terms from the Colonel for their liquidation as one of several steps toward preparing the rest of Hill and Range for sale. On March 8, 1972, in a letter to Parker, Jean outlined a tax strategy that included loaning money to the artist over the next three years to pay liquidation taxes and offering to continue to manage the copyrights for a 5 percent administration fee. The strategy would afford Elvis a net gain of approximately three-quarters of a million dollars.[12]

By July, however, it was unclear who would buy out whom. Freddy was acting as the Colonel's advocate, further fueling interfamily tensions. Jean had a clear advantage, since the artist was in debt to Hill and Range for nearly a million dollars, taking loans against future royalties to support his lavish lifestyle.[13]

In the end, Jean and Julian bought out Elvis's publishing interest. Elvis formally terminated employment and resigned as an officer on the boards of the companies on September 30, 1972. Liquidation cash in the amount of $313,000 for Gladys Music and $425,000 for Elvis Presley Music was distributed to Elvis during 1972 with another $100,000 provided for Colonel Parker and $200,000 for Elvis the following year to jump-start a pension fund.[14] Meanwhile, Hill and Range continued to benefit from Elvis's successes. Three-quarters of the songs used in the January 1974 worldwide broadcast from Hawaii were from Hill and Range or its affiliates.[15]

Talks went on for years with PolyGram about acquiring the Hill and Range parent company to supplement those foreign companies it had already purchased in the mid-1960s. Jean finally decided that if he wanted to conclude the deal, he would have to fly to Europe and not return until the deal was done. He did this in 1975, taking Tom Levy, Paul Weiss, and Bud Hicks along with him to hammer out the final details in Germany. They had convinced the chief counsel and director of PolyGram, Wolfgang Hicks, and Heinz Voigt, director of all music publishing activities at Polygram, to alter their vacation schedules so they could be available for two days, during which time they negotiated the entire deal.[16]

Much as he had with Leiber and Stoller, Jean planted himself in the hotel suite and devoted himself to making sure Tom and Bud were comfortable and had enough food, drink, and coffee to keep working. He did not meddle or get in their way. He had faith in the talent he had hired to do the best possible job for him. Running largely on adrenalin, they concluded the deal at the end of the two days, Bud and Tom unable to focus their eyes to read a newspaper for days after. The sale of all Hill and Range assets to Chappell and Company/ PolyGram GmbH/Polygram B.V. was concluded July 1, 1975. Jean and Julian retained a 25 percent interest in the catalog, which included everything except the Elvis Presley and Hank Williams properties.[17] As much as Jean loved the music business, he was glad to finally be free of it.

Although they had retired from the music industry, Jean and his brother had not retired from business. Over several decades they had amassed a sizeable private art collection. Becoming professional art dealers seemed to be the next logical step in their careers. Around 1973, Jean leased a building on the corner 77th Street and Madison Avenue, and Susan began remodeling it to create the Aberbach Fine Art gallery. For decades, Jean and Julian had been purchasing fine art, initially as a means of sheltering their investments. Very quickly the activity took on life of its own. Here was a new world to conquer, a new way to channel their business energies that was every bit as lucrative as music and just as challenging.[18]

The business of art wasn't much different than the business of music. Money follows the trends. The challenge was anticipating where the market would go and what would be popular tomorrow. And like with music, if you were smart, that popularity could be engineered to some extent. Someone looking to make a killing in the art market would know how to recognize new talented artists destined to resonate with the public. They would win their trust and promote them to achieve their fullest potential. These were talents Jean Aberbach had honed well in the music business.

Their business strategy concerning art was exactly the same as they had used for music. They shrewdly targeted an artist, absorbed most of his work, promoted it to greater value, and then profited in its trade. Not long after they had bought their first works in 1949, the brothers had begun to collect most of the works of Parisian painter Gen Paul. After accumulating approximately thirty pieces of his work, they traded most of them for their next major focus— Bernard Buffet. This intensely expressive French painter had won the Grand Prix de la Critique in 1947. Ultimately they donated all his works to museums and colleges throughout the country. Several can be found today at the Fine Arts Museum of San Francisco and at the Hirshhorn in Washington, D.C.[19]

The brothers then turned their attention to the short-lived COBRA school, a collection of artists from Copenhagen, Brussels, and Amsterdam. They acquired works of Dane Asger Jorn, the Dutchman Karel Appel, and Belgians Pierre Alchinsky and Corneille (aka Cornelis van Beverloo). Jean and Julian recognized these works as the next logical step in postmodern art that preserved, yet extended, classical traditions. This group of artists recorded to canvas the direct expression of the subconscious. Jorn's work, for example, was rife with artistic references, symbols, myth, and magic—always fascinating topics for Jean.

Loosely connected to this school was the French artist Jean Dubuffet. His works centered on the unadulterated purity of artistic expression that is found in the art of children and madmen. Dubuffet's paintings resembled everything from graffiti scratched on walls to chalk drawings on a sidewalk, suggesting just how much strange—often profound—artwork can be found in everyday life. The weird awkwardness of the tools and surfaces used, and the naïve or obsessed subject matter fascinated the brothers. Jean and Julian acquired many of his works.

They also captured some of the most important works by Dada/surrealist Max Ernst, Bible-inspired Marc Chagall, French *Fauvre* artist Henri Matisse, sculptor Henri Moore, and the disturbing works of Englishman Francis Bacon. Even many well known works by the father of modern art, Pablo Picasso, were among their acquisitions. In truth, a large number of the most important works of the twentieth century passed through their hands at one time or another.[20]

They searched out the "classic standards" of modern art, enjoying this chase as much as they had their quest for enduring songs. During the 1960s Jean and Julian actively collected the works of abstract expressionists. Many of the startling works by Willem de Kooning, Jackson Pollock, Mark Rothko, Robert Motherwell, Jasper Johns, Clifford Still, and Ashile Gorky were made even more powerful by the sheer size of the canvas used. At that time the brothers resided in a building called the Beresford. Neighbors like Lauren Bacall and Richard Burton and writers Adolph Green and Dorothy Fields must have been mystified to witness the comings and goings from their apartments. As the artwork came in, the furniture went out, until all they had left were bare walls. One painting by Clifford Still was so tall that Jean had the carpet cut away—and still it could only fit by leaning it against the wall.[21]

Similarly, their penthouse Hill and Range offices were stuffed full of art. From 1958 forward, on average Hill and Range was borrowing nearly a quarter of a million dollars a year (or the equivalent of $1.75 million in today's money) on expected music publishing returns of probably twice or three times that.[22] Not all of it was going back into the music business. From time to time the company would present artworks to employees as bonuses. For appreciation of his "fine work as a professional manager and for the affection for which he was held by the stockholders," Freddy Bienstock was awarded works by Gen Paul, Diego Rivera, and Pablo Picasso.[23]

Whether it was music or art, Jean was driven by impulse, and his impulses were mostly right. It was not long before others in the music world began to seek out his expertise. When the works could no longer be contained at their living quarters and place of work, Jean became a "committee of one," acquiring works to grace the hall of the National Music Publishers' Association offices. He loaned the organization paintings, and it paid the insurance. Later, Jean was given complete autonomy to buy paintings for the organization.[24]

To the uninitiated, some of the works seemed incomprehensible. The gamble, however, paid off. In one instance, Jean purchased a work for the organization that he later wanted back. He obtained it by trading one by abstract expressionist Lee Krasner. Years later the organization was approached to lend the Krasner painting to a gallery for a showing in Houston. When they asked Jean how much they should insure this painting for (originally bought for $2,500), Jean replied "$85,000." The value of the painting had increased more than thirty times its initial investment![25]

Preferring classic art to soup cans, Jean and Julian avoided the hysterical pop art craze, but their tastes encompassed most other trends and all the traditional media. They collected sculpture and between them accumulated many of the rough, spindly bronze works of Swiss painter-sculptor Alberto Giacometti. As with music, their enthusiasms ran so closely in parallel that the brothers sometimes settled ownership in a coin toss when both were attracted to the same work.[26]

As in music, both Jean and Julian were quiet operators in the art world. Neither became swept up in artistic social circles, but they counted many of the art industry's top business people among their close confidantes. These included the owners of the prestigious Pierre Matisse, Stephan Hahn, and the Marlborough galleries. Sometimes they were asked to participate in or to help negotiate complicated deals between collectors. Other times, they would be asked to scout works for galleries, acquiring several of Francis Bacon's important works for the Marlborough Gallery on a trip to Europe. This gave them a chance to also seed their own collections. It was a perfect relationship, one that kept them not only in the know, but also one that allowed them to influence, to some small degree, those artworks they felt merited mass exposure. At the same time, they struck up personal relationships with artists such as Henri Moore, Alberto Giacometti, Karl Appel, Paul Klee, and Wassilli Kandinsky. Jean's own reputation also grew with the investor elite, the distinguished author and *Forbes* columnist Martin Sosnoff calling Jean "my favorite art dealer" when Jean acquired Bacon's disturbing "Study on a Pope" for a staggering $5.72 million in 1989. "You gotta buy the best and keep your fingers crossed," Jean once quipped to the writer."[27]

Unlike Julian, who gravitated more toward proven artists, Jean was interested in capturing inspiring younger artists on their way up just like he had captured songwriters and performers on their way up. One such find was Austrian Friedrich Hundertwasser, whose spirit, as much as his artwork, attracted Jean. This was a man who resigned his post as guest lecturer at the prestigious Hamburg School of Applied Arts after having been restrained from painting all the surfaces of the building in an endless, rainbow-colored spiral. Profiled as a militant ecologist, architect, and social radical, Hundertwasser initiated a movement called transautomatism—a sort of spontaneous, free creative expression that rebelled against artistic conventions and academic traditions—anything that restrained individual creative potential. He appeared nude in public at times to defend his ideas—one of which was a "nonpolluting toilet"—a standard model that simply had no flushing mechanism![28]

Hundertwasser's impulsive zest for life infused Jean's, exciting him in the same way that western music had fifteen years earlier. Taken with these whimsical, free-spirited works, Jean picked up two of them in the late 1950s, probably anticipating the artist's growing celebrity after a successful retrospective at the 1962 Venice Biennial. He eventually collected half the artist's oeuvre, representing him exclusively in the United States. He became not only a close friend, but the artist's chief benefactor. Jean was picky, selecting the thirty paintings the artist himself considered his best works. Jean's support and encouragement so inspired him that Hundertwasser bought a large wooden schooner and sailed away to New Zealand, where he purchased 8,000 acres, planted 20,000 trees, and dubbed the region "Aberbach Valley."[29]

When Jean saw something he liked, something that had an immediate effect on him, he did not hesitate. During the 1960s he developed an intense interest in Native American artwork, collecting most of the best works of one of the genre's leading painters, Fritz Sholder. His works were featured at the Smithsonian in 1972, in a show he shared with another up-and-coming Native American talent, a Caddo-Kiowa painter from Oklahoma known as T. C. Cannon. Jean immediately saw his potential, asked to meet the artist, and after sharing dinner with him, asked which paintings were available. It turns out most were, to which Jean replied, "I'll buy them all!" Jean devoted the next several years exclusively representing and promoting the works of T. C. Cannon, until the artist's untimely death in a car crash in 1978.[30]

Jean's main focus of attention settled on a young Colombian artist he'd stumbled onto one rainy night in 1968 at a group show at the Metropolitan Museum of Modern Art. As a whole, the show was disappointing, until he turned a corner and was faced with a painting that left him nearly breathless. The delicate lines and shades of the figures were unusual. Form and color were balanced in a way he'd never seen before. The work was profoundly graceful. Glancing left, then right, he assured himself no one else was watching and leaned forward to read the inscription: "The Presidential Family, Botero '67, Colombian."[31] He immediately decided to keep his deep interest in this artist secret, until he could establish a relationship with him. In an article for the *Yale Literary Review* years later, Jean described the experience: "I walked back into the darkness and the rain, and my cheeks reached out for the raindrops and my heart was filled with happiness and expectation."[32]

Beginning his career as an illustrator in Medellín, Colombia, Fernando Botero studied in Spain, Paris, and Italy, returning home to become counted as one of the most promising artists in his country. In the United States he was little known, despite the fact that he won a Guggenheim award in 1950, won second prize at the National Salon in Bogotá in 1957, participated in New York group shows, and had one of his works acquired and displayed at the Museum of Modern Art in 1961. With little money, Botero took up residence in a loft in Greenwich Village in 1963, where his affinity for exaggerated yet delicate figures began to coalesce.

Jean conducted several weeks of correspondence through the Colombian embassy only to be told that they were unable to divulge the artist's current address. Another few months passed before a disappointing phone call informed him that the artist had nothing at this time to show him. Weeks later he received an invitation to the artist's studio on 14th Street in New York, but he was dismayed when presented with a simple *bodegon*—a still life probably of a sidebar in a tavern laden with a fruit bowl and water pitchers. Jean declined, saying he would rather wait for a family picture. He expected a bright family scene similar to that of *The Presidential Family* that he had viewed that night at the Met. A few months later, however, the artist presented him with the dark, subdued tones of *The Widower*. Nevertheless, Jean bought it, along with another work, and came back monthly to buy more, two at a time.

Coming from South America, Botero did not know how to build an art career in the United States. While he was getting some exposure in Europe, these opportunities were barely providing enough to pay the bills. Jean recognized this and began to counsel him on how to further his career. They shared lunch every few weeks, and Jean would advise him to contact this person or pursue that strategy.

Before long, Jean was bringing powerful members of the New York art community down to Botero's loft. Jean convinced Frank Lloyd, owner of the Marlborough Gallery (and considered one of the most powerful people in the art world), to promote Botero's works, which was a huge break for the struggling artist. Soon Botero was on the road to international success.

Jean profited handsomely by his investment in this genuine talent, purchasing works for $2,000 and $3,000 apiece that appreciated enormously as soon as association with a major gallery was confirmed. Nevertheless, as with Hundertwasser, the relationship was much more than just a commercial venture. Botero considered Jean a mentor who provided important encouragement and support at a low point in his career. He describes his life as two distinct eras—the time before Aberbach, and the time after.[33]

"The most important thing that he gave me was a lot of enthusiasm," recalls Botero. "Because he was telling me all the time, 'You are going to succeed! Your work is going to be very appreciated.' And he was so enthusiastic with the work he saw every time he came. That, of course, gave me a great push to do more work! And to try to do better work! There were not that many people who were

Jean Aberbach and Fernando Botero. Courtesy of Rampage Studios.

giving me this kind of enthusiasm and support. That was surprising to me. I met important people every day, but not many people were willing to put all his money and enthusiasm behind the work of an artist. And that's what he did."[34]

When the Aberbach Fine Art gallery opened in 1973, Jean turned his full attention to representing artists. By this time, Botero was already exclusively represented by the Marlborough Gallery. Nevertheless, like a father looking proudly on his son's achievements, Jean continued to counsel Botero and promote his work, reveling in the artist's growing success, which eventually brought international acclaim from the highest levels of the art world. They shared a friendship that went well beyond business. They spent social time together. As a token of his appreciation, the artist did a figurative painting of Jean's daughter

By Fernando Botero. *Joachim Jean Aberbach and His Family.* Oil on canvas, 1970. Copyright 2008, Fernando Botero.

Anne, which led to the commissioning of *Joachim Jean Aberbach and His Family,* one of only a handful of portraits the artist ever chose to do.

When Jean judged a Botero, or any piece of music or artwork, he knew what he was buying. He had done his homework to understand the value of the work. Jean's real talent, though, was how he maneuvered the supporting chess pieces into a deliberate design. Jean excelled in art for the same reasons he had in music. Whether the talent was a young songwriter or a painter, the same strategy of careful selection, personal and emotional investment, subtle influence, and patience applied. By generating interest among the most important gallery owners and art critics, Jean developed a strong interest in Botero's work. The artist would go on to be internationally acclaimed as one of the century's most important artists.

Jean was one of those people who could perceive the wholeness of life much as he could the wholeness of an artwork—a tapestry of color, composition, and tension. He chose to pepper the tapestry of his life with many unselfish acts, such as purchasing a dialysis machine for house counselor Lew Dreyer when he was diagnosed with kidney failure. He never forgot a birthday. He could be found handing out $50 bills to a taxi driver who was about to be married, or casting off workday affairs to play chess with his son David's friends.[35]

The canvas of Jean's life was also marred by some disappointments. When Max Dreyfus died at the age of ninety, Freddy encouraged Jean to make an overture to acquire Max's share of Chappell Music. Jean thought he would finally become a major stockholder in the world's most successful music publishing company, only to learn that Max gave explicit directions on the disposition of his business interest.[36] His widow was instructed that no part of his Chappell interest should be sold to the Aberbach brothers. Jean was dumbstruck. Max apparently never forgot the sting of Jean moving out to pursue his own career.[37]

In the end, Jean got what he wanted. While the company was sold to Polygram GmbH, by this time Chappell Music also had been acquired by that company.[38] So although Jean had been prohibited from purchasing Chappell himself, he was still more than a little pleased that Hill and Range properties had achieved a level of parity with those of his mentor. Country, western, and rhythm and blues tunes were rolled into the Chappell catalog, where today they stand side by side with the works of Rodgers and Hammerstein, Cole Porter, and George and Ira Gershwin—equal partners in the legacy of American music in the twentieth century. They ended up right where Jean always thought they belonged.

The partnership model Jean and Julian promoted also proved to be a double-edged sword. It provided unprecedented opportunity to writers who were able, for the first time, to participate equally in the success of their intellectual properties. Bob Wills, Ernest Tubb, Hank Snow, Red Foley, and Marty Robbins all proudly incorporated their own publishing companies in partnership with the

Aberbachs. Using this cooperative legal device, Hill and Range outpaced their competitors at every turn, providing unprecedented freedom and security to their songwriters, most of who remained with them until they closed the company.

This partnership device, however, may have hastened the passing of an era that depended on artistic guidance and promotional support from music publishers. If an artist could own half their music publishing, why couldn't they own it all? By 1960 the industry was shifting away from the notion that the song was the star, with the artist simply a vehicle for interpretation, to a model where the artist and the artist's songs were a unique creative package. In the early 1960s, managers like Brian Epstein determined that talented artists like the Beatles no longer had to share any part of their intellectual property but could own and control their publishing rights in their entirety. This signaled vast changes in the industry. Record companies became primarily investors and distribution pipelines, and music publishers were increasingly relegated to the role of administrative accounting house.[39]

But in their time, the Aberbach brothers, as part of a trusted inner circle, changed music history. Together with Steve Sholes and Tom Parker they developed a star-making business model that they proved out with Eddy Arnold and later perfected with Elvis Presley. This fueled the successful transition of country and western music (and to some extent rhythm and blues, and gospel music) from rural niche markets into the popular mainstream. Funneling country, blues, and gospel-tinged popular music his way, they proved not only that Elvis had no equal, but that music had no color.

One story holds special prominence in Jean's memoir sketches. It is clear that Jean intended it as the centerpiece of the autobiography he never completed. It is a morbid little story, but it clearly demonstrates Jean's view on life: "If someone dies, people say he is not dying, as long as he continues to live in the memory of his friends and family. When they are talking about him he continues to live. I once attended a funeral of a man whose eulogy consisted almost exclusively of the fact that he loved to eat sauerkraut. If that is the best that can be said about a man on his passing, then the man's life was empty. He was nothing, vacant. A man who lives his life like this will not live again. He is eaten up—finished."[40]

Jean learned many lessons during his long life, but the most important was that the greatest challenges come from within. Jean understood that his mission was to make a life worth living, one that used the full range of his natural gifts, and was guided by his instincts, hopes, and dreams. It's what drove this restless giant.

The beauty found in a song, or the grace found in a painting, are not qualities confined to those works. The passion that yields a fine work of art or

The Jean Aberbach Family, at their New York City home, 1990. Courtesy of Susan Aberbach.

produces a great song emanates from the creator, not the thing. Jean did not work in musical notes or in wood, bronze, or canvas. Instead, his palette was the vast array of genuine, colorful, interesting people that peppered his life. He illuminated his world with them, their spirits fueling the passion that spilled over into everything he did.

Whether it was music, art, family, deal making, celebration, chess, or a simple walk in the park, Jean lived his life with passion. He was sure that by doing so, he would not waste the gifts given to him and would be remembered for all his goodness and flaws, failures and successes, long after he was gone. Jean embraced the full measure of life's palette, trusting that he would be presented with opportunities and choices that would complete the canvas of his life. They did. By being fearless in that pursuit, in the end he counted few regrets.

It is easy to live. You wake up every day, the clock turns, and you place your head on a pillow at night. It is not so easy to live life with passion. A life filled with passion challenges you to stretch your talents and intellect every waking moment. It makes you strive for perfection, even knowing it can never be achieved. It requires you to accept your shortcomings, that you be humbled by your failures, and rise up every day to overcome them.

That is the art of life. You must open your eyes every day to a world of adventure and wonderment. You must bound down the mountain with abandon and let the wind and snow sting your face. You must brave the storm boldly, letting your cheeks reach out to saturate you with every raindrop of life. You must follow the path wherever it takes you and stay in constant motion, always restless to exceed yourself. Every day, you must get up, gaze out, set your sights beyond the horizon, and strive for giant things. Only then can you be sure that you have truly lived.

Jean left us on May 24, 1992, at the age of eighty-two, having demonstrated to us the art of life.

APPENDIX A   Chart Hits: 1954–75

Between 1954 and 1975, Hill and Range contributed at least 254 hits to the *Billboard* Top 40 pop charts, almost half of which were in the Top 10, and twenty-seven of which became number 1 hits.

Activity peaked in 1959 with twenty-seven Top 40 hits and dropped off steadily until the company and its many international subsidiaries was sold to Polydor in two installments. In 1968 most of their European companies were sold, and in 1975 the company divested itself of all copyrights except those contained in the Hank Williams Music Catalog and the properties co-owned with Elvis Presley that were contained in Elvis Presley Music and Gladys Music corporations.

Hill and Range's success is remarkable. Weekly presence on the pop charts was equivalent to contributing an average of two of the Top 40 hits every week over that twenty-two year period.

Song Title	Author(s)	Chart Debut	Highest Position	Weeks on Chart
Let Me Go, Lover!	Carson, Hill	12/18/1954	6	12
No More	Robertson, Blair	12/25/1954	6	13
Ling Ting Tong	Godwin	12/25/1954	28	2
Tweedlee Dee	Scott	1/15/1955	14	11
Plantation Boogie	Hornton, Dee	2/12/1955	19	15
It May Sound Silly	Hunter	3/26/1955	11	7
Hummingbird	Robertson	7/9/1955	7	13
Wake the Town and Tell the People	Gallop, Livingston	8/13/1955	5	12

Suddenly There's a Valley	Myer, Jones	10/1/1955	9	10
Black Denim Trousers and Motorcycle Boots	Leiber, Stoller	11/12/1955	38	1
Sixteen Tons	Travis	12/3/1955	17	1
Nuttin' for Christmas	Tepper, Bennett	12/31/1955	36	1
Seven Days	Carrol, Taylor	2/11/1956	17	2
The Poor People of Paris	Lawrence, Monnot	2/18/1956	1	20
Ninety-Nine Years	Wayne, Brooks	2/25/1956	23	4
A Tear Fell	Burton, Randolph	3/3/1956	5	17
Ask Me	Modugno, Giant, Baum, Kaye	3/3/1956	18	0
Blue Suede Shoes	Perkins	3/10/1956	2	17
I Was the One	Schroeder, DeMetrius, Blair, Peppers	3/17/1956	19	10
I Want You, I Need You, I Love You	Mysels, Kosloff	6/2/1956	1	19
I Almost Lost My mind	Hunter	6/9/1956	1	19
Treasure of Love	Shapiro, Stallman	6/9/1956	16	12
My Baby Left Me	Crudup	6/9/1956	31	3
Allegheny Moon	Hoffman, Manning	6/16/1956	2	22
Glendora	Stanley	6/23/1956	8	12
You Don't Know Me	Walker, Arnold	7/28/1956	14	17
Don't Be Cruel	Blackwell, Presley	8/4/1956	1	24
Hound Dog	Leiber, Stoller	8/4/1956	1	24
Tonight You Belong to Me	Rose, David	8/25/1956	4	17
Chains of Love	Nugetre	9/29/1956	20	8
I Can't Love You Enough	Burton, Plummer, Baker	10/13/1956	22	2
Love Me Tender	Presley, Matson	10/20/1956	1	19
I Walk the Line	Cash	10/20/1956	17	11
Love Me	Leiber, Stoller	11/24/1956	2	14
Poor Boy	Presley, Matson	1/5/1957	24	3
Since I Met You, Baby	Hunter	1/5/1957	34	2
Too Much	Rosenberg, Weinman	1/26/1957	1	14
Butterfly	Lowe, Mann	2/23/1957	1	14
Lucky Lips	Leiber, Stoller	3/2/1957	25	5
Gone	Rogers	3/9/1957	4	19

All Shook Up	Presley, Blackwell	4/6/1957	1	0
Rock-a-Billy	Harris, Deane	4/13/1957	10	12
Peace in the Valley	Dorsey	4/29/1957	25	1
C.C. Rider	Willis, Hancock, Matthews	5/13/1957	12	8
Searchin'	Leiber, Stoller	5/20/1957	3	22
Young Blood	Leiber, Stoller, Pomus	5/20/1957	8	11
Wondering	Werner	6/3/1957	12	5
Teddy Bear	Mann, Lowe	6/24/1957	1	18
Loving You	Wayne, Silver	7/8/1957	20	13
Honeycomb	Merrill	8/19/1957	1	23
Jailhouse Rock	Leiber, Stoller	10/14/1957	1	19
Treat Me Nice	Leiber, Stoller	10/21/1957	18	6
Great Balls of Fire	Hammer, Blackwell	12/2/1957	2	13
Wild Is the Wind	Washington, Tiomkin	12/16/1957	22	7
I Beg of You	McCoy, Owens	2/3/1958	8	7
This Little Girl of Mine	Charles	2/17/1958	26	3
We Belong Together	Andriani	3/3/1958	32	6
Breathless	Blackwell	3/10/1958	7	9
Wear My Ring around Your Neck	Carroll, Moody	4/21/1958	2	13
Skinny Minnie	Haley, Keefer, Cafra, Gabler	4/21/1958	22	6
Doncha' Think It's Time	Otis, Dixon	5/5/1958	15	0
Sugar Moon	Wills, Walker	5/12/1958	5	12
What Am I Living For?	Jay, Harris	5/12/1958	9	17
Hang Up My Rock and Roll Shoes	Willis	5/26/1958	24	2
Padre	Webster, Romans	6/2/1958	13	11
Yakety Yak	Leiber, Stoller	6/9/1958	1	15
Hard Headed Woman	DeMetrius	6/30/1958	1	14
Rebel Rouser	Eddy, Hazelwood	7/7/1958	6	12
Don't Ask Me Why	Wise, Weisman	7/14/1958	25	4
Judy	Riedel	7/28/1958	22	1
Tears on My Pillow	Lewis, Bradford	8/18/1958	4	0
Summertime Blues	Cochran, Capehart	8/25/1958	8	12
Tom Dooley	Warner, Lomax	10/6/1958	1	18
There Goes My Heart	Davis, Silver	10/20/1958	19	8

One Night	Bartholomew, King	11/10/1958	4	14
I Got Stung	Schroeder, Hill	11/10/1958	8	12
I Cried a Tear	Julia, Jay	12/28/1958	6	15
Goodbye, Baby	Engvick, Katz, Hamilton	12/28/1958	8	13
C'mon Everybody	Byers	1/5/1959	35	1
May You Always	Markes, Charles	1/19/1959	11	12
Petite Fleur	Bechet	2/2/1959	5	10
I'm a Man	Pomus, Shuman	2/2/1959	31	3
Don't Take Your Guns to Town	Cash	2/2/1959	32	6
Charlie Brown	Leiber, Stoller	2/9/1959	2	12
Plain Jane	Pomus, Shuman	2/23/1959	38	2
I Need Your Love Tonight	Wayne, Reichner	3/30/1959	4	10
Lipstick on Your Collar	Lewis, Goehring	6/1/1959	5	12
Along Came Jones	Leiber, Stoller	6/1/1959	9	8
Hushabye	Pomus, Shuman	6/15/1959	20	9
There Goes My Baby	Patterson, Treadwell, Nelson	6/29/1959	2	14
Forty Miles of Bad Road	Eddy, Casey	6/29/1959	9	11
Big Hunk o' Love	Schroeder, Wyche	7/13/1959	1	10
What'd I Say	Charles	7/20/1959	6	11
Caribbean	Torok	8/31/1959	27	6
Poison Ivy	Leiber, Stoller	9/7/1959	7	11
Primrose Lane	Shanklin, Callender	9/7/1959	8	15
Hey, Little Girl	Byers	9/14/1959	20	9
You're Gonna Miss Me	Curtis	9/21/1959	34	4
Don't You Know	Charles	10/5/1959	2	15
Dance With Me	Lebish, Treadwell, Nahan, Glick	11/2/1959	15	9
El Paso	Robbins	11/30/1959	1	16
Hound Dog Man	Pomus, Shuman	11/30/1959	9	11
I'm Movin' On	Snow	12/14/1959	40	1
Go, Jimmy, Go	Pomus, Shuman	12/21/1959	5	11
Not One Minute More	Robertson, Dinning, Blair	12/28/1959	16	8
Just Come Home	Sigman, Monnot	1/4/1960	35	3
Lonely Blue Boy	Wise, Weisman	1/18/1960	6	10
Run Red Run	Leiber, Stoller	1/25/1960	36	1

This Magic Moment	Pomus, Shuman	3/14/1960	16	6
El Matador	Bowers, Burgess	3/14/1960	32	5
Stuck on You	Schroeder, McFarland	4/11/1960	1	13
Big Iron	Robbins	4/11/1960	26	4
Fame and Fortune	Wise, Weisman	4/25/1960	17	7
Dutchman's Gold	Capehart	5/30/1960	30	3
Please Help Me, I'm Falling	Robertson, Blair	6/13/1960	8	15
Pennies from Heaven	Burke, Johnston	6/20/1960	24	6
It's Now or Never	Schroeder, Gold	7/25/1960	1	16
Devil or Angel	Carter	9/5/1960	6	13
Save the Last Dance for Me	Pomus, Shuman	9/19/1960	1	14
New Orleans	Tepper, Bennett	10/31/1960	6	11
I Gotta Know	Evans	11/28/1960	20	8
I Count the Tears	Pomus, Shuman	12/31/1960	17	7
Lovey Dovey	Ertegun, Curtis	1/9/1961	25	4
Spanish Harlem	Leiber, Stoller	1/30/1961	10	10
Don't Worry	Robbins	2/13/1961	3	12
Surrender	DeCurtis, Pomus, Shuman	2/20/1961	1	11
No One	Cochran, Mascheroni	2/20/1961	34	2
Lonely Man	Benjamin, Marcus	3/13/1961	32	2
Runaway	Shannon, Crook	3/27/1961	1	12
One Mint Julep	Toombs	3/27/1961	8	9
Just for Old Time's Sake	Tepper, Bennett	4/17/1961	20	7
Flaming Star	Wayne, Edwards	4/24/1961	14	5
Stand by Me	King, Glick	5/22/1961	4	11
Wild in the Country	Weiss, Peretti, Creatore	6/19/1961	26	2
Together	DeSylva, Brown, Henderson	7/3/1961	6	9
Wooden Heart	Wise, Weisman, Twomey	7/17/1961	1	12
I'm Gonna Knock on Your Door	Schroeder, Wayne	7/24/1961	12	8
Little Sister	Pomus, Shuman	8/28/1961	5	10
His Latest Flame	Pomus, Shuman	9/4/1961	4	7
Mexico	Tepper, Bennett	9/11/1961	7	10

Sweets for My Sweet	Pomus, Shuman	9/25/1961	16	9
Missing You	Sovine, Noe	9/25/1961	29	3
Tonight (Is So Right for Love)	Wayne, Silver	11/13/1961	8	8
Just Out of Reach	Shelton	11/13/1961	24	7
Can't Help Falling in Love	Creatore, Peretti, Weiss	12/18/1961	2	0
Rock-a-Hula Baby	Wise, Weisman, Fuller	12/18/1961	23	0
Baby, It's You	David, Bacharach, Williams	1/6/1962	8	11
Let Me In	Merrill	2/10/1962	4	12
What's Your Name?	Johnson	2/24/1962	7	9
Good Luck Charm	Schroeder, Weisman, Gold	3/24/1962	1	11
Anything That's Part of You	Wise, Weisman	4/7/1962	31	5
I Wish That We Were Married	Weiss, Lewis	4/21/1962	16	8
Don't Play That Song	Ertegun, Nelson	5/19/1962	11	7
Follow That Dream	Wise, Weisman	5/19/1962	15	7
That's Old Fashioned	Giant, Baum, Kaye	6/2/1962	9	7
Any Day Now	Hilliard, Bacharach	6/2/1962	23	6
Lemon Tree	Holt	6/9/1962	35	2
She's Not You	Leiber, Stoller	8/11/1962	5	9
Devil Woman	Robbins	8/18/1962	16	7
King of the Whole Wide World	Batchelog, Roberts	10/6/1962	30	4
Return to Sender	Blackwell, Scott	10/27/1962	2	14
Zip-a-Dee Doo-Dah	Gilbert, Wrubel	12/8/1962	8	7
Spanish Lace	Hoffman, Manning	12/15/1962	31	2
Ruby Baby	Leiber, Stoller	1/26/1963	2	11
Little Town Flirt	Shannon, McKenzie	1/26/1963	12	7
One Broken Heart for Sale	Blackwell, Scott	2/23/1963	11	0
Can't Get Used to Losing You	Pomus, Shuman	3/23/1963	2	12
Young and in Love	Sherman, Roberts	4/6/1963	17	6
Every Step of the Way	Carson	6/8/1963	30	4
Hopeless	Pomus, Shuman	7/6/1963	13	8

Hootenanny	Goehring, Deane, Horther	7/27/1963	38	2
Mean Woman Blues	DeMetrius	9/28/1963	5	10
It's All Right	Charles	10/12/1963	4	11
Cry to Me	Russell	10/26/1963	23	6
Your Other Love	Pomus, Shuman	11/9/1963	28	4
Drip Drop	Leiber, Stoller	11/23/1963	6	9
Good News	Gottlieb	2/15/1964	11	7
Kissin' Cousins	Wise, Starr	3/7/1964	12	7
My Bonnie	Charles	3/7/1964	26	2
It Hurts Me	Byers, Daniels	3/14/1964	29	0
Understand Your Man	Cash	3/14/1964	35	3
Twist and Shout	Russell, Medley	3/21/1964	2	9
Suspicion	Pomus, Shuman	3/21/1964	3	10
My Heart Cries for You	P. Faith, C. Sigman	3/21/1964	38	0
Little Children	Shuman, McFarland	5/2/1964	7	12
Today	Dorsey	5/16/1964	17	9
Wrong for Each Other	Pomus, Shuman	5/16/1964	34	4
Kiss Me Quick	Pomus, Shuman	5/23/1964	34	2
Viva Las Vegas	Pomus, Shuman	5/30/1964	29	4
Reach Out for Me	David, Bacharach	11/7/1964	20	6
Love Potion Number Nine	Leiber, Stoller	12/19/1964	3	11
Keep Searchin' (We'll Follow the Sun)	Shannon	12/19/1964	9	10
I Go to Pieces	Shannon	1/23/1965	9	9
The "In" Crowd	Page	1/23/1965	13	7
Don't Let Me Be Misunderstood	Caldwell, Marcus, Benjamin	3/6/1965	15	6
Do the Clam	Weisman, Wayne, Fuller	3/13/1965	21	6
Stranger in Town	Shannon	3/13/1965	30	4
Cast Your Fate to the Wind	Werber, Guaraldi	4/10/1965	10	11
Mrs. Brown, You've Got a Lovely Daughter	Peacock	4/17/1965	1	11
Crying in the Chapel	Glenn	5/8/1965	3	11
Easy Question	Blackwell, Scott	7/3/1965	11	6
Don't Just Stand There	Tubb, Henley	7/17/1965	8	8

The "In" Crowd	Page	8/21/1965	5	12
I'm Yours	Robertson, Blair	9/18/1965	11	7
Ring Dang Doo	Byers, Tubert	11/13/1965	33	3
Puppet on a String	Tepper, Bennett	12/4/1965	14	6
Flowers on the Wall	DeWitt	12/11/1965	4	9
My Love	Robbins	1/15/1966	1	10
It Was a Very Good Year	Drake, Shane	1/15/1966	28	4
Somewhere There's a Someone	Knight	3/5/1966	32	4
Mama	O'Currran, Brooks	6/4/1966	22	5
Dedicated Follower of Fashion	Davies	6/18/1966	36	1
Sweet Dreams	Leiber, Stoller	7/23/1966	15	7
Distant Shores	Guercio	8/13/1966	30	2
Sunny Afternoon	Davies	8/27/1966	14	7
I Really Don't Want to Know	Barnes, Robertson	9/24/1966	22	5
All I See Is You	Westlake, Weisman	10/1/1966	20	5
Dandy	Davies	10/15/1966	5	8
I Just Don't Know What to Do with Myself	David, Bacharach, Williams	10/22/1966	26	5
Spinout	Wayne, Weisman, Fuller	11/5/1966	40	2
Look What You've Done	Johnston, Farrell	1/14/1967	32	4
Indescribably Blue	Glenn	2/18/1967	33	4
I Found a Love	Schofield, Pickett, West	4/22/1967	32	2
Mirage	Giant, Baum, Kaye	5/6/1967	10	8
I Had a Dream	Charles	9/2/1967	17	5
I Love You	Barton, Talley, Owen	5/25/1968	14	10
Sky Pilot	Burdon, Briggs, Weider, Jenkins, McCulloch	6/22/1968	14	10
Folsom Prison Blues	Cash	6/29/1968	32	6
Turn Around, Look at Me	Capeheart	7/13/1968	7	11
Atlantis	Kouta, Stein	4/26/1969	7	10
Love Me Tonight	Robertson	6/7/1969	13	0
Let Me	Presley, Matson	6/14/1969	20	8
Get Together	Powers	8/2/1969	5	12
Easy Come, Easy Go	Weisman, Wayne	2/28/1970	9	0

Come and Get It	Spencer, Spencer	3/7/1970	7	11
Reflections of My Life	Campbell, McAleese	4/4/1970	10	11
Amazing Grace	Newton	1/9/1971	15	11
Chick a Boom (Don't Ya Jes' Love It)	Merrill	4/10/1971	9	11
Sooner or Later	Gilbert, Wolcott	6/19/1971	9	9
Stop, Look, Listen	Byers	7/17/1971	39	0
I'm Comin' Home	Rich	10/23/1971	40	0
How Do You Do?	Mac Gimsey	6/17/1972	8	12
Take It Easy	DeBru, Taylor, Mizzy	6/24/1972	12	8
I'm Still in Love with You	Walker	7/15/1972	3	11
Let's Pretend	Nolan	5/12/1973	35	7
Angel	Tepper, Bennett	7/21/1973	20	10
Ecstasy	Pomus, Shuman	9/22/1973	31	6
The Lord's Prayer	Carey	3/9/1974	4	11

Companies

Jean and Julian Aberbach created partnership companies around the world with some of the most talented and prolific songwriters and performers in popular music history. Their efforts institutionalized a trend that fueled a fundamental revolution in the music industry. Increasingly, artists began to demand equity ownership in their careers and greater control over their creative work and business affairs.

NORTH AMERICAN COMPANIES

Companies	Affiliation	Incorporation Date	Notable Stockholders, Board Members, or Associates
Aberbach (Canada), Ltd.	CAPAC	15 Aug. 1955	T. St. Clair Low
Aberbach, Inc. (Calif.)	BMI	13 Sept. 1948	
Aberbach, Inc. (N.Y.)	BMI	7 June 1960	
Affiliated Music Enterprises, Inc.	BMI	14 Oct. 1953	Kurt Jadassohn (affiliates include Gospel Advocate Co., Inc.; Tharon and Murl Guffey; Happy Hearts Music; Scared Music Foundation; L. O. Sanderson; Stamps-Baxter Music & Printing Co., including Samuel W. Beazley & Son and Sisk Music Co.; Herbert G. Tovey; LaVerne Wright; Zondervan Music Publishing; Diadem Productions, Inc.; Harper Kreiser; and Good News Broadcasting Association, Inc.)

Agrun Music Corp.	ASCAP	18 July 1957	Ross Jungnickel, Inc.
Aida Music, Inc.	ASCAP	6 Jan. 1959	Connie Francis
Alamo Music, Inc.	ASCAP	28 July 1947	Rodeheaver Gospel Music
And Music Co., Inc.	BMI	29 Dec. 1958	Johnny Nash, Peter Dean, Robert Altfield
Anne-Rachel Music Corporation			
Ark-La-Tex Publishing Co., Inc.	BMI	10 Nov. 1952	Webb Pierce
Arlington Music, Inc.	BMI	13 Jan. 1959	George Hamilton, IV and Connie B. Gay
Artists Consultants, Inc.		25 Feb. 1958	
Atzal Music, Inc.			
Belinda (Canada) Ltd.	CAPAC	14 Sept. 1960	
Benmed Music, Inc.	BMI	7 Sept. 1962	Bennie Benjamin, Jean Medlin, Sol Marcus
Bennie Benjamin Music, Inc.	ASCAP	6 Feb. 1958	Bennie Benjamin
Big Top Record Distributors, Inc.		25 Feb. 1958	
Big Top Records, Inc.		25 Feb. 1958	
Bob Wills Music, Inc. (Calif.)	BMI	17 May 1946	Bob Wills
Bob Wills Music, Inc.(N.Y.)	BMI	7 June 1960	Bob Wills
Brakenbury Music, Inc.	BMI	30 Nov. 1959	Jack Good, William Davidson, Irving Gamow
Brenner Music, Inc.	BMI	27 Oct. 1949	
Brittany Music, Inc. (Calif.)	BMI	15 Apr. 1946	
Brittany Music, Inc. (N.Y.)	BMI	7 June 1960	
C.M.A. Music, Inc.	ASCAP	6 Feb. 1959	Chubby Jackson
Canford Music, Inc.	BMI	9 Apr. 1953	Shirley Wolf, Sy Soloway, Reginald John Connelly
Charles Emmerich Kalman, Inc.	ASCAP	5 Dec. 1956	
Charles N. Daniels, Inc.	ASCAP	6 Mar. 1947	
Cindy Music, Inc.	ASCAP	26 Apr. 1957	
Copar-Forrest Music Corp.	ASCAP	2 Oct. 1961	
Cornell-Kingsway Music Corp.	ASCAP	2 Oct. 1961	
December Music, Inc.	ASCAP	16 Jan. 1959	

Derby Music, Inc.	ASCAP	7 Oct. 1957	Al Cohn
Dolfi Music, Inc.	ASCAP	5 Aug. 1959	
Efsee Music, Inc.	BMI	6 Jan. 1959	Connie Francis
Eleventh Floor Music, Inc.	ASCAP	5 Aug. 1959	
Elton Britt Music, Inc. (Calif.)	BMI	30 June 1948	Elton Britt
Elton Britt Music, Inc. (N.Y.)	BMI	7 June 1960	Elton Britt
Elvis Presley Music, Inc.	BMI	6 Dec. 1955	Elvis Presley (VP), Tom Parker (2nd VP)
Ernest Tubb Music, Inc. (Calif.)	BMI	11 Dec. 1946	Ernest Tubb
Ernest Tubb Music, Inc. (N.Y.)	BMI	7 June 1960	Ernest Tubb
European Plays and Television Corporation of New York		14 Aug. 1952	
Everglades Music, Inc.		27 Mar. 1952	
Fabulous Music, Inc.	BMI	20 May 1959	
Flamingo Music, Inc.	ASCAP	9 Apr. 1953	Sam Coslow
Frankie Avalon Music, Inc.	BMI	19 Jan. 1959	Frankie Avalon
Galli Music, Inc.	ASCAP	4 Sept. 1964	Sergio Franchi
Gibson Music, Inc.	BMI	27 Apr. 1960	
Gladys Music, Inc.	ASCAP	16 Nov. 1956	Elvis Presley, Tom Parker
Granville Music, Inc.	BMI	5 Aug. 1959	
Graybar Music, Inc	BMI	19 Sept. 1961	
Gretbert Music, Inc.	BMI	4 Sept. 1964	Sergio Franchi
Hallowell Music, Inc.	BMI	12 Nov. 1957	
Hanks Music, Inc.			
Hank Snow Music, Inc.	BMI	30 Apr. 1956	Hank Snow, Ted Daffan, Blanche Snow
Hill and Range Songs, Inc.	BMI	9 Dec. 1944	
Hill and Range Songs, Inc. (Real Estate Division)	BMI	9 Dec. 1944	
Hill and Range Songs Enterprises, Ltd.		18 Dec. 1947	
Home Folks Songs, Inc. (Calif.)	BMI	11 Sept. 1947	
Home Folks Songs, Inc. (N.Y.)	BMI	7 June 1960	

Imogen Music, Inc.	ASCAP	29 Aug. 1960	Jack Good, William Davidson, Irving Gamow
J & E Music Co., Inc.	ASCAP	29 Dec. 1958	Johnny Nash, Peter Dean, Robert Altfield
Janique Music, Inc.	BMI	20 Sept. 1960	
Joaneline Music, Inc.	BMI	18 Sept. 1961	Harry R. Webb, Dorothy Webb, Peter Gormley, Michael Simkins
Johnny Cash Music, Inc.	BMI	25 Nov. 1957	Johnny Cash
Johnny Mathis Music, Inc.	ASCAP	23 Oct. 1957	Johnny Mathis
Josephine Music, Inc.	ASCAP	28 Oct. 1959	Josephine Peoples, Otis Blackwell
Kalith Music, Inc.	BMI	29 Sept. 1958	
Kenny Lynch Music, Inc.	BMI	7 Nov. 1963	
Kentucky Music, Inc. (Calif.)	BMI	26 June 1947	
Kentucky Music, Inc. (N.Y.)	BMI	7 June 1960	
Kidd Music, Inc.	BMI	18 Mar. 1960	
L & M Music, Inc.	ASCAP	14 Nov. 1960	
Laren Music, Inc.	ASCAP	17 Nov. 1958	
Lemon Music Corp.	ASCAP	6 Sept. 1962	
Looman Music, Inc.	BMI	14 Nov. 1960	
Louisiana Music, Inc.	BMI	28 Mar. 1949	
Luriline Music, Inc.	BMI	25 Sept. 1961	
MacGibbon Music, Inc.	ASCAP	26 Sept. 1960	
Mahalia Jackson Music, Inc.	BMI	4 Mar. 1959	
Mantel Music. Inc.	BMI	17 Nov. 1958	
Mantovani Music, Inc.	ASCAP	1 Jan. 1959	Annunzio Mantovani
May Music, Inc.	ASCAP	22 Apr. 1959	
Monfry Music, Inc.	ASCAP	4 Nov. 1959	
Multihon Music, Inc.	BMI	27 Nov. 1959	
Municipal Musical Instrument Corp.	BMI		
New Wave Music, Inc.	BMI	5 Aug. 1959	
Noma Music, Inc.	BMI	23 Oct. 1957	
November Music, Inc.	BMI	8 July 1959	
Osvaldo Farres Music, Inc.	BMI	28 Jan. 1949	Osvaldo Farres
Parliament Music, Inc.	ASCAP	11 Mar. 1958	
Pentagon Music, Inc.	BMI	10 Oct. 1958	

Picture Music, Inc.	ASCAP	24 Mar. 1960	
Pine Bluff Music, Inc.	ASCAP	29 Sept. 1959	
Plan Two Music, Inc.	ASCAP	4 Sept. 1959	
Progressive Music Publishing Co., Inc.	BMI	20 Nov. 1957 (reincorporated 17 Sept. 1962)	Ahmet and Nesuhi Ertegun
Questar Music, Inc.	ASCAP	19 Sept. 1961	
Quintet Music, Inc.	BMI	25 Sept. 1957	Jerry Leiber, Mike Stoller
Reg Connelly Music, Inc.	ASCAP	9 Apr. 1953	
Renoir Music, Inc.	BMI	26 Mar. 1959	
Rio Grande Music, Inc.	BMI	22 Apr. 1949	
Rosarita Music, Inc.	ASCAP	15 Mar. 1954	
Ross Jungnickel, Inc.	ASCAP	24 Apr. 1925	
Rumbalero Music, Inc.	BMI	29 Oct. 1948	
St. Louis Music Corp.	BMI	8 Aug. 1947	
Saline Music, Inc.	ASCAP	30 Dec. 1958	Johnny Cash
Second Music Pub. Co, Inc.	ASCAP	18 May 1956	
Semprini Music, Inc.	BMI	13 Jan. 1959	
The Shadows Music, Inc.	BMI	19 June 1961	Peter Gormley
Shenandoah Music, Inc.	BMI	17 June 1947	
Show Music Pub., Inc.	BMI	21 May 1956	
Sigma Music, Inc.	ASCAP	17 Nov. 1950	
Silvertowne Music, Inc.	ASCAP	30 Dec. 1960	
Sito Music, inc.	BMI	6 Nov. 1959	Otis Blackwell, Josephine Peoples
SJW Music Inc.	BMI	2 Nov. 1961	
Sky Hi Music, Inc.	ASCAP	4 Aug. 1962	
Skyrock Music, Inc.	ASCAP	18 July 1960	
Southwind Music, Inc.	BMI	25 Nov. 1957	Johnny Cash
Stock Music, Inc.	BMI	12-May-59	
Tarrytown Music, Inc.	BMI	11 Mar. 1958	
Tenson Music, Inc.	ASCAP	16 Oct. 1958	
Three Bells Music, Inc.	BMI	29 Sept. 1959	
Thunderbird Productions, Inc.		30 Oct. 1962	
Tiger Music, Inc.	BMI	4 Nov. 1955	Quintet Music (Leiber and Stoller) and Progressive Music (Erteguns & Aberbachs)

Trans-Pacific Music, Inc.	BMI	20 Mar. 1962	
Two Worlds Music, Inc.	ASCAP	23 June 1960	Sid Wayne
Two-Penny Music, Inc.	ASCAP	27 June 1957	Jerry Leiber, Mike Stoller
Valley Publishers, Inc.	BMI	21 Feb. 1953	
Wickham Music, Inc.	ASCAP	26 Jan. 1962	
Wooftie Music, Inc.	ASCAP	3 Nov. 1960	Chubby Jackson

INTERNATIONAL COMPANIES

Australia
Aberbach (Australia) PTY, Ltd.
Belinda Music (Australia) PTY, Ltd.
Benday Music (Australia) PTY, Ltd.
Johnny Devlin Music PTY, Ltd.
Kalmann Music (Australia) PTY, Ltd.
Lonnie Lee Music PTY, Ltd.
Progressive Music (Australia) PTY, Ltd.
A. Schroeder Music (Australia) PTY. Ltd.
T.M. Music (Australia) PTY. Ltd.
George Wiener Music (Australia) PTY, Ltd.
Williams-Conde Music PTY, Ltd.

Austria
Aberbach (Wien) GmbH

Belgium
Belindamusic SPRL
Dolfimusic SPRL

Brazil
Aberbach Editora Musical Ltda.
Editora Musical Walden Ltda.

British Isles
Aberbach (London), Ltd.
Aberbach (London Properties), Ltd.
Ambrose Music, Ltd.
Anita Music, Ltd.
Belinda (London), Ltd.
Belinda (Recordings), Ltd.

Benday Music, Ltd.
Cardinal Music, Ltd.
Coronet Music, Ltd.
December Music, Ltd.
Design Music, Ltd.
Elstree Music, Ltd.
Enquiry Music, Ltd.
Fabienne Music, Ltd.
Fiesta Music, Ltd.
Figure Music, Ltd.
Jack Good Music Publishing Co., Ltd.
Hill and Range Songs (London), Ltd.
Joaneline Music, Ltd.
June Music, Ltd.
Kalith Music, Ltd.
Kalmann Music, Ltd.
Kenmoss Music, Ltd.
Kenny Lynch Music, Ltd.
Kieron Music, Ltd.
Knox Music, Ltd.
Lark Music, Ltd.
Jeff Leigh Music, Ltd.
Lewman Music, Ltd.
Linvoy Music, Ltd.
Ludix Music, Ltd.
The Manor Music Co., Ltd.
Marilyn Music, Ltd.
Johnny Mathis Music, Ltd.
Maycroft Music, Ltd.
Page Music, Ltd.
Parkgate Music, Ltd.
Peterman & Co., Ltd.
Progressive Music, Ltd.

Riverdale Music, Ltd.
Ronny Music (London), Ltd.
Roosevelt Music, Ltd.
Scan Music, Ltd.
Sea-Lark Music, Ltd.
Semprini Music, Ltd.
Seventeen Savile Row, Ltd.
The Shadows Music, Ltd.
Vincent Shepherd Enterprises, Ltd.
S-P-R Music, Ltd.
Starfire Music, Ltd.
Stork Music Publishing Co., Ltd.
T.M. Music, Ltd.
Tollie Music, Ltd.
Tone Music, Ltd.
Vicki Music, Ltd.
West One Music, Ltd.

Canada
Aberbach (Canada), Ltd.
Belinda (Canada), Ltd.

France
Editions Associées, SARL
Editions Barton, SARL
Cirque-Brunel (Société Civile Immobilière)
Editions Colby, SARK
Editions Fiesta, SARL
Merry Music, SARL
Editions Pigalle, SARL
Pigalle Champs-Elysées (Société Civile Immo-
bilière)
Editions Progressive, SARL
Editions Ronny, SARL
Editions Roosevelt, SARL

Germany
Aberbach (Hamburg), GmbH
Musikverlag Barton, GmbH
Bella-Ton Musikverlag, GmbH
Benday Musikverlag, GmbH

Musikverlag Colby (Hamburg), GmbH
Fein (Hamburg), GmbH
Hanseatic Musikverlag, GmbH
Harmonie, Verlagsgesellschaft für Literatur
und Kunst, GmbH
Kalmann Music, Inc. (Deutschland), GmbH
Musikverlag Lark, GmbH
Musikverlag Progressive, GmbH
Rondo-Verlag, GmbH
Ronny (Hamburg) Musikverlag, GmbH
T.M. Musikverlag, GmbH
Tonika Verlag Horst Bussow

Holland (The Netherlands)
Aberbach (Holland), NV
Belinda (Amsterdam), NV
Progressive Music Publishing Company
(Holland), NV

Israel
Aberbach (Israel) Co., Ltd.

Italy
Aberbach (Roma) Editori di Musica, SpA
Edizioni Barton, SRL
Edizioni Colby, SRL
Edizioni Progressive, SRL
Resolute-Case Editrice Musicale, SRL
Edizioni Ronny, SRL
Edizioni Roosevelt, SRL

Japan
Aberbach Tokyo Kabushiki Kaisha
Hill and Range Songs (Japan) KK

Mexico
Aberbach de Mexico, SA

New Zealand
Belcas Music, Ltd.

Scandinavia

Barton (Scandinavia) AB
Belinda (Scandinavia) AB
Cedarwood (Scandinavia) AB
Lois (Scandinavia) AB
Robert Mellin (Scandinavia) AB
Progressive Musikförlåg AB

South Africa

Aberbach (South Africa) (PTY.), Ltd.
Belinda (Johannesburg) (PTY.), Ltd.

Plymouth Music (PTY.), Ltd.
Progressive-Africa (PTY.), Ltd.
Telstar Records (PTY.), Ltd.
Tennessee Music (PTY.), Ltd.

Spain

Aberbach (Madrid), SA

Switzerland

Aberbach (Alpina), GmbH

NOTES

Except as otherwise noted, all interviews were conducted by the author.

CHAPTER 1. NO WRONG TURNS

In addition to his own memoir sketches, sources for Jean's early life include several interviews with his wife Susan, brother Julian, and cousin John Schmetterling that took place over 1992 and 1993.

CHAPTER 2. HAPPENSTANCE

1 Roger Manvell and Heinrich Fraenkel, *The German Cinema.*
2 "[A]ccidentally turned the wrong way, entering the business of Willi Meisel—the filmmaker. He was hired on the spot. That was in 1932. About 6 months later, a man came to Berlin representing Campbell Connelly to get the representation of Meisel's work for France. He asked Jean to come to Paris" (Julian Aberbach interview, December 23, 1992). "Paris—Jacques Rosenberg: How we met in Berlin at a barber shop" (Jean Aberbach memoir sketches, date unknown).
3 Jean Aberbach memoir sketches, date unknown.

CHAPTER 3. THE REVOLVING DOOR

In addition to his own memoir sketches, sources for Jean's Paris years include several interviews with his wife Susan and brother Julian that took place over 1992 and 1993. Background material on Campbell, Connelly & Co. was derived from a summary of company history supplied by Mick Booth.

CHAPTER 4. DESTINY

1. Fritz Spielman interview, December 19, 1992.
2 Russell Sanjek, *Pennies from Heaven,* 109.
3 Ibid., 111.
4 Ibid., 193.
5 Russell Sanjek, *American Popular Music and Its Business,* 98. Using the CPI method and 1938 as the date, this calculates to approximately $195,000 in 2003 money.

6   Ibid., 91.

7   Sanjek, *Pennies*, 108.

8   Nat Shapiro, *Popular Music*, 5.

9   Sanjek, *American Popular Music*, 96.

10 Jean continued independent representation of Éditions Salabert the whole time he was working for Chappell, eventually also adding Julian to the arrangement. In a letter of agreement dated January 1, 1945, made between him and Julian (operating under the alias "Jerome J. Brooks"), Jean excludes revenue from a transaction he secured years earlier with Lowes, Inc., from their joint representation agreement with Éditions Salabert. All other revenue would be equally shared. Since the agreement indicates that the arrangement would be automatically renewed year to year, these and other evidence suggest that prior contract arrangements with other companies survived throughout Jean's staff tenure at Chappell; Hill and Range Songs corporate records.

CHAPTER 5. EYE OF THE NEEDLE

1   All facts and statistics on the fate of the *St. Louis* are from Arthur D. Morse, *While Six Million Died*, 270–88, or from Haskel Lookstein, *Were We Our Brother's Keepers?* 81–103.

2   Israel Gutman, ed., *Chronicle of the 20th Century*, 494.

3   Jacques Adler, *The Jews of Paris and the Final Solution*, 5.

4   Paul Webster, Petain's Crime: The Full Story of French Collaboration in the Holocaust, 31.

5   "[T]hey got their visa, they took a boat *Le Gras* [sic] and came to the United States. And on the way back, the boat struck a mine and sank" (Julian Aberbach interview, May 31, 1993).

CHAPTER 6. AMBITION

1   Russell Sanjek, *From Print to Plastic: Publishing and Promoting America's Popular Music (1900–1980)*, 17.

2   Ibid., 21.

3   Of his early career, Julian recalls: "He had a good position but was not making very much money" (Julian Aberbach interview, December 23, 1992). "$50 a week. And his job, at that particular time, was to visit the big band leaders and try to get the latest song that they published played on the air. . . . That was his job" (Julian Aberbach interview, May 31, 1993). Within two years, Fritz Spielman was amazed at his progress: "He was still working for Max Dreyfus. But you know he was not any more a lieutenant. He was already looking out for songs for motion pictures for Max Dreyfus" (Fritz Spielman interview, December 19, 1992). "He had an executive position at Chappell. And he was working directly with Mr. Dreyfus. And at one time he was the head of a whole company [division]" (Freddy Bienstock interview, April 29, 1993). Wife Susan recalls how Jean revered Dreyfus: "Jean always used to say that he modeled himself after Max Dreyfus. He had tremendous respect for the man and always wanted to be like him" (Susan Aberbach interview, December 10, 1992).

4   Sanjek, *Pennies*, 176.

5   Ibid., 179, 181.

6   David Ewen, *All the Years of Popular Music*, 303–4.

7   Sanjek, *American Popular Music*, 105.

8   "The Cockeyed Mayor of Kaunakakai" (1935, words by R. Alex Anderson and Al Stillman, music by R. Alex Anderson); "Let's Dance" (1935, words by Fanny Baldridge, music by Gregory Stone and Joseph Bonine).

9 "(Allá En) El Rancho Grande" (1934, Spanish words by Pedro Berrios, music by Xavier Cugat, English words by Stanley Adams); "My Shawl (Ombo)" (1934, Spanish words and music by María Grever, English words by Stanley Adams); "What a Diff'rence a Day Made" (1934, Spanish words and music by María Grever, English words by Stanley Adams).

10 Shapiro, *Popular Music*, 70, 104, 106.

11 Except otherwise noted, all references to Peer works taken from Ewen, *All the Years of Popular Music*.

12 Sanjek, *Pennies*, 288–89.

13 Fred Rose's ability to craft songs was legendary in Nashville. "See, he did this thing called 'Freddie Rose's Song Shop.' And people would call in and suggest titles, and he would write the songs right there on the air!" (Chet Atkins interview, January 20, 1993).

14 Elizabeth Schlappi, *Roy Acuff: The Smokey Mountain Boy*, 42–43; Paul Kingsbury, *The Grand Ole Opry History of Country Music*, 70.

CHAPTER 7. THE REBBE SLEEPS

1 Most material on cowboys in film comes from Buck Rainey, "The 'Reel' Cowboy," in Charles W. Harris and Buck Rainey, *The Cowboy: Six-Shooters, Songs, and Sex*.

2 Laurence Zwisohn, liner notes to Sons of the Pioneers, *Wagons West;* also letter from Bob Nolan toTim Spencer, Inc., Record No. 260e, July 7, 1948, Hill and Range corporate records.

3 Ace Collins, *The Stories behind Country Music's All-Time Greatest 100 Songs*, Boulevard Books, 22.

4 Sanjek, *Pennies*, 219.

5 Sanjek, *American Popular Music*, 131–32.

6 Sanjek, *Pennies*, 187.

7 Ewen, *All the Years*, 391, 578.

8 Collins, *Stories behind Country Music*, 32–33.

9 Stanley Green, *The Rodgers and Hammerstein Story*, 109.

10 Shapiro, *Popular Music*, 5–6.

11 Richard Rodgers, *Musical Stages*, 283.

12 Richard Maurice Hurst, *Republic Studios: Between Poverty Row and the Majors*, 147, 151.

CHAPTER 8. BETTING THE FARM

1 Hill and Range corporate records, Record No. 195.

2 Zwisohn, liner notes to Sons of the Pioneers, *Wagons West*.

3 The service company King cofounded with Blink is known by a confusing array of names. It is sometimes referred to collectively as Standard Transcriptions, but Russell Sanjek provides its full name as Standard Radio Transcription Service. At other times, he uses Standard Radio Library. It probably refers to the collective catalog repository of its transcribed works (Sanjek, *Pennies*, 758). Hill and Range corporate records contain numerous documents with letterhead "Standard Radio Electrical Transcriptions," with a location of 6404 Hollywood Boulevard, Hollywood, California, which was Gerald King's record label attached to the service firm. King and Blink signed their contracts and informally referred to themselves as "Standard Radio." For the purposes of reference in this book, the abbreviated name "Standard Radio" or "Standard" may be used.

4 Robert W. Phillips, *Roy Rogers*, 14.

5 Hill and Range Songs corporate records, letter of agreement with BMI by Bob Burton, March 15, 1944.
6 Hill and Range Songs corporate records, various documents dated December 12, 1944.
7 Zwisohn, liner notes to Sons of the Pioneers, *Wagons West*.
8 Jean Aberbach, from the transcript of his 80th birthday party video in the possession of Susan Aberbach; also "went right through the roof!" (Grelun Landon interview, August 18, 1993).
9 That Jean's work at Chappell funded the early years of Hill and Range is also asserted in the Freddy Bienstock interview, April 29, 1993.
10 Wills's most creative period was the late 1930s and early 1940s. Biographer Charles R. Townsend refers to them as his "glory years" (Townsend, *San Antonio Rose: The Life and Music of Bob Wills*, 151–56).
11 Ibid., 239.
12 Al Quaglieri in the liner notes for *Spadella! The Essential Spade Cooley* (Columbia Legacy, 1994); also Sanjek, *Pennies*, 219–20.
13 Collins, *Stories behind Country Music*, 47.
14 Joel Whitburn, *Top Country Singles: 1944–1988*.
15 Julian Aberbach interview, May 31, 1993.
16 Jean Aberbach memoir sketches, date unknown.

CHAPTER 9. HARDY'S HORSEMEAT

1 "Chicken scratch" music among the Pima Indians is now well documented (Townsend, *San Antonio Rose*, 28; for sources, see p. 33, fn. 52).
2 Ibid., 149, 190.
3 Ibid., 212.
4 Ibid., 241.
5 Sheet Music, Rider B, Record No. 167, Hill and Range corporate records.
6 Whitburn, *Top Country Singles*, week of July 7, 1945, 513.
7 Letter of assignment from Julian as Jerome J. Brooks/Biltmore Music to Adolf Aberbach for Normandy Music, October 1944, Hill and Range Songs corporate records.
8 Julian Aberbach interview, December 23, 1992.
9 Letter from Gerald King, August 5, 1946, proposing settlement, Hill and Range corporate records.
10 Jean Aberbach memoirs, date unknown.

CHAPTER 10. A VIEW FROM THE BRIDGE

1 Various songwriter agreements, Hill and Range corporate records.
2 Julian made it clear that Max was candidly informed and fully aware of Jean's activities with Hill and Range in California from 1946 forward (Julian Aberbach interview, December 23, 1992).
3 Hill and Range Songs corporate records: Biltmore folder, 1945.
4 Lawrence Zwisohn interview, August 15 1997.
5 Fred Fox interview, October 1997. Fred Fox was the son of the founder of Sam Fox Publishing.
6 According to Fred Fox, he and others were against the sale of this song (Fred Fox interview, October 1997).
7 Stanley Green, *The Rodgers and Hammerstein Story*, 113.
8 Jean Aberbach memoir sketches, date unknown.

CHAPTER II. THE HIRED BAND

1 Zwisohn, liner notes to *Wagons West*.

2 Jean Aberbach memoir sketches, date unknown.

3 Julian Aberbach interview, January 3, 1993.

4 Daffan would later sign an exclusive songwriter agreement with Hill and Range and also contribute greatly to Hank Snow Music, Inc., which Hank Snow co-owned with Hill and Range. Snow Music was formed in the mid-1950s, and Daffan held a 25 percent stake.

5 Cindy Walker interview, December 17, 1993.

6 They did pick up one other tune written exclusively by one of Wills's cowriters, "There's an Empty Chair at the Christmas Table." Cliff Sundin reminds Julian to thank Jean for the title suggestion in a letter dated September 9, 1945 (Hill and Range corporate records).

7 Sanjek, *Pennies*, 181.

8 Hill and Range corporate records, Biltmore Folder, 1944–1945.

9 Mitch Miller states that Jean undoubtedly learned the business technique of partnering companies directly from Max Dreyfus (Mitch Miller interview, January 29, 1993).

10 In a promotional pamphlet for the series, Tiffany Music, Inc., asserts Columbia was scheduled to release only two Wills recordings a year. The list of recordings during 1945 detailed by Townsend *San Antonio Rose*, suggests that this was not a great exaggeration. See the Tiffany promotional insert in Townsend, 250–51.

11 Ibid., 241.

12 Rodgers, *Musical Stages*, 283.

13 Hill and Range corporate records, Record No. 267a, April 24, 1946.

14 Jean Aberbach memoir sketches, date unknown.

CHAPTER 12. NASHVILLE STEAMROLLER

1 American Music "became the biggest name in country and western music." Laurence Zwisohn interview, August 15, 1997; "He had a number of important writers under exclusive contract" (Julian Aberbach interview, January 3, 1993).

2 Whitburn, *Top Country Singles*, 513.

3 Peter Guralnick, *Lost Highway*, 31, and Paul Kingsbury and Alanna Nash, *Will the Circle Be Unbroken*, 135.

4 Ronnie Pugh, *Ernest Tubb*, 54–56, and 84–85.

5 This event is said to have been the brainchild of promoters Connie B. Gay, Oscar Davis, and Abe Lackman. Fred Rose acted as consultant on this event, which was originally created for a venue in Washington, D.C. (John Rumble, *Fred Rose and the Development of the Nashville Music Industry, 1942–1954*, 248).

6 "Ernest was a very, very fine person—very down to earth. And I've often said, he was the most unselfish person I'd ever known. He would plug other artists and their records and leave his go!" (Hank Snow interview, January 20, 1993).

7 From an interview with Townsend Miller, quoted in the essay "Ernest Tubb" in Bill C. Malone and Judith McCulloh, eds., *Stars of Country Music*, 225.

8 Guralnick, *Lost Highway*, 25, and Hank Snow, Hank Snow Story, 290–91.

9 Johnny Cash was among those encouraged by Tubb to sign with Hill and Range "As far as Johnny Cash is concerned, he was anxious to create a music publishing company and was very unsure who to entrust with the partnership. He consulted with Ernest Tubb, who had an excellent experience with us. He recommended my brother and myself

very highly to Johnny Cash, who came to see me in Los Angeles and we organized a music publishing company together" (Julian Aberbach interview, January 5, 1993).

10 Pugh, *Ernest Tubb*, 90–93.

11 Ibid., 91.

12 Ibid., 117–18.

13 Sylvester Cross "became a music publisher—an illegitimate music publisher. He had a number of important writers under exclusive Bob Nolan, Tim Spencer, Ernest Tubb and Merle Travis . . . he approached me" (Julian Aberbach interview, January 3, 1993).

14 "[A]s he always needed money, I bought a great number of important songs" (Julian Aberbach interview, January 3, 1993).

15 Julian asserts that while they were not legally bound to redress Sylvester Cross's deficiencies, they felt ethically bound, and that this was the Aberbachs' manner of doing business. "After his [Cross's] death, American Music was acquired by Hill and Range. This was relatively simple because he had failed to pay writers royalties and Hill and Range made up for the difference" (Julian Aberbach interview, January 3, 1993).

16 Hill and Range corporate records, 1947.

17 Guralnick, *Lost Highway*, 109–10; John Morthland, *The Best of Country Music*, 151–52.

18 Ralph Rinzler, "Bill Monroe," in Bill C. Malone and Judith McCulloh's *Stars of Country Music*, 203, 218; Ace Collins, *The Stories*, 261; Paul Kingsbury and Alanna Nash, *Will the Circle Be Unbroken*, 188–91.

19 Morthland, *The Best*, 154.

20 "All of these writers switched to Hill and Range" (Julian Aberbach interview, January 3, 1993).

21 Paul Kingsbury, *The Grand Ole Opry*, 64–65, 69.

22 Kingsbury, *Grand Ole Opry*, 65, 77.

23 Rumble, *Fred Rose*, 68, 147.

24 Ewen, *All the Years*, 579.

25 Rumble, *Fred Rose*, 147–48.

26 Kingsbury, *Grand Ole Opry History*, 69–72.

27 Rumble, *Fred Rose*, 128.

28 Ibid., 219.

29 John Rumble asserts that prior to the inception of the new policy that afforded artists direct payments from BMI for their writer's share, Rose's policy was to divide Acuff-Rose's BMI royalties with the songwriters, providing equal shares to the publisher and writer on a song-by-song basis (ibid., 148). Thus, if the publisher's share was $1.00 and the author/composer share was $1.00, then BMI paid the publisher $2.00 and Acuff-Rose paid the author/composer $1.00, keeping $1.00 for itself. This was no more or less than what the law at the time dictated, but it was still less than what the Aberbachs were willing to wager.

30 Kingsbury, *Grand Ole Opry*, 77–78.

31 Paul Kingsbury and Alanna Nash, *Will the Circle Be Unbroken*, 130.

32 Justin Tubb interview, January 20, 1993.

33 Hank Snow, *The Hank Snow Story*, 290–91; "very unsure who to entrust with the partnership. He consulted with Ernest Tubb. . . . He recommended my brother and myself very highly to Johnny Cash" (Julian Aberbach interview, January 5, 1993). A partnership company was set up with Cash, but left to lapse during his drug-ridden unproductive years (letter from Bob Nolan to Grelun Landon, November 6, 1957, Hill and Range corporate records).

34 Chet Atkins interview, January 20, 1993.

35 Percentages are derived from John Rumble's calculations of 690 Top 10 hits surveyed

between the years 1944 and 1954. Hill and Range had no hits in 1944 as it was not yet incorporated. Peer ranks as the fourth company. Except for an overwhelming forty-six hits in 1944, and a spike in 1951 to sixteen, it ranged from only one to nine hits in any other year, probably because by this time Ralph Peer had turned the bulk of his attention away from American folk music to explore South American Latin music (Rumble, *Fred Rose*, 212–31).

36 Roger M. Williams in "Hank Williams" from Bill C. Malone and Judith McCulloh, eds., *Stars of Country Music*, 239.

37 Jean Aberbach memoir sketches, date unknown.

CHAPTER 13. THE DISAPPEARING ACT

1 Chet Atkins interview, January 20, 1993.

2 Sanjek, *Pennies*, 293.

3 Ibid., 217–21, 286.

4 Pugh, *Ernest Tubb*, 135–7

5 "Auf Wiedersehen, My Dear" was cowritten with Al Hoffman, Al Goodhart, and Milton Brown.

6 Standard songwriter's agreement with Jay Glass, Steve Nelson, and Fred Wise, March 26, 1947 (Hill and Range corporate records).

7 The 1949 contract with BMI allowed the Aberbach brothers to operate ASCAP firms, but prohibited them from exploiting songs published through ASCAP (Advance Agreement between Hill and Range Songs, Inc., and Broadcast Music, Inc., March 29, 1949, Hill and Range corporate records).

8 "What is significant, though, is that based upon new repertoire, Hill & Range was the most active publisher (Ed Cramer interview, January 12, 1993). By 1956, Hill and Range was their seventh-highest-paid affiliate. Sanjek, *Pennies*, 425.

9 Sanjek, *Pennies*, 279.

10 Country Music Hall of Fame website, available at http://www.countrymusichalloffame. com/inductees/steve_sholes.html (accessed July 10, 2009).

11 Streissguth, *Eddy Arnold*, 70–73.

12 Ibid., 69–70.

13 "Steve was a great man, and [the work at] RCA Victor killed him. He got a raw deal. They would move everybody up around him but Steve would plod along. He was not a real happy man" (Charlie Grean interview, March 16, 1994).

14 Townsend Miller's "Ernest Tubb" in Bill C. Malone and Judith McCulloh's *Stars of Country Music*, 226.

15 Sanjek, *Pennies*, 219.

16 Ibid., 219.

17 Julian's friendship with Sholes was cultivated only after he emerged from his tour of duty in March 1944 and began working again in the music business.

18 Zwisohn, *Wagons West*.

19 *Ibid.;* also "Jean [visited] a little more. He was a little more active in coming around than Julian. But most of time, we would see them together. . . . [Jean] brought the best material all the time. . . . I think he had kind of a knack" (Charlie Grean interview, March 16, 1994).

20 "Chet [Atkins] had sent a demonstration record of him playing guitar. . . . I think he was working in Springfield at the time. I just couldn't believe the technique! Geez! This guy is fabulous! Nobody plays like this!" (Charlie Grean interview, March 16, 1994).

21 "Jean signed me up when I went on RCA. He signed me up [by phone] as a Hill and Range writer. He came to Chicago with Mr. Sholes. That's when I first met him, August

1947. [Q: Jean or Julian?] Jean. The heavier one" (Chet Atkins interview, January 20, 1993); see also Chet Atkins, *Country Gentleman*, 133–34.

22 Streissguth, *Eddy Arnold*, 45–46.

23 Eddy Arnold interview, January 19, 1993; Kingsbury, *Grand Ole Opry History*, 80–81; Streissguth, *Eddy Arnold*, 95–96.

24 Streissguth, *Eddy Arnold*, 62–63; and Eddy Arnold interview, January 19, 1993.

25 Kingsbury, *Grand Ole Opry History*, 80.

26 Eddy Arnold interview, January 19, 1993.

27 Alanna Nash, *The Colonel*, 28–30.

28 Dirk Vellenga with Mick Farren, *Elvis and the Colonel*, 54, 63; Peter Guralnick, *Last Train to Memphis*, 165; Alanna Nash, *The Colonel*, 95.

29 Streissguth, *Eddy Arnold*, 53–55.

30 Minutes, November 11, 1947, Hill and Range corporate records; Julian Aberbach interview, December 23, 1992, and Eddy Arnold interview, January 19, 1993. Alanna Nash, *The Colonel*, pp.110–11.

31 Julian Aberbach interview, December 23, 1992.

32 Eddy Arnold interview, January 19, 1993.

33 Ibid.

34 While Julian recounts that the transferred song was "Fool That I Am," which became a chart hit in August 1947, the only Floyd Hunt song that apparently ended up in the Chappell catalog was his "Old Memories" (Hill and Range corporate records).

35 Streissguth, *Eddy Arnold*, 95–96.

36 It was acquired from Leeds Music on April 24, 1947, along with representation of a release against any claims by Red Foley. It is possible the lyrics and music preexisted in some nascent form, and were collected into Foley's firm—then later recast and polished into the hit by Nelson and Hilliard (Hill and Range corporate records).

37 Charlie Grean interview, March 16, 1994.

38 "I instinctively knew that there would be jealousy and troubles at Chappell" (Jean Aberbach, memoir sketches, date unknown).

39 Julian Aberbach interview, May 31, 1993.

CHAPTER 14. WALTZING TO THE BRINK

1 Julian Aberbach interview, January 15, 1993.

2 Agreement between BMI and Hill and Range, March 29, 1949 (Hill and Range corporate records).

3 Julian Aberbach interview, January 15, 1993.

4 Streissguth, *Eddy Arnold*, 222.

5 Ibid., 223; also two agreements engaging Jenny Lou Carson, dated April 4, 1949, were negotiated and signed by Jean creating her partnership corporation and binding her to it with an exclusive songwriter's agreement (corporate resolution, April 18, 1949, Hill and Range corporate records).

6 Colin Escott, *Hank Williams: The Biography*, 142.

7 Songwriter's agreement between Henry "Redd" Stewart and Ernest Tubb Music/Hill and Range Songs, June 1, 1947, Hill and Range corporate records.

8 Pugh, *Ernest Tubb*, 126.

9 Ace Collins, *The Stories*, 54; Colin Escott, *Hank Williams*, 142.

10 Johnny Tyler, "Oakie Boogie" sheet music in Hill and Range promotional collection donated by Ken Nelson, Capitol Records, Country Music Hall of Fame Archives.

11 Wade Hall, *Hell Bent for Music*, 146–47.

12 Collins, *The Stories*, 55.

13 Colin Escott states that "Tennessee Waltz" was another Acuff-Rose "hit by happenstance," asserting that neither Fred Rose, his son Wesley, nor their song plugger Mel Foree played any role in the success of the song (Escott, *Hank Williams*, 142); "Tennessee Waltz" appears to have been one property that was not effectively managed or promoted. The important "Lovesick Blues" can be counted as yet another (Rumble, *Fred Rose*, 141–42; 320, fn. 30). These accounts cast some doubt on the consistency and effectiveness of Acuff-Rose promotional practices.

14 Collins, *The Stories*, 55; Stewart's exclusive songwriter's agreement was found, but King's was not. However, Hill and Range corporate minutes record the date that King's agreement was dissolved, so we are certain it existed (corporate minutes, January 13, 1953, Hill and Range corporate records). Since the standard engagement was for three years, we can assume King's agreement was in place not earlier than January 13, 1950.

15 While King in his autobiography cites that they conveyed the work to Rose around Christmas of 1946, the registered copyright date for the work is 1948, at least a year later (Hall, *Hell Bent for Music*, 146).

16 From an interview by author Ronnie Pugh with Pee Wee King, November 18, 1993 (Pugh, *Ernest Tubb*, notes to ch. 13, 339, n. 25).

17 Ewen, *All the Years*, 458; Frankie Laine interview, September 15, 1993.

18 Sanjek, *Pennies*, 235.

19 According to Ace Collins, at the time of the writing of his book in 1996, the Patti Page version was the best-selling single ever recorded by a female singer and the sixth best-selling pop single released before 1954 (Collins, *The Stories*, 56).

20 Rumble, *Fred Rose*, 227.

21 Hall, *Hell Bent*, 148.

22 Agreement between Hill and Range Songs, Inc., and Broadcast Music, Inc., March 29, 1949; attorney Milton Rudin recalls the case also involved a song with "Roses" in the title (Milton Rudin interview, August 15, 1994).

23 Apparently, there was ample evidence available to support litigation for more than a year, so there must have been reasonable merit on both sides. So bitter was Wesley Rose he "took delight" in personally serving the legal papers (Rumble, Fred Rose, 264).

CHAPTER 15. KEYHOLE LOGIC

1 Rumble, *Fred Rose*, 266.

2 "Then the automation thing started. . . . You know, we had a lot of foul ups the first year or so" (Grelun Landon interview, August 18. 1993).

3 Milton Rudin interview, August 15, 1994.

4 Jean Aberbach memoir sketches, date unknown.

5 Norman Tyre interview, August 17, 1993.

6 Julian Aberbach interview, January 5, 1993.

7 Hill and Range corporate records, Record No. 260a, May 14, 1946.

8 "If you wanted works of ASCAP writers, you weren't going to say 'No, I can't take them because I only have a BMI company'" (Thea Zavin interview, July 22, 1993).

9 History of Wall Drug, available at http://www.walldrug.com/t-history.aspx (accessed July 10, 2009).

10 It is unclear whether Nolan was ever completely clear about how publishing worked. Laurence Zwisohn states that as late as 1969, he was unaware that he could have been paid his writer's share directly had he only joined ASCAP during his career (Lawrence Zwisohn interview, August 15, 1997).

11 Tim Spencer was a signatory to the arrangements made to separate Nolan's work from his own (Hill and Range corporate records, Record Nos. 260, May 14, 1946; 260a [no date]; and 260e, July 12, 1948).

12 Sanjek, *Pennies*, 175–82.

13 This loophole generated much media attention and is usually referred to as the "twilight zone" clause (Sanjek, *Pennies*, 188).

14 Ed Cramer interview, January 12, 1993.

15 "They put their house in order, until they only had to face Tim Spencer" (Milton Rudin, August 15, 1994).

16 Between June 2, 1952, and November 11, 1952, almost 700 copyrights and most song-writer agreements were ratified (Hill and Range corporate records).

17 Details of this episode are from Milton Rudin interview, August 15, 1994.

18 Sanjek, *Pennies*, 189–90.

19 "Sidney Kaye told me that he thought that Jean Aberbach was the most knowledgeable person in the music business at that time in the United States. And that's a strong statement for someone to make who was then actually running BMI but who had experience in other areas as well" (Ed Cramer interview, January 12, 1993).

20 Jean Aberbach memoir sketches, date unknown.

CHAPTER 16. JOHNNY TAPS

1 Sanjek, *Pennies*, 206.

2 Ibid., 299–303.

3 Ibid., 302.

4 Ibid., 294.

5 Jean specifically paired ASCAP pop writers with songwriters and performers in the country and western field. Ben Weisman recalls, "He would say 'OK, Weisman, we want to you write something for Conway Twitty.' . . . All the songs you see, they would not have been possible without Jean's guidance" (Ben Weisman interview, December 21, 1992).

6 Alamo was incorporated in New York on July 28, 1947. It was owned personally by Jean and Julian paying them weekly salaries a year later (corporate resolution, June 25, 1948).

7 Rumbalero was cited in the BMI agreement of March 29, 1949. Jean bought out the Cuban partner for $20,000.

8 Ben Weisman interview, December 21, 1992.

9 Charlie Grean interview, March 4, 1994.

10 Sanjek, *Pennies*, 425.

11 "Tuxedo Junction" was written by Buddy Feyne, Erskine Hawkins, William Johnson, and Julian Dash; "Jersey Bounce" was written by Robert B. Wright, Bobby Plater, Tiny Bradshaw, and Edward Johnson (corporate minutes, December 30, 1952, and April 1, 1953).

12 Hill and Range corporate records, Record No. 155, January 9, 1953.

13 "Renewal copyrights were something Jean knew a lot about. He had taken on a Supreme Court case that involved renewals" (Tom Levy interview, May 6, 1993). "On a great number of songs we were able to acquire the renewal rights" (Julian Aberbach interview, January 15, 1993).

14 Sanjek, *Pennies*, 420–21.

15 According to the Hill and Range Stock Ledger and Transfer Record, the first certificates were issued on December 10, 1952 (Hill and Range corporate records, 1952).

16 "Lee Eastman bought the Ross Jungnickel company. My recollection was that he trans-

ferred all of the catalog out of Ross Jungnickel to one of the other Lee Eastman companies and just bought a shell. So it wasn't a catalog that they bought. It was seniority in the company that they bought. That was what was so irritating to everybody. They [ASCAP] then had to later change the rules about seniority" (Milton Rudin interview, August 15, 1994).

17 Milton Rudin interview, August 15, 1994.

18 Stan Cornyn (with Paul Scanlon), Exploding: The Highs, Hits, Hype, Heroes, and Hustlers of the Warner Music Group, 9.

19 Sanjek, *Pennies*, 105–7. The comedies were "Follow Through," "Good News," "Three Cheers," "Hold Everything," and the revue "George White's Scandals" (Cornyn, *Exploding*, 7).

20 Sanjek, *Pennies*, 217–18, 227–29.

21 Ewen, *All the Years*, 369–70.

22 Milton Rudin interview, August 15, 1994.

23 United States Court of Appeals Ninth Circuit, No. 13880, Marie Ballentine, as Guardian of the Estate of Stephen William Ballentine, Appellant, v. Marie De Sylva, Appellee; Marie De Sylva, Appellant, v. Marie Ballentine, as Guardian of the Estate of Stephen William Ballentine, Appellee, 226 F.2d 623; 1955 U.S. App. LEXIS 4751; 106 USP.Q. (BNA)347, August 25, 1955.

24 Supreme Court of the Unites States, No. 214: *Miller Music Corp. v. Charles N. Daniels, Inc.*, 362 US 373; 80 S. Ct. 792; 4 L. Ed. 2d 804; 1960 US LEXIS 2009; 125 USP.Q. (BNA) 147, February 24–25, 1960, Argued; April 18, 1960, Decided.

25 Milton Rudin interview, August 15, 1994.

26 Jean Aberbach memoir sketches, date unknown.

27 Milton Rudin interview, August 15, 1994.

CHAPTER 17. MR. BRUMS

1 Peter Guralnick, *Last Train To Memphis*, 167.

2 Peter Guralnick and Ernst Jorgenson, *Elvis, Day by Day*, 12.

3 Nash, *The Colonel*, 111–12.

4 Peter Guralnick, *Lost Highway*, 39–40.

5 Tubb also emulated Rodger's style while building a regional career in Texas (Guralnick, *Lost Highway*, 39–40).

6 Snow, *Hank Snow Story*, 278–79.

7 Ibid., 294–96.

8 Ibid., 290–93.

9 Snow writes of his second RCA session: "This time I did have what I considered excellent material. I had songs I'd written and songs that had been sent to me from Hill and Range publishers by the Aberbach brothers" (Snow, *Hank Snow Story*, 316–22).

10 Diskin ultimately gave up any interest in the venture, paving the way for a Snow-Parker alliance (Nash, *The Colonel*, 161–62).

11 Peter Guralnick, *The Last Train to Memphis*, 168.

12 "The firing left Parker humiliated and deeply wounded" (Nash, *The Colonel*, 112); "it must have come as a terrible blow to Parker to be abandoned so abruptly by his protégé, in a manner that left him unavoidably exposed to the glare of the show biz spotlight" (Guralnick, *Last Train to Memphis*, 168); "Arnold's letter comes out of the blue, leaving Parker both emotionally shaken and at professional loose ends" (Peter Guralnick and Ernst Jorgenson, *Elvis, Day by Day*, 12). On the other hand, all the authors point out that Parker was always thinking "two steps ahead." Either Parker anticipated the Arnold breakup, or more likely, he had always had an exit plan in place.

13 Jean Aberbach memoir sketches, date unknown.

14 Nash, *The Colonel,* 112.

15 Pugh, *Ernest Tubb,* 195–96.

16 Snow laments that he was too busy to scrutinize the Colonel's bookkeeping practices, but that he was "shocked and discouraged," believing that it was largely his money rather than their shared investments that kept the venture afloat (Snow, *Hank Snow Story,* 382–83).

CHAPTER 18. DIAMOND IN THE ROUGH

1 Colin Escott, *Hank Williams,* 239–42.

2 Nash, *The Colonel,* 120–22.

3 Guralnick, *Last Train to Memphis,* 62–65, 89–95, 100.

4 Paul Ackerman was reviewing Elvis's first release, known as "Sun 209" (Guralnick and Jorgensen, *Elvis Day by Day,* 19).

5 Octavo agreements were made with Ira Stanphill's Hymntime Publishing with the Sacred Music Foundation and with the Rodeheaver Company (which included songs like "Take Up Thy Cross"), as well as 121 hymns from the Basilian Press (corporate minutes of December 12, 1952). "Swing Low, Sweet Chariot" and "Go Down Jordan" are listed in corporate records as having been acquired April 1, 1952, with a resolution to print sacred octavos on May 1, 1952 (ibid.). Songwriters included V. B. (Vep) Ellis, Karl Davis—of Karl and Harty fame—Joe E. Parks, Truman Darnell, Don Grashey, and Jim Amadeo; publishers included Don Robey's Lion Publishing Company, the John M. Henson Publishing Company, James D. Vaughan Music Publishing, Bowles Music Company, the Roberta Martin Studio of Gospel Music, and Dr. Herbert G. Tovey's Tennessee Music and Printing Company.

6 Anthony Heilbut, *The Gospel Sound,* 31. "We got Stamps-Baxter music into BMI. The contract lasted for 30 years" (Julian Aberbach interview, May 31, 1993).

7 Anthony Heilbut, *The Gospel Sound,* 21–35. Hill and Range paid the customary rates of six cents per sheet music (regular piano and orchestrations), sixty-two and half percent of net foreign revenue from orchestrations and piano copies, and for synch and records, fifty percent of net performance fees on three cents network and two cents independent station use (Hill and Range corporate records, 1951–1952). A signed general agreement was executed on August 26, 1952.

8 Sanjek, *Pennies,* 240–41; Ed Ward, Geoffrey Stokes and Ken Tucker, *Rock of Ages,* 64–71.

9 Grelun Landon interview, August 18, 1993.

10 Guralnick, *Last Train to Memphis,* 146, 155; Guralnick and Jorgensen, *Elvis, Day by Day,* 24; Chick Crumpacker, who became the national country and western promotional manager for RCA, reported that RCA was keenly aware of Sun's sudden success and were not at all happy about it (Guralnick, *Last Train to Memphis,* 122).

11 Guralnick and Jorgensen, *Elvis Day by Day,* 26.

12 Nash, *The Colonel,* 116–17.

13 Guralnick and Jorgensen, *Elvis Day by Day,* 21–22.

14 Elvis is not mentioned in connection with the January 4, 1955, daybook entry. It simply references meetings with Parker. This entry, however, is made only a few days after Elvis's Eagles Hall radio show. The very next day after Jean and Parker's lunch meeting, both men set off on a flurry of activities clearly connected with Elvis Presley.

15 Guralnick and Jorgensen, *Elvis Day by Day,* 27–31.

16 "1:30 arrival Chicago . . . Colored publishers" (Jean Aberbach daybook entry, January 25, 1955).

17 Copyright transfer agreement between Lester Melrose, individually and doing business as Wabash Music, and St. Louis Music, dated February 22, 1955, including song list (Hill and Range corporate records, Record No. 13085).

18 Guralnick and Jorgensen, *Elvis Day by Day*, 39; "Hill and Range put out a songbook. That was the deal I got signed on down in Mississippi. And Sam was ok with it" (Grelun Landon interview, August 18, 1993).

19 "Parker Dinner" (Jean Aberbach daybook, June 5, 1955); Guralnick and Jorgensen, *Elvis Day by Day*, 45. Investing directly into the record deal invited restraint of trade lawsuits from other publishers that could damage their core business.

20 Stock shares issued November 20, 1950 (Hill and Range corporate records); Jorgensen, *Elvis Presley*, 21–25.

21 Ewen, *All the Years*, 560. Snow, *Hank Snow Story*, 384.

22 Guralnick and Jorgensen, *Elvis Day by Day*, 41.

23 "Steve Sholes Family dinner, Kay Birthday" Jean Aberbach daybook, July 7, 1955; Guralnick and Jorgensen, *Elvis Day by Day*, 41.

24 Letter to Sam Phillips/Hi-Lo Publishers outlining terms for use of copyright for the folio, July 13, 1955. This deal was consummated October 3, 1955, when Marion Keisker, office manager for Sun Records, returned the signed agreement papers (Hill and Range corporate records); Guralnick and Jorgensen, *Elvis Day by Day*, 44.

25 Sanjek, *Pennies*, 344. Jean Aberbach daybook, July 14 and August 9, 1955. Jean might also have seen Clark as another source for song properties held by independent labels that were about to get national exposure.

26 Guralnick and Jorgensen, *Elvis Day by Day*, 49.

27 "Lew—Elvis Pressley, W. Morris, Bill Randle" and "Gre: Rush Pressley folio Marks Song" (Jean Aberbach daybook, October 24, 1955).

28 Nash, *The Colonel*, 118; Guralnick and Jorgensen, *Elvis Day by Day*, 53–55.

29 Guralnick, *Last Train*, 226. The agreement was made between Hill and Range and Elvis Presley, Vernon Presley, and Gladys Presley. Hill and Range would take a ten percent administration fee deducted from all revenue. Elvis Presley acknowledges receipt of funds totaling $2,000. The payment was construed as a nonrefundable bonus, but the standard clause designating it as such was struck. Renewal is detailed in Clause 29. It will be renewed by a letter of request secured by a $1,000 check. The contract also named the board of directors for the Elvis Music Publishing Company: "EP hereby designates Elvis Presley as Pres and Director, and Vernon Presley as VP and Director; H&R hereby designates Joachim Jean Aberbach as Secretary and Director, and Julian J. Aberbach as Treasurer and Director" (Elvis Presley general agreement, November 21, 1955, Record No. 14180, Hill and Range Songs corporate records).

30 This rate probably remained in place until the five-year deal on the folio was renegotiated, after which time the rate was standardized to five cents (Inventory Document No. 6248, Graceland Archives).

31 Mitch Miller interview, January 29, 1993.

32 Elvis Presley general agreement, November 21, 1955, Record No. 14180, Hill and Range Songs corporate records.

33 Julian Aberbach interview, January 15, 1993.

34 Mitch Miller interview, January 29, 1993.

35 Sanjek, *Pennies*, 342; Nash, *The Colonel*, 118; Jean Aberbach daybook, 1955 and 1956. Minutes of the Board, Hill and Range corporate records, 1955 and 1956.

36 "We invested only $2500 that we gave to Elvis Presley and it goes for opening up the

new publishing company which was called Elvis Presley Music" (Julian Aberbach interview, January 22, 1993).

37 Elvis Presley general agreement, November 21, 1955, Record No. 14180, Hill and Range Songs corporate records.

38 Jean Aberbach memoir sketches, date unknown.

CHAPTER 19. UNDER PRESSURE

1 As one of the most progressive and prolific producers, it was assumed Mitch Miller was favoring BMI for song selection, but the evidence proved otherwise. "When I would listen to songs, I didn't think 'This is BMI' or 'This is ASCAP.' In fact, I had this big percentage of hits, more than anyone. And I was accused of favoring BMI. Oh, God, yes! So the lawyers at Columbia right away came in—I did five percent BMI! I never knew it was BMI— I just listened to the song! The percent was way lower than most record companies. [Q: So you were being falsely accused?] Yes. In fact they went in front of Congress and said that I was favoring BMI songs! So the lawyers came in and counted every song I recorded! [Q: And it turned out to be only five percent?] Yes! Unbelievable!" (Mitch Miller interview, January 29, 1993).

2 Leo Feist interview, December 29, 1992.

3 Ward, Stokes, and Tucker, *Rock of Ages*, 46, 52.

4 Sanjeck, *Pennies*, 222, 230–31.

5 Jean Aberbach daybook, January 25, 1955, and February 2, 1956; Ewen, *Popular Music*, 457, 461.

6 Fred Bronson, *Billboard's Hottest 100 Hits*, 113.

7 Clark, *Penguin Encyclopedia of Popular Music*, 64–65; Ward, Stokes, and Tucker, *Rock of Ages*, 93 fn.

8 Ward, Stokes, and Tucker, *Rock of Ages*, 53.

9 Jean Aberbach daybook, January 25, 1955.

10 On April 25, 1955, Hill and Range conveyed the mechanical rights for T-Bone Walker's "I'm Still in Love with You" to Capitol (Record No. 13443, Hill and Range Songs corporate records). He did the same for Ivory Joe Hunter's "I Almost Lost My Mind" on June 15, 1955 (Record No. 13446, Hill and Range Songs corporate records).

11 Sanjek, *Pennies*, 376. Also, Jean's daybook entry for January 5, 1955 (Jean Aberbach Archives), notes "Julian, deliver EMI stock."

12 Sanjek, *Pennies*, 425.

13 Julian Aberbach interview, May 31, 1993.

14 Jean declared to colleague Leo Feist "I'm not a publisher, I'm a banker" (Leo Feist interview, December 29, 1992).

15 Mitch Miller interview, January 29, 1993.

16 Ward, Stokes, and Tucker, *Rock of Ages*, 87–88.

17 Mike Stoller interview, August 17, 1993.

18 This date coincides with Tennessee Ernie Ford's recording session, but neither tune was used. "2:30, Capitol; I'd Be a Fool to Let You Go; Ten Ernie; I Won't Be Ashamed to Pray; Dave Dexter" (Jean Aberbach daybook, September 15, 1955).

19 Ewen, *Popular Music*, 416; http://www.ernieford.com/SixteenTons.htm.

20 "My first response at the time was just negative" (Mike Stoller interview, August 17, 1993).

21 "Quintet, Mr. Stoller; Sam Clark, Elvis Pressley" (Jean Aberbach daybook, August 9, 1955).

22 Jean Aberbach daybook, August 12 and 14, 1955; Mike Stoller interview, August 17, 1993.

23 Mike Stoller interview, August 17, 1993.

24 Jean Aberbach daybook, September 1 and 2, 1955; Mike Stoller interview, August 17, 1993.

25 Mike Stoller interview, August 17, 1993.

26 Jean Aberbach 1955 daybook, September 19 and 27, 1955.

27 Jorgensen, *Elvis Presley*, 38.

28 At first, writer Don Robertson was disappointed his tunes were being placed with this unknown artist. Robertson would eventually write and record demos for Elvis that included "They Remind Too Much of You," "Anything That's Part of You," "Starting Today," "There's Always Me," "Love Me Tonight," "I Met Her Today," "What Now, What Next?" "Where To," and "I'm Counting on You." He is also noted as the originator of the Floyd Cramer's "slip-note" piano style that permeated many of Elvis's tunes (Don Robertson interview, August 15, 1993).

29 Jorgensen, *Elvis Presley*, 35–40; Guralnick, *Last Train*, 238–39, 244.

30 Jorgensen, *Elvis Presley*, 37; Jean Aberbach daybook, February 1 and 2, 1956. "Steve Sholes, Hickory House 5pm." However, the latter date conflicts with the Hickory House promotional event noted as February 1 in Guralnick and Jorgensen, *Elvis Day by Day*, 61, so the meeting was probably just dinner between Sholes and Jean.

31 "I Forgot to Remember to Forget" was the only song excluded in the Standard Administration contract for Hi-Lo music sealed at the time of the Elvis RCA Record deal. Apparently it ended up in the E. B. Marks catalog (Jorgensen, *Elvis Presley*, 27).

32 Roy Brown first recorded "Good Rockin' Tonight" in 1948 for DeLuxe records, an outfit started in Linden, New Jersey, by brothers David and Jules Braun. By this time, however, Syd Nathan was well along the way to absorbing them, having bought a controlling interest in that company and elbowed the brothers out in 1949. Brown continued recording for the DeLuxe label, signing with King in 1952. Therefore the song remained completely under Syd Nathan's control (*King/Federal/DeLuxe Story*, available at http://www.bsnpubs.com/king/kingstory.html [accessed July 10, 2009]; and Clark, *Penguin Encyclopedia of Popular Music*, 167).

33 The disposition of other tunes at that time is unconfirmed. Their current representation suggests they were not at any time connected to Hill and Range. "Trying to Get to You" ended up with Red Storming Music, Slow Dancing Music LLC, and You Look Good Music Publishing (publishing concerns seemingly connected to producer Bobby Shad). "Baby, Let's Play House," first recorded on Excello records, ended up in Embassy Music and LPGV Music; "I Don't Care If the Sun Don't Shine," however, ended up with Universal Polygram International, which may indicate some connection, since parts of the Hill and Range catalog were sold off to Polygram in the 1970s.

34 Jean Aberbach daybook, January 31, 1956.

35 Freddy is mentioned several times in connection with Elvis (Jean Aberbach daybook, February 17 and 25, March 6 and 15, 1956); "Freddy Raise or Bonus" (Jean Aberbach daybook, April 1, 1956); "Julian back; discuss Freddy, Grelun S[alary?] with Julian" (Jean Aberbach daybook, April 5, 1956).

36 Jean Aberbach daybook, May 10, 11, and 28, 1956.

37 Guralnick and Jorgensen, *Elvis Day By Day*, 67; Nash, *The Colonel*, 136–38.

38 Jorgensen, *Elvis Presley*, 48.

39 Invoice 838, June 5, 1956, Hill and Range corporate records.

40 Guralnick and Jorgensen, *Elvis Day By Day*, 81. Nash, *The Colonel*, 140.

41 Mike Stoller interview, August 17, 1993.

42 Guralnick and Jorgensen, *Elvis Day By Day*, 80.

43 Six of thirteen songs ended up half-owned in Elvis Presley Music. Another three were owned or co-owned by Hill and Range. (Jorgensen, *Elvis Presley*, 60–61.)

44 " . . . they copied, note for note, from the demos!" (Ben Weisman interview, December 21, 1992); "The arranger would copy from the demo" (Winfield Scott interview, October 5, 1993).

45 Jorgensen, *Elvis Presley*, 55.

46 Guralnick and Jorgensen, *Elvis Day By Day*, 84–89; Jorgensen, *Elvis Presley*, 68; Sanjek, *Pennies*, 342.

47 There was a flurry of meetings with Joe Hazen throughout November, leading up to delivery of the tunes for Loving You (Jean Aberbach daybook, November 8, 9, 13, 12, 14, 15, and December 10, 1956); Guralnick and Jorgensen, *Elvis Day by Day*, 93.

48 Jorgensen, *Elvis Presley*, 78–81.

49 Ibid., 84–85.

50 Guralnick and Jorgensen, *Elvis Day by Day*, 92–93.

51 Jorgensen, *Elvis Presley*, 68–70, 75.

52 "I think he was concerned that he was expecting us to jump immediately to write the songs, and we hadn't. So he, in effect, he locked us in the dungeon until we came up with the goods. And then we got out, and were finally free and had a good time that evening." (Mike Stoller interview, August 17, 1993.)

53 Freddy Bienstock interview, April 29, 1993.

54 Ben Weisman interview, December 21, 1992.

55 Ben Weisman interview, January 8, 1994.

56 [Q: So you were signed exclusively to Hill and Range?] Scott: "On a first-refusal basis only." [Q: So that if they couldn't do anything with the song with any of the artists, then you were free to go somewhere else?] Scott: "Correct" (Winfield Scott interview, October 5, 1993).

57 Ibid.

58 Contract with the U.S. Dept. of Agriculture, August 5, 1952, Hill and Range corporate records.

59 "My brother suggested to Steve Nelson and Jack Rollins to write a song for Christmas about a snowman. And they had the idea to have the snowman come to life" (Julian Aberbach interview, January 15, 1993). Hill and Range also published another seasonal novelty, "Jingle-Bell Rock," through Cornell Music in 1958.

60 Says writer Don Robertson, "They would express an opinion, and very often they were excellent suggestions, but usually not specific. Like not 'Why don't you change this line to these words' but 'There's something that does not seem quite right about this line' or 'Maybe could you change the ending?' It would be that rather than a specific suggestion. And so often they were right! I would go home and come back with a much better product that way" (Don Robertson interview, August 15, 1993).

61 Ben Weisman interview, January 8, 1994.

62 See "About Country Music" at http://countrymusic.about.com/library/blctaug23.htm and the RCA Victor Index, and http://rcs.law.emory.edu/rcs/labels/r/r945.htm.

63 "You see, she refused Jean. She would not change a word or note on that song. She refused to do it" (Ben Weisman interview, January 8, 1994).

64 Jorgensen, *Elvis Presley*, 61, 75.

65 Ibid., 54–55.

66 Ibid., 89–94.

1 Guralnick and Jorgensen, *Elvis, Day by Day*, 102.
2 Ibid., 108.
3 The Danny Thomas event was on June 28, 1957, at Russwood Park in Memphis. Mention of plans to build the youth center is made on August 14, 1957, and the donation of $1,050 for the football game was made December 1, 1957 (ibid., 107–15).
4 Ibid., 103.
5 "The Colonel didn't like Steve [Sholes]. Steve did something to the Colonel and the Colonel damn near drummed him right out of RCA . . . real bad situation. Steve was a very decent person. A very good, honorable, decent person" (Lamar Fike interview, January 22, 1993).
6 Guralnick and Jorgensen, *Elvis Day by Day*, 105.
7 Ibid., 110; Jorgensen, *Elvis Presley*, 95–98.
8 Guralnick and Jorgensen, *Elvis Day by Day*, 112.
9 Jorgensen, *Elvis Presley*, 105.
10 Ibid., 129.
11 Ibid., 129–30.
12 Ibid., 106–11.
13 Nash, *The Colonel*, 146; Lamar Fike interview, January 22, 1993.
14 Winfield Scott interview, October 5, 1993.
15 Peter Guralnick, *Careless Love*, 33–35.
16 Guralnick and Jorgensen, *Elvis Day by Day*, 145–46.
17 Mike Stoller interview, August 17, 1993.
18 Alex Halberstadt, *Lonely Avenue*, 75, 103.
19 The original Drifters were responsible for hits such as "Money, Honey," "Honey, Love," and the classic doo-wop version of Irving Berlin's "White Christmas." McPhatter started the group in 1953 but exited for military service two years later. Irwin Stambler, *The Encyclopedia of Pop, Rock, and Soul*, 192.
20 Halberstadt, *Lonely Avenue*, 107–10; Jorgensen, *Elvis Presley*, 119–20; Leiber and Stoller, *Hound Dog*, 102–3.
21 Ibid., 130–32.
22 The $2,000 bonus—large for the time—was offered "in consideration of his excellent cooperation in the exploitation of musical compositions owned by Johnny Mathis Music, Inc., and Noma Music Inc." (board minutes, February 11, 1959, Hill and Range corporate records).
23 Ross collaborated with Julius Dixon on the first two, and with Fred Neil on the latter (Mark Ribowsky, *He's a Rebel*, 62–63).
24 According to writer Mark Ribowsky, Case believed Spector would be a fountainhead of hits for the company (ibid., 67).
25 Leiber and Stoller, *Hound Dog*, 170–74, 176–77.
26 "Hill and Range had an affiliated label, outside {other than} Big Top, that we had produced records for, and they called, and we were busy on a number of other productions. And they asked if we could do a singer named Ray Peterson. And I remember Jerry said, 'We'll oversee and check the mixes, but we had a very talented young fellow—because we had signed Phil as a writer, as you know, everything. So we sent Phil to do that, and Phil made a big hit, with "Corina Corina." And that's how he got involved with Hill and Range" (Mike Stoller interview, August 17, 1993.)
27 Ward, Stokes, and Tucker, *Rock of Ages*, 226–27.
28 Jean Aberbach memoir sketches, date unknown.

29 "He was just shy of his 21st birthday! I remember, because he tried to disavow his contract, claiming he was under age! Well, he was thinking about California law, not New York law. But since he was an unethical person, we let him go" (Mike Stoller interview, August 17, 1993). "Someone apparently removed from our files. . . . It didn't take Dick Tracy to figure out who it might have been" (Jerry Leiber and Mike Stoller with David Ritz, *Hound Dog*, 177).

30 According to Johnny Bienstock, Big Top was incorporated in 1957 or 1958, and Colonel Parker suggested the name (Johnny Bienstock interview, January 6, 1993). But Bienstock believes Jean's anger was over having to give up half interest in the company to the Colonel if Elvis were signed. This is possible, but recognizing a conflict of interest in competing with the very companies they depended on to market their songs was probably a more powerful motivator.

31 Ribowsky, *He's a Rebel*, 103.

32 Smith's recording may have contributed to the decision to close Big Top. The label had wooed Smith, lead singer of the Chantels, away from reputedly mob-connected Morris Levy's Roulette records, who was said to have made "intimidating noises" over the arrangement (ibid., 106–7).

33 Ibid., 173–75.

34 Johnny Bienstock interview, January 6, 1993.

35 Figures were derived from a partial catalog listing of Hill and Range sheet music, housed in Hill and Range professional catalogs contributed by Ken Nelson to the Country Music Hall of Fame, as compared with the electronic Top 40 listings compiled by Archie Gramble and available at *Pop Song Database,* http://www.gramble.com/music/top40.html (accessed July 10, 2009). Calculations showed Hill and Range had twenty-five number 1 hits during this period. Variations in song titles may obscure other Hill and Range hits.

36 "Charlie Brown" and "Poison Ivy" are trademark Leiber and Stoller tunes. They also contributed "There Goes My Baby," with credits also going to Benjamin Nelson, Lover Patterson, and George Treadwell. Treadwell and Nathan are credited with them for "Dance with Me," Jerry N. Capehart and Eddie Cochran wrote "C'mon Everybody," Doc Pomus and Mort Shuman contributed "I'm a Man," jazz trumpet giant Edmond Hall contributed the instrumental "Petite Fleur," and George Goehring and Edna Lewis wrote "Lipstick on Your Collar." Ray Charles, Hank Snow, Marty Robbins, and Johnny Cash wrote their own tunes.

37 BMI, *Pop Hits: 1940–1974,* various; also fn. 36; List of corporations, Hill and Range corporate records.

38 Nash, *The Colonel,* 208; Leonard Feist Jr. interview, December 29, 1992.

39 Phil Spector interview, August 16, 1993.

40 Tom Levy interview, May 6, 1993.

CHAPTER 21. THE ART OF LIFE

1 Julian Aberbach interview, December 16, 1992.

2 Susan Aberbach interview, November 23, 1992.

3 Ibid.

4 Julian Aberbach interview, December 23, 1992.

5 Since Hill and Range and Elvis Presley were 50/50 partners in the publishing companies, if Elvis obtained $400,000 from royalties during 1965 as distribution accounts credit to him that year, then so did Hill and Range (Jorgensen, *Elvis Presley,* 198).

6 Julian Aberbach interviews, January 15 and May 31, 1993.

7   Growing difficulties of doing business in Europe is noted in corporate minutes, "Resolution," June 1, 1960, Hill and Range corporate records. Corporate consolidation began in June of 1970 with Aberbach, Inc., Ark-La-Tex Publishing, Big Top records, Brenner Music, Brittany Music, Home Folks Music, Kentucky Music, Progressive Music Publishing (formerly PMPC), Rio Grande Music (formerly Jenny Lou Carson Music), Rumbalero Music, St. Louis Music Corporation, and Bob Wills Music—all being folded into Hill and Range (board minutes, June 24, 1970, Hill and Range corporate records). *Billboard* also reports "Publisher buys share of Quintet Co." (*Billboard*, September 11, 1971, p. 4). Previously their interest was shared with the Erteguns, under the banner of Progressive Music.

8   Heinz Voigt interview, January 21, 1994.

9   Julian claims that not only did they sell Belinda Music to Freddy, but also underwrote the loans with which he acquired it. "In the end, when he wanted to leave, we sold him our firm in England with a loan from us—guaranteed by us!" (Julian Aberbach interview, December 10, 1992). This may have been at the heart of the misunderstanding between the cousins, where Jean and Julian felt that by this goodwill gesture Freddy would be in their debt and his attention to their interests would supersede his own ambitions.

10 Guralnick, *Careless Love*, 379–80.

11 Roger Hilburn, "Elvis: Waning Legend in His Own Time?" *Los Angeles Times*, January 19, 1975.

12 *Letter from Jean Aberbach to Tom Parker*, March 8, 1972, Hill and Range corporate records.

13 In a letter to Tom Diskin, Freddy requested a copy of the "Exact ground rules in the acquisition of the Presley and Gladys catalogs. I have advised Jean and Julian to send in a specimen contract in the event that they would be the purchasers, so that we can then use this contract if we decide to buy and know that we will be fully protected. It is quite possible that by now you have received this contract in which case . . . send it to me as soon as possible. If we then decide to go ahead and acquire Jean and Julian's half, I have told the Potentate that I can arrange all of the financing and that I felt, off the top of my head, that Elvis should get an additional 10 percent of the shares, Lisa Marie five percent, the Potentate 25 percent and we 10 percent. . . . we will have a 10 percent management fee [on] $500,000–$600,000 per year publisher's fees, less 10 percent management. [need to pay back $900,000 loan (presumably from Jean and Julian) and to buy out their shares.] From Carbert Music, Inc., 1619 Bway." (Letter from Freddy Bienstock to Tom Diskin, July 5, 1972, Hill and Range corporate records.) A subsequent letter dated August 18, 1972 reiterates the recommendations and reminds the Colonel that they are starting from scratch, with the value of the company dependent on the quality of copyrights they can find for Elvis that he will be willing to promote.

14 On February 13, 1972, the Colonel warned Elvis to avoid recording commitments until after the company was established. By February 1973, the Colonel and Freddy had resolved to establish Elvis's own publishing company, which was in place by mid-September 1973. A letter from Freddy to the Colonel dated January 14, 1973 (artifact 3460, Graceland Archives), indicates that they organized two companies, one BMI and one ASCAP, with shareholders defined as sixty percent Elvis, twenty-five percent Col, fifteen percent Freddy and that the affairs of the company would be handled by the Hudson Bay Music Co. for a ten percent management fee (Guralnick and Jorgensen, *Elvis Day by Day*, 231).

15 Other publishers included were Acuff-Rose for the "American Trilogy," Press Music for "Suspicious Minds," Don C. Publications for "My Way," and Combine Music for "Burnin' Love."

16 Tom Levy interview, May 16, 1993.

17 Purchase Agreement between Hill and Range Songs, Inc. and Chappell & Co./Polygram GmbH., July 1, 1975 (Hill and Range corporate records).

18 "He found himself with a pretty sizable collection and he was faced with 'Well, what do I do now?' and it was a pretty easy move for both he and my uncle" (David Aberbach interview, October 27, 1993).

19 Julian Aberbach interview, January 3, 1993.

20 Julian Aberbach interview, January 5, 1993.

21 Most of these artworks were ultimately donated to universities, the University of California at Berkeley receiving the best (Susan Aberbach interview, April 12, 2005).

22 Between September 1958 and September 1960 the Aberbach brothers had borrowed $471,000 from banks against presumed royalties of at least twice that much (board minutes, 1958–1960, Hill and Range corporate records).

23 The company was generous in its appreciation of its employees. During banner year 1956, cash bonuses ranged from $3,000—the equivalent of nearly $20,000 in today's money—for Grelun and Freddy to $500 for key supporting staff. All other employees got a full week's pay. Paul Case got a bonus of $2,000 in 1959 for his excellent work in nurturing and promoting Johnny Mathis. (Board minutes, March 21, 1957, Hill and Range Songs corporate records.)

24 Leo Feist interview, December 29, 1992.

25 Ibid.

26 "At one point, I was collecting jointly with my brother and particularly sculpture by Alberto Giacometti. By that time, we had assembled five pieces and were then trying to divide them. They were a dog, a tall woman (6 feet) with a double bass, the cat, a particularly beautiful woman of Venice with a turban, and a small walking man. In the exchange, which was made by the flip of a coin, I received the tall woman and the dog, and my brother kept the woman of Venice, the cat, and the walking man" (Julian Aberbach interview, January 5,1993). During the 1960s, Jean traded some of his for some important works by "magic realists" Paul Delvaux and Henri Magritte, including "The Great Sirens" (1947), one of the masterpieces of the surrealist school.

27 Martin Sosnoff, "The Art of the Real," *Washington Post,* November 20, 1989.

28 Jean-Louis Ferrier, *Art of the 20th Century,* 117.

29 Julian Aberbach interview, January 3, 1993.

30 Joram Harel interview, November 27, 1994.

31 Fernando Botero: *The Presidential Family,* (MOMA-P0742) 1967. They also collected works by Wilfredo Lam and Matta. After meeting Botero, Jean took trips throughout Central and South America, one in April 1972 to study South American colonial architecture and paintings.

32 J. Jean Aberbach, "Fernando Botero," *Yale Literary Magazine* 149, No. 3 (December 1981): 13.

33 Fernando Botero interview, May 12, 1993.

34 Ibid.

35 "Dreyer developed a kidney problem and needed dialysis and the Aberbachs bought the dialysis machine for his home" (Thea Zavin interview, July 22, 1993); Susan Aberbach interview, November 23, 1992; "He also was extremely generous. Jean was a very generous man. He would give presents and so forth." Freddy Bienstock interview, April 29, 1993. "It was very important to him to help other people who were struggling.

He was definitely not greedy. He was very generous. And he would walk around . . . anybody he had an interaction with he would be completely generous with. He was always over tipping waiters and waitresses and cab drivers—enormously over tipping them! Hotel doormen in the city loved him. He was constantly giving them Mets tickets and huge tips—for no occasion or anything. He was just handing out $10s and $20s everywhere he went. And it really wasn't even to be a big shot or anything—it was just to be cool to these people, because he understood what they were going through. He really understood what they were going through. He had been through it himself. He had come from a position of no money and worked his way up to where he was and never forgot where he came from." (Jason Aberbach interview, May 18, 1993.)

36 For his entire lifetime, Jean never forgot Max's birthday. It was noted every year in his daybooks, as were the many gifts and cordial social times Jean spent with Max and his wife. In a letter, date unknown but late in his life, Max wrote a warm letter to Jean declaring "If I am an inspiration to you, then you are no less to me" (letter from Max Dreyfus to Jean Aberbach, date unknown, Susan Aberbach Archives).

37 In an ironic twist, it took Jean several more years to recognize that he had visited the same wrath on his cousin Freddy for more or less the same reasons, and that he had allowed business to soil a lifelong friendship with someone who had simply learned well from him and followed in his own footsteps. "My problem with him was that eventually, I went out on my own, and did quite well, and he resented that" (Freddy Bienstock interview, April 29, 1993).

38 Heinz Voigt interview, January 21, 1994.

39 "You asked me what the Aberbachs impact was on the music business. Well, I'll tell you. More than the renewals issue, and more than even country music—they set a precedent in the music business—which in essence forced other publishers to adopt the same. While it was not their intention to do so, the Aberbachs introduced the concept of the artist as a percentage owner in his own work. And that made them hungry for more knowledge on how they could better control the rights to their work. It was the first wholesale effort to bring the artist into the ownership loop. I think that hurt the record industry far more than their getting a few renewal copyrights. Sure you had people like Rodgers and Hammerstein setting up their own company. And there was always, of course, Irving Berlin. But that was different than setting up a company for, say, Tim Spencer, who sang backup on Roy Rogers records. These were not Berlin and Gershwin—these were not the greats. That was the major impact of the Aberbachs." (Milton Rudin interview, August 15, 1994.)

40 Jean Aberbach memoir sketches, date unknown.

BIBLIOGRAPHY

Aberbach, J. Jean. *Memoir Sketches*. Susan Aberbach Archives, date unknown.

———. *Daybooks, 1956–57*. Susan Aberbach Archives.

———. "On Fernando Botero." *Yale Literary Magazine* 149, No. 3 (December 1981): 5–13.

Adler, Jacques. *The Jews of Paris and the Final Solution*. New York: Oxford University Press, 1987.

Atkins, Chet. *Country Gentleman*. Chicago: Henry Regnery, 1974.

Bronson, Fred. *Billboard's Hottest 100 Hits*. New York: *Billboard* Books, 1991.

Clark, Donald. *Penguin Encyclopedia of Popular Music*. New York: Penguin, 1989.

Collins, Ace. *The Stories behind Country Music's All-Time Greatest 100 Songs*. New York: Boulevard, 1996.

Cornyn, Stan, with Paul Scanlon. *Exploding: The Highs, Hits, Hype, Heroes, and Hustlers of the Warner Music Group*. New York: HarperCollins, 2002.

Cusic, Don. *Cowboys and the Wild West*. New York: Facts on File, 1994.

Escott, Colin. *Hank Williams: The Biography*. Boston: Little, Brown, 1995.

Ewen, David. *All the Years of Popular Music*. Englewood Cliffs, N.J.: Prentice-Hall, 1977.

———. *Men of Popular Music*. Chicago: Ziff-Davis, 1944.

Ferrier, Jean-Louis. *Art of the 20th Century*. Paris: Chêne-Hachette, 1999.

Freedman, Michael. *Jerome Kern: A Biography*. London: Robson, 1978.

Gramble, Archie, The Pop Song Database [website]. Available at http://www.gramble.com/music/top40.html.

Green, Stanley. *The Rodgers and Hammerstein Story*. New York: John Day, 1963.

Grendysa, Peter, and Robert Pruter. Liner notes to *Atlantic Rhythm and Blues, 1947–1974*. New York: Atlantic, 1991.

Guralnick, Peter. *Careless Love: The Unmaking of Elvis Presley*. New York: Little, Brown, 1999.

———. *Last Train to Memphis*. Boston: Little, Brown, 1994.

———. *Lost Highway*. New York: HarperPerennial, 1994.

Guralnick, Peter, and Ernst Jorgensen. *Elvis Day by Day: The Definitive Record of His Life and Music*. New York: Ballantine, 1999.

Gutman, Israel, ed. *Chronicle of the 20th Century*. New York: Dorling Kindersley, 1995.

Halberstadt, Alex. *Lonely Avenue*. New York: Da Capo Press, 2007.

Hall, Wade. *Hell Bent for Music: The Life of Pee Wee King*. Lexington: University Press of Kentucky, 1996.

Harris, Charles, and Buck Rainey. *The Cowboy*. Norman: University of Oklahoma Press, 1976.

Heilbut, Anthony. *The Gospel Sound: Good News and Bad Times*. New York: Limelight Editions, 1978.

Hill and Range corporate records. New York: Aberbach Families Archives, 1944–75.

Hurst, Richard Maurice. *Republic Studios: Between Poverty Row and the Majors*. Metuchen, N.J.: Scarecrow Press, 1979.

Jasen, David. *Tin Pan Alley*. New York: Donald I. Fine, 1988.

Jorgensen, Ernst. *Elvis Presley: A Life in Music: The Complete Recording Sessions*. New York: St. Martin's Press, 1998.

Kingsbury, Paul, *The Grand Ole Opry History of Country Music*. New York: Villard, 1995.

Knight, Wayne. Liner notes to *Spade Cooley: King of Western Swing, Premier Show July 21, 1951*. Itasca, Ill.: Collectors Choice, 1997.

Lax, Roger, and Frederick Smith. *The Great Song Thesaurus*. New York: Oxford University Press, 1984.

Leiber, Jerry, and Mike Stoller, with David Ritz. *Hound Dog*. New York: Simon and Schuster, 2009.

Lookstein, Haskel. *Were We Our Brother's Keepers?* New York: Hartmore House, 1985.

Malone, Bill C., and Judith McCulloh, eds. *Stars of Country Music*. Urbana: University of Illinois Press, 1975.

Manvell, Roger, and Heinrich Fraenkel. *The German Cinema*. London: Dent, 1971.

Morse, Arthur D. *While Six Million Died*. Toronto: Random House, 1967.

Nager, Larry. *Memphis Beat*. New York: St. Martin's Press, 1998.

Nash, Alanna. *The Colonel*. New York: Simon & Schuster, 2003.

Phillips, Robert W. *Roy Rogers*. Jefferson, N.C.: McFarland,1995.

Pugh, Ronnie. *Ernest Tubb: The Texas Troubadour*. Durham, N.C.: Duke University Press, 1996.

Quaglieri, Al. Liner notes for *Spadella! The Essential Spade Cooley*. New York: Columbia Legacy, 1994.

Rainey, Buck. "The 'Reel' Cowboy." In Charles W. Harris and Buck Rainey, eds, *The Cowboy: Six-Shooters, Songs, and Sex*. Norman: University of Oklahoma Press, 1976.

Ribowsky, Mark. *He's a Rebel*. New York: Cooper Square Press, 2000.

Rodgers, Richard. *Musical Stages*. New York: Da Capo Press, 1975.

Rumble, John. *Fred Rose and the Development of the Nashville Music Industry, 1942–1954*. Unpublished Ph.D. diss., Vanderbilt University, Nashville, Tenn., 1980.

Sanjek, Russell. *American Popular Music and Its Business: The First Four Hundred Years, Vol. 3, From 1900 to 1984*. New York: Oxford University Press, 1988.

———. *From Print to Plastic: Publishing and Promoting America's Popular Music (1900–1980)*. Brooklyn, N.Y.: Institute for Studies in American Music, Brooklyn College, 1983.

———. *Pennies from Heaven: American Popular Music and Its Business*. New York: DaCapo Press, 1996.

Schlappi, Elizabeth. *Roy Acuff: The Smokey Mountain Boy*. Gretna, LA: Pelican Publishing Company, 1978.

Shapiro, Nat. *Popular Music: An Annotated Index of American Popular Songs*. New York: Adrian Press, 1965.

Sherwood, Robert E. *Tovarich Notes*. New York: Samuel French, 1935.

Snow, Hank with Jack Ownbey and Bob Burris. *The Hank Snow Story*. Urbana: University of Illinois Press, 1994.

Stambler, Irwin. *The Encyclopedia of Pop, Rock and Soul*. New York: St. Martin's Press, 1989.

Streissguth, Michael. *Eddy Arnold*. New York: Schirmer Books, 1997.

Townsend, Charles R. *San Antonio Rose: The Life and Music of Bob Wills*. Urbana: University of Illinois Press, 1976.

Vellenga, Dirk with Mick Farren. *Elvis and the Colonel*. New York: Delacorte Press, 1988.

Ward, Ed, Geoffrey Stokes, and Ken Tucker. *Rock of Ages: The History of Rock & Roll*. New York: Rolling Stone Press, 1986.

Webster, Paul. *Petain's Crime: The Full Story of French Collaboration in the Holocaust*. Chicago: Ivan R. Dee, 1991.

Whitburn, Joel. *Top Country Singles: 1944–1988*. Menomonee Falls, Wisc.: Record Research, 1989.

Zwisohn, Laurence. Liner notes to the CD Box Collection: *Sons of the Pioneers: Wagons West*. Holste-Oldendorf, Germany: Bear Family Records, 1993.

INDEX

in film music, 7–10; works for Salebert, 17–23, 25, 29, 31

Aberbach, Julian (brother), 2–5, 13, 31–32, 70, 76–79, 102–5, 126–29, 144–46, 150–55, 158–60, 173, 175–76, 186–87, 199, 213, 225, 232; acquires first hit, 68–72, 75, 78–79, 90–93, 102–3; Army service, 37–38, 62–63; artist relations and joint publishing companies, 107–13; and Elvis Presley, 186–88, 203; escape from Europe, 34–35; establishes SEMI, 15–17; first paintings, 195; as Jerome J. Brooks, 62, 66–67, 75–76; negotiates "Let Me Go, Lover," 213; pursues Elvis Presley folio, 182; recommends signing Hank Snow, 165–66; recommends divesting foreign subsidiaries, 232; reticence to relinquish songs to Chappell Music, 124–26; sends first royalties to Elvis, 203; works with King and Blink, 64–67, 76–77, 95–98

Aberbach Fine Art, 234, 240
Aberbach, Susan (wife), 229–30, 234, 243
"Aberbach Valley," 237
Abramson, Herb, 182, 193
a cappella, 43, 192
Acuff, Roy, 47–49, 86, 96, 102, 105–8, 110–11, 121, 128, 131, 172
Acuff-Rose Publishing, 47, 49–50, 86–87, 89, 96, 105–8, 110–11, 117, 128–35, 157, 172–73
Adams, Vee and Abbott, 120
Adamson, Harold, 84
"Adios," 46, 92
Aeolian Company, 40
Ahlert, Fred, 148
"Ain't That Loving You, Baby," 220
Airlane Music, 92
Alamo Music, 110, 114, 151–53, 210
Alchinsky, Pierre, 235
Alden-Rochelle v. ASCAP, 149
"(Allá en) El Rancho Grande," 44
Allan, Fleming, 95
Allan, Lewis, 44
"All Dressed Up (Spic and Spanish)," 44
Allen, Rex, 51
Allen, Rosalie, 114
Allen, Sam, 95
Allen, Steve, 205
"All Shook Up," 220
"Amber Tresses Tied with Blue," 45
American Composers Alliance, 150
American Federation of Musicians, 43, 70, 113

American Music, Inc., 67, 88, 95, 99, 102–3, 110, 128, 138–40, 196
American Society of Composers, Authors and Publishers. See ASCAP
Ames, Pearl, 229
"Among My Souvenirs," 84
"Andantino in D-Flat," 158
Anderson, Deacon, 94
Andrea Doria (ship), 204
Andreoli, Pete, 226
Andrews, Thomas E., 100
Andrews Sisters, 54
Annie Get Your Gun (musical), 83
"Another Kiss," 84
"Answer the Phone," 91
"Anytime," 125, 128
"Any Time," 153
"A Penny for Your Thoughts," 129
Appalachian music, 45, 103
"April Showers," 157
Arch of Triumph (film), 84
Ark-La-Tex Music, 110, 173
Armstrong, Louis, 46, 157
Arnold, Eddy: and Fred Forster, 120–24; Hill and Range relationship, 122–25, 134, 161–62, 171, 231, 242; managed by "Colonel" Tom Parker, 121–23, 161–62, 167–69, 171, 179; popularity, 119, 173–74, 176–77; songs, 91, 106, 119–20, 125, 128–29, 134, 152, 176–77, 201, 211; "Tennessee Plowboy" reference, 122, 162
Arnold, Gene, 176
Arodin, Sidney, 45
"Arrivederci, Roma," 228
Arthur Godfrey Show, The, 182
artist and repertoire (A&R), 103, 150, 198
ASCAP: background and profile, 26–28; board, 27–28, 41–42, 45, 159; collection limitations, 26, 54–55, 149; companies, 139, 152–53, 160; competition and differences with BMI, 42–43, 47, 82, 113, 115, 137–40, 142, 145, 191, 199; discourages payola, 38; and Elvis Presley, 186, 219; firms, 152, 154, 227; and Fred Rose, 110; and Hill and Range, 82–83, 114, 151–53, 157, 186, 195, 219, 227; and Max Dreyfus/Chappell Music, 26–28, 42, 60, 134, 139, 152; members, 41, 55, 152; membership, 43, 49; rating system disparity, 27, 43, 149, 153–55; relationship to film industry, 60, 114, 149; restricts membership and repertoire, 41–42, 45, 113, 151–52, 213; seniority, 26–27, 43, 149, 153–55, 157, 159–60; songwriters,

Cohen, Mickey, 87
Collie, Biff, 178–79
Colombo, Russ, 114
Columbia Pictures, 91, 93–94
Columbia Records, 104, 115, 193, 198, 213;
    OKeh label, 69–70, 72, 89, 213
Connelly, Reg, 13, 194
Cook's Hoedown Club, 179
Cooley, Spade, 63, 66–69, 72, 89, 119, 151,
    164–65
"Cool Water," 53, 103
Copas, Lloyd "Cowboy," 130–31, 173
Copland, Aaron, 150
Coral Records, 131
Corneille (aka Cornelis van Beverloo), 235
"Corrina, Corrina," 225
Cotton, James, 174
Cotton Bowl, 206
"Cotton Eyed Joe," 94
Country Barn Dance, 67, 72
"Cowbell Polka," 67
"Cowboy Camp Meetin'," 94, 117
Cowboy Ramblers, 70. See also Boyd, Bill
"Cow Cow Boogie," 156
Cowtown Jamboree (concert production),
    166
Crawford Music, 83
Crew Cuts, The, 193
Cromwell Music Catalog, 208
Crosby, Bing, 38, 43–44, 52–53, 55, 82, 114,
    116, 119
Crosby, Bob, 25, 66
Cross, Sylvester, 67, 88, 95, 99–100, 102–3,
    105, 128, 138, 180
Crudup, Arthur "Big Boy," 175, 180, 200
"Crying in the Chapel," 228
Crystals, The, 226
Cugat, Xavier, 44, 46
Current Writers Group, 154
cut-in, 29, 38, 187

Dada, 235
"Daddy Bluegrass," 104. See also Monroe,
    Bill
"Da Doo Ron Ron (When He Walked Me
    Home)," 226
Daffan, Ted, 72, 80, 89
Daladier, Édouard, 35
Dalhart, Vernon, 162
Damone, Vic, 91
"Dance with Me," 223, 227
Daniels, Charles N., 158–59
"Danny," 219
Darby, Ken, 204

Darin, Bobby, 220
David, Emmanuel, 195
David, Mack, 201
Davis, Jimmie, 121
Davis, Jimmy, 43
Day, Anita, 133
Decca Records, 43, 52–53, 64, 72, 89,
    100–101, 108, 116, 130
"'Deed I Do," 47
"Deep in the Heart of Texas," 42
"Deep Water," 94
DeMetrius, Claude, 207, 219
Denny, Jim, 166
De Rose, Peter, 153
De Sylva, Brown & Henderson, 155
De Sylva, Buddy G., 84, 155, 160
De Sylva v. Ballentine, 191
"Detour," 89
Dexter, Al, 43, 90, 96
Diamonds, The, 193
Dilbeck, Tommy, 125
"Dim, Dim the Lights," 224
Diskin, Tom, 167, 170
Disney, 84, 201
"Divorce Me C.O.D.," 105
"Dixie," 233
Dixon, Floyd, 198
"Do I Love You?" 226
"Don't," 218–19
"Don't Be Ashamed of Your Age," 90, 94
"Don't Be Cruel," 205–6, 214, 220
"Don't Fence Me In," 59
"Don't Leave Me Now," 214
"Don't Look Now (But Your Broken Heart
    Is Showin')," 109
"Don't Sit under the Apple Tree (with
    Anyone Else but Me)," 54
"Don't Take Your Guns to Town," 227
DooTone, 193
Dorsey, Jimmy, 46
Dorsey, Tommy, 75, 116, 199, 209
Dowd, Tom, 193
"Down in Mexico," 204, 206
"Down t' Uncle Bill's," 45
Drake, Ervin, 208
Dreyer, Lew, 184, 229, 241
Dreyfus, Max: as ASCAP board member,
    26, 42–44, 149–50; background, 25–29;
    as Chappell Music director, 21, 58–60, 79;
    dismisses Jean over "Bouquet of Roses,"
    124–26; hires Jean, 25; influence on Jean,
    29–30, 40–41, 50, 59, 92, 94, 165, 241; re-
    jects hillbilly, country and western music,
    41–42, 44–45, 59, 61, 83–85

BAR BISZICK-LOCKWOOD founded Music Access, Inc., the first national service bureau for music clips, and she helped establish the non-profit World Music Institute. She lives in Redmond, Washington, where she works as a program manager at Microsoft.

THE UNIVERSITY OF ILLINOIS PRESS

IS A FOUNDING MEMBER OF THE

ASSOCIATION OF AMERICAN UNIVERSITY PRESSES.

COMPOSED IN 9.75/13.5 ICS SCALA

BY JIM PROEFROCK

AT THE UNIVERSITY OF ILLINOIS PRESS

DESIGNED BY COPENHAVER CUMPSTON

MANUFACTURED BY THOMSON-SHORE, INC.

UNIVERSITY OF ILLINOIS PRESS

1325 SOUTH OAK STREET

CHAMPAIGN, IL 61820-6903

WWW.PRESS.UILLINOIS.EDU

Carl Ruggles: Composer, Painter, and Storyteller   *Marilyn Ziffrin*

Never without a Song: The Years and Songs of Jennie Devlin, 1865–1952
   Katharine D. Newman

The Hank Snow Story   *Hank Snow, with Jack Ownbey and Bob Burris*

Milton Brown and the Founding of Western Swing   *Cary Ginell, with special assistance
   from Roy Lee Brown*

Santiago de Murcia's "Códice Saldívar No. 4": A Treasury of Secular Guitar Music
   from Baroque Mexico   *Craig H. Russell*

The Sound of the Dove: Singing in Appalachian Primitive Baptist Churches
   Beverly Bush Patterson

Heartland Excursions: Ethnomusicological Reflections on Schools of Music   *Bruno Nettl*

Doowop: The Chicago Scene   *Robert Pruter*

Blue Rhythms: Six Lives in Rhythm and Blues   *Chip Deffaa*

Shoshone Ghost Dance Religion: Poetry Songs and Great Basin Context   *Judith Vander*

Go Cat Go! Rockabilly Music and Its Makers   *Craig Morrison*

'Twas Only an Irishman's Dream: The Image of Ireland and the Irish in American
   Popular Song Lyrics, 1800–1920   *William H. A. Williams*

Democracy at the Opera: Music, Theater, and Culture in New York City, 1815–60
   Karen Ahlquist

Fred Waring and the Pennsylvanians   *Virginia Waring*

Woody, Cisco, and Me: Seamen Three in the Merchant Marine   *Jim Longhi*

Behind the Burnt Cork Mask: Early Blackface Minstrelsy and Antebellum American
   Popular Culture   *William J. Mahar*

Going to Cincinnati: A History of the Blues in the Queen City   *Steven C. Tracy*

Pistol Packin' Mama: Aunt Molly Jackson and the Politics of Folksong   *Shelly Romalis*

Sixties Rock: Garage, Psychedelic, and Other Satisfactions   *Michael Hicks*

The Late Great Johnny Ace and the Transition from R&B to Rock 'n' Roll
   James M. Salem

Tito Puente and the Making of Latin Music   *Steven Loza*

Juilliard: A History   *Andrea Olmstead*

Understanding Charles Seeger, Pioneer in American Musicology   *Edited by Bell Yung
   and Helen Rees*

Mountains of Music: West Virginia Traditional Music from Goldenseal   *Edited by
   John Lilly*

Alice Tully: An Intimate Portrait   *Albert Fuller*

A Blues Life   *Henry Townsend, as told to Bill Greensmith*

Long Steel Rail: The Railroad in American Folksong (2d ed.)   *Norm Cohen*

The Golden Age of Gospel   *Text by Horace Clarence Boyer; photography by Lloyd Yearwood*

Aaron Copland: The Life and Work of an Uncommon Man   *Howard Pollack*

Louis Moreau Gottschalk   *S. Frederick Starr*

Race, Rock, and Elvis   *Michael T. Bertrand*

Theremin: Ether Music and Espionage   *Albert Glinsky*

Poetry and Violence: The Ballad Tradition of Mexico's Costa Chica   *John H. McDowell*

The Bill Monroe Reader   *Edited by Tom Ewing*